CENSORED 2014
FEARLESS SPEECH IN FATEFUL TIMES

The Top Censored Stories and Media Analysis of 2012–13

Mickey Huff and Andy Lee Roth
with Project Censored

Foreword by
Sarah van Gelder
Cartoons by
Khalil Bendib

Seven Stories Press
New York

Seven Stories Press

140 Watts Street

New York, NY 10013

www.sevenstories.com

ISBN 978-1-60980-494-7 (paperback)

ISBN 978-1-60980-495-4(electronic)

ISSN 1074-5998

9 8 7 6 5 4 3 2 1

Book design by Jon Gilbert

Printed in the USA

"Project Censored continues to be an invaluable resource in exposing and highlighting shocking stories that are routinely minimized or ignored by the corporate media. The vital nature of this work is underscored by this year's NSA leaks. The world needs more brave whistle blowers and independent journalists in the service of reclaiming democracy and challenging the abuse of power. Project Censored stands out for its commitment to such work."—Deepa Kumar, author of *Islamophobia and the Politics of Empire* and associate professor of Media Studies and Middle Eastern Studies at Rutgers University

"Project Censored interrogates the present in the same way that Oliver Stone and I tried to interrogate the past in our *Untold History of the United States*. It not only shines a penetrating light on the American Empire and all its deadly, destructive, and deceitful actions, it does so at a time when the Obama administration is mounting a fierce effort to silence truth-tellers and whistleblowers. Project Censored provides the kind of fearless and honest journalism we so desperately need in these dangerous times."—Peter Kuznick, professor of history, American University, and coauthor, with Oliver Stone, of *The Untold History of the United States*

"At a time when the need for independent journalism and for media outlets unaffiliated with and untainted by the government and corporate sponsors is greater than ever, Project Censored has created a context for reporting the complete truths in all matters that matter. . . . It is therefore left to us to find sources for information we can trust. . . . It is in this task that we are fortunate to have an ally like Project Censored."—Dahr Jamail

"Activist groups like Project Censored . . . are helping to build the media democracy movement. We have to challenge the powers that be and rebuild media from the bottom up."—Amy Goodman

"Project Censored is one of the organizations that we should listen to, to be assured that our newspapers and our broadcasting outlets are practicing thorough and ethical journalism."—Walter Cronkite

"[*Censored*] should be affixed to the bulletin boards in every newsroom in America. And, perhaps read aloud to a few publishers and television executives."—Ralph Nader

"[*Censored*] offers devastating evidence of the dumbing-down of mainstream news in America. . . . Required reading for broadcasters, journalists, and well-informed citizens."—*Los Angeles Times*

"One of the most significant media research projects in the country."—I. F. Stone

"A terrific resource, especially for its directory of alternative media and organizations. . . . Recommended for media collections."
—*Library Journal*

"[Project Censored's] efforts to continue globalizing their reporting network could not be more timely or necessary."—Kristina Borjesson

"A distant early warning system for society's problems."—*American Journalism Review*

"Project Censored goes where the media conformist angels fear to tread. . . . It's the kind of journalism we need."—Norman Solomon

"Project Censored shines a spotlight on news that an informed public must have . . . a vital contribution to our democratic process."
—Rhoda H. Karpatkin, president, Consumer's Union

"Hot news, cold truths, utterly uncensored."—Greg Palast

"Buy it, read it, act on it. Our future depends on the knowledge this collection of suppressed stories allows us."—*San Diego Review*

"Those who read and support Project Censored are in the know."
—Cynthia McKinney

Contents

FOREWORD: Solutions in a Time of Climate Meltdown:
The Most Censored (and Indispensible) Story by Sarah van Gelder 13

INTRODUCTION by Andy Lee Roth and Mickey Huff 25

SECTION I: CENSORED NEWS AND MEDIA ANALYSIS

INTRODUCTION 35

NOTE ON RESEARCH AND EVALUATION
OF CENSORED NEWS STORIES 39

CHAPTER 1: Top 25 Censored Stories from 2012–13
and Censored News Clusters 41

The Top 25

Top 25 Story Summaries, compiled by Andy Lee Roth 41
1. Bradley Manning and the Failure of Corporate Media 41
2. Richest Global 1 Percent Hide Trillions in Tax Havens 42
3. Trans-Pacific Partnership Threatens a Regime
   of Corporate Global Governance 43
4. Obama's War on Whistleblowers 44
5. Hate Groups and Antigovernment Groups on Rise across US 44
6. Billionaires' Rising Wealth Intensifies Poverty and Inequality 46
7. Merchants of Death and Nuclear Weapons 47
8. Bank Interests Inflate Global Prices by 35 to 40 Percent 48
9. Icelanders Vote to Include Commons in Their Constitution 49
10. A "Culture of Cruelty" along Mexico–US Border 50
11. Bush Blocked Iran Nuclear Deal 50
12. The US Has Left Iraq with an Epidemic of
    Cancers and Birth Defects 52
13. A Fifth of Americans Go Hungry 53
14. Wireless Technology a Looming Health Crisis 54
15. Food Riots: The New Normal? 55
16. Journalism Under Attack Around the Globe 56
17. The Creative Commons Celebrates Ten Years of
    Sharing and Cultural Creation 57
18. Fracking Our Food Supply 57
19. The Power of Peaceful Revolution in Iceland 58

20. Israel Counted Minimum Calorie Needs in Gaza Blockade 59
21. Monsanto and India's "Suicide Economy" 60
22. Pennsylvania Law Gags Doctors to Protect
    Big Oil's "Proprietary Secrets" 61
23. Transaction Tax Helps Civilize Wall Street and
    Lower the National Debt 62
24. Widespread GMO Contamination: Did Monsanto
    Plant GMOs Before USDA Approval? 63
25. Israel Gave Birth Control to Ethiopian Immigrants
    Without Their Consent 63

Censored News Clusters

Whistleblowers and Gag Laws
    by Brian Covert 65

Plutocracy, Poverty, and Prosperity
    by James F. Tracy 85

Human Rights and Civil Liberties
    by Susan Rahman and Donna Nassor 101

Technologies and Ecologies of War
    by Targol Mesbah and Zara Zimbardo 113

Health and the Environment
    by Susan Rahman and Liliana Valdez-Madera 127

Iceland, the Power of Peaceful Revolution, and the Commons
    by Andy Lee Roth 143

CHAPTER 2: Déjà Vu: What Happened to Previous Censored Stories?
by Mickey Huff and Nolan Higdon with Andrew O'Connor-Watts,
Jen Eiden, Allen Kew, Emmie Ruhland, Aaron Hudson, Rex Yang,
Sam Park, Amitai Cohen, Michael Kolbe, and Matthew Carhart 155

CHAPTER 3: Can't Touch This: Junk Food News and News Abuse
by Mickey Huff, Michael Kolbe, Nolan Higdon, Sam Park,
Jennifer Eiden, and Kimberly Soiero 177

CHAPTER 4: Media Democracy in Action: Free Press and
Free Speech Advocates that Make a Difference
compiled by Mickey Huff, with contributions by Daniel Ellsberg, On
Civil Courage; Josh Wolf, Journalism that Matters; William Creely,
Foundation for Individual Rights in Education; Christopher M. Finan,
American Booksellers Foundation for Free Expression; Acacia O'Connor,
National Coalition Against Censorship and Kids' Right to Read; Tony Diaz,
Librotraficante; Beau Hodai, DBA Press; Sunsara Taylor, Stop Patriarchy;
John Collins, *The Weave*; and Ken Walden, What the World Could Be 207

SECTION II: CRITICAL THINKING, MEDIA LITERACY, AND NARRATIVES OF POWER

INTRODUCTION...249

CHAPTER 5: Digging Deeper: Politico-Corporate Media Manipulation, Critical Thinking, and Democracy
by Elliot D. Cohen..251

CHAPTER 6: Diffusing Conspiracy Panics: On the Public Use of Reason in the Twenty-First Century Truth Emergency
by James F. Tracy...271

CHAPTER 7: Censorship That Dares Not Speak its Name: The Strange Silencing of Liberal America
by John Pilger..287

CHAPTER 8: Screening the Homeland: How Hollywood Fantasy Mediates State Fascism in the US of Empire
by Rob Williams..297

SECTION III: CASE STUDIES OF "UNHISTORY" IN THE MAKING—AND HOW TO BUILD A BETTER FUTURE

INTRODUCTION...311

CHAPTER 9: Exposing The Financial Core of the Transnational Capitalist Class
by Peter Phillips and Brady Osborne..313

CHAPTER 10: Apple Exposed: The Untold Story of Globalization
by Nicki Lisa Cole and Tara Krishna..331

CHAPTER 11: The "New" American Imperialism in Africa: Secret Sahara Wars and AFRICOM
by Brian Martin Murphy..353

CHAPTER 12: The Sixth Mass Extinction
by Julie Andrzejewski and John C. Alessio..365

CHAPTER 13: The New Story: Why We Need One and How to Create It
by Michael Nagler...387

Acknowledgments and Judges..407

Report From The Media Freedom Foundation President
by Peter Phillips 413

How To Support Project Censored...419

No News Is Good News
by Marcia Annenberg, cover artist..421

About The Editors 423

Index...425

There's a time when the operation of the machine becomes
so odious, makes you so sick at heart, that you can't take part.
You can't even passively take part. And you've got to put your
bodies upon the gears and upon the wheels . . . upon the
levers, upon all the apparatus, and you've got to make it stop.
And you've got to indicate to the people who run it, to the
people who own it, that unless you're free, the machine will
be prevented from working at all.

MARIO SAVIO
University of California–Berkeley
December 2, 1964

Everyone has the right to freedom of opinion and expression; this right includes freedom to hold opinions without
interference and to seek, receive and impart information and
ideas through any media and regardless of frontiers.

THE UNIVERSAL DECLARATION OF
HUMAN RIGHTS, ARTICLE 19
United Nations General Assembly
adopted 1948

In Memoriam

BRIAN MARTIN MURPHY
July 14, 1948–June 14, 2013
Intrepid journalist, cherished colleague, inspiring teacher,
fearless truth-teller

As a Canadian journalist covering the wars in southern Africa for Inter Press Service during the 1980s, I saw Project Censored was one of the few media outlets in the US consistently featuring coverage of those underreported wars. I paid attention. When I was working with the filmmaking company Media Education Foundation, part of a national initiative defining and promoting media literacy, the publication of Project Censored's annual book was one of our reference points.

When I joined the faculty of the Department of Communication Studies at Niagara University, we decided to completely redesign the program as a degree in Communicating for Social Justice. In ten years, that redesign has become a model for many other communication departments.

At every step, Project Censored's work has been an example of the fearless truth-telling to which all social-justice advocates and students of journalism should be exposed. Today, Project Censored is integrated into our curriculum, with at least one course a year doing research to contribute to the list of contenders for the Top 25 underreported stories. Our students' successes are a testament to Project Censored's value as a media literacy teaching tool, introducing a whole new generation to what *real* press freedom looks like.

—Brian Martin Murphy
July 30, 2012

FOREWORD

Solutions in a Time of Climate Meltdown
The Most Censored (and Indispensible) Story

Sarah van Gelder

The most censored story of our lifetime is hiding in plain sight. We humans are disrupting the climate of the planet to the point at which the world our children and grandchildren will inhabit may be unrecognizable.

The risk we are taking is not something discussed in polite company, much less in the corporate press. Instead of covering the many facets of this impending crisis and the options for mobilizing a response, the corporate press has largely served up a diet of distortion and distraction. Even the progressive media has a mixed record on covering the climate crisis.

Yet stories that explore the depth of—and solutions to—the climate crisis are essential to any prospect that we will respond at the scale needed.

After years of record-breaking fires, droughts, heat waves, and storms, public opinion is beginning to move toward greater comprehension, although still at a rate that is dangerously slow. While 97 percent of peer-reviewed scientific studies conclude that the Earth is warming because of human influences,[1] just 42 percent of the general public believes the world is warming because of human activity.[2] And though journalists cover at length the stories of particular wildfires, droughts, megastorms, floods, and other events exacerbated by the shifting climate, until recently, the corporate media have neglected to explore something that scientists are warning about and

13

that many people perceive with their own senses: that these are not isolated incidents, but signs of a long-term and accelerating disruption in climate stability.

The hard truth is that scientists predict a temperature rise of six degrees Celsius by the end of the century, unless we take action. This level of heating will hobble agriculture, deplete water supplies, and move shorelines. It will make many areas uninhabitable and cause famine, widespread extinctions, and massive movements of climate refugees. And it will be largely irreversible for centuries thereafter.[3]

WHAT CORPORATE POWER MEANS

Why have we been unable to take action in the face of a threat larger and more long-lasting than terrorism?[4] The climate crisis highlights a systemic flaw in human society today: the power of large corporations over our economy, governance, and way of life overwhelms other forces in our public and private lives.

Corporations dealing in fossil fuel are among the biggest and most powerful on the planet. Together with other large corporations, as well as the think tanks and lobbyists they fund, they have undermined efforts to reach international climate agreements, and to get government action on renewable energy and energy efficiency, smart transportation options, and other policies that could counter the threat of climate disruption. With a focus on making the most money possible for shareholders and executives, the fate of human and other life on the planet just doesn't show up on the quarterly balance sheet. With billions of dollars in profits and a Supreme Court friendly to the power of big corporations, their influence on government goes largely unchecked.

An economy that concentrates wealth and power more each year, while undermining our world's capacity to support life, especially goes unquestioned when the media is owned by big corporations that rely on corporate advertising.

We also have a cultural flaw. Influenced by billions of dollars of advertising, popular culture has come to equate having lots of stuff with success and happiness. Those at the top can accumulate with abandon and without considering the implications for the future.

Meanwhile, people in the 99 percent increasingly struggle just to get by. Other values that are just as much a part of the founding culture of the United States—frugality, community, neighbor-helping-neighbor, contribution to the whole—have been pushed aside by the advertising-driven impulse to buy. The production and eventual disposal of all that stuff exacts a price on the finite resources and energy capacities of the planet, and the bill is coming due.

CLIMATE COVERAGE: THE GOOD, THE BAD, AND THE UGLY

Facing the dire reality of a destabilized climate is not easy, and some of the country's most influential media don't even try. The Wall Street Journal's notoriously right-wing opinion section published a column on May 9, 2013, titled "In Defense of Carbon Dioxide."[5] The piece celebrates rising levels of carbon dioxide as a boon to plant life. Columbia Journalism Review columnist Ryan Chittum, who is a former Wall Street Journal writer himself, called it "shameful even by the dismal standards of that page."[6]

According to a January 2013 Media Matters report, not a single climate scientist appeared as a guest on the influential Sunday morning television talk shows, nor were any climate scientists quoted, over the previous four years.[7] Most of those invited to speak on global warming were either media figures or politicians, but, among the politicians, not a single one was a Democrat. Climate change deniers on the shows went unchallenged. The nightly news shows had somewhat more coverage, and most of that was driven by extreme weather events, according to the report. But this coverage, too, was biased: 60 percent of the politicians on the air were Republicans.

Most journalists want to be perceived as objective, and so for years much of the climate reporting included an ersatz balance: climate deniers were given equal time even though they were a tiny fraction of the scientific community; the fact that many were funded by the fossil fuel lobby was rarely mentioned. The New York Times is among those that now explicitly reject this he-said-she-said approach.[8]

The result of this distorted coverage is that precious years, during which a well-informed people might have acted, have been lost to confusion produced by so-called "objective" journalism.

There's an additional, less recognized flaw with journalism as currently practiced. Journalists are considered objective when their reporting accepts the dominant worldview as a given, without questioning beliefs and assumptions that may or may not hold up to scrutiny. The good journalist, in other words, goes along with the worldview of the powerful. Today, that worldview includes the assumption that all growth is good and can go on indefinitely, that a rising tide will lift all boats (an ironic phrase in this time of sea-level rise), that technology and free enterprise will solve any problem, and that the Earth will provide all we need.

Real objective journalism would question these assumptions, especially those contradicted by the evidence on the ground—and in the glaciers.

Although some of the media has flouted their responsibility to truth-telling, others have been extraordinary. *Rolling Stone* published a game-changing piece by Bill McKibben on the math of climate change, which shows that most of the world's fossil fuel reserves must remain in the ground if we are to avert climate catastrophe.[9] And among Project Censored's Top 25 stories is Nafeez Mosaddeq Ahmed's article from the *Guardian* on the likelihood of food shortages becoming the new normal, in large part because of the impact of climate change on crop yields.[10] *The Guardian*'s coverage of the climate crisis has been among the best and most consistent among the large newspapers. (Full disclosure: I occasionally write a column for the *Guardian*). And there are some extraordinary blogs like *Inside-ClimateNews*, *Grist*, *Climate Progress*, *Climate Wire*, and *Real Climate*, which are out in front on climate coverage.

Project Censored has highlighted some of the key climate stories of the last decade. Among the Project's annual list of the censored stories over the past years are independent journalists' reports on the disruption to marine species resulting from global warming,[11] the role of excessive consumption in the climate crisis,[12] and the flaws in World Bank cap-and-trade schemes, which result in the displacement of indigenous farmers.[13]

Still, there is a mixed record among the progressive press on climate coverage. Perhaps this is a reflection of a split within the progressive world, which until recently was divided between those who focus on the environment and those who focus on politics and social justice. Much of the progressive press has left climate change to environmental magazines.

The implicit view that environmental issues are for backpackers, conservationists, and middle-class white folks is outdated and dangerous. The climate crisis is changing everyone's life—*especially* the poor and vulnerable.

MAKING SOLUTIONS VISIBLE

More truly objective reporting on the climate crisis and its systemic causes would be a huge improvement over what we find now. But still it would be just half the story. The other half is the solutions. We need much more reporting on solutions, and not just to keep despair from sending us screaming into those rising seas. We need solutions journalism because it is the only way we can develop the global consensus we need to take action and the knowledge base that makes that action effective.

Over just a few hundred years, we clever humans have transformed our world, creating a vast fossil fuel–driven industrial economy that permits high-consumption lifestyles (for some). Yet until recently, we lacked an understanding of what industrialization was doing to the prospects for our children and their children.

But we have the smarts to create a world in which the climate is stable, diverse species thrive, and all people have a shot at a good life. The means to do that are as diverse as the factors that cause the problem. Renewable energy can displace carbon-based fuels. Buildings can be built or retrofitted for super-efficiency. Organic fertilizers can build the fertility and resilience of the soil while safely storing carbon, replacing the chemical fertilizers that are a major contributor to the climate crisis. Fuel-efficient vehicles, fast trains, and bicycles can replace gas-guzzlers. A greater appreciation of time well spent with family and friends, and of the satisfaction of meaningful work, can replace an obsession with owning and using up *stuff*.

Each of these shifts improves our chances of stabilizing the climate, and most of them have multiple benefits: they improve health, clean up air and water, improve community life, create new economic opportunities, and promote equity. And some do all of these at once. But the potential of these solutions can't be fulfilled unless people find out about them. That's why the media is so important.

With international talks at a standstill and little national leadership on this issue, the focus of action has shifted, becoming much more bottom-up. Local and state governments (and an exceptional few national governments) around the world are instituting policies, like carbon taxes, that help shift the market toward cleaner energy sources. Policy makers are rethinking the use of economic growth and the gross domestic product as a measure of progress. Inventors and entrepreneurs are coming up with new ways to produce clean energy or to cut the inefficient use of energy.

Importantly, there is a climate justice movement happening that few know exists—a movement founded in the grassroots and especially in communities that are often ignored by the corporate media: Appalachia, indigenous communities, youth, farmers, fishermen, and small businesses. It's a movement that doesn't separate environmental concerns from human concerns, but that recognizes that they are one and the same.

At the forefront of this movement are young people, ranchers, tribal leaders, people living near refineries, those resisting hydraulic fracturing (also known as fracking), and others who are most affected by the fossil fuel industry. People are using their bodies to block the building of tar sands pipelines, to stop mountaintop removal, to prevent drilling in their communities—both to protect their land, water, and health, and to protect the climate.[14]

The 350.org campaign, headed up by Bill McKibben, is spurring actions around the world, including civil disobedience in front of the White House aimed at convincing President Barack Obama to reject the Keystone XL pipeline.

Others are responding to the climate crisis through changes in their own lives. Many are finding much greater satisfaction in ways of life focused on community or personal development. Young people are seeking out livelihoods that allow them to contribute to a more sustainable planet and to ride out the storms they see on the horizon. There's extraordinary interest in developing local food systems. These deeper cultural shifts offer another part of the solutions matrix.

These new policy initiatives, innovations, social movements, and lifestyle shifts are rarely covered, but with all that's at stake, these responses deserve to be front-page news. We need this sort of reporting to seek out the many solutions, investigate which ones are working, and tell the stories through the media now available. Out of those many stories and many solutions, the answers can emerge. If these answers spread, are replicated, and inspire others, we have a shot at preserving a healthy planet and our own future.

WHAT SOLUTIONS JOURNALISM MAKES POSSIBLE

The truth is that there is no shortage of solutions—whether it's Germany's turn to solar power or the carbon-storing power of restored soils. But given the shortage of stories about solutions, it's little wonder that so many people—once they understand the implications of the climate crisis—leap right from denial to despair. When stories of people taking action are censored, when the innovations that could help us tackle the greatest crisis humanity has ever faced go unreported, when the ordinary people and grassroots leaders working to build a sustainable future go unquoted, people are left isolated and feeling powerless.

That's what makes solutions journalism so important at this point in human history.

When the myriad efforts to build a sustainable world are covered, the rapid evolution of our society toward solutions becomes possible.[15] The best innovations can travel quickly and build on one another—bike lanes in one city become a linked system of bike lanes and public transit in another. A public food forest, where all are free to harvest fresh fruits and nuts, sparks the same idea in another community. One city sets out to be carbon neutral, to reduce asthma and heart disease, and inspires other cities to follow suit. If they encounter these sorts of stories, people don't feel alone, powerless, and even foolish when they pick up a shovel and plant a tree, start an urban garden, or risk arrest blockading a tar sands pipeline. They see their work as part of a much larger fabric of change—one with real possibility for a better world.

So here's where solutions journalism is at its best. Just as an individual coal plant is not the whole picture in terms of the climate crisis, the individual windmill is not the whole solution. To meet its potential, solutions journalism must investigate not only the individual innovations, but also the larger pattern of change—the emerging ethics, institutions, and ways of life that are coming into existence.

UN-CENSORING SOLUTIONS-FOCUSED JOURNALISM

	PROBLEM-FOCUSED	SOLUTIONS-FOCUSED
News Stories	Corn Belt Fears Large Crop Loss from Heat Wave, Drought Conditions[16]	Germany Swaps Nuclear Power for Wind and Solar[19]
	Old Ways of Life are Fading as the Arctic Thaws[17]	Why We're Putting Ourselves on the (Pipe)line With the Tea Party[20]
	Methane Emissions Higher than Thought Across Much of US[18]	How Bicycling is Transforming Business[21]
Stories with context, analysis, implications	Climate and Capitalism in Copenhagen[22]	How Thoughtful Farming Could Curb Climate Change, Feed the World[25]
	Western Lifestyle Unsustainable, Says Climate Expert Rajendra Pachauri[23]	Less Work, More Living[26]
	The World Bank and Climate Change: Sustainability or Exploitation?[24]	Religion, Science and Spirit: A Sacred Story for Our Time[27]

The change will not happen from the top down—most of the leaders of big government, big business, and even big religion are too entrenched in the status quo to offer much help on this score.

Instead, it is the actions of millions of ordinary people that have the best chance of transforming our society to one that can live within its ecological means and meet the needs of humans and other life forms. To do that, we need evidence-based stories of practical, feasible innovations. But we also need to see the larger picture that they are a part of, the new ways of doing business[28] that are rooted in community and work in harmony with our ecosystems, along with the emerging values and ways of life that create genuine well-being without compromising the life-sustaining capacity of the planet. We need to experience the democratic impulse, which, at times, can overcome the top-down power of giant corporations.[29]

Journalists, it has been said, write the first draft of history. In that spirit, discerning these patterns of change—which ones have promise, which ones are taking hold—is an inexact science. But a bottom-up global process thrives when the first draft is available, and all of those with a stake in the future can see that they, themselves, are its authors.

Bainbridge Island, Washington
May 17, 2013

SARAH VAN GELDER is cofounder and executive editor of *YES! Magazine* and Yes-Magazine.org, which feature powerful ideas and practical actions for a more just and sustainable world. *YES!* covers issue ranging from prison alternatives to do-it-yourself culture, from climate justice to the cooperatives movement. Sarah edited *This Changes Everything: Occupy Wall Street and the 99% Movement* and coedited *Making Peace: Healing a Violent World.* She has lived in China, India, and Central America, and has cofounded a cohousing community, organized low-income tenants, and collaborated with the Suquamish tribe to win the return of the land where Chief Seattle once lived.

Notes

1. Suzanne Goldenberg, "Climate research nearly unanimous on human causes, survey finds," *Guardian*, May 15, 2013, http://www.guardian.co.uk/environment/2013/may/16/climate-research-nearly-unanimous-humans-causes.
2. "Climate Change: Key Data Points from Pew Research," April 2, 2013, http://www.pewresearch.org/2013/04/02/climate-change-key-data-points-from-pew-research.
3. Joe Romm, "An Illustrated Guide to the Science of Global Warming Impacts: How We Know Inaction Is the Gravest Threat Humanity Faces," *Climate Progress*, September 28, 2011, http://thinkprogress.org/climate/2011/09/28/330109/science-of-global-warming-impacts.
4. Mark Townsend and Paul Harris, "Now the Pentagon Tells Bush: Climate Change Will Destroy Us," *Guardian*, February 21, 2004, http://www.guardian.co.uk/environment/2004/feb/22/usnews.theobserver.
5. Harrison H. Schmitt and William Happer, "In Defense of Carbon Dioxide," *Wall Street Journal*, May 8, 2013, http://online.wsj.com/article/SB10001424127887323528404578452483656067190.html.

6. Ryan Chittum, "The WSJ Editorial Page Hits Rock Bottom," *Columbia Journalism Review*, May 9, 2013, http://www.cjr.org/the_audit/the_wsj_editorial_page_hits2.php.

7. Jill Fitzsimmons, "Warmest Year On Record Received Cool Climate Coverage," Media Matters, January 8, 2013, http://mediamatters.org/research/2013/01/08/study-warmest-year-on-record-received-cool-clim/192079.

8. Margaret Sullivan, "He Said, She Said, and the Truth," *New York Times*, September 15, 2012, http://www.nytimes.com/2012/09/16/public-editor/16pubed.html. For more on climate change denial front groups, like the Exxon Mobile–funded Heartland Institute (Heartland.org), see Sourcewatch.org by the Center for Media and Democracy, http://www.sourcewatch.org/index.php?title=Heartland_Institute.

9. Bill McKibben, "Global Warming's Terrifying New Math," *Rolling Stone*, July 19, 2012, http://www.rollingstone.com/politics/news/global-warmings-terrifying-new-math-20120719.

10. Nafeez Mosaddeq Ahmed, "Why Food Riots Are Likely to Become the New Normal," *Guardian*, March 6, 2013, http://www.guardian.co.uk/environment/blog/2013/mar/06/food-riots-new-normal, analyzed as *Censored* story #15 in this volume. For more on Ahmed's writing on climate issues, see the foreword of *Censored 2013: Dispatches from the Media Revolution*, Mickey Huff and Andy Lee Roth with Project Censored (New York: Seven Stories Press, 2012), 11–19.

11. *Censored* story #2, "Oceans in Peril," *Censored 2013*, 87–89.

12. *Censored* story #21, "Western Lifestyle Continues Environmental Footprint," *Censored 2011: The Top 25 Censored Stories of 2009–10*, Mickey Huff, Peter Phillips, and Project Censored (New York: Seven Stories Press, 2010), 113–116.

13. *Censored* story #15, "World Bank's Carbon Trade Fiasco," *Censored 2010: The Top Censored Stories of 2008–09*, Peter Phillips and Mickey Huff with Project Censored (New York: Seven Stories Press, 2011), 67–72.

14. See *Censored* story #18, "Fracking Our Food Supply," in this volume.

15. Sarah van Gelder, "Is There Inspiration in Your Media Diet?," *YES! Magazine*, February 10, 2013, http://www.yesmagazine.org/people-power/sarah-van-gelder-inspiration-media-diet-solutions-journalism.

16. Christine Stebbins, "Corn Belt Fears Large Crop Loss from Heat Wave, Drought Conditions," *Insurance Journal*, July 9, 2012, http://www.insurancejournal.com/news/midwest/2012/07/09/254790.htm.

17. Steven Lee Myers, Andrew C. Revkin, Simon Romero, and Clifford Krauss, "Old Ways of Life are Fading as the Arctic Thaws," *New York Times*, October 20, 2005, http://www.nytimes.com/2005/10/20/science/earth/20arctic.ready.html?ref=thebigmelt.

18. "Methane Emissions Higher than Thought across Much of U.S.," ScienceDaily, May 15, 2013, http://www.sciencedaily.com/releases/2013/05/130515165021.htm.

19. Oliver Lazenby, "Germany Swaps Nuclear for Solar and Wind Power," *YES! Magazine*, June 7, 2012, http://www.yesmagazine.org/issues/making-it-home/renewable-power-for-germany.

20. Will Wooten, Candice Bernd, and Ron Seifert, "Why We're Putting Ourselves on the (Pipe)Line With the Tea Party," *YES! Magazine*, August 24, 2012, http://www.yesmagazine.org/planet/why-we-put-ourselves-on-the-pipeline-with-the-tea-party-keystone.

21. Jay Walljapser, "How Bicycling Is Transforming Business," *YES! Magazine*, December 31, 2012, http://www.yesmagazine.org/happiness/how-bicycling-is-transforming-business.

22. Walden Bello, "Climate and Capitalism in Copenhagen," *YES! Magazine*, December 2, 2009, http://www.yesmagazine.org/new-economy/climate-and-capitalism-in-copenhagen.

23. James Randerson, "Western Lifestyle Unsustainable, Says Climate Expert Rajendra Pachauri," *Guardian*, November 29, 2009, http://www.guardian.co.uk/environment/2009/nov/29/rajendra-pachauri-climate-warning-copenhagen, included in "Western Lifestyle Continues," *Censored 2011*.

24. Mary Tharin, "The World Bank and Climate Change: Sustainability or Exploitation?," *Upside Down World*, February 11, 2009. Also see "World Bank's Carbon Trade Fiasco," *Censored 2010*.

25. Nora Doyle-Burr, "How Thoughtful Farming Could Curb Climate Change, Feed the World," *Christian Science Monitor*, March 28, 2012, http://www.csmonitor.com/Science/2012/0328/How-thoughtful-farming-could-curb-climate-change-feed-the-world.

26. Juliet Schor, "Less Work, More Living," *YES! Magazine*, September 2, 2011, http://www.yesmagazine.org/issues/new-livelihoods/less-work-more-living.
27. David Korten, "Religion, Science, and Spirit: A Sacred Story for Our Time," *YES! Magazine*, January 17, 2013, http://www.yesmagazine.org/happiness/religion-science-and-spirit-a-sacred-story-for-our-time. For more on this theme, see Michael Nagler's chapter, "The New Story," in this volume; and see the work of Kenn Burrows (with Michael Nagler) published in *Censored 2013*, ch. 10; and Kenn Burrows in *Censored 2012: Sourcebook for the Media Revolution*, ed. Mickey Huff and Project Censored (New York: Seven Stories Press, 2011), ch. 4.
28. See, for example, *Censored* story #7, "2012: The International Year of Cooperatives," *Censored 2013*, 62, 79–80; and the spring 2013 issue of *YES! Magazine*, with the theme "How Cooperatives Are Driving the New Economy."
29. For additional recent examples of the democratic impulse in action, see the Censored News Cluster on "Iceland, the Power of Peaceful Revolution, and the Commons," in ch. 1 of this volume.

Introduction

Andy Lee Roth and Mickey Huff

FEARLESS SPEECH: CRITICAL AND AFFIRMATIVE

Thirty years ago, in October and November 1983, the French philosopher Michel Foucault gave a series of lectures at the University of California–Berkeley. No doubt aware of the campus having been the locus of the 1964–65 free speech movement, Foucault chose to focus his Berkeley lectures on the origins of our contemporary understanding of "free speech."[1]

Tracing the history of this idea back to fifth century BCE Athens, Foucault explained how the Greek term *parrhesia*—conventionally translated into English as "free speech"—literally meant, "to say everything." As such it could carry either a negative meaning—as in "chattering," indiscriminately—or a positive one, "to tell the truth."[2] As truth-telling, *parrhesia* amounted to a moral activity that was "an essential characteristic of Athenian democracy."[3]

In Foucault's analysis, five distinct elements (italicized in the following quotation) defined *parrhesia* as a specific kind of verbal activity:

> The speaker has a specific relation to truth through *frankness*, a certain relationship to his own life through *danger*, a certain type of relation to himself or other people through *criticism* (self-criticism or criticism of other people) and a specific relation to moral law through *freedom* and *duty*.[4]

Thus Foucault suggested, by tracing contemporary conceptions of "free speech" back to their Athenian roots, we might reconceive it as *fearless* speech, "the courage to speak the truth in spite of some danger."[5]

The independent journalists whose reportage features in *Censored 2014* each demonstrate that this is a robust, living tradition. Journalists committed to fearless speech risk their freedom and, far too often, their lives, in order to bring us the truth from places and in situations where those wielding power would prefer that silence reigned, as documented in *Censored 2014* story #16, "Journalism Under Attack Around the Globe." Even more frequently, in the course of their work as truth-tellers, journalists give voice to others—themselves engaged in fearless speech—who might otherwise go unheard. As Brian Covert documents in this year's Censored News Cluster on "Whistleblowers and Gag Laws," without the dedicated reporting of independent journalists such as Kevin Gosztola, Glenn Greenwald, and Janet Reitman, we would know at best an incomplete story about Bradley Manning and the trial that is ongoing as this volume goes to press: quite simply, the corporate media have failed to cover the whole Manning story.

Criticism—particularly the critique of those who wield their power indiscriminately or selfishly—is another characteristic of fearless speech, identified by Foucault in his Berkeley lectures, and evident in the independent journalism that Project Censored highlights in this volume. From the causes and consequences of wealth inequality—as reported, for example, by Carl Herman (story #2, "Richest Global 1 Percent Hide Trillions in Tax Havens") and George Monbiot (story #6, "Billionaires' Rising Wealth Intensifies Poverty and Inequality")—to immigration (e.g., Erika L. Sánchez, story #10, "A 'Culture of Cruelty' along Mexico–US Border") and the environment (e.g., Elizabeth Royte, story #18, "Fracking Our Food Supply"), our best independent investigative reporters speak "from 'below'" to hold accountable those "above."[6]

While true to Foucault's exploration of the ancient roots of fearless speech, an exclusive focus on criticism gives an incomplete view of journalistic duty, as practiced by today's independent press and broadcasters and celebrated by Project Censored. As heralded by Sarah van Gelder in her foreword, voiced by journalists across this year's Top 25, and resounded in our book's concluding chapter, "The New Story" by Michael Nagler, independent journalism in 2014 is as much about realistic *solutions* as it is oriented to systemic problems. "Solutions journalism," van Gelder writes, "must investigate not only the individual innovations, but also the larger pattern of change—the emerging ethics, institutions, and ways of life that are coming into existence." To be effective, critique requires the balance of affirmation.[7] Affirmation also requires courage. In an era when "hope" and "change" may seem like nothing more than a deeper gloss of campaign rhetoric, reporting news stories of genuine change and valid hope takes a certain kind of fearlessness. So, we would expand Foucault's anatomy of fearless speech to encompass affirmative truthtelling, as is found here in Jessica Conrad's reportage on the people of Iceland voting to treat their nation's natural resources as a commons (story #9) and independent press accounts of the Creative Commons celebrating its tenth anniversary (story #17). The truth to which we need access in order to fulfill our duties and our potential—as family members, as community members, and as citizens—includes not only knowledge of power and its abuses, but also exemplars of human activity, relationships, and institutions at their very best.

FATEFUL TIMES AND CYNICISM

The "fateful times" that comprise the second half of our book's theme this year certainly include economic inequalities, environmental crises, and the scourge of war. But even the most in-depth journalism on these topics, or the most sophisticated analyses of their interconnectedness, will not help if those reports and analyses leave their audiences disenchanted or cynical.

As teachers and in our public work for Project Censored, we regularly encounter evidence of this dangerous result. For example, when independent journalists first began to document how Central Intelligence Agency (CIA) officials had consulted on the production of the movie *Zero Dark Thirty*, we posted one such report on Project Censored's Facebook page.[8] Within minutes, a person following our posts wrote in response, "This is news?" Similarly, during a classroom discussion of the revelation that Barack Obama's administration had demanded—and the Associated Press had provided—the phone records for a number of AP journalists, a student seemed intent on closing down further discussion by posing the cynical question, "Why are you surprised?"[9]

The more we learn about climate-induced species extinctions, the consolidation of a nearly incomprehensible amount wealth in the hands of a global "superclass," or a "new" imperialism in Africa—to name just three of the crucial topics, expertly addressed by authors in subsequent sections of *Censored 2014*—the greater the risk that we too may respond cynically, "This is news?" or "Why are you surprised?" Those afflicted are too "cool" (read: jaded) to get upset about the latest environmental catastrophe or political scandal: they have effectively turned away from politics.

In many ways, the corporate media encourage such responses. But, we confess to being surprised when we recently read—in the *New York Times*, no less—that conspiracy theories and those who advocate them are to blame for cynicism about politics. In "Sure You Saw a Flying Saucer," Maggie Koerth-Baker drew on psychological research to show that those who believe in conspiracy theories are "more likely to be cynical about the world in general and politics in particular." She continued,

> Conspiracy theories also seem to be more compelling to those with low self-worth, especially with regard to their sense of agency in the world at large. Conspiracy theories appear to be a way of reacting to uncertainty and powerlessness.[10]

From this perspective, the problem is that, although conspiracy theories give their believers a *feeling* of being in control, they do not actually confer greater control. "Psychologists aren't sure whether powerlessness causes conspiracy theories or vice versa," Koerth-Baker wrote. "Either way, the current scientific thinking suggests these beliefs are nothing more than an extreme form of cynicism, a turning away from politics and traditional media."[11]

At the risk of identifying ourselves as suffering from low self-worth or powerlessness, we note that, by emphasizing psychological rather than sociological or historical understandings of conspiracy theories, Koerth-Baker offers at best a partial understanding of the links between conspiracy theories and political cynicism. Kathryn Olmsted, a historian at University of California–Davis, provided useful counterpoint to the predominating low self-worth explanation—though Koerth-Baker paraphrased Olmsted, rather than quoting her directly: "[C]onspiracy theories wouldn't exist in a world in which real conspiracies didn't exist."[12]

INSIDE *CENSORED 2014*

We organized *Censored 2014* into three primary sections.

Section I features our listing and summaries of the Top 25 Censored Stories for 2012–13, as well as in-depth analyses of those stories in the form of Censored News Clusters by Brian Covert, James F. Tracy, Susan Rahman and Donna Nassor, Targol Mesbah and Zara Zimbardo, Susan Rahman and Liliana Valdez-Madera, and Andy Lee Roth, who each contribute news clusters that "connect the dots," by identifying overarching themes that link individual stories and by offering background analysis of the *types* of stories most likely to be underreported or censored in corporate coverage.

Three additional chapters add breadth to this first section's analysis of the Top 25 stories.

Chapter 2 revisits six selected Top 25 Censored Stories from previous years, focusing on their subsequent corporate coverage and the extent to which they have either become part of broader public discourse, or have remained "censored" by corporate media. Mickey Huff and Nolan Higdon work with Project Censored intern researchers and writers Andrew O'Connor-Watts, Jen Eiden, Allen Kew, Emmie Ruhland, Aaron Hudson, Rex Yang, Sam Park, Amitai Cohen, Michael Kolbe, and Matthew Carhart to bring us up-to-date on news media coverage of key past stories addressing the emerging police state, Federal Bureau of Investigation–involved and subsequently thwarted terror plots, economic global ruling elites, the US and al-Qaeda in Syria, sexual assaults on women in the US military, and President Obama's use of drones and the ongoing assassination campaign.

Chapter 3 features Project Censored's annual review of Junk Food News, News Abuse, and the ongoing problem of Infotainment. Project Censored interns Michael Kolbe, Sam Park, and Kimberly Soiero, Jen Eiden, along with Mickey Huff and Nolan Higdon, survey a year's worth of establishment news coverage to contrast the corporate lowlights, distractions, and propaganda with the independent press's stellar alternatives. From the Korean rapper Psy's dance craze and the return of MC Hammer to election debates involving Big Bird and national lamentations over the Twinkie, this year's offerings, from the insipid to mendacious, are so far off the infotainment charts that "U Can't Touch This."

Chapter 4, "Media Democracy in Action," takes readers on a tour through the "no-spin" zone—territory that increasingly appears outside the range of corporate news media. Daniel Ellsberg's essay, "On Civil Courage," sets the tone for this chapter on free press and free speech advocates who make a difference, and really connects with Foucault's analysis of *parrhesia*, or fearless speech, outlined earlier. "Media Democracy in Action" also features Josh Wolf of Journalism that Matters, William Creely with the Foundation for Individual Rights in Education, Christopher M. Finan of the American Booksellers Foundation for Free Expression, Acacia O'Connor on the National Coalition Against Censorship and the Kids' Right to Read Project, Tony Diaz of Librotraficante, Beau Hodai of the Center for Media and Democracy and DBA Press on "Dissent or Terror," Sunsara Taylor on Stop Patriarchy, John Collins and *The Weave*, and Ken Walden on "What the World Could Be." This chapter is meant to inspire us to action and further build community around free speech, free press, and free thought ideals.

Section II addresses the importance of critical thinking and media literacy in addressing narratives of power. Crucial skills for all community members and citizens, critical thinking and media literacy go to the heart of Project Censored's ongoing mission to educate students about the importance of a truly free press for democratic self-government. Do you know the Disney origins of our misconception about lemmings? Using the myth of lemmings' alleged inclination to collective suicide as its organizing metaphor, in Chapter 5, Elliot D. Cohen identifies six critical thinking skills and illustrates their effective use by applying them to corporate news coverage on a range of contemporary issues. Cohen not only invites us to dig deeper, he provides the tools to do the heavy lifting in developing independence of thought.

In Chapter 6, James F. Tracy deepens the analysis of conspiracy theories, cynicism, and public use of reason by looking at the phenomenon of conspiracy panics. He draws on the work of Erich Fromm and C. Wright Mills, among others, to address "the prevailing myth of terrorism as an existential threat to the Western world," and at the same time goes beyond even historian Kathryn Olmsted's observation, calling for the public use of reason in identifying and understanding actual national and international conspiracies as state/corporate crimes against democracy, thus providing a platform from which to safely and openly discuss significant yet controversial matters.

In Chapter 7, John Pilger provides a candid insider's view of censorship within liberal and progressive circles among those who normally decry such censorious actions. Pilger discusses how his documentary *The War You Don't See*, documenting the many failures of the press in wartime, became the film some liberal foundations didn't want people to see in the US. In Chapter 8, Rob Williams concludes the section with a critical analysis of two recent Hollywood films, *Zero Dark Thirty* and *Argo*, showing how "political interests are quick to exploit Hollywood's uniquely powerful reach to propagandize, rather than to educate."

The third and final section of *Censored 2014* offers four case studies of "unhistory" in the making, while this section's fifth and ultimate chapter provides a positive alternative. As in *Censored 2013*, we adapt Noam Chomsky's term "unhistory" to convey the importance of bringing to public attention and holding in collective memory a range of issues, events, and sociohistorical patterns that the corporate media and power elite might otherwise prefer—or actively encourage—the public to ignore or forget.[13]

Thus, whereas establishment academics often analyze "power elites" in the abstract, in Chapter 9, Peter Phillips and Brady Osborne examine the transnational "superclass" in specific detail, summarizing their findings from an exhaustive analysis of the 161 specific individuals who represent "the financial core of the world's transnational capitalist class." Though followers of Project Censored may feel like they have learned all they need to know about the problematic role of Apple and its subcontractors in China, Nicki Lisa Cole and Tara Krishna deepen our understanding in Chapter 10, "Apple Exposed." By examining Chinese news coverage—some of which they translate into English for a first time here—Cole and Krishna find that US reporting on Apple in China "has been clouded by a Western lens, and that it has overwhelmingly ignored the voices of workers themselves, rural Chinese citizens affected by environmental pollution, and those displaced by ongoing construction of new factories."

In Chapter 11, Brian Martin Murphy, who served for six years as editor in chief of Inter Press Service's African bureau, surveys the recent history of conflict in Saharan Africa to put the current crisis in Mali into perspective. His account illuminates standing US interests in the region and disentangles the indigenous Tuareg role, two angles of the Mali story that are crucial to a deep understanding of ongoing events in the region, but which US corporate media coverage either obscures or omits.

In "The Sixth Mass Extinction," our penultimate chapter (in perhaps more ways than one), Julie Andrzejewski and John C. Alessio amplify the theme of climate change addressed in Sarah van Gelder's foreword. Andrzejewski and Alessio identify obstacles to assessing and taking seriously what we know scientifically about the impact of climate change on animal extinction. In keeping with our focus on critique and affirmation, they provide six important steps that we can take to "reverse the forces driving the extinction process."

Finally, shifting from the threats and challenges of "unhistory" to building a better future, Michael Nagler of the Metta Center for Nonviolence explains why we need a "new story" and explains how to tell it, using the Center's clear and realistic "Roadmap" as a guide. Nagler's chapter brings *Censored 2014* full circle, back to the keynote of Sarah van Gelder's foreword heralding solutions journalism, providing powerful ideas and practical actions for a better future.

NOW'S THE TIME

The cover of *Censored 2014* features detail from artist Marcia Annenberg's striking piece, "No News Is Good News." We do not believe there is a more salient image to convey the theme of this year's book, "Fearless Speech in Fateful Times." In "No News Is Good News," the cord, which pulls back the veil to reveal the day's news, is adorned by a bow that features the US flag's stars and stripes. Truth-telling—including whistleblowing and other forms of fearless speech—is patriotic, as those who engage in fearless speech remind us when they invoke defense of the Constitution, protection of the commonwealth, and informing the public as the driving motivations for their selfless acts of civil courage.

As Project Censored's associate director and director, and as coeditors of *Censored 2014*, the message of Annenberg's artwork, with the creativity and integration of history behind it, reminds us of two crucial insights integral for building a better future. First, in the hands of *independent* journalists—who number too many for even such an extensive volume as this to identify and appreciate completely—the US has a robust free press worthy of the loftiest ideals expressed in the US Constitution and Article 19 of the Universal Declaration of Human Rights. Second, and related, given the urgency of those journalists' dispatches and our authors' keen analyses, we hope that *Censored 2014* will inspire you, too, with our abiding feeling that, more than ever, *now* is the time to do something good in service of a better future, for ourselves, our communities, and the world.

Notes

1. Michel Foucault, *Fearless Speech*, ed., Joseph Pearson (Los Angeles, Semiotext(e), 2001).
2. Ibid., 11–14.
3. Ibid., 22; as Foucault states in a subsequent lecture, members of Greco-Roman culture understood *parrhesia* as "not primarily a concept or theme, but a *practice*," 106, emphasis original.
4. Ibid., 19, emphases added. Foucault uses male pronouns here and throughout the lectures, but obviously, in contemporary context, fearless speech is not exclusively a male domain.
5. Ibid., 16.
6. Foucault: "The *parrhesia* comes from 'below,' as it were, and is directed toward 'above,'" ibid., 18; again, "[T]he king or tyrant generally cannot use *parrhesia* for he risks nothing," 16.
7. Thanks to Steve Sherwood for teaching me [ALR] this simple but crucial point, back when we were graduate students in sociology at University of California–Los Angeles.
8. See, for example, Adrian Chen, "Newly Declassified Memo Shows CIA Shaped *Zero Dark Thirty*'s Narrative," *Gawker*, May 6, 2013, http://gawker.com/declassified-memo-shows-how-

cia-shaped-zero-dark-thirty-493174407. For more on this topic, see Rob Williams, "Screening the Homeland," in this volume.

9. "Chris Hedges: Monitoring of AP Phones a 'Terrifying' Step in State Assault on Press Freedom," *Democracy Now!*, May 15, 2013, http://www.democracynow.org/2013/5/15/chris_hedges_monitoring_of_ap_phones.
10. Maggie Koerth-Baker, "Sure You Saw a Flying Saucer," *New York Times Magazine*, May 26, 2013, 16.
11. Ibid.
12. Ibid.
13. Noam Chomsky, "Anniversaries from 'Unhistory,'" *In These Times*, February 6, 2012, http://inthesetimes.com/article/12679/anniversaries_from_unhistory. See also *Censored 2013: Dispatches from the Media Revolution*, Mickey Huff and Andy Lee Roth with Project Censored (New York: Seven Stories, 2012), 25, 217, 333–4.

CENSORED NEWS AND MEDIA ANALYSIS

All censorships exist to prevent anyone from challenging current conceptions and existing institutions. All progress is initiated by challenging current conceptions, and executed by supplanting existing institutions. Consequently, the first condition of progress is the removal of censorship. There is the whole case against censorships in a nutshell.

—George Bernard Shaw[1]

The first chapter of *Censored 2014* summarizes and analyzes the twenty-five most important censored news stories for 2012–13. The presentation of this year's Top 25 stories extends the tradition originated by Professor Carl Jensen and his Sonoma State students in 1976, while reflecting how the expansion of the Project to include affiliate faculty and students from campuses across the country and around the world—initiated several years ago as outgoing director Peter Phillips passed the reins to current director Mickey Huff—has made the Project even more diverse and robust.

During this year's cycle, Project Censored reviewed 233 Validated Independent News stories (VINs) representing the collective efforts of 219 college students and 56 professors from 18 college and university campuses that participate in our affiliate program, with 13 additional community evaluators. A perusal of the credits for this year's Top 25 gives evidence of how the affiliates program extends Project Censored's ability to "ensure progress by removing censorships." We look forward to doubling the size of the affiliates program in the next year, and we invite interested faculty and students to visit our website in order to learn how to get involved.

Of course, no matter how robust our network, Project Censored could not exist without the dedicated efforts of the independent journalists and news organizations that publish and broadcast the news stories that we bring to broader public attention. Although many of the Top 25 stories can be interpreted as emphasizing "what's wrong" in the world today, we hope that our annual list is also understood as a celebration and appreciation of the good work that these independent reporters and news organizations do.

Those familiar with Project Censored's work know that we define *censorship* as "anything that interferes with the free flow of information in a society that purports to have a free press."[2] This broader conception of censorship includes

> the subtle yet constant and sophisticated manipulation of reality by mass media. . . . Such manipulation can take the form of political pressure (from government officials and powerful individuals), economic pressure (from advertisers and funders), and legal pressure (from the threat of lawsuits from deep-pocket individuals, corporations, and institutions). Censorship includes stories that were never published, but also those that get such restricted distribution that few in the public are likely to know about them.[3]

By this standard, each of the news stories in our listing of the Top 25 for 2012–13 is a censored story, whether the story has received no corporate coverage at all, or—in cases where the story has received corporate coverage—that coverage is *partial* in one or both senses of the term, i.e., incomplete and/or biased.

Two stories on US drone policy and targeted killings do not appear in this year's Top 25 despite having garnered tremendous support from affiliate campuses' faculty and students and our distinguished panel of judges during this year's story selection process. Although *Democracy Now!* and the *Huffington Post*'s Lindsay Wilkes-Edrington deserve credit for their early coverage of Jeremy Scahill and Rick Rowley's new film, *Dirty Wars*, before *Censored 2014* went to press, the corporate media—perhaps spurred by independent news coverage and growing public concern—has come round to provide some coverage of this important documentary.[4] Similarly, Michel Chossudovsky's Global Research article on Yemeni and Pakistani children killed by US drone strikes brought vital attention to this topic before corporate media did so.[5]

Because these stories eventually gained traction in the corporate media—the *New York Times* and *Washington Post* deserve credit for their coverage[6]—we chose not to include them in this year's Top 25, even though it is obvious that US drone policy is one of the most important ongoing news stories about which all Americans ought to be informed.[7] For more on this topic, see Chapter 2, "Déjà Vu: What Happened to Previous Top Censored Stories?"

Section I begins with a brief "Note on Research and Evaluation," which explains Project Censored's methodology and story selection process, followed by summaries of the Top 25 stories themselves. Then we present this year's Censored News Clusters, highlighting major themes in this year's news cycle that the corporate media frequently overlook in the course of their 24/7 competition to be first, often at the expense of being most thorough or informative. Brian Covert provides perspective on "Whistleblowers and Gag Laws"; James F. Tracy on "Plutocracy, Poverty, and Prosperity"; Susan Rahman and Donna Nassor cover "Human Rights and Civil Liberties"; Targol Mesbah and Zara Zimbardo analyze the "Technologies and Ecologies of War"; Susan Rahman and Liliana Valdez-Madera address "Health and the Environment"; and Andy Lee Roth examines "Iceland, the Power of Peaceful Revolution, and the Commons."

Beyond Chapter 1, the media analysis in this section includes the aforementioned "Déjà Vu," Chapter 2; an examination of corporate Junk Food News and News Abuse, Chapter 3; and "Media Democracy in Action," Chapter 4, our survey of free speech and free press organizations that make a difference.

We hope you will agree that this year's Top 25 stories demonstrate how today's independent journalists, as well as Project Censored, strive tirelessly to remove censorship, challenge current conceptions and existing institutions, and, thereby, ensure progress.

Notes

1. "The Author's Apology" (1902) to *Mrs. Warren's Profession* (1894) in *Plays by George Bernard Shaw* (New York: Penguin, 1960), 41. We are grateful to John K. Roth for bringing this quotation to our attention.
2. See *Censored 2013: Dispatches from the Media Revolution*, Mickey Huff and Andy Lee Roth with Project Censored (New York: Seven Stories, 2012), 30. Also see Antoon De Baets, "Censorship Backfires: A Taxonomy of Concepts Related to Censorship," in *Censored 2013*, 223–234.
3. Ibid, 31.
4. "Dirty Wars: Jeremy Scahill and Rick Rowley's New Film Exposes Hidden Truths of Covert U.S. Warfare," *Democracy Now!*, January 22, 2013, http://www.democracynow.org/2013/1/22/dirty_wars_jeremy_scahill_and_rick; Lindsay Wilkes-Edrington, "'Dirty Wars,' Sundance Documentary, Investigates Joint Special Operations Command," *Huffington Post*, January 28, 2013, http://www.huffingtonpost.com/2013/01/28/dirty-wars-sundance-docum_n_2538914.html. On subsequent corporate coverage, see, for example, Jeremy Egner, "Snapshot: Jeremy Scahill: His Target is Assassinations," *New York Times Magazine*, June 9, 2013, http://www.nytimes.com/2013/06/09/movies/jeremy-scahill-on-his-documentary-dirty-wars.html.
5. Michel Chossudovsky, "The Children Killed by America's Drones," Global Research, January 26, 2013, http://www.globalresearch.ca/the-children-killed-by-americas-drones-crimes-against-humanity-committed-by-barack-h-obama/5320570.
6. At the *Washington Post*, Greg Miller and Karen DeYoung, among others, deserve credit for their reporting on US drone strikes and targeted killings. At the *Times*, Scott Shane, Jo Becker, and others also merit recognition. See, e.g., Mark Mazzetti, Charlie Savage, and Scott Shane, "How a U.S. Citizen Came to Be in America's Cross Hairs," *New York Times*, March 9, 2013, http://www.nytimes.com/2013/03/10/world/middleeast/anwar-al-awlaki-a-us-citizen-in-americas-cross-hairs.html.
7. Peter Scheer, "Connecting the Dots Between Drone Killings and Newly Exposed Government Surveillance," *Huffington Post*, June 8, 2013, http://www.huffingtonpost.com/peter-scheer/drones-surveillance_b_3408487.html. For example, describing Americans' "collective discomfort" with the US government's paradigms of targeted killing and domestic surveillance, Peter Scheer wrote, "The logic of warfare and intelligence has flipped. . . . Warfare has shifted from the scaling of military operations to the selective targeting of individual enemies. Intelligence gathering has shifted from the selective targeting of known threats to wholesale data mining for the purpose of finding hidden threats."

A Note on Research and Evaluation of *Censored* News Stories

How do we at Project Censored identify and evaluate independent news stories, and how do we know that the Top 25 stories that we bring forward each year are not only relevant and significant, but also trustworthy? The answer is that each candidate news story undergoes rigorous review, which takes place in multiple stages during each annual cycle. Although adapted to take advantage of both the Project's expanding affiliates program and current technologies, the vetting process is quite similar to the one Project Censored founder Carl Jensen established thirty-seven years ago.

Candidate stories are initially identified by Project Censored professors and students, or nominated by members of the general public, who bring them to the Project's attention through our website.[1] Together, faculty and students vet each candidate story in terms of its importance, timeliness, quality of sources, and corporate news coverage. If it fails on any one of these criteria, the story does not go forward.

Once Project Censored receives the candidate story, we undertake a second round of judgment, using the same criteria and updating the review of any competing corporate coverage. Stories that pass this round of review get posted on our website as Validated Independent News stories (VINs).[2]

In early spring, we present all VINs in the current cycle to the faculty and students at all of our affiliate campuses, and to our national and international panel of judges, who cast votes to winnow the candidate stories from nearly 300 down to 25.

Once the Top 25 have been determined, students in Peter Phillip's Media Censorship course at Sonoma State University, and Project Censored student interns working with Mickey Huff at Diablo Valley College, begin another intensive review of each story using LexisNexis and ProQuest databases.

The Top 25 finalists are then sent to our panel of judges, who vote to rank them in numerical order. At the same time, these experts—including communications and media studies professors, professional journalists, and a former commissioner of the Federal Communications Commission, among others—offer their insights on the stories' strengths and weaknesses.[3]

Thus, by the time a story appears in the pages of *Censored*, it has undergone at least five distinct rounds of review and evaluation.

Although the stories that Project Censored brings forward may be socially and politically controversial—and sometimes even psychologically challenging—we are confident that each is the result of serious journalistic effort and, so, deserves greater public attention.

Notes

1. For information on how to nominate a story, see "How To Support Project Censored," at the back of this volume.
2. Validated Independent News stories are archived on the Media Freedom International website: http://www.mediafreedominternational.org/category/validated-independent-news.
3. For a complete list of the national and international judges and their brief biographies, see the acknowledgments section of this book.

CHAPTER 1

The Top Censored Stories and Media Analysis of 2012–13

Compiled by Andy Lee Roth

1. Bradley Manning and the Failure of Corporate Media

In February 2013, United States military intelligence analyst Bradley Manning confessed in court to providing vast archives of military and diplomatic files to the anti-secrecy group WikiLeaks, saying he wanted the information to become public "to make the world a better place" and that he hoped to "spark a domestic debate on the role of the military in (US) foreign policy." The 700,000 released documents revealed a multitude of previously secret crimes and acts of deceit and corruption by US military and government officials.

According to Manning's testimony in February 2013, he tried to release the Afghanistan and Iraq War Logs through conventional sources. In winter 2010, he contacted the *Washington Post*, the *New York Times*, and *Politico* in hopes that they would publish the materials. Only after being rebuffed by these three outlets did Manning begin uploading documents to WikiLeaks. Al Jazeera reported that Manning's testimony "raises the question of whether the mainstream press was prepared to host the debate on US interventions and foreign policy that Manning had in mind."

Indeed, US corporate media have largely shunned Manning's case, not to mention the importance of the information he released. When corporate media have focused on Manning, this coverage has often emphasized his sexual orientation and past life, rather than his First Amendment rights or the abusive nature of his imprisonment, which includes almost three years without trial and nearly

41

one year in "administrative segregation," the military equivalent of solitary.

In his February 2013 court appearance, Manning pled guilty to twelve of the twenty-two charges against him, including the capital offense of "aiding and abetting the enemy." He faces the possibility of a life sentence without parole. His severe treatment is a warning to other possible whistleblowers.

For sources and further analysis, see page 65 and the "Whistleblowers and Gag Laws" News Cluster.

2. Richest Global 1 Percent Hide Trillions in Tax Havens

The global 1 percent hold twenty-one to thirty-two trillion dollars in offshore havens in order to evade taxes, according to James S. Henry, the former chief economist at the global management consulting firm, McKinsey & Company. Based on data from the Bank for International Settlements, the International Monetary Fund, the World Bank, and 139 countries, Henry found that the top 1 percent hid more than the total annual economic output of the US and Japan combined. For perspective, this hidden wealth is at least seven times the amount—$3 trillion—that many estimates suggest would be necessary to end global poverty.

If this hidden wealth earned a modest rate of 3 percent interest and that interest income were taxed at just 30 percent, these investments would have generated income tax revenues between $190 and $280 billion, according to the analysis.

Domestically, the Federal Reserve reported that the top seven US banks hold more than $10 trillion in assets, recorded in over 14,000 created "subsidiaries" to avoid taxes.

Henry identified this hidden wealth as "a huge black hole in the world economy that has never before been measured," and noted that the finding is particularly significant at a time when "governments around the world are starved for resources, and we are more conscious than ever of the costs of economic inequality."

For sources and further analysis, see page 85 and the "Plutocracy, Poverty, and Prosperity" News Cluster.

3. Trans-Pacific Partnership Threatens a Regime of Corporate Global Governance

The Trans-Pacific Partnership (TPP), branded as a trade agreement and negotiated in unprecedented secrecy, is actually an enforceable transfer of sovereignty from nations and their people to foreign corporations.

As of December 2012, eleven countries were involved—Australia, Brunei, Canada, Chile, Malaysia, Mexico, New Zealand, Peru, Singapore, Vietnam, and the United States—with the possibility of more joining in the future due to inclusion of an unusual "docking agreement."

While the public, US Congress, and the press are locked out, 600 corporate advisors are meeting with officials of signatory governments behind closed doors to complete text for the world's biggest multinational trade agreement, which aims to penalize countries that protect their workers, consumers, or environment.

Leaked text from the thirty-chapter agreement has revealed that negotiators have already agreed to many radical terms, granting expansive new rights and privileges for foreign investors and their enforcement through extrajudicial "investor-state" tribunals. Through these, corporations would be given special authority to dispute laws, regulations, and court decisions. Foreign firms could extract unlimited amounts of taxpayer money as compensation for "financial damages" to "expected future profits" caused by efforts to protect domestic finance, health, labor, environment, land use, and other laws they claim undermine their new TPP privileges.

There is almost no progressive movement or campaign whose goals are not threatened, as vast swaths of public-interest policy achieved through decades of struggle are targeted. Lori Wallach, director of Public Citizen's Global Trade Watch, reported that once this top-secret TPP is agreed to, its rules will be set in stone. No rule can be changed without all countries' consent to amend the agreement. People of the world will be locked into corporate domination.

For sources and further analysis, see page 85 and the "Plutocracy, Poverty, and Prosperity" News Cluster.

4. Obama's War on Whistleblowers

Obama signed both the Whistleblower Protection Enhancement Act, expanding whistleblower protections, in November 2012, and the National Defense Authorization Act (NDAA) furthering these protections in January 2013. His NDAA signing statement, however, undermines these protections, stating that those expanded protections "could be interpreted in a manner that would interfere with my authority to manage and direct executive branch officials." Thus, in his signing statement, Obama promised to ignore expanded whistleblower protections if they conflicted with his power to "supervise, control, and correct employees' communications with the Congress in cases where such communications would be unlawful or would reveal information that is properly privileged or otherwise confidential."

Despite rhetoric to the contrary, the Obama administration is targeting government whistleblowers, having invoked the otherwise dormant Espionage Act of 1917 seven times. The Obama justice department has also used the Intelligence Identities Protection Act to obtain a conviction against Central Intelligence Agency (CIA) whistleblower John Kiriakou for exposing the waterboarding of prisoners, ironically making Kiriakou the first CIA official to be sentenced to prison in connection with the torture program. The justice department charged former National Security Agency senior executive Thomas Drake with espionage for exposing hundreds of millions of dollars of waste.

The highly visible prosecution of Bradley Manning has become what some may argue to be the most effective deterrent for government whistleblowers. Manning admitted to leaking troves of classified documents to WikiLeaks, but pleaded not guilty on counts of espionage.

For sources and further analysis, see page 65 and the "Whistleblowers and Gag Laws" News Cluster.

5. Hate Groups and Antigovernment Groups on Rise across US

The Southern Poverty Law Center (SPLC), which monitors hate

groups and antigovernment groups, released a report showing that 1,360 radical, antigovernment "patriot" groups and 321 militias actively operate within the United States. Released in March 2013, these statistics show an 813 percent rise in the number of such groups since 2008, with increasing numbers each year. Hate groups are most prevalent in California, with eighty-four total; Texas was second among states with sixty-two.

The SPLC counted over 1,000 hate groups in the US in 2012. By the SPLC's standards, hate groups "have beliefs or practices that attack or malign an entire class of people, typically for their immutable characteristics," and their activities can include "criminal acts, marches, rallies, speeches, meetings, leafleting or publishing."

With the numbers of Patriot groups now much higher now than they were during the peak of the militia movement in the 1990s, the threat of domestic terror attacks is very real. After the SPLC's report was released, the Center's president, Richard Cohen, sent a letter to the US attorney general as well as the Homeland Security secretary requesting them to "create a new task force to ensure the government is devoting the resources needed to address domestic terrorism."

Hate groups are now transitioning from racist hatred to hatred focused on the government and its representatives. The patriot and militia groups are some of the fastest growing groups, and their goals and rhetoric must be understood in order to implement successful strategies to counter their behavior if it should become violent, according to the SPLC. The SPLC also identified "sovereign citizens," who often operate as "lone wolves," breaking away from the group to perform the violent acts. Unfortunately, with the use of social media and the Internet, hate groups are able to recruit and spread their beliefs more readily than in the past.

Corporate media have paid scattered attention to the SPLC report and its findings. Both the *New York Times* and MSNBC covered the report on the day the SPLC issued it, but otherwise, establishment media have done little to shed light on this subject.

For sources and further analysis, see page 101 and the "Human Rights and Civil Liberties" News Cluster.

6. Billionaires' Rising Wealth Intensifies Poverty and Inequality

As a direct result of existing financial policies, the world's one hundred richest people grew to be $241 billion richer in 2012. This makes them collectively worth $1.9 trillion, just slightly less than the United Kingdom's total economic output.

A few of the policies responsible for this occurrence are the reduction of tax rates and tax enforcement, the privatization of public assets, wage controls and the destruction of collective bargaining. These same policies that are building up the richest people are causing colossal hardships to the rest of the world's population.

George Monbiot has attributed this situation to neoliberal policies, which produce economic outcomes contrary to those predicted, and even promised, by advocates of neoliberal policy and *laissez faire* markets. In consequence, across the thirty-four countries that constitute the Organ-

isation for Economic Co-operation and Development (OECD), taxation has decreased among the rich and increased among the poor. Despite what neoliberals claimed would happen, the spending power of the state and of poorer people has diminished, contracting demand along with it.

Wage inequality and unemployment have both skyrocketed, making the economy increasingly unstable with monumental amounts of debt. Monbiot observed, "The complete failure of this world-scale experiment is no impediment to its repetition. This has nothing to do with economics. It has everything to do with power."

For sources and further analysis, see page 85 and the "Plutocracy, Poverty, and Prosperity" News Cluster.

7. Merchants of Death and Nuclear Weapons

The Physicians for Social Responsibility released a study estimating that one billion people—one-seventh of the human race—could starve over the decade following a single nuclear detonation. A key finding was that corn production in the United States would decline by an average of 10 percent for an entire decade, with the most severe decline (20 percent) in the fifth year. Another forecast was that increases in food prices would make food inaccessible to hundreds of millions of the world's poorest: the 925 million people in the world who are already chronically malnourished (with a baseline consumption of 1,750 calories or less per day) would be put at risk by a 10 percent decline in their food consumption.

The International Campaign to Abolish Nuclear Weapons (ICAN) released its 180-page study showing that nuclear-armed nations spend over $100 billion each year assembling new warheads, modernizing old ones, and building ballistic missiles, bombers, and submarines to launch them. The US still has about 2,500 nuclear weapons deployed and 2,600 more as backup. Washington and Moscow account for 90 percent of all nuclear weapons. Despite a White House pledge to seek a world without nuclear weapons, the 2011 federal budget for nuclear weapons research and development exceeded $7 billion and could (if the Obama administration has its way) exceed $8 billion per year by the end of this decade.

Nuclear-armed nations spend over $100 billion each year on weapons programs. The institutions most heavily involved in financing nuclear arms makers include Bank of America, BlackRock, and JPMorgan Chase in the United States; BNP Paribas in France; Allianz and Deutsche Bank in Germany; Mitsubishi UFJ Financial Group in Japan; Banco Bilbao Vizcaya Argentaria (BBVA) and Banco Santander in Spain; Credit Suisse and UBS in Switzerland; and Barclays, HSBC, Lloyds, and Royal Bank of Scotland in Britain.

For sources and further analysis, see page 113 and the "Technologies and Ecologies of War" News Cluster.

8. Bank Interests Inflate Global Prices by 35 to 40 Percent

A stunning 35 to 40 percent of everything we buy goes to interest. As Ellen Brown reported, "That helps explain how wealth is systematically transferred from Main Street to Wall Street." In her report, Brown cited the work of Margrit Kennedy, PhD, whose research in Germany documents interest charges ranging from 12 percent for garbage collection, to 38 percent for drinking water, and 77 percent for rent in public housing. Kennedy found that the bottom 80 percent pay the hidden interest charges that the top 10 percent collect, making interest a strongly regressive tax that the poor pay to the rich.

Drawing on Kennedy's data, Brown estimated that if we had a financial system that returned the interest collected from the public directly to the public, 35 percent could be lopped off the price of everything we buy. To this end, she has advocated direct reimbursement. According to Brown, "We could do it by turning the banks into public utilities and their profits into public assets. Profits would return to the public, either reducing taxes or increasing the availability of public services and infrastructure."

For sources and further analysis, see page 86 and the "Plutocracy, Poverty, and Prosperity" News Cluster.

9. Icelanders Vote to Include Commons in Their Constitution

In October 2012, Icelanders voted in an advisory referendum regarding six proposed policy changes to the nation's 1944 Constitution. In response to the question, "In the new Constitution, do you want natural resources that are not privately owned to be declared national property?," Iceland's citizens responded with a decisive "yes." Eighty-one percent of those voting supported the commons proposal.

The constitutional reforms are a direct response to the nation's 2008 financial crash, when Iceland's unregulated banks borrowed more than the country's gross domestic product from international wholesale money markets. As Jessica Conrad of *On the Commons* reported, "It is clear that citizens are beginning to recognize the value of what they share together over the perceived wealth created by the market economy."

After the October vote, Prime Minister Jóhanna Sigur ardóttir said, "The people have put the parliament on probation."

For sources and further analysis, see page 143 and the "Iceland, the Power of Peaceful Revolution, and the Commons" News Cluster.

10. A "Culture of Cruelty" along Mexico–US Border

Migrants crossing the Mexico–US border not only face dangers posed by an unforgiving desert but also abuse at the hands of the US Border Patrol. During their journey through the desert, migrants risk dehydration, starvation, exhaustion, and the possibility of being threatened and robbed. Unfortunately, the dangers continue if they come in contact with the Border Patrol. In "A Culture of Cruelty," the organization No More Deaths revealed human rights violations by the US Border Patrol including limiting or denying migrants water and food, verbal and physical abuse, and failing to provide necessary medical attention. Female migrants face additional violations including sexual abuse, according to No More Deaths. As Erika L. Sánchez reported, "Dehumanization of immigrants is actually part of the Border Patrol's institutional culture. Instances of misconduct are not aberrations, but common practice." The Border Patrol has denied any wrongdoing and has not been held responsible for these abuses.

Public debate on immigration tends to ignore not only the potential dangers of crossing the desert, but also the reasons for the migration of undocumented immigrants to the US. The North American Free Trade Agreement (NAFTA), signed by US president Bill Clinton and Mexican president Carlos Salinas in 1994, displaced many Mexican farmers and workers from their farms. Lack of employment resulting from NAFTA continues to motivate many to migrate to the US.

For sources and further analysis, see page 101 and the "Human Rights and Civil Liberties" News Cluster.

11. Bush Blocked Iran Nuclear Deal

According to a former top Iranian negotiator, Seyed Hossein Mousavian, in 2005 Iran offered a deal to the United States, France, Germany, and the United Kingdom that would have made it impossible for Iran to build nuclear weapons. At that time, Iran did not have the capability to fabricate fuel rods. The offer included the plan to ship its uranium to an "agreed upon country" for enrichment in exchange for yellowcake, the raw material used to make fuel rods. Once uranium

is fabricated into fuel rods, it is practically impossible to reconvert for military purposes. As Gareth Porter reports for *Consortium News*, Mousavian's account makes it clear that President George W. Bush's administration "refused to countenance any Iranian enrichment capability, regardless of the circumstances."

The French and German governments were prepared at the time to discuss the offer and open up negotiations, but the UK vetoed the proposal at the insistence of the United States. "They were ready to compromise but the US was an obstacle," Mousavian reported in his 2012 memoir, *The Iranian Nuclear Crisis*.

The continuation of these negotiations could have headed off the current political crisis over the Iranian nuclear program, if not eliminated the threat of war and the strain of strict economic sanctions.

After the US and the UK rejected the offer, the European Union stated that more time was required to consider the proposal, but Mousavian's team learned later that the EU had no intention of revisiting the proposal.

Mousavian quoted Francois Nicoullaud, the French ambassador to Iran, as saying that "for the United States the enrichment in Iran is a red line the EU cannot cross." British representative to the International Atomic Energy Agency (IAEA) Peter Jenkins recalled that "the British objective was to eliminate entirely Iran's enrichment capability," at the urging of the United States. One proposal placed a ceiling on the number of centrifuges and the scale of production so that it remained well below the levels necessary for the production of weaponry. Then British and American teams ignored these negotiations to put pressure on Iran with the threat of referral to the United Nations Security Council. As Iranian presidential elections approached, the talks were abandoned.

Now a visiting research scholar at Princeton University's Woodrow Wilson School of Public and International Affairs, Mousavian was arrested by the Mahmoud Ahmadinejad administration on charges of espionage in April 2007.

For sources and further analysis, see page 113 and the "Technologies and Ecologies of War" News Cluster.

12. The US Has Left Iraq with an Epidemic of Cancers and Birth Defects

High levels of lead, mercury, and depleted uranium are believed to be causing birth defects, miscarriages, and cancer for people living in the Iraqi cities of Basra and Fallujah. Researchers have claimed that the United States bombings of Basra and Fallujah are to blame for this rapidly increasing health crisis.

A recent study showed more than 50 percent of babies born in Fallujah have a birth defect, while one in six pregnancies ends in a miscarriage. While there is no conclusive evidence to show that US military attacks directly caused these health problems among Iraqi citizens, the immense increase of birth defects and miscarriages after the attacks has been enough to concern a number of researchers.

Military officials continue to dodge questions about the attacks, and about use of depleted uranium in particular, while maintaining silence about the health crisis. Instead, the US government has dismissed the reports as controversial and baseless.

For sources and further analysis, see page 113 and the "Technologies and Ecologies of War" News Cluster.

13. A Fifth of Americans Go Hungry

An August 2012 Gallup poll showed that 18.2 percent of Americans lacked sufficient money for needed food at least once over the previous year. To make matters worse, the worst drought in half a century impacted 80 percent of agricultural lands in the country, increasing food prices. Despite this, in 2012, Congress considered cutting support for Supplemental Nutrition Assistance Program (SNAP)— the official name of its food stamp program—as part of the 2013 Farm Bill.

Proposed Senate cuts would cost approximately 500,000 households about ninety dollars a month in nutritional assistance. Proposed cuts in the House of Representatives would go much further than the ones in the Senate, and would have removed at least 1.8 million people from SNAP. Republicans controlling the House have been eager to cut spending and were the primary supporters of food stamp cuts.

Opponents have expressed concern over the harm the cuts would cause to society's more vulnerable members, including seniors, children, and working families. Rising food prices would hit Southern states the hardest, while Mountain-Plains and Midwest states would be least affected. Despite all the food hardship, the National Resources Defense Council reported that 40 percent of food in the country goes to waste.

For sources and further analysis, see page 86 and the "Plutocracy, Poverty, and Prosperity" News Cluster.

14. Wireless Technology a Looming Health Crisis

As a multitude of hazardous wireless technologies are deployed in homes, schools, and workplaces, government officials and industry representatives continue to insist on their safety despite growing evidence to the contrary. Extensive deployment of "smart grid" technology hastens this looming health crisis.

By now many residents in the United States and Canada have smart meters—which transfer detailed information on residents' electrical usage back to the utility every few minutes—installed on their dwellings. Each meter has an electronic cellular transmitter that uses powerful bursts of electromagnetic radio frequency (RF) radiation to communicate with nearby meters, which together form an interlocking network. Such information can easily be used to determine individual patterns of behavior based on power consumption.

Utilities sell smart grid technology to the public as a way to "empower" individual energy consumers, allowing them to access information on their energy usage so that they may eventually save money by programming "smart" (i.e., wireless-enabled) home appliances and equipment to run when electrical rates are lowest. In other words, a broader plan behind smart grid technology involves a tiered rate system for electricity consumption that will be set by the utility, to which customers will have no choice but to conform.

For sources and further analysis, see page 127 and the "Health and the Environment" News Cluster.

15. Food Riots: The New Normal?

Reduced land productivity, combined with elevated oil costs and population growth, threaten a systemic, global food crisis. Citing findings from a study by Paul and Anne Ehrlich, published by the Royal Society, Nafeez Mosaddeq Ahmed identified the links among intensifying economic inequality, debt, climate change, and fossil fuel dependency to conclude that a global food crisis is now "undeniable."

"Global food prices have been consistently higher than in preceding decades," reported Ahmed, leading to dramatic price increases in staple foods and triggering food riots across the Middle East, North Africa, and South Asia. The crux of this global phenomenon is climate change: severe natural disasters including drought, flood, heat waves, and monsoons have affected major regional food baskets. By mid-century, Ahmed reported, "world crop yields could fall as much as 20–40 percent because of climate change alone."

Industrial agricultural methods that disrupt soil have also contributed to impending food shortages. As a result, Ahmed reported, global land productivity has "dropped significantly," from 2.1 percent during 1950–90 to 1.2 percent during 1990–2007.

By contrast with Ahmed's report, corporate media coverage of food insecurity has tended to treat it as a local and episodic problem. For example, an April 2008 story in the *Los Angeles Times* covered food riots in Haiti, which resulted in three deaths. Similarly, a March 2013 *New York Times* piece addressed how the loss of farmland and farm labor to urbanization contributed to rising food costs in China. Corporate media have not connected the dots to analyze how intensifying inequality, debt, climate change, and consumption of fossil fuels have contributed to the potential for a global food crisis in the near future.

For sources and further analysis, see page 127 and the "Health and the Environment" News Cluster.

16. Journalism Under Attack Around the Globe

The world is a more dangerous place for journalists. Journalists are increasingly at risk of being killed or imprisoned for doing their jobs, a situation that imperils press freedom. From 2011 to 2012, the number of journalists behind bars because of their work increased from 53 to 232, and the 70 journalists killed in the line of duty during 2012 represents a 43 percent increase, compared with 2011, according to a study by the Committee to Project Journalists (CPJ). Over the past two decades, a journalist is killed once every eight days.

The CPJ also published a Risk List, identifying the ten countries worldwide where press freedom suffered the most in 2012. Notably, half of the nations on the Risk List—Brazil, Turkey, Pakistan, Russia, and Ecuador—"practice some form of democracy and exert significant influence on a regional or international stage."

"When journalists are silenced, whether through violence or laws, we all stand to lose because perpetrators are able to obscure misdeeds, silence dissent, and disempower citizens," said CPJ deputy director Robert Mahoney.

The CPJ has been a leader in advocating for full implementation of a five-year-old UN resolution calling for protection of journalists in conflict zones, in order to guarantee a free and safe press. Article 19 of the 1948 Universal Declaration of Human Rights includes the freedom to "impart information and ideas through any media and regardless of frontiers," making freedom of press a transnational right.

The New York Times ran a story on the CPJ report on February 15, 2013, noting the alarming rise in the number of journalists killed and imprisoned during 2012. However, the *Times'* report did not address the possible UN resolution or freedom of press as a transnational right.

Dave Lindorff, of *ThisCantBeHappening!*, writes that "the incidence of journalists killed by US forces in recent US conflicts has been much, much greater than it ever was in earlier wars, such as the one in Vietnam, or in Korea or World War II," begging the question of whether some of the deaths have been "deliberate, perhaps with the intent of keeping journalists in line."

For sources and further analysis, see page 65 and the "Whistleblowers and Gag Laws" News Cluster.

17. The Creative Commons Celebrates Ten Years of Sharing and Cultural Creation

Creative Commons (CC) is celebrating ten years of helping writers, artists, technologists, and other creators share their knowledge and creativity with the world. CC provides free, public, and standardized licenses that allow creators to share their material with others and help create a balance between the open nature of public domain (e.g., the Internet) and copyright laws. The first CC licenses were issued in December 2002, and they now number in the millions. For example, governments and libraries make their information available to the public using CC tools. YouTube now has over four million videos available under Creative Commons, allowing everyone to use, remix, and edit them.

A strong push for copyright reform is currently occurring around the world—coming both from the increased recognition of public/user rights as well as the need for author protection. Creative Commons and the free culture movement envision a new world in which partnership premised on shared benefits replaces the false battle between self-interest and community. To imitate or steal an idea is one thing, but to transform or remix content, while crediting its originator, is something new and completely different. Collaboration is the center of community, and CC tools offer a major step toward a more collaborative and abundant world.

For sources and further analysis, see page 143 and the "Iceland, the Power of Peaceful Revolution, and the Commons" News Cluster.

18. Fracking Our Food Supply

The effects of hydraulic fracturing (or "fracking") on food supply and the environment are slowly emerging. The fracking process runs contrary to safe sustainable food production. In the agriculturally and energy-rich region called the Marcellus Shale, a tug-of-war between food producers and energy companies has begun.

Chemicals used in the fracking process contaminate surrounding land, water, and air. Ranchers in Pennsylvania, North Dakota, Louisiana, and New Mexico have been reporting health problems and incidents of dead and tainted livestock, due to elevated levels of contaminants from nearby wells.

While no long-term research on the effects of fracking on humans, livestock, or plants exists, a peer-reviewed report by Michelle Bamberger and Robert E. Oswald has linked fracking to illness in animals. They believe chemicals leaking from fracking sites could start appearing in human food supplies, because of a lack of regulation and testing.

There is an absence of both adequate disclosures by energy companies and timely regulation by government to protect the environment and landowners. Secrecy shrouding the fracking process and Bush-era loopholes obscure consumer knowledge of food safety.

A lack of whistleblowers has been attributed to fear of retaliation, nondisclosure agreements, or involvement in active litigation. While some fear that the early warnings will be ignored, two major agricultural insurance companies now refuse to cover damages from fracking.

For sources and further analysis, see page 127 and the "Health and the Environment" News Cluster.

19. The Power of Peaceful Revolution in Iceland

Iceland is experiencing one of the greatest economic comebacks of all time, reported Alex Pietrowski.

After privatization of the nation's banking sector, completed in 2000, private bankers borrowed $120 billion (ten times the size of Iceland's economy), creating a huge economic bubble that doubled housing prices and made a small percentage of the country's population exceedingly wealthy. When the bubble burst, the bankers left the nation on the verge of bankruptcy and its citizens with an unpayable debt.

In October 2008, Iceland's people took to the streets in response to the economic crisis caused by the banksters. Over a span of five months, the main bank of Iceland was nationalized, government officials were forced to resign, the old government was liquidated, and a new government was established. By March 2010, Iceland's people voted to deny payment of the €3,500 million debt created by the bankers, and about 200 high-level executives and bankers responsible for the economic crisis in the country were either arrested or faced criminal charges.

In February 2011, a new constitutional assembly settled in to rewrite the tiny nation's constitution, which aimed to avoid entrapment by debt-based currency foreign loans. In 2012, the Paris-based Organisation for Economic Co-operation and Development expected Iceland's economy to outgrow the euro and the average for the developed world.

For sources and further analysis, see page 143 and the "Iceland, the Power of Peaceful Revolution, and the Commons" News Cluster.

20. Israel Counted Minimum Calorie Needs in Gaza Blockade

Declassified documents reveal that the Israeli military calculated how many calories a typical Gazan would need to survive, in order to determine how much food to supply the Gaza Strip during Israel's 2007–2010 blockade. The Israeli human rights group Gisha, which campaigns against Israel's Gaza blockade, fought a legal battle to force the Israeli Ministry of Defense to release the documents.

Israel began its blockade in September 2007, identifying Gaza as a "hostile territory" that had been "seized" by Hamas. Israel claimed that the blockade was necessary to weaken Hamas. Critics accused the Israeli government of targeting Gaza's more than 1.5 million people in its failed effort to overthrow Hamas.

In the food calculation, Israel applied the average daily requirement of 2,279 calories per person to determine that it would allow roughly 1,836 grams of food per person, per day. Food imports to Gaza were cut by nearly 75 percent, from 400 trucks per day to 106 trucks per day, five days a week, from the start of the blockade.

"How can Israel claim that it is not responsible for civilian life in Gaza when it controls even the type and quantity of food that Palestinian residents of Gaza are permitted to consume?" asked Sari Bashi, Gisha's executive director, in a statement. After Gisha published the documents, Israeli defense ministry official Guy Inbar defended the Israeli research paper as something "that came up in two discussions" but was "never made use of."

These developments occurred against the backdrop of a diplomatic cable from 2008 showing that Israel informed US officials that it would keep Gaza's economy "on the brink of collapse" while avoiding a humanitarian crisis.

For sources and further analysis, see page 101 and the "Human Rights and Civil Liberties" News Cluster.

21. Monsanto and India's "Suicide Economy"

Monsanto has a long history of contamination and cover-up. In India, another Monsanto cover-up is ongoing. Since 1995, nearly 300,000 Indian farmers have committed suicide due to massive debt. Monsanto has argued that these suicides have no single cause. However, there is clear evidence that Monsanto's Bt cotton is implicated. Physicist and author Vandana Shiva has been monitoring what is going on in these rural farming towns. Shiva noted, "The price per kilogram of cotton seeds [has gone] from 7 to 17,000 rupees. . . . Monsanto sells its GMO seeds on fraudulent claims of yields of 1,500 kg/year when farmers harvest 300–400 kg/year on an average." Shiva and other critics have concluded that Monsanto's profit-driven policies have led to a "suicide economy" in India.

A new documentary film, *Dirty White Gold* by Leah Borromeo, goes beyond the issue of farmer suicides to explain how the global fashion industry and international consumer habits contribute to Indian farmers' hardships. *Dirty White Gold* examined the cotton supply chain, with the aim of generating support for legislation that will, in Borromeo's words, "make ethics and sustainability the norm in the fashion industry."

Monsanto's horrific impact in India is also showcased in an earlier documentary, *Bitter Seeds*, directed by Micha X. Peled, which follows a teenage girl whose father committed suicide due to debt. *Bitter Seeds* showcased the major problems people in India are having, and how Monsanto lies directly to Indian farmers, going as far as making up fictitious farmers who "have success" with the new Bt cotton. Monsanto has claimed that there has also been a 25 percent reduction in pesticide costs. In *Bitter Seeds*, both of these claims were proven false.

For sources and further analysis, see page 127 and the "Health and the Environment" News Cluster.

22. Pennsylvania Law Gags Doctors to Protect Big Oil's "Proprietary Secrets"

In communities affected by hydraulic fracturing, or "fracking," people understand that this process of drilling for natural gases puts the environment and their health at risk. In February 2013, legislators in Pennsylvania—a state on the forefront of a national debate over fracking—passed a law that requires oil companies to disclose the identity and amount of chemicals used in fracking fluids to health professionals who request the information so that they can diagnosis or treat patients who may have been exposed to hazardous chemicals. However, as Kate Sheppard reported for *Mother Jones*, a provision in the new bill requires those health professionals to sign a confidentiality agreement stating that they will not disclose that information to anyone else—not even their own patients. The companies deem the chemical ingredients used in the process as "proprietary secrets."

The crucial provision gagging doctors was added after the bill was introduced, so many lawmakers did not recognize the broad, problematic alterations to the proposed law. Pennsylvania State Senator Daylin Leach told *Mother Jones*, "The importance of keeping it as proprietary secret seems minimal when compared to letting the public know what chemicals they and their children are being exposed to."

An addendum to the *Mother Jones* report noted that Patrick Henderson, the energy executive for Pennsylvania Governor Tom Corbett, said that others' interpretation of the law is inaccurate. Doctors will still be allowed to share information with their patients. However, Kate Sheppard reported, "the actual terms of the confidentiality agreements have not yet been drafted, and there seems to be pretty wide confusion in the state about what exactly the bill as signed into law would mean."

Under the Obama administration, the Environmental Protection Agency has pressed oil companies to voluntarily provide information about fracking fluids, but the industry has largely rebuffed those appeals.

For sources and further analysis, see page 65 and the "Whistleblowers and Gag Laws" News Cluster.

23. Transaction Tax Helps Civilize Wall Street and Lower the National Debt

In February 2013, United States senators Tom Harkin (D-Iowa) and Peter DeFazio (D-Oregon) introduced a bill to implement a new tax of three basis points (that is, three pennies for every hundred dollars) on most nonconsumer stock trades. If made law, the tax could generate $350 billion in federal revenues over the next ten years.

Describing the proposed tax as a "simple matter of fairness and fiscal sanity," Senator Harkin elaborated, "We need the new revenue generated by this tax in order to reduce deficits (after sequestration) and maintain critical investments in education, infrastructure, and job creation. . . . Wall Street (investors) can easily bear this modest tax."

Because the tax is percentage-based, large transactions would be harder hit; most middle-class investors would see minimally increased charges. The tax would also help curb overzealous market speculation by discouraging the large-sum, short-term, risky trading that tends to put the economy in a fragile state.

This bill has been proposed in previous congressional sessions, yet it has been underreported in the corporate media, making it hard to gain public support.

France recently became the first country in Europe to pass such a tax. French finance minister Pierre Moscovici said the law marks "the first step toward fiscal reform and a move toward justice." Ten other European countries are discussing similar laws. For the US, the Harkin–DeFazio transaction tax would be a major step in civilizing speculative investment, stabilizing the economy, and reducing the national debt.

For sources and further analysis, see page 86 and the "Plutocracy, Poverty, and Prosperity" News Cluster.

24. Widespread GMO Contamination: Did Monsanto Plant GMOs Before USDA Approval?

Monsanto introduced genetically modified alfalfa in 2003—a full two years before it was deregulated, according to recently released evidence. Global Research reported that a letter from Cal/West Seeds indicated that "evidence of contamination was withheld and the USDA turned a blind eye to proof of contamination," thus allowing widespread GMO contamination of GMO-free crops. The Cal/West Seeds letter to the United States Department of Agriculture (USDA) stated they found the Round-up Ready gene in foundation production lots seeds in 2005: according to the letter, the GMO-contaminated foundation seed originated in 2003 from a field in Solano County, California. The letter stated, "Cal/West Seeds had zero access to Roundup Ready seed at that time; therefore we assume the contamination originated from an external source."

Alfalfa is a perennial plant that grows for more than two years and may not need to be replanted each year like annuals. As a perennial, it is exceptionally vulnerable to contamination. This genetically modified alfalfa could quickly spread to crops across the US, threatening the integrity of organic products—including organic meat and dairy products, if those animals are fed alfalfa believed to be GMO-free, but are in fact carrying Monsanto's patented genetically modified trait.

In 2010, the USDA released a Final Environmental Impact Statement that acknowledged awareness of the GMO alfalfa spreading its traits to non-GMO alfalfa as far back as 2003. Not only was the USDA aware of the scandal, but the agency also deregulated genetically modified alfalfa with full awareness of the environmental dangers and contamination concerns.

For sources and further analysis, see page 128 and the "Health and the Environment" News Cluster.

25. Israel Gave Birth Control to Ethiopian Immigrants Without Their Consent

In January 2013, Israel acknowledged that medical authorities have been giving Ethiopian immigrants long-term birth-control injections, often without their knowledge or consent. The Israeli government had previously denied the charges, which were first brought to light by investigative reporter Gal Gabbay in a December 8, 2012, broadcast of Israeli Educational Television's news program, *Vacuum*. In January, the Israeli Health Ministry's director-general, Ron Gamzu, ordered all gynecologists to stop administering the drugs.

Gabbay interviewed over thirty women from Ethiopia in an attempt to discover why birth rates in the immigrant community were so low. Israeli medical authorities had been injecting women of Ethiopian origin with a drug alleged to be Depo-Provera, a highly effective and long-lasting form of contraception. In some cases, the drugs were reportedly administered to women waiting in transit camps for permission to immigrate to Israel. Writing for the *Electronic Intifada*, Ali Abunimah makes the case that, "if the allegations are proven, this practice may fit the legal definition of genocide."

Nearly 100,000 Ethiopian Jews have moved to Israel under the Law of Return since the 1980s, but some rabbis have questioned their Jewishness. In May 2012, Israeli prime minister Benjamin Netanyahu ignited controversy when he warned that illegal immigrants from Africa "threaten our existence as a Jewish and democratic state."

For sources and further analysis, see page 102 the "Human Rights and Civil Liberties" News Cluster.

Whistleblowers and Gag Laws

Brian Covert

Censored #1

Bradley Manning and the Failure of Corporate Media

Kevin Gosztola, "The US Press Failed Bradley Manning," *FireDogLake*, February 28, 2013, http://dissenter.firedoglake.com/2013/02/28/the-us-press-failed-bradley-manning/.

Glenn Greenwald, "Bradley Manning: The Face of Heroism," *Guardian*, February 28, 2013, http://www.guardian.co.uk/commentisfree/2013/feb/28/bradley-manning-heroism-pleads-guilty.

Janet Reitman, "Did the Mainstream Media Fail Bradley Manning?," *Rolling Stone*, March 1, 2013, http://www.rollingstone.com/politics/news/did-the-mainstream-media-fail-bradley-manning-20130301.

"The Case of the US vs. Bradley Manning," *Al Jazeera English*, March 9, 2013, http://www.aljazeera.com/programmes/listeningpost/2013/03/201339107329512.html.

Student Researcher: Amanda Renteria (San Francisco State University)

Faculty Evaluator: Kenn Burrows (San Francisco State University)

Censored #4

Obama's War on Whistleblowers

Dana Liebelson, "Why Is Obama Bashing a Whistleblower Law He Already Signed?," *Mother Jones*, January 10, 2013, http://www.motherjones.com/politics/2013/01/obama-whistleblower-protections-signing-statement.

Glenn Greenwald, "Kiriakou and Stuxnet: The Danger of the Still-Escalating Obama Whistleblower War," *Guardian*, January 27, 2013, http://www.guardian.co.uk/commentisfree/2013/jan/27/obama-war-on-whistleblowers-purpose?INTCMP=SRCH.

Paul Harris, "Barack Obama's 'Extreme' Anti-Terror Tactics Face Liberal Backlash," *Guardian*, February 9, 2013, http://www.guardian.co.uk/world/2013/feb/09/barack-obama-extreme-anti-terror-tactics-liberal-backlash?INTCMP=SRCH.

Ed Pilkington, "Bradley Manning Prosecution to Call Full Witness List Despite Guilty Plea," *Guardian*, March 1, 2013, http://www.guardian.co.uk/world/2013/mar/01/bradley-manning-prosecution-guilty-plea.

Student Researchers: Shannon Polvino, William Scannapieco, Kathyrn La Juett, and Justin Lewis (State University of New York–Buffalo)

Faculty Evaluator: Michael I. Niman (State University of New York–Buffalo)

Censored #16

Journalism Under Attack Around the Globe

Roy Greenslade, "Journalism Under Attack Across the Globe Imperils Press Freedom," *Guardian*, February 14, 2013, http://www.guardian.co.uk/media/greenslade/2013/feb/14/press-freedom-censorship.

"Attacks on the Press: Journalism on the Frontlines in 2012," Committee to Project Journalists, http://cpj.org/2013/02/attacks-on-the-press-in-2012.php.

Dave Lindorff, "Incidents Raise Suspicions on Motive: Killing of Journalists by US Forces a Growing Problem," *ThisCantBeHappening!*, November 22, 2012, http://www.thiscantbehappening.net/node/1438.

Student Researcher: Qui Phan (College of Marin)

Faculty Evaluator: Andy Lee Roth (College of Marin)

Censored #22

Pennsylvania Law Gags Doctors to Protect Big Oil's "Proprietary Secrets"

Kate Sheppard, "For Pennsylvania's Doctors, a Gag Order on Fracking Chemicals," *Mother Jones*, March 23, 2012, http://www.motherjones.com/environment/2012/03/fracking-doctors-gag-pennsylvania.

Christopher Banks, "Pennsylvania Law Gags Doctors," *Liberation News*, June 13, 2012, http://www.pslweb.org/liberationnews/news/pennsylvania-law-gags-doctors.html.

Student Researcher: Lyndsey Casey (Sonoma State University)

Faculty Evaluator: Peter Phillips (Sonoma State University)

RELATED VALIDATED INDEPENDENT NEWS STORY

Prominent Establishment Journalists Turn Whistleblowers Over News Censorship

Glenn Greenwald, "Why Didn't CNN's International Arm Air Its Own Documentary on Bahrain's Arab Spring Repression?" *Guardian*, September 4, 2012, http://m.guardian.co.uk/world/2012/sep/04/cnn-international-documentary-bahrain-arab-spring-repression?cat=world&type=article.

J. D. Heyes, "Bombshell: CNN Takes Money from Foreign Dictators to Run Flattering News Stories About Them," *Natural News*, October 4, 2012, http://www.naturalnews.com/037423_CNN_payola_news_stories.html.

Michael Krieger, "Former Reporter Amber Lyon Exposes Massive Censorship at CNN," *Liberty Blitzkrieg*, September 4, 2012, http://libertyblitzkrieg.com/2012/09/04/meet-amber-lyon-former-reporter-exposes-massive-censorship-at-cnn/.

Abby Martin, "*NY Times* Peddles War Propaganda/Interview with Daniel Simpson," *Breaking the Set*, Russia Today, September 18, 2012, http://www.youtube.com/watch?v=-CuEqywX1VQ.

Student Researcher: Brittany Cocilova (Florida Atlantic University)

Faculty Advisor: James F. Tracy (Florida Atlantic University)

On May 3, 2013, journalists around the world commemorated the twentieth anniversary of World Press Freedom Day, a yearly international day of journalistic reflection and action that has its roots, like much else of human culture, in Africa.

It was in 1991 that dozens of journalists from all across the African continent gathered in the southern African nation of Namibia—then recently liberated from the occupation of the apartheid regime of South Africa—to find solutions to the crisis of news censorship, the jailing and killing of reporters, and the very real threats to the pursuit of truth and freedom of expression in their respective countries.

The result of the African journalists coming together was a bold, uncompromising statement, the Declaration of Windhoek on Promoting an Independent and Pluralistic African Press, that would speak directly to the important work of journalists, press freedom advocates, and media activists around the world for many years to come.[1] The spirit of that declaration evolved into World Press Freedom Day, as later adopted by the United Nations.

In the Central American nation of Costa Rica, site of the official UN-sponsored World Press Freedom Day events for 2013, journalists and others commemorated the day with especially timely discussions on the "safety of journalists, the issue of impunity, and online safety" of news media organizations.[2]

Who should be on an official state visit in San José, the Costa Rican capital, on the twentieth anniversary of World Press Freedom Day but Barack Obama, president of the United States?[3]

Every year since taking office in 2009, President Obama had issued official statements on the annual World Press Freedom Day, stressing the importance of an independent news media, unfettered by government interference, and honoring journalists worldwide who had been persecuted or killed in the line of work.[4] Those honored by President Obama in the past have included slain reporters who covered "crime, corruption, and national security in their home countries . . . and hundreds more each year who face intimidation, censorship, and arbitrary arrest—guilty of nothing more than a passion for truth and a tenacious belief that a free society depends on an informed citizenry."[5]

No such statement of support for freedom of the press, however, was announced by the Obama White House in 2013.[6]

Instead, the extent of President Obama's official concern for a free press this year consisted of two sentences spoken during a media briefing in San José, just across town from the concurrent UN-sponsored World Press Freedom Day conference. "I'm proud to be here as you host World Press Freedom Day," President Obama stated, and then, pointing to members of the US media elites traveling with him: "So, everybody from the American press corps, you should thank the people of Costa Rica for celebrating free speech and an independent press as essential pillars of our democracy."[7]

Just how "thankful" the American news media back home should be became clear exactly one week later on May 10: the US Department of Justice under President Obama notified the Associated Press news agency that day that it had been spying on the company in a national security investigation, secretly seizing the company's phone records as well as the work and personal phone records of individual AP reporters. The AP called it a "massive and unprecedented intrusion" into a company's newsgathering operations, and a firestorm of protest ignited across the spectrum of mainstream and independent/ alternative news media in the US.[8]

The following group of stories on the issue of "censoring the news about censorship," highlighted this year by Project Censored, could not come at a more critical time. We are seeing a war on truth on all fronts in the US—against journalists and media companies, against those who would blow the whistle on government and military corruption, and against truth-tellers in general—with the Obama administration's heavy-handed actions against the Associated Press and others in the media being just a part of a much larger international trend.

But is this critical message about the war on truth in all its manifestations reaching the public? The censored stories presented here indicate that, by and large, the message is not making it past the self-censoring filters of the US corporate-dominated news media. This is alarming indeed for a nation professing to be the world's most open, democratic society and home to the freest press on the planet.

Censored #1: Bradley Manning and the Failure of Corporate Media

Nowhere is the war on truth more clearly seen than in the case of Bradley Manning, an intelligence analyst with the United States Army who is at the center of the largest leak of classified documents in US history. The Manning case shows in stark relief both the US government's relentless pursuit of a legitimate whistleblower and the US corporate media's relentless retreat from the story.

Private First Class Manning, at age twenty-two, was arrested in May 2010 at the US military base in Iraq where he was stationed, on

suspicion of leaking of about 700,000 pages of confidential documents and video footage of US military helicopter attacks to the WikiLeaks whistleblower organization. The leaking had helped to shine a much-needed international spotlight on the US wars in Afghanistan and Iraq—especially on the killing of civilians by US soldiers—and on how the US government conducts its foreign policy behind the scenes.

In February 2012, Manning was ordered to stand trial in a US military court on twenty-two charges of leaking confidential government documents; the most serious charge, "aiding the enemy," carried a possible sentence of life in prison.[9] The US Army had also charged Manning on multiple counts of violating the 1917 US Espionage Act, a World War I–era law that carries very stiff punishment—including a possible death penalty—for exposing "national defense" information.[10]

A sign of how the US corporate media would treat Manning's court martial came some months later in November 2012, when Manning, then held prisoner for more than 900 days without trial, spoke publicly for the first time since his arrest.[11]

In a pretrial hearing at Fort Meade, Maryland, he detailed the physical and psychological trauma he had suffered due to inhumane treatment by the US military while in detention. But these newsworthy developments in Manning's case were unreported for the most part by major US news companies, according to the New York–based media watch group Fairness and Accuracy in Reporting (FAIR). FAIR found that the *New York Times* published just a brief Associated Press wire story on Manning's testimony, and that only one of the big three corporate television networks, CBS, reported the Manning trial at all. PBS mentioned it in passing.[12] "[T]he minimal attention to Manning's trial last week tells us how little corporate media care about the mistreatment of a government whistleblower," concluded FAIR.[13]

In February 2013, Manning pled guilty to ten of the twenty-two charges he faced of releasing secret government documents to WikiLeaks, but not to the charge of aiding the enemy.

In his statement to the court, Manning said he was motivated by his conscience to blow the whistle: "I believed that if the general public, especially the American public, had access to the information . . . this could spark a domestic debate on the role of the military and our foreign policy in general as well as it related to Iraq and Afghanistan," he said. "No one associated with [WikiLeaks] pressured me into giving any more information. . . . I take full responsibility for my actions."[14]

Manning denied in his testimony that anything damaging to US government interests was released in the US State Department cables he leaked, though he conceded they "might be embarrassing."[15] But the bigger embarrassment may have been for the US corporate press.

Manning testified that before leaking documents to WikiLeaks, he had tried going through the proper news company channels:

> I then decided to contact the largest and most popular newspaper, the *New York Times*. I called the public editor number on the *New York Times* website. The phone rang and was answered by a machine. I went through the menu to the section for news tips. I was routed to an answering machine. I

left a message stating I had access to information about Iraq and Afghanistan that I believed was very important. However, despite leaving my Skype phone number and personal e-mail address, I never received a reply from the *New York Times*. I attached a text file I drafted while preparing to provide the documents to the *Washington Post*. It provided rough guidelines saying "It's already been sanitized of any source identifying information. You might need to sit on this information—perhaps 90 to 100 days to figure out how best to release such a large amount of data and to protect its source. This is possibly one of the more significant documents of our time removing the fog of war and revealing the true nature of twenty-first century asymmetric warfare. Have a good day."[16]

Manning never heard back from them, later sent the information he had on to WikiLeaks, and the rest is history.

As the pretrial phase of Manning's court martial is headed toward the scheduled June 2013 start of the main trial proceedings (as we go to press on this book), the big question, especially for US independent journalists and reporters from other countries who covered the trial regularly, was: Where is the American press?[17] The big media companies were noticeably absent from or negligent in covering what was surely one of the most important legal cases in United States history.

One of those companies, the *New York Times*—which had actually cooperated with WikiLeaks and Julian Assange in 2010 by publishing thousands of documents originally leaked by Manning—now found no stomach to stand by Manning in court, or even to be bothered at one point with covering the whistleblower's legal proceedings at all. *The Times* had to be shamed into covering the Manning trial more consistently by its own public editor, who wrote: "In failing to send its own reporter to cover the fascinating and important pretrial testimony of Bradley Manning, the *New York Times* missed the boat. . . . *The Times* should be there."[18]

Other corporate news media did not fare much better. Kevin Gosztola, a Chicago-based writer for the progressive news website *FireDogLake*, was one of a handful of independent journalists and activists who turned up day after day at the Manning hearings to record every development of the trial. At the same time, Gosztola was also monitoring the US so-called mainstream print and broadcast media's attendance at the trial, which he found to be nonexistent at worst and spotty at best.[19]

Gosztola spoke for many in and outside the media field when he said that as an institution, "the US press failed Bradley Manning" from the very beginning of the whole whistleblowing affair for which he now stood trial.[20] Many contend that Manning's status as a modern-day folk hero is well deserved, and that, far from being treated like a criminal, he should be credited with having done a great public service as a whistleblower in what is proving to be an increasingly dangerous environment to report the truth.[21]

Censored #4: Obama's War on Whistleblowers

The Bradley Manning case stands out as a prime example of official persecution of a legitimate whistleblower, but it is by no means the only one.

During his first election campaign, Barack Obama promised more protection for whistleblowers—those within government who would take risks to make unauthorized leaks of information. Obama as candidate promised to "strengthen whistleblower laws to protect federal workers who expose waste, fraud, and abuse of authority in government [and] ensure that federal agencies expedite the process for reviewing whistleblower claims and whistleblowers have full access to courts and due process."[22]

The Government Accountability Project, a Washington DC–based nonprofit organization that promotes and defends whistleblower protections, credits Obama as president with mostly keeping his campaign promises to protect whistleblowers. But in one area—national security—the Obama administration is seen as being "dangerously contradictory" by aggressively prosecuting leakers of classified information and going after the journalists to whom they leak.[23]

The Obama administration has far surpassed what past US administrations have done by presiding over the prosecution of seven persons for whistleblowing and other offenses under the Espionage Act. As of this writing (May 2013), the seven persons are:

▸ **Thomas Drake:** Former senior executive at the National Security Agency (NSA), the US government's electronic-spying agency. Indicted in 2010 in connection with the leaking of top-secret documents about an NSA program, which he felt violated citizens' privacy rights, to a newspaper reporter at the *Baltimore Sun*.[24] Felony charges were dropped in 2011 in exchange for a misdemeanor plea by Drake.

▸ **Shamai Leibowitz:** Israeli lawyer/activist in the US working secretly under contract for the Federal Bureau of Investigation (FBI) as a Hebrew-language translator. Concerned about possible plans for a military attack on Iran, he leaked FBI transcripts of wiretapped conversations of diplomats at the Israeli embassy in Washington DC to the blog *Tikun Olam*.[25] Sentenced in 2010 to twenty months in federal prison. He served out his sentence and was released in 2011.

▸ **Bradley Manning:** Charged by the US Army for whistleblowing offenses (see *Censored* story #1, above).

▸ **Stephen Kim:** South Korean–born and US Ivy League–educated analyst who worked on a contract basis with the US State Department. Indicted in 2010 for having passed nonclassified information concerning North Korea to a Fox News correspondent, who later reported it on television, citing an anonymous source. Kim faces a sentence of up to fifteen years in prison; he has pled not guilty to the charges and his court case continues.[26] (Following the AP phone records firestorm in May 2013, it was revealed that the Fox News reporter, James Rosen, had had his movements at the State Department, as well as his phone and e-mail records, monitored by government investigators at the time in 2009.)[27]

▸ **Jeffrey Sterling:** Former Central Intelligence Agency (CIA) case officer. Indicted in 2010 for having leaked information on Iranian nuclear research to *New York Times* reporter James Risen for a chapter in Risen's book *State of War*.[28] Facing a sentence of up to 120 years, Sterling pled not guilty. Risen was subpoenaed three times to force him to testify as to whether or not Sterling was his source; Risen has refused to comply. Pretrial rulings by the judge on evidentiary issues have posed a major setback for the Justice Department in the case. The government is reportedly appealing the rulings as it moves ahead with prosecuting Sterling.[29]

▶ **John Kiriakou:** Former CIA case officer and analyst. Well known as the first US government official who, in 2007, exposed to the media the CIA's "waterboarding" interrogation technique on al-Qaeda prisoners as a form of torture.[30] Kiriakou was initially charged in 2012 under the Espionage Act for leaking the names of CIA colleagues to journalists, including a *New York Times* reporter, for which he faced up to fifty years in prison. Kiriakou pled guilty to a lesser charge and was sentenced in January 2013 to thirty months in prison. He is currently an inmate at a federal prison in Pennsylvania.[31]

▶ **James Hitselberger:** Former Arabic-language specialist who worked for a private company on contract to the US Navy. Though not technically a whistleblower, he was "quietly indicted" under the Espionage Act in late 2012 for taking classified documents from a US naval base in Bahrain where he worked, including some documents that ended up in a collection of his papers at Stanford University.[32] He was reported to be under house arrest in Virginia in 2013 as his trial proceeds.[33]

To be sure, the big corporate media companies have published news reports on these and other whistleblower cases as the lawsuits have come up. But what have been missing from the US press overall are context and consistency: the much wider context of a systematic war on whistleblowers and truth-tellers with the aim of silencing them, and consistency in reporting that wider context over time.

And the war looks to get worse before it gets better. In January 2013, President Obama issued a memorandum, barely reported by the US corporate media, that seeks new rules to allow federal agencies to fire employees without appeal if their work is deemed to be "national security sensitive."[34] This could affect thousands of US government workers, and there are concerns that it would also give the Obama administration yet another weapon in its war on whistleblowers.[35]

If the final goal of the US government has been to put a "chilling effect" on the press to keep the truth unreported and to deter potential whistleblowers from coming forward, then it has succeeded in at least one noteworthy case.

"I heard from various news sources that the FBI [under George W. Bush] had been monitoring my phone and Internet communications with certain people as part of its leak investigation into our [2005] NSA story," says Eric Lichtblau, Pulitzer Prize–winning reporter for the *New York Times*. A fear of getting subpoenaed led Lichtblau to quit writing national security stories for the *Times* and move on to another beat before the Obama administration took over in 2009. "While the Justice Department never made good on the threat, it certainly made it more difficult to do my job in dealing with confidential sources when you realize you may be forced to testify before a grand jury or risk going to jail to protect a source."[36]

Censored #16: Journalism Under Attack Around the Globe

The domestic war on whistleblowers in the United States is, in turn, part of a much broader pattern of increasing repression of the news media and freedom of expression internationally.

In this digital age, the world has indeed become a smaller place yet at the same time a more dangerous one, if we are to believe the latest reports from press-support organizations and news media around the globe. Are those dangers to journalists in doing their work consistently reflected in news reporting by the US establishment media with the proper context, as they appear to be in other countries? Once again, we see a huge gap between the reality and the reporting in the United States.

Across the board, 2012 was reported by several organizations and institutions to be the deadliest year yet for journalists in various parts of the world, a sign of increasing danger to media workers and ultimately of a growing trend of censoring and gagging of news reporters. The Austria-based International Press Institute documented a record-high killing of 132 journalists worldwide in 2012 in the line of work, with the rate showing no sign of slowing down as of mid-2013 (forty-eight journalists killed).[37] Similar results were found by the France-based organization Reporters Without Borders in its "World Press Freedom Index" for 2013.[38]

The United Nations Educational, Scientific and Cultural Organization (UNESCO) also documented a rise in the number of media professionals killed on a global scale, along with an increase in "nonfatal attacks" such as journalists being injured, raped, kidnapped, intimidated, harassed, or illegally arrested in the course of their work.[39] Like other parties, UNESCO attributed these rising numbers in large part to the growing problem of impunity—that is, when no one is brought to justice for crimes against journalists. Most of the reporters, UNESCO noted, were not killed while covering war zones but rather while reporting on corruption or illegal activities at the local level. Increasingly, covering human rights issues and even environmental issues are proving to be more fatal for journalists than before, UNESCO found.

The US-based Committee to Protect Journalists (CPJ) issued its own report in February 2013, "Attacks on the Press."[40] It documented seventy journalists killed in 2012 in the course of their work, a jump of almost 50 percent over the year before.[41] CPJ also identified a record-high 232 journalists imprisoned around the world in 2012, a climbing figure "driven in part by the widespread use of charges of terrorism and other anti-state offenses against critical reporters and editors."[42]

The New York Times followed up by publishing an article on the release of the CPJ report.[43] But the Times' reporting was all too typical of the poor US corporate media coverage of this important issue, lacking in quantity (at a mere 440 words) as well as in quality (the deeper implications for press freedom of more journalists getting killed). Most noticeably absent from the Times story was any mention at all of the landmark United Nations resolution on journalists' safety passed just a few months before, which recognized the severity of the crisis in journalism and which was heralded by media workers and press-support organizations around the world.

In September 2012, the forty-seven–member United Nations Human Rights Council passed a resolution that for the first time called on nations to "promote a safe and enabling environment for journalists to perform their work independently and without undue interference." It also called on countries to fight impunity in cases of attacks against journalists, by "ensur[ing] accountability through the conduct of impartial, speedy and effective investigations" into such attacks and "bring[ing] to justice those responsible."[44]

The New York Times and the US corporate press failed to give this important development the prominent coverage it deserved. But if

US establishment media reporting of the important UN resolution on journalists' safety was sparse in 2012, acknowledgment of Article 19 of the UN Universal Declaration of Human Rights—upon which this and other resolutions and press freedom principles are based—has been nearly nonexistent.

Article 19 of the Universal Declaration of Human Rights, passed by the United Nations in 1948, reads:

> Everyone has the right to freedom of opinion and expression; this right includes freedom to hold opinions without interference and to seek, receive and impart information and ideas through any media and regardless of frontiers.[45]

Article 19 is worth noting here because it affirms freedom of the press as a basic human right, not just the civil right of a nation. Several UN press freedom–related resolutions of the past are based on Article 19, as is the groundbreaking Windhoek Declaration of 1991 by African journalists, which evolved into World Press Freedom Day.

Inspired by the Windhoek Declaration, journalists in other regions of the world—Europe, Asia, the Middle East, and Latin America and the Caribbean—also have drawn up similarly strong statements of press principles.[46] Conspicuously missing from that list of regions is North America, where a kind of Windhoek Declaration is arguably most needed in the world today.

When more news reporters and other media professionals in the United States see themselves and their important public service role as one vital part of the larger international picture, and can stand side by side with their colleagues around the world in times of danger, then we may finally begin to see US news reporting that truly informs the public whenever journalism comes under threat of attack anywhere on the globe.

Censored #22: Pennsylvania Law Gags Doctors to Protect Big Oil's "Proprietary Secrets"

Attacking or killing journalists after they report the truth is one way to censor news; another is to use "prior restraints" under the law *before* the truth is reported. Those in the media profession are no strangers to legal restraints being used to bind and gag them beforehand, based on what they might report. Now, however, that kind of gag is being extended in the US to persons in the medical profession.

Under a controversial new law that went into effect in 2012 in the state of Pennsylvania, doctors must sign a confidentiality agreement before a corporation will release any information to the doctors concerning the chemicals used in deep underground drilling of oil and natural gas, a practice known as hydraulic fracturing or "fracking"—even when that information directly affects the health of the doctors' patients.

The text of the law, Act 13, stipulates that a fracking company must "identify the specific identity and amount of any chemicals claimed to be a trade secret or confidential proprietary information to any health professional who requests the information in writing," but only "if the health professional executes a confidentiality agreement and provides a written statement of need for the information" for treating patients.[47]

Like other states, Pennsylvania is undergoing a virtual gold rush of fracking by oil and gas companies. There are an estimated 5,000 oil and gas drilling wells located around the state, and the number of sites continues to grow.[48] The drilling, which is done with toxic chemicals, has led medical professionals, local residents, and activists alike to raise serious environmental concerns about contaminated groundwater and about the resulting outbreaks of health problems among people living near the drilling sites.[49]

This puts medical professionals in a bind: doctors in Pennsylvania can be sued by patients for not informing them of the health risks of fracking, which may involve naming the actual "secret" chemicals used at local fracking sites. As one Pennsylvania doctor put it: "What is the big secret here that they [fracking companies] are unwilling to tell people, unless they know that if people found out what's really in these chemicals, they would be outraged?"[50]

There has been some decent reporting of this "doctor gag rule" in the US corporate press, including, for example, by the New York-based website *International Business Times*[51] as well as by the *Los Angeles Times*.[52] But by and large, considering the huge implications this case has for the wider issue of creeping corporate control over public health matters, the doctor gag rule has not garnered nearly the amount of sustained, consistent coverage in the corporate media that it deserves.

This is especially true of one related aspect that appears to have gone unreported in the national media: the possible linking of the doctor gag rule on fracking with the gagging of whistleblowers and activists in Pennsylvania's agricultural industry.[53]

Pennsylvania is one of several US states that in the past few years has moved to pass agricultural gag laws—so-called "ag-gag laws"—at the behest of the powerful industrial agricultural lobby. These are laws that would make it a crime for anyone to expose conditions at factory farms where animals are killed and processed for human consumption.

Under House Bill 683, introduced into the Pennsylvania state legislature in February 2013, it would be a felony offense for anyone who "records an image of, or sound from, the agricultural operation by leaving a recording device on the agricultural operation," or anyone who "uploads, downloads, transfers or otherwise sends recorded images of, or sound from, the agricultural operations over the Internet in any medium."[54]

Public concerns are now being raised about such factory farms that are located in the same rural areas of Pennsylvania where fracking operations are also being carried out by oil and natural gas drilling companies. HB 683 deals specifically with gags on exposing industrial farming practices. But there are concerns that if this ag-gag bill is passed into law, it could someday be expanded in scope to include the legal gagging of activists and whistleblowers who expose operations at rural oil and gas fracking sites in Pennsylvania as well.

This is an important case worth keeping an eye on for the future, as a sign of where the ongoing war on truth in the United States is taking us.

RELATED VALIDATED INDEPENDENT NEWS STORY

Prominent Establishment Journalists Turn Whistleblowers over News Censorship

What happens when journalists themselves blow the whistle on censorship within their own ranks? Ask two such journalists who worked for some of the biggest names in American news.

Amber Lyon, a reporter for CNN, produced a one-hour documentary in 2011 titled *iRevolution: Online Warriors of the Arab Spring*, on how social media were playing a part in the then-unfolding Arab Spring uprisings in the Middle East. It included a thirteen-minute segment shot in Bahrain featuring dramatic footage and interviews.[55]

Lyon said she was later pressured by CNN during the editing process to include Bahraini government denials and untruths about the Arab Spring uprising in that country.[56]

The documentary aired once that summer on the US domestic edition of CNN, but not on the network's overseas arm, CNN International (CNNi), which is widely watched in the Middle East.[57] When she raised questions about it, Lyon said, she was warned by the president of CNNi to drop the subject and not talk about it publicly;[58] she later received a similar threat from CNN's business department.[59]

US journalist Glenn Greenwald has suggested that it had something to do with pressure put on CNN by the government of Bahrain, a close United States ally, in conjunction with a high-priced US public relations firm, in an effort to nip Bahrain's Arab Spring in the bud.[60]

In response, CNN admitted that it has carried advertising by a Bahraini government agency but strongly denied any connection between that and Lyon's report not airing.[61] Lyon was later laid off from CNN and has been reporting independently since then.

The second journalist, Daniel Simpson, was a British writer based in Serbia who worked as the Balkans correspondent for the *New York Times* for about a year starting in 2002, reporting mostly on political developments.[62]

But Simpson would later recall how *Times* editors leaned on him to slant his stories more in line with the *Times*' conventional wisdom of geopolitics in the Balkan region and in keeping with Bush administration positions in its newly declared war on terror.

This included at one point, he said, being urged by the US embassy in the Serbian capital of Belgrade, as well as by a *Times* colleague in New York, reporter Judith Miller, to dig up evidence that would link the Bosnian Serb Republic to suspected weapons of mass destruction in Iraq.[63] Simpson said that Miller (who would later be discredited for her reporting on Iraq) "wanted me to say [in an article] that Serbs were selling Saddam Hussein 'weapons of mass destruction' delivery systems. Now, it turned out that what they were actually selling was spare parts for planes . . ."[64]

Fed up, he says, with what he called the "propaganda" and spin being put out by the US government in the war on terror and the supportive role played by the *Times* and other corporate media, he left the

Times and the news business entirely.

Simpson today is quite open about once having fabricated part of a story that was published on the front page of the *Times*, and about having used a fake identity in a letter to the editor that he sent to the *Times*, later published by the paper while he was still working there.[65] These actions strain Simpson's journalistic credibility and cannot be defended.

But at the very least, the claim of self-censorship and institutional bias at the *New York Times*, and the credible evidence of news censorship at CNN, both deserve to be covered and debated widely in the US establishment press, not dismissed or ignored as they have been.

BRIAN COVERT is an independent journalist and author based in Kawanishi, western Japan. He has worked for United Press International news service in Japan, as staff reporter for three of Japan's English-language daily newspapers, and as contributor to Japanese and overseas newspapers and magazines. He contributed a chapter to *Censored 2013* on the Fukushima nuclear disaster and news censorship in Japan. He is currently a lecturer in the Department of Media, Journalism, and Communications at Doshisha University in Kyoto.

Notes

1. United Nations, "Declaration of Windhoek," http://www.un.org/en/events/pressfreedomday/windhoek.shtml.
2. United Nations Educational, Scientific and Cultural Organization (UNESCO), "Safe to Speak: Securing Freedom of Expression in All Media—World Press Freedom Day," May 2–4, 2013, http://www.unesco.org/new/fileadmin/MULTIMEDIA/HQ/CI/CI/pdf/WPFD/wpfd2013_agenda_en.pdf.
3. Keith Koffler, "Obama Schedule: Friday, May 3, 2013," White House Dossier.com, http://www.whitehousedossier.com/2013/05/02/obama-schedule-friday-3-2013/.
4. White House, "Statement by the President on World Press Freedom Day," May 3, 2012, http://www.whitehouse.gov/the-press-office/2012/05/03/statement-president-world-press-freedom-day. See also similar statements for the years 2009 to 2011 on the White House website, http://www.whitehouse.gov/ (search term: World Press Freedom Day).
5. White House, "Statement by the President in Honor of World Press Freedom Day," May 1, 2009, http://www.whitehouse.gov/the_press_office/Statement-by-the-President-in-honor-of-World-Press-Freedom-Day/.
6. Finding from search of archives on the White House website, http://www.whitehouse.gov/ (search term: World Press Freedom Day). Accessed on May 28, 2013.
7. Barack Obama, "President Obama Holds a Press Conference with President Chinchilla," video and transcript, White House, May 3, 2013, http://www.whitehouse.gov/photos-and-video/video/2013/05/03/president-obama-holds-press-conference-president-chinchilla. See also UNESCO, "Who Will Expose the Hidden Truths?," World Press Freedom Day, May 4, 2013, http://www.unesco.org/new/en/unesco/resources/who-will-reveal-the-hidden-truths/.
8. Mark Sherman, "Gov't Obtains Wide AP Phone Records in Probe," Associated Press, May 13, 2013, http://bigstory.ap.org/article/govt-obtains-wide-ap-phone-records-probe.

9. "Bradley Manning: Charge Sheet," *Guardian*, March 4, 2011, http://www.guardian.co.uk/law/interactive/2011/mar/04/bradley-manning-charge-sheet.
10. "Primary Documents—US Espionage Act, 15 June 1917," FirstWorldWar.com, http://www.firstworldwar.com/source/espionageact.htm.
11. Ed Pilkington, "WikiLeaks Suspect Bradley Manning Gives Evidence for First Time," *Guardian*, November 29, 2012, http://www.guardian.co.uk/world/2012/nov/29/wikileaks-bradley-manning-gives-evidence.
12. Fairness and Accuracy in Reporting, "Turning Their Back on Bradley Manning: Whistleblower Speaks—But Press Doesn't Listen," December 4, 2012, http://fair.org/take-action/media-advisories/turning-their-back-on-bradley-manning/.
13. Ibid.
14. Charlie Savage, "I Did It to Make the World a Better Place: Manning," *New York Times*, as published in *Sydney Morning Herald*, March 1, 2013, http://www.smh.com.au/world/i-did-it-to-make-the-world-a-better-place-manning-20130301-2f9y3.html. See also Alexa O'Brien, "Pfc. Bradley E. Manning's Statement for the Providence Inquiry," February 28, 2013, http://www.alexaobrien.com/secondsight/wikileaks/bradley_manning/pfc_bradley_e_manning_providence_hearing_statement.html.
15. O'Brien, "Pfc. Bradley E. Manning's Statement for the Providence Inquiry."
16. Ibid.
17. Al Jazeera English, "The Case of the US vs Bradley Manning," *Listening Post* program, March 9, 2013, http://www.aljazeera.com/programmes/listeningpost/2013/03/201339107329512.html.
18. Margaret Sullivan, "The *Times* Should Have a Reporter at the Bradley Manning Hearing," *New York Times*, December 5, 2012, http://publiceditor.blogs.nytimes.com/2012/12/05/the-times-should-have-a-reporter-at-the-bradley-manning-hearing/.
19. Kevin Gosztola, "MSNBC Doesn't Cover Bradley Manning's Statement or Guilty Pleas at All," *FireDogLake*, March 2, 2013, http://dissenter.firedoglake.com/2013/03/02/msnbc-doesnt-cover-bradley-mannings-statement-or-guilty-pleas-at-all/. See also Kevin Gosztola, "A Shame There Aren't More Journalists Covering Bradley Manning's Court Martial," *FireDogLake*, March 16, 2013, http://dissenter.firedoglake.com/2013/03/16/a-shame-there-arent-more-journalists-covering-bradley-mannings-court-martial/. For a revealing interview with Gosztola on media coverage of the Manning trial, see Arun Rath, "Why Foreign Media Cover the Bradley Manning Trial," Public Radio International, *The World* program, March 15, 2013, http://www.theworld.org/2013/03/foreign-media-manning-trial/.
20. Kevin Gosztola, "The US Press Failed Bradley Manning," *FireDogLake*, February 28, 2013, http://dissenter.firedoglake.com/2013/02/28/the-us-press-failed-bradley-manning/. See also Janet Reitman, "Did the Mainstream Media Fail Bradley Manning?," *Rolling Stone*, March 1, 2013, http://www.rollingstone.com/politics/news/did-the-mainstream-media-fail-bradley-manning-20130301.
21. Glenn Greenwald, "Bradley Manning: The Face of Heroism," *Guardian*, February 28, 2013, http://www.guardian.co.uk/commentisfree/2013/feb/28/bradley-manning-heroism-pleads-guilty. [Ed. note: the Manning trial was just getting underway when this book was going to the publisher and off to print.]
22. Change.gov: The Office of the President-Elect, "The Obama-Biden Plan: Spend Taxpayer Money Wisely—Protect Whistleblowers," http://change.gov/agenda/ethics_agenda/.
23. Tom Devine, "Obama's Dangerously Contradictory Stance on Whistleblowing," *Guardian*, April 16, 2013, http://www.guardian.co.uk/commentisfree/2013/apr/16/obama-contradictory-stance-whistleblowing.
24. Jane Mayer, "The Secret Sharer: Is Thomas Drake an Enemy of the State?," *New Yorker*, May 23, 2011, http://www.newyorker.com/reporting/2011/05/23/110523fa_fact_mayer.
25. Richard Silverstein, "Why I Published US Intelligence Secrets about Israel's Anti-Iran Campaign," *Truthout*, October 14, 2011, http://www.truth-out.org/news/item/3499:why-i-published-us-intelligence-secrets-about-israels-antiiran-campaign.
26. Stephen Kim Legal Defense Trust, http://stephenkim.org/.

27. Ann E. Marimow, "A Rare Peek into a Justice Department Leak Probe," *Washington Post*, May 20, 2013, http://www.washingtonpost.com/local/a-rare-peek-into-a-justice-department-leak-probe/2013/05/19/0bc473de-be5e-11e2-97d4-a479289a31f9_story.html.

28. Warren Richey, "Former Covert CIA Agent Charged with Leaking Secrets to Newspaper," *Christian Science Monitor*, January 6, 2011, http://www.csmonitor.com/USA/Justice/2011/0106/Former-covert-CIA-agent-charged-with-leaking-secrets-to-newspaper.

29. Josh Gerstein, "Feds: Judge's Ruling Destroyed Case against Alleged Leaker," *Politico*, January 6, 2012, http://www.politico.com/blogs/under-the-radar/2012/01/feds-judges-ruling-destroyed-case-against-alleged-109921.html. See also Charlie Savage, "Nine Leak-Related Cases," June 20, 2012, *New York Times*, http://www.nytimes.com/2012/06/20/us/nine-leak-related-cases.html.

30. Joby Warrick and Dan Eggen, "Waterboarding Recounted," *Washington Post*, December 11, 2007, http://www.washingtonpost.com/wp-dyn/content/article/2007/12/10/AR2007121002091.html.

31. "Defend John Kiriakou" support website, http://www.defendjohnk.com/index.html.

32. John Diedrich, "Ex-Wisconsin Man Charged in Espionage Case," *Milwaukee Journal Sentinel*, November 12, 2012, http://www.jsonline.com/news/wisconsin/former-wisconsin-man-charged-in-national-espionage-case-vc7k4vp-179024791.html. See also Jesselyn Radack, "Obama's 7th Espionage Act Case Against a Non-Spy," *Daily Kos*, April 9, 2013, http://www.dailykos.com/story/2013/04/09/1200306/-Obama-s-7th-Espionage-Act-Case-Against-a-Non-Spy; and Aaron Sekhri, "Tinker, Sailor, Soldier, Spy," *Stanford Daily*, November 12, 2012, http://www.stanforddaily.com/2012/11/12/tinker-sailor-soldier-spy/.

33. Josh Gerstein, "Judge Orders Release of Linguist for Navy," *Politico*, December 19, 2012, http://www.politico.com/blogs/under-the-radar/2012/12/judge-orders-release-of-linguist-for-navy-152440.html. See also Ryan Abbott, "Linguist in State Secrets Jam Gets House Arrest," Courthouse News Service, December 21, 2012, http://www.courthousenews.com/2012/12/21/53358.htm.

34. Barack Obama, "Presidential Memorandum—Rulemaking Concerning the Standards for Designating Positions in the Competitive Service as National Security Sensitive and Related Matters," White House, January 25, 2013, http://www.whitehouse.gov/the-press-office/2013/01/25/presidential-memorandum-rulemaking-concerning-standards-designating-posi.

35. Margaret Talev, "Obama Memo on 'Sensitive' Jobs Stirs Whistle-Blower Fears," *Bloomberg*, February 27, 2013, http://www.bloomberg.com/news/2013-02-27/obama-memo-on-sensitive-jobs-stirs-whistle-blower-fears.html.

36. Molly Redden, "Is the 'Chilling Effect' Real? National-Security Reporters on the Impact of Federal Scrutiny," *New Republic*, May 15, 2013, http://www.newrepublic.com/article/113219/doj-seizure-ap-records-raises-question-chilling-effect-real.

37. International Press Institute, "2012 Deadliest Year on Record for Journalists," November 21, 2012, http://www.freemedia.at/home/singleview/article/2012-deadliest-year-on-record-for-journalists.html. See also International Press Institute, "IPI Death Watch," http://www.freemedia.at/our-activities/death-watch.html.

38. Reporters Without Borders, "2013 World Press Freedom Index: Dashed Hopes After Spring," http://en.rsf.org/press-freedom-index-2013,1054.html.

39. UNESCO, "The Safety of Journalists: Why Should You Care?," http://www.unesco.org/new/en/communication-and-information/resources/news-and-in-focus-articles/in-focus-articles/2012/the-safety-of-journalists-why-should-you-care/.

40. Committee to Protect Journalists, "Attacks on the Press: Journalism on the Front Lines in 2012," http://cpj.org/2013/02/attacks-on-the-press-in-2012.php.

41. Committee to Protect Journalists, "Attacks on the Press—Killed in 2012: A Worldwide Roundup," http://cpj.org/2013/02/attacks-on-the-press-killed-in-2012.php.

42. Committee to Protect Journalists, "Attacks on the Press—Prison Census 2012: A Worldwide Roundup," http://cpj.org/2013/02/attacks-on-the-press-prison-census-2012-a-worldwid.php.

43. Rick Gladstone, "Report Sees Journalists Increasingly Under Attack," *New York Times*, February 14, 2013, http://www.nytimes.com/2013/02/15/world/attacks-on-journalists-rose-in-2012-group-finds.html?_r=0.

44. United Nations Office for the High Commissioner for Human Rights, "Human Rights Council Adopts 11 Texts on Safety of Journalists, Transitional Justice, Corruption and Terrorist Hostage-

Taking," September 27, 2012, http://www.ohchr.org/en/NewsEvents/Pages/DisplayNews.
aspx?NewsID=12596&LangID=E. See also Helena Williams, "UN Human Rights Body Throws
Weight behind Safety for Journalists," International News Safety Institute, September 28, 2012,
http://newssafetyblog.org/2012/09/28/un-human-rights-body-throws-weight-behind-safety-
for-journalists/.

45. United Nations, "The Universal Declaration of Human Rights" (full text), http://www.un.org/
en/documents/udhr/index.shtml.
46. UNESCO, "Along the Freedom Road 1989–1998," http://www.unesco.org/webworld/fed/
temp/communication_democracy/along.htm.
47. Pennsylvania General Assembly, text of amended Act No. 13, February 14, 2012, http://www.
legis.state.pa.us/WU01/LI/LI/US/HTM/2012/0/0013..HTM.
48. Christopher Banks, "Pennsylvania Law Gags Doctors," Liberation News, June 13, 2012, http://
www.pslweb.org/liberationnews/news/pennsylvania-law-gags-doctors.html.
49. Ellen Cantarow, "The Downwinders: Fracking Ourselves to Death in Pennsylvania," Al Jazeera
English, May 11, 2013, http://www.aljazeera.com/indepth/opinion/2013/05/201357123155791818
.html. For additional coverage of fracking, see the Censored News Cluster, "Health and the Environment," in this volume.
50. Kate Sheppard, "For Pennsylvania's Doctors, a Gag Order on Fracking Chemicals," Mother
Jones, March 23, 2012, http://www.motherjones.com/environment/2012/03/fracking-doctors-
gag-pennsylvania.
51. Pierre Bertrand, "Pennsylvania Fracking Bill Puts Gag Order on Doctors, Union Says," International Business Times, March 28, 2012, http://www.ibtimes.com/pennsylvania-fracking-bill-
puts-gag-order-doctors-union-says-431144.
52. Neela Banerjee, "Pennsylvania Law on Fracking Chemicals Worries Doctors," Los Angeles
Times, April 21, 2012, http://articles.latimes.com/2012/apr/21/nation/la-na-adv-fracking-doc-
tors-20120422.
53. Jacob Chamberlain, "Fracking Activists Could Face Felony Charges as 'Ag-Gag' Laws Spread,"
Common Dreams, May 9, 2013, https://www.commondreams.org/headline/2013/05/09-10.
54. "Pennsylvania House Bill 683," LegiScan.com, http://legiscan.com/PA/text/HB683/
id/775868.
55. "'iRevolution' Documentary, Bahrain Segment," AmberLyonLive.com, http://amberlyonlive.
com/bahrain-coverage/.
56. Glenn Greenwald, "Why Didn't CNN's International Arm Air its Own Documentary on Bahrain's Arab Spring Repression?," Guardian, September 4, 2012, http://www.guardian.co.uk/
world/2012/sep/04/cnn-international-documentary-bahrain-arab-spring-repression.
57. Ibid.
58. Ibid.
59. Ibid.
60. Ibid.
61. "CNN International's Response to the Guardian—Update," CNN, September 5, 2012, http://
cnnpressroom.blogs.cnn.com/2012/09/05/cnn-internationals-response-to-the-guardian/.
62. "Daniel Simpson," archive listing of published articles, New York Times, http://topics.nytimes.
com/topics/reference/timestopics/people/s/daniel_simpson/index.html.
63. Daniel Simpson, "Weapons of Mass Delusion in the Balkans," RoughGuideDarkSide.com,
http://www.roughguidedarkside.com/2002/11/02/wmd-balkans-judy-miller-nytimes/.
64. "NYT Propaganda" segment (interview with Daniel Simpson), Breaking the Set, Russia Today,
September 18, 2012, http://rt.com/shows/breaking-set-summary/usa-dictaors-nyt-propagan-
da/.
65. Daniel Simpson, "Why I Made Stuff Up for the New York Times," RoughGuideDarkSide.com,
September 3, 2012, http://www.roughguidedarkside.com/2012/09/03/why-i-made-stuff-up-
for-the-new-york-times/. See also Daniel Simpson, "FAQ: A Rough Guide to the Dark Side,"
July 13, 2012, YouTube.com, http://www.youtube.com/watch?v=2czK3CrebfY.

Plutocracy, Poverty, and Prosperity

James F. Tracy

Censored #2

Richest Global 1 Percent Hide Trillions in Tax Havens

Carl Herman, "1% Hide $21 Trillion and US Big Banks Hide $10 Trillion; Ending World poverty: $3 Trillion," *Washington's Blog*, July 24, 2012, http://www.washingtonsblog.com/2012/07/1-hide-21-trillion-us-big-banks-hide-10-trillion-ending-world-poverty-3-trillion.html.

James S. Henry, "The Cost of Offshore Revisited," Tax Justice Network, July 2012, http://www.taxjustice.net/cms/upload/pdf/Price_of_Offshore_Revisited_120722.pdf.

Student Researcher: Lyndsey Casey (Sonoma State University)

Faculty Evaluator: Peter Phillips (Sonoma State University)

Censored #3

Trans-Pacific Partnership Threatens a Regime of Corporate Global Governance

Kevin Zeese, "Obama's 'Employment Creation' Program: Massive Outsourcing of American Jobs," *Global Research*, September 10, 2012, http://www.globalresearch.ca/obamas-employment-creation-program-massive-outsourcing-of-american-jobs/5304005.

Lori Wallach, "Breaking '08 Pledge, Leaked Trade Doc Shows Obama Wants to Help Corporations Avoid Regulations," *Democracy Now!*, June 14, 2012, http://www.democracynow.org/2012/6/14/breaking_08_pledge_leaked_trade_doc.

Andrew Gavin Marshall, "The Trans-Pacific Partnership: This Is What Corporate Governance Looks Like," *Truthout*, November 20, 2012, http://truth-out.org/news/item/12857-the-trans-pacific-partnership-this-is-what-corporate-governance-looks-like.

Lori Wallach, "Can a 'Dracula Strategy' Bring Trans-Pacific Partnership into the Sunlight?," *Yes! Magazine*, November 21, 2012, http://www.yesmagazine.org/new-economy/can-dracula-strategy-bring-trans-pacific-partnership-into-sunlight.

Student Researcher: Kyndace Safa (College of Marin)

Community Researcher: Tricia Boreta

Faculty Evaluators: Susan Rahman (College of Marin); Andy Lee Roth (Sonoma State University)

Censored #6

Billionaires' Rising Wealth Intensifies Poverty and Inequality

George Monbiot, "Bang Goes the Theory," Monbiot.com, January 14, 2013, http://www.monbiot.com/2013/01/14/bang-goes-the-theory/.

Student Researcher: Paige Fischer (Sonoma State University)

Faculty Evaluator: Peter Phillips (Sonoma State University)

Censored Story #8

Bank Interests Inflate Global Prices by 35 to 40 Percent

Ellen Brown, "It's the Interest, Stupid! Why Bankers Rule the World," Global Research, November 8, 2012, http://www.globalresearch.ca/its-the-interest-stupid-why-bankers-rule-the-world/5311030. Originally posted at Web of Debt, November 8, 2012, http://webofdebt. wordpress.com/2012/11/08/its-the-interest-stupid-why-bankers-rule-the-world/.

Student Researcher: Cooper Reynolds (Sonoma State University)

Faculty Evaluator: Peter Phillips (Sonoma State University)

Censored Story #13

A Fifth of Americans Go Hungry

Mike Ludwig, "Millions Go Hungry as Congress Considers Food Stamp Cuts and Drought Threatens Crops," *Truthout*, August 23, 2012, http://truth-out.org/news/item/11067-millions-go-hungry-as-congress-considers-food-stamp-cuts-and-drought-threatens-crops.

Student Researcher: Noah Tenney (Sonoma State University)

Faculty Evaluator: Andy Lee Roth (Sonoma State University)

Censored #23

Transaction Tax Helps Civilize Wall Street and Lower the National Debt

George Zornick, "Financial Transactions Tax Introduced Again—Can It Pass This Time?," *Nation*, February 28, 2013, http://www.thenation.com/blog/173134/financial-transactions-tax-introduced-again-can-it-pass-time.

"Lawmakers Introduce Targeted Wall Street Trading Tax," *Albany Tribune*, February 28, 2013, http://www.albanytribune.com/28022013-lawmakers-introduce-targeted-wall-street-trading-tax.

Gregory Heires, "As the Misguided $1.4 Trillion Cuts Begin, a Wall Street Tax Looks Like a No-Brainer," *Reader Supported News*, March 7, 2013, http://readersupportednews.org/pm-section/78-78/16370-as-the-misguided-14-trillion-cuts-begin-a-wall-street-tax-looks-like-a-no-brainer.

Helene Fouquet and Adria Cimino, "French Lawmakers Pass Trading Transaction Tax," *Bloomberg Businessweek*, August 1, 2012, http://www.businessweek.com/news/2012-07-31/french-lawmakers-pass-budget-bill-including-transaction-tax.

Student Researcher: Marisa Soski (San Francisco State University)

Faculty Evaluator: Kenn Burrows (San Francisco State University)

Over the past four decades, the wealth controlled by a small transnational elite has gradually increased and now amasses at a spectacular pace. In 2012, the world's 100 wealthiest people became $241 billion richer and are presently worth a total $1.9 trillion.[1] In the shadow of such opulence, however, close to 870 million of the world's inhabitants—roughly one in eight—suffer from "chronic undernourishment," according to the Food and Agriculture Organization of the United Nations.[2]

In the US alone, over 200,000 families fell below the poverty line in 2011, a demarcation underneath which 10.4 million families—or 47.5 million Americans—now exist. In other words, close to one-third of all working families in the US lack the very basic resources to make ends meet. In contrast, as the Working Poor Families Project reported, "higher income families receive a [much] larger share of income relative to families at the bottom of the income distribution."[3] The news generated by corporate media all too frequently fail to capture the magnitude of this profound crisis. Because such media are first and foremost concerned with mesmerizing constituents of a lucrative advertising demographic, they seldom focus on poverty and economic inequality—the root causes of the street crime regularly highlighted in the local papers and broadcast news.

Further, since Americans often lack a genuine historical compass and are regularly bombarded with an array of bizarre and horrific reports purporting to be news, they are unlikely to recognize that things haven't always been this way. Indeed, from a historic perspective such socioeconomic conditions seem a world away from the widely held notion of prosperity America once exemplified. For example, in the period immediately following World War II through the early 1970s, the average US family saw its annual income grow in accord with the gross domestic product (GDP).

In addition, most households carried little debt and credit purchases were hardly the routine occurrence or affirmation of lifestyle they have become today. The greater degree of economic enfranchisement and equality was largely due to a very different political-economic arrangement that included higher rates of unionization and greater tax rates on wealthy individuals and corporations that provided for the emergence and growth of a distinct middle class—a taken-for-granted American institution that is now increasingly a thing of the past.

"The experience of the two postwar eras is a story of two entirely different societies," economics writer Robert Kuttner explained.

The first era was one of broadly shared gains. Between 1947 and 1973, productivity rose by 103.5 percent and median family income rose by almost exactly the same amount, 103.9 percent. But between 1973 and 2003 productivity rose by 71.3

percent, while median family income rose by just 21.9 percent. Factor out the extra hours worked by wives, and median family income rose scarcely at all.[4]

Between 2000 and 2006 American worker productivity increased by close to 20 percent yet wages paid to workers in nonsupervisory roles remained stagnant.[5] And, as *Censored* story #13, below, suggests, since 2007 the US has been in an economic tailspin not experienced since the Great Depression.

These dramatic changes can be further explained through a sociological lens by considering the closely intertwined elements of social class and economic institutions. Beginning in the 1970s, the United States and many of those constituting the "power elite" or "governing class"—chronicled by political sociologists C. Wright Mills and G. William Domhoff, a half-century ago[6]—had begun to unilaterally abandon their implicit pact with working people. The captains of industry that roved the halls of government and the Pentagon, while holding sway in the boardrooms of major corporations, vigorously fought unionization, promoted a wasteful armaments industry, and started the long process of exporting the country's manufacturing base overseas—an undertaking that has since rendered America a shadow of its former self.

Within the scope of human affairs, the economy's foremost ideational doppelgängers are political thought and public opinion. In order to change the nation's political economy, key individuals articulating the wishes of influential quarters within the governing class understood that any program to shift wealth upward must be accompanied by a far-reaching ideological campaign. In 1971, future Supreme Court Justice Lewis F. Powell Jr. wrote a detailed memorandum to Eugene B. Sydnor Jr., chairman of the Chamber of Commerce's education committee. In it, Powell urged an ambitious campaign to contest what he saw as a wide-scale espousal of liberal and leftist precepts and ideas on college campuses, in mass media, and elsewhere throughout America's opinion-generating apparatus.

Powell argued that those concerned with defending the capitalist system must regain the higher ground in academe especially, thereby influencing the broader field of ideas. In his view, the Chamber of

Commerce should advocate for the inclusion of free-market-minded scholars within the formal academy and even consider setting up think tanks promoting free enterprise-friendly concepts. "Reaching the campus and the secondary schools is vital for the long-term," Powell wrote.

Reaching the public generally may be more important for the shorter term. The first essential is to establish the staffs of eminent scholars, writers and speakers, who will do the thinking, the analysis, the writing and the speaking. It will also be essential to have staff personnel who are thoroughly familiar with the media, and how most effectively to communicate with the public.[7]

With neoliberal tenets now commonplace throughout the business community and broader culture, Powell's then seemingly improbable plan has been fully realized. Further abetted by the increasing sophistication and scope of information technology, the power elite that once confined themselves to the nation-state have become a truly global phenomenon.[8] Unlike their human counterparts, rendered finite through modest economic means and everyday drudgery, the supranational global overlords defy time and space, flying above perceived reality while cloaking themselves in the widely propagated myth of free market capitalism. "Their companies are transnational but they are transcendent," historian David Noble declared. "They have overcome their mortality, the constraints of space and time, the particulars of place and the moment. Thus they live in their godliness, their virtual divinity, the culmination of a thousand years of earnest expectation."[9] The plans they have for humanity and other life on Earth, suggested in byzantine financial maneuverings and all-encompassing trade deals, portend a continued global transformation in accord with their vision—exclusive corporate control over the Earth's broad expanse of material and human resources.

In their examination of the 1 percent, Project Censored's Peter Phillips and Kimberly Soeiro pointed to the worldwide "superclass," an idea, developed by David Rothkopf, designating an international elite whose constituents exert their power through wealth and position or, to a lesser degree, cultural, scientific, or artistic talent and contributions frequently appropriated by the superelites.[10] Like the globe-trotting *Übermensch* described by Noble, "the superclass constitutes approximately o.oooi percent of the population," Phillips and Soeiro explain, or 6,ooo to 7,ooo people.

> They are the Davos-attending, Gulfstream/private jet–flying, money-incrusted, megacorporation-interlocked, policy-building elites of the world. . . . They are 94 percent male, predominantly white, and mostly from North America and Europe. [They] are the people setting the agendas at the G8, G2o, NATO, the World Bank, and the WTO.[11]

Through their intricate monetary designs and international accords, those comprising this superclass and their immediate subordinates symbolically coordinate much of our material existence. Such a predicament could not be possible without a severely censored news media that keeps the broader public from knowing the frequency and degree to which it is methodically swindled.

This year's top Censored stories addressing "Plutocracy, Poverty, and Prosperity" suggest the increasingly close relationship between information and economic inequality. Indeed, as the methods for transferring wealth upward are further perfected, and as the walls and bars of economic imprisonment thicken, the news and information that might illuminate such processes are largely purged from the public mind, thereby deterring the possibilities for collective action and meaningful reform encompassed in, for example, the recent Occupy movement. Yet because most of the large media outlets that Americans rely on for their news are owned, managed, and overseen by corporate board members constituting the 1 percent, it is not surprising that important news of their repeated con games and criminality is trivialized or ignored altogether.

Censored Story #2: Richest Global 1 Percent Hide Trillions in Tax Havens

Despite their already exorbitant wealth, the world's richest institutions and individuals have sheltered $21 trillion and $10 trillion respectively—a total $31 trillion—in offshore tax havens and in over 14,000 funding entities to avoid paying their fair share of taxes. The figure is more than the total annual GDP of the US and Japan combined, Carl Herman reported.[12]

An especially important observation in the report is that while this gigantic fortune parked in various accounts fortifies the wherewithal of the extraordinarily privileged, it simultaneously impedes economic productivity and the real potential for eradicating world poverty that kills one million children per month. Indeed, researchers estimate that such poverty could be ended for one to three trillion dollars. Further, curbing poverty through development aid and investment tends to reduce the rate of population growth and would thus diminish such loss of life.

Over the past two decades, Herman wrote, "more human beings have died from preventable poverty than from all wars, murders, and violent deaths of any kind in all human history." Nonetheless, the US government has failed to uphold the promise to end global poverty made at the 1990 World Summit for Children. This abdication of responsibility might be considered alongside the wanton misuse of American military forces overseas and those profiting from such murder and destruction—many of whom are the same entities allowed to float their riches offshore with impunity.

In reality, there is a profound inverse correlation between such economic imbalances—a heaven and hell dichotomy of sorts reflected in the apparent transcendence of the lavish Hyde Park penthouse, the villa in Monaco, the private jet, versus the bottomless despair and misery of the sub-Saharan farmer driven off his land, or the Chinese sweatshop employee made to work and live in squalor for close to nothing. To be sure, much of the foundation for such increasingly bleak boundaries may be found in the wherewithal to shelter oneself from taxation as much as in the broad and elaborate trade agreements forged by global elites behind closed doors.

Censored Story #3: Trans-Pacific Partnership Threatens a Regime of Corporate Global Governance

Modernity is characterized by a system of representative governance capable of articulating and exerting the popular will while preserving the basic constitutional rights and freedoms of all citizens. In this way, the inordinate power of corporations may be held in check, thereby providing a more level economic playing field for all. In many ways, C. Wright Mills's theoretical model of a power elite remains applicable to today's condition, where over half a century of movement through revolving doors—some of which now go to lobbying firms—have brought about an almost thoroughly corporatized state that acts mostly on behalf of its intercontinental masters. As plans for a Trans-Pacific Partnership (TPP) suggest, however, the now familiar public-private coziness at the national level may be merely the end of the beginning. "What makes the TPP unique," Andrew Gavin Marshall wrote,

> is not simply the fact that it may be the largest "free trade agreement" ever negotiated, nor even the fact that only two of its roughly twenty-six articles actually deal with "trade," but that it is also the most secretive trade negotiations in history, with no public oversight, input, or consultations.[13]

Incorporating the US, Canada, Mexico, Peru, Chile, New Zealand, Australia, Brunei, Singapore, Vietnam, and Malaysia, the TPP became a priority for the Obama administration when it took office in 2009. Yet the true power interests that are intimately involved in shaping the massive pact include about 600 corporations that stand to profit enormously once the deal is sealed.

While the TPP was initially conceived as a counterbalance to China's economic might, it has been redesigned "to be a structure on to which other nations, including possibly South Korea and eventually even China, could be bolted," Asian Development Bank's Iwan Azis observed.[14]

The TPP predictably received rave reviews from major transnationals and their lobby groups, yet many independent observers found the accord unsettling at best. In May 2012, over thirty legal scholars from nations falling under TPP provisions signed a letter to US Trade Representative Ron Kirk stating their "profound concern and disappointment at the lack of public participation, transparency and open government processes in the negotiations." Along these lines, leading international trade lawyer Gary Horlick remarked, "This is the least transparent trade negotiation I have ever seen."[15]

Kevin Zeese at Global Research wrote that the TPP will be a logical extension of the North American Free Trade Agreement (NAFTA) that displaced several hundred thousand US manufacturing jobs, increased income inequality, and threw up additional barriers to worker unionization.[16] Yet among the TPP's most ominous features is its expansion of an already functioning corporate-controlled court system that gives major transnationals the ability to sue governments for any lost profits incurred while adhering to the environmental, health, and worker safety laws protecting the natural resources and citizenry of host countries. As with most international trade deals, this requirement will also tend to further transfer governments' autonomy over their own affairs to corporate elites accountable to no one but their shareholders.[17]

Censored Story #6: Billionaires' Rising Wealth Intensifies Poverty and Inequality

As suggested in *Censored* story #2, the world's richest individuals and institutions are busy giving taxation authorities the slip in part because over the past few years alone they've simply become much wealthier. This is largely the manifestation of the very neoliberal policies—cutting taxes on the rich, accelerated deregulation and privatization, reducing social programs, relaxing laws protecting workers—they have since the late 1970s steadfastly promoted through sponsorship of endowed university professorships and "free market"–oriented think tanks that Lewis Powell called for in 1971.

George Monbiot has argued that the neoliberal economic programs test-piloted forty years ago by Latin American dictatorships and proffered with the underlying notion that economic growth would arise through lower taxes and a more "flexible" labor force have had the exact opposite effect.[18] The undermining of postwar economic policies—which had reined in elites, compelled a broader distribution of wealth, and created a more robust working class with consistently rising incomes—opened the ground for elites to advocate trimming government and scaling back unions as means to unparalleled growth and decreased unemployment.

The results have been spectacular for the 1 percent. Yet for the overwhelming majority they have been disastrous. The loss of unionized jobs has contributed to wage suppression in most every occupation while "free trade" deals such as NAFTA and the impending TPP brought geo-economic forces to bear on workers. "As wages stagnated," Monbiot contended, "people supplemented their incomes with debt. Rising debt fed the deregulated banks, with consequences of which we are all aware."[19] Even though the consequences have intensified wealth accumulation among an infinitesimally small stratum, citizens remain largely unaware of the extent to which they are fleeced, quite literally on an everyday basis.

Censored Story #8: Bank Interests Inflate Global Prices by 35 to 40 Percent

In our present economic system, two out of every five dollars spent on ordinary goods and services ends up in the bank accounts of the most well-to-do institutions and individuals on the planet. This is essentially due to the fact that banking itself is a private, for-profit enterprise beholden only to the lenders, financiers, and bondholders who run it. A study conducted by German professor Margrit Kennedy, and brought to the attention of alternative media readerships by financial author and attorney Ellen Brown, noted that while 1 percent of the world's population now owns 42 percent of the wealth, the bottom 80 percent yield to such hidden charges that bolster the very wealthy merely for sitting on their assets.[20]

Many harbor the false understanding that interest is paid only on a debt that has not been satisfied within a particular time frame. Yet the prices of many goods and services, from running water to sewer and garbage collection, include interest charges necessary to keep money in circulation and banks solvent. The higher up the wealth chain a family is, the greater the chance that they take in more interest than they pay out. Within our monetary system, Kennedy explained in her study, we allow the operation of a hidden redistribution mechanism which constantly shuffles money from those who have less money than they need to those who have more money than they need. This is a different and far more subtle and effective form of exploitation than the one Marx tried to overcome.[21]

Indeed, not only is this a stealth form of confiscation, "baked into the cake," it's an extremely regressive wealth transfer, unwittingly forfeited by the least well-off.

Left unregulated and to its own devices, the present financial system will weave its way into almost all facets of everyday existence. Kennedy and Brown's solution, of which the latter has written extensively, involves de-privatizing the banking system that holds the 99 percent captive and making those interest payments and fees something the public once again owns.

Such an undertaking doesn't have to be national in scope. While Iceland's electorate provides an important example of economic enfranchisement and resilience stemming from its full-scale rejection of private banks' unwarranted claims on the public purse, North Dakota's booming economy, low unemployment, and consistent state budget surpluses are due to the fact that it possesses a state-owned bank.[22] While North Dakota is rich in natural resources, "[a]ccess to credit is the enabling factor that has fostered both a boom in oil and record profits from agriculture in" the state, Brown noted. "The Bank of North Dakota does not compete with local banks but partners with them, helping with capital and liquidity requirements. It participates in loans, provides guarantees, and acts as a sort of mini-Fed[eral Reserve] for the state."[23]

Beyond North Dakota, Montana's example has inspired fifteen states to consider legislation that would change banking policy or establish public banks that could contribute to ending Wall Street's control over Main Street and the cycle of indebtedness that hinders economic development and further jeopardizes living standards.[24] The fact that such profit schemes exist to fleece the broader public, as tens of millions across the US lack the simple means to adequately feed themselves, should be cause for serious alarm. Yet such activities and conditions are seldom the focus of corporate media overwhelmingly concerned with the latest murder rampage, "terrorist" threat, or celebrity breakup.

Censored Story #13: A Fifth of Americans Go Hungry

As suggested thus far, the United States, once regarded as the upholder of freedom and prosperity, has been rotting from within over the past several decades and now has in many respects the distinctive qualities of an unindustrialized peripheral country. This observation is confirmed in unemployment numbers reminiscent of the Great Depression—as much as 23 percent—yet allayed in the public mind through the deceptive bookkeeping methods of federal government statisticians.[25]

In this way, an August 2012 Gallup Poll revealed that 18.2 percent of the public find it routinely difficult to feed their families. Nevertheless, both the US House of Representatives and Senate are proposing cutbacks in the Supplemental Nutrition Insurance Program (SNAP) that may reduce or eliminate aid to as many as 1.8 million already struggling people. Such measures will only further America's already precipitous decline toward conditions resembling Dickensian England. "In 15 states," Mike Ludwig wrote at *Truthout*, "at least 1 in 5 Americans polled in the first half of 2012 reported struggling to pay for food during the past 12 months."[26] Recall that just forty years ago a majority of families looked forward to the security of a modestly expanding income in accord with rising GDP and accompanied by little-to-no debt.

The proposed cuts come at a particularly difficult time as food prices increased in the wake of the most severe drought in fifty years. Opponents of the reductions point to how such measures will hit the most vulnerable especially hard—particularly seniors, children, and working poor families. Even in light of those grave socioeconomic disparities, brought on largely through a corrupt financial system, misplaced economic priorities, and the abandonment of honest governance, those comprising the 1 percent and working in its interests are quick to resist even modest attempts to level the playing field, such as an extremely small tax on investment transactions.

Censored Story #23: Transaction Tax Helps Civilize Wall Street and Lower the National Debt

The prospect of a modest tax on the routine stock transactions that benefit the financial industry and super elites has been discussed in Congress over the past several years as a potential means of revenue. Such a tax at a proposed rate of 0.03 percent (three cents for every $100 of equity value traded) could generate $350 billion in revenue over a ten-year period for a severely indebted and overstretched federal government forced to curtail programs for the most disadvantaged.

Even though such a measure would likely receive broad support from a public well aware of wealth and income disparities between the 99 percent and their ultra-wealthy counterparts, it has received little coverage in corporate media for obvious reasons. This blackout suggests the ways that such media serve their corporate masters. By keeping such anticipated legislation buried, the public has no way of knowing about it, much less advocating their congresspersons for its passage.

The traditional "buy and hold" investor who purchases securities for the long haul would barely notice the small tax. Instead, "high frequency traders" who buy and sell gargantuan volumes of equities and derivatives throughout the course of a day in order to benefit from often modest, split-second fluctuations in price would be the ones to feel the tax most keenly. In other words, the tax would fall most heavily on the likes of Goldman Sachs, JPMorgan Chase, Citibank, and the various hedge funds taking in massive profits through their hefty buy-and-dump transactions and attendant market manipulation as government regulators awaiting passage from their positions through the revolving door to industry often look the other way.

JAMES F. TRACY, PHD, is associate professor of media studies at Florida Atlantic University. His scholarly and critical writings have appeared in a wide variety of academic journals, edited volumes, and alternative news and analysis outlets. Tracy is the editor of Union for Democratic Communications' journal *Democratic Communiqué*. He is also a regular contributor to the Center for Research on Globalization's website GlobalResearch.ca, and a contributor to Project Censored's 2012 publication, *Censored 2013: Dispatches From the Media Revolution.*

Notes

1. Matthew G. Miller and Peter Newcomb, "Billionaires Worth $1.9 Trillion Seek Advantage in 2013," Bloomberg, January 2, 2013, http://www.bloomberg.com/news/2013-01-01/billionaires-worth-1-9-trillion-seek-advantage-in-2013.html.
2. "Globally Almost 870 Million Chronically Undernourished," United Nations Food and Agricultural Organization, October 9, 2012, http://www.fao.org/news/story/en/item/161819/icode/.
3. Brandon Roberts, Deborah Povich and Mark Mather, "Low Income Working Families: The Growing Economic Gap," Working Poor Families Project, Winter 2012–13, http://www.workingpoorfamilies.org/wp-content/uploads/2013/01/Winter-2012_2013-WPFP-Data-Brief.pdf.
4. Robert Kuttner, *The Squandering of America: How the Failure of Our Politics Undermines Our Prosperity* (New York: Alfred A. Knopf, 2007), 21.
5. Ibid.
6. C. Wright Mills, *The Power Elite* (New York: Oxford University Press, 1956); William G. Domhoff, *Who Rules America?* (Englewood Cliffs NJ: Prentice-Hall, 1967).
7. "Confidential Memorandum: Attack on American Free Enterprise System," Lewis F. Powell Jr. to Eugene B. Sydnor Jr., August 23, 1971, 19–21. Available at http://research.greenpeaceusa.org/?a=view&d=5971, accessed May 27, 2013.
8. For more on this theme, see Peter Phillips and Brady Osborne's "Exposing the Financial Core of the Transnational Capitalist Class," ch. 9 in this volume.

9. David Noble, "Prologue," in *Global Productions: Labor in the Making of the "Information Society,"* ed. Gerald Sussman and John Lent (Cresskill, NJ: Hampton Press, 1998), ix–x.

10. David Rothkopf, *Superclass: The Global Power Elite and the World They Are Making* (New York: Farrar, Strauss and Giroux, 2009).

11. Peter Phillips and Kimberly Soeiro, "The Global 1 Percent Ruling Class Exposed," in *Censored 2013: Dispatches From the Media Revolution*, Mickey Huff and Andy Lee Roth with Project Censored (New York: Seven Stories Press, 2012), 235–258. Also see Phillips and Osborne, "Exposing the Financial Core," ch. 9 in this volume.

12. Carl Herman, "1% Hide $21 Trillion and US Big Banks Hide $10 Trillion; Ending World poverty: $3 Trillion," *Washington's Blog*, July 24, 2012, http://www.washingtonsblog.com/2012/07/1-hide-21-trillion-us-big-banks-hide-10-trillion-ending-world-poverty-3-trillion.html.

13. Andrew Gavin Marshall, "The Trans-Pacific Partnership: This Is What Corporate Governance Looks Like," *Truthout*, November 20, 2012, http://truth-out.org/news/item/12857-the-trans-pacific-partnership-this-is-what-corporate-governance-looks-like.

14. Ibid.

15. Ibid.

16. Kevin Zeese, "Obama's 'Employment Creation' Program: Massive Outsourcing of American Jobs," Global Research, September 10, 2012, http://www.globalresearch.ca/obamas-employment-creation-program-massive-outsourcing-of-american-jobs/5304005.

17. Ibid.

18. George Monbiot, "Bang Goes the Theory," Monbiot.com, January 14, 2013, http://www.monbiot.com/2013/01/14/bang-goes-the-theory/.

19. Ibid.

20. Ellen Brown, "It's the Interest, Stupid! Why Bankers Rule the World," Global Research, November 8, 2012, http://www.globalresearch.ca/its-the-interest-stupid-why-bankers-rule-the-world/5311030. Originally posted at Web of Debt, November 8, 2012, http://webofdebt.wordpress.com/2012/11/08/its-the-interest-stupid-why-bankers-rule-the-world/.

21. Margrit Kennedy, *Interest and Inflation Free Money: Creating an Exchange Medium that Works for Everybody and Protects the Earth* (Seva International, 1995), 10, http://kennedy-bibliothek.info/data/bibo/media/GeldbuchEnglisch.pdf.

22. On Iceland, see *Censored* stories #9 and #19 and the Censored News Cluster, "Iceland, the Power of Peaceful Revolution, and the Commons," in this volume.

23. Ellen Brown, "North Dakota's 'Economic Miracle,' It's Not Oil," *YES! Magazine*, August 31, 2011, http://www.yesmagazine.org/new-economy/the-north-dakota-miracle-not-all-about-oil.

24. "State-Owned Financial Institutions 2012 Legislation," National Conference of State Legislatures, January 16, 2013, http://www.ncsl.org/issues-research/banking/state-owned-financial-institutions-2012-legis.aspx.

25. The unemployment rate was roughly 25 percent in 1933—the most severe year of the Depression. This is an estimate as the US government did not collect such statistics until 1940. Irving Bernstein, "Americans in Depression and War," US Department of Labor, http://www.dol.gov/oasam/programs/history/chapter5.htm. Independent economist John Williams used the Bureau of Labor Statistics U6 alternate measure of unemployment that includes all able-bodied and employable workers, including "short-term discouraged," "marginally attached," and "part-time" workers, to arrive at a figure of 13.6 percent. Williams includes long-term discouraged workers to arrive at a much higher figure of 23 percent. John Williams, "April Employment and Unemployment, M3 and Monetary Base," *Shadow Government Statistics*, May 3, 2013, http://www.shadowstats.com/article/no-521-april-employment-and-unemployment-m3-and-monetary-base. See also John Williams, "Alternate Employment Charts," May 3, 2013, http://www.shadowstats.com/alternate_data/unemployment-charts.

26. Mike Ludwig, "Millions Go Hungry as Congress Considers Food Stamp Cuts and Drought Threatens Crops," *Truthout*, August 23, 2012, http://truth-out.org/news/item/11067-millions-go-hungry-as-congress-considers-food-stamp-cuts-and-drought-threatens-crops.

Human Rights and Civil Liberties

Susan Rahman and Donna Nassor

Censored #5

Hate Groups and Antigovernment Groups on Rise across US

Brian Levin, "U.S. Hate and Extremist Groups Hit Record Levels, New Record Says," *Huffington Post*, March 8, 2012, http://www.huffingtonpost.com/brian-levin-jd/hate-groups-splc_b_1331318.html.

Mark Potok, *Intelligence Report: The Year in Hate and Extremism*, Southern Poverty Law Center, Spring 2013, http://www.splcenter.org/home/2013/spring/the-year-in-hate-and-extremism.

LaurieInQueens, "'Patriot' Groups At All-Time High, Hate Groups Up Again: Report," *National Memo*, March 7, 2013, http://www.nationalmemo.com/patriot-groups-at-all-time-high-hate-groups-up-again-report/.

Student Researchers: Sunnie Ayers (Sonoma State University); Jackson Hand and Amanda Baron (College of Marin)

Community and Faculty Evaluators: Ben Parry (Sonoma State University); Andy Lee Roth (College of Marin)

Censored #10

A "Culture of Cruelty" along Mexico–US Border

Erika L. Sánchez, "Ripped Off by Smugglers, Groped by Border Patrol: The Nightmares Women Migrants Face," *AlterNet*, June 26, 2012, http://www.alternet.org/immigration/156035/ripped_off_by_smugglers,_groped_by_border_patrol%3A_the_nightmares_women_migrants_face?page=entire.

No More Deaths, "A Culture of Cruelty," September 21, 2011, http://www.nomoredeaths.org/cultureofcruelty.html.

Student Researcher: Marylyn Phelps (Santa Rosa Junior College)

Faculty Evaluator: Susan Rahman (Santa Rosa Junior College)

Censored #20

Israel Counted Minimum Calorie Needs in Gaza Blockade, Documents Reveal

John Glaser, "Israel Counted Minimum Calorie Needs in Gaza Blockade, Documents Reveal," Antiwar.com, October 17, 2012, http://news.antiwar.com/2012/10/17/israel-counted-minimum-calorie-needs-in-gaza-blockade-documents-reveal.

"Israel Forced to Release Study on Gaza Blockade," BBC News, October 17, 2012, http://www.bbc.co.uk/news/world-middle-east-19975211.

"Israel Set Calorie Limit during Gaza Blockade," Al Jazeera English, October 18, 2012, http://www.aljazeera.com/news/middleeast/2012/10/2012101711552984539.html.

"Israel Calculated Palestinian Calories for Gaza Blockade," *Ma'an News Agency*, October 17, 2012, http://www.maannews.net/eng/ViewDetails.aspx?ID=529743.

Student Researchers: Mohamed Duple (College of Marin); Liliana Valdez-Madera (Santa Rosa Junior College)

Faculty Evaluator: Susan Rahman (College of Marin)

Censored #25

Israel Gave Birth Control to Ethiopian Immigrants without Their Consent

Alistair Dawber, "Israel Gave Birth Control to Ethiopian Jews without Their Consent," *Independent*, January 27, 2013, http://www.independent.co.uk/news/world/middle-east/israel-gave-birth-control-to-ethiopian-jews-without-their-consent-8468800.html.

Ali Abunimah, "Did Israel Violate the Genocide Convention by Forcing Contraceptives on Ethiopian Women?" *Electronic Intifada*, January 28, 2013, http://electronicintifada.net/blogs/ali-abunimah/did-israel-violate-genocide-convention-forcing-contraceptives-ethiopian-women.

Beth Brogan, "Israel Admits Forced Birth Control For Ethiopian Immigrants," Common Dreams, January 29, 2013, http://www.commondreams.org/headline/2013/01/29-0.

Student Researchers: Shanti Williams (College of Marin); Elizabeth Saechao (Sonoma State University)

Faculty Evaluator: Andy Lee Roth (College of Marin); Noel Byrne (Sonoma State University)

INTRODUCTION

We have come so far since the 1965 Civil Rights Act, people frequently assert from across the political spectrum in the United States. But is it true? That is debatable. Although people can now sit together at lunch counters and on buses, research also documents huge increases in black and brown people incarcerated for offenses—including various types of drug possession—that have only recently been considered crimes for which the offender must serve time.[1] The US incarcerates people at a rate that is higher than ever—with lifelong repercussions for those subject to imprisonment, not least of which is the denial of their civil liberties.[2]

Each of the independent news stories in this Censored News Cluster deals with hatred, racism, bigotry, and hegemony. These stories show how the maintenance of power, in the US and in Israel, partly depends on the ability and willingness of the powerful to restrict or violate the human rights and civil liberties of those they deem "Other."

Censored #5: Hate Groups and Antigovernment Groups on Rise across US

Corporate media pump doubts over public safety and fear of terrorists into the minds of American public. The basic message is that we have much to fear but our government is ever vigilant to protect us from the bad guys.

Censored story #5 covers the rise of hate groups in the US, suggesting that we do have something to fear, but that this rise may be an unintended consequence of US policies. Laws intended to keep Americans safe may actually be alienating the very people who join "patriot" and militia groups. In March 2013, the Southern Poverty Law Center (SPLC), which monitors hate groups and antigovernment groups, released a report showing 1,360 radical, antigovernment patriot groups and 321 militias actively operating within the US. SPLC statistics indicate an 813 percent rise in the number of such groups since 2008.[3] Hate groups are most prevalent in California, with eighty-two documented groups; Texas stands second among states with sixty-two.[4]

By the SPLC's standards, hate groups "have beliefs or practices that attack or malign an entire class of people, typically for their immutable characteristics," and their activities can include "criminal acts, marches, rallies, speeches, meetings, leafleting or publishing."[5]

With the numbers of patriot groups now higher than during the peak of the 1990s militia movement, the threat of non-Islamic domestic terrorism is real and growing, according to the SPLC. As the SPLC released its report, the Center's president, J. Richard Cohen, sent a letter to the US attorney general and the homeland security secretary urging the Departments of Justice and Homeland Security "to establish an interagency task force to assess the adequacy of the resources devoted to responding to the growing threat of non-Islamic domestic terrorism."[6]

According to the SPLC report, hate groups are now transitioning from racist hatred to hatred focused on the government and its representatives.[7] As Brian Levin reported,

> While hate groups and right-wing extremists, with some notable exceptions, have largely been unsuccessful in carrying out violence, analysts are increasingly concerned due to:

1. A steady stream of thwarted violent plots,
2. Several notable spontaneous violent encounters with police,
3. The rapid increase in groups, [and]
4. Widespread political, economic and social distress.[8]

As Cohen and the SPLC argued, "serious questions have been raised about the level of resources that are now being devoted to assessing the threat of non-Islamic terrorism."[9]

Corporate media paid scattered attention to the SPLC report. Both the *New York Times* and MSNBC covered the report on the day the SPLC issued it. Otherwise, establishment media have done little to shed light on this subject. In some cases, corporate media actually contribute to the problem. As the Southern Poverty Law Center noted, the growth in extremism

> has been aided by mainstream media figures and politicians who have used their platforms to legitimize false propaganda about immigrants and other minorities and spread the kind of paranoid conspiracy theories on which militia groups thrive.[10]

Individuals that identify with patriot groups often seek to preserve a strong white nationalism, which they perceive as threatened by cultural shifts in today's society. These shifts include the election of Barack Obama as America's first black president, changes in the nation's demographics (with the loss of its white majority predicted by 2043), and, in his second term, President Obama's agenda for gun control and immigration reform.[11] Of course, change is nothing new in the US. From the abolition of slavery through the civil rights movement to the present, greater inclusivity appears as a threat to those who would maintain the status quo. Perhaps corporate media pay less attention to (white) militia groups because, in a way, these organizations do the ruling class's dirty work.

Censored #10: A "Culture of Cruelty" along Mexico–US Border

US treatment of immigrants crossing the Mexico–US border shows that we do not see all people as equal. US policies have left many citizens of Central American countries without adequate work.[12] As *Censored* story #10 documents, when immigrants travel to the US in hopes of economic opportunity, they encounter what the organization No More Deaths has dubbed a "culture of cruelty."

Drawing on the work of No More Deaths, Erika L. Sánchez reported how migrants crossing the Mexico–US border face not only the dangers posed by an unforgiving desert but also abuse at the hands of the US Border Patrol. Crossing the desert, migrants risk dehydration, starvation, exhaustion, and the possibility of being threatened and robbed; the dangers continue if they come in contact with the Border Patrol, Sánchez reported.[13] In "A Culture of Cruelty," the organization No More Deaths revealed human rights violations by the US Border Patrol including limiting or denying migrants water and food, verbal and physical abuse, and failing to provide necessary medical attention; female migrants face additional risks, including sexual abuse, according to No More Deaths.[14] Sánchez reported, "Dehumanization of immigrants is actually part of the Border Patrol's institutional culture. Instances of misconduct are not aberrations, but common practice."[15] The Border Patrol denies any wrongdoing and has not been held responsible for these abuses. No More Deaths reported 179 human remains found in the desert in 2012 alone.[16]

Public debate on immigration tends to ignore not only the potential dangers of crossing the desert, but also the reasons for the migration of undocumented immigrants to the US. The North American Free Trade Agreement (NAFTA), signed by US President Bill Clinton and Mexican President Carlos Salinas in 1994, displaced many Mexican farmers and workers from their farms. Lack of employment resulting from NAFTA continues to motivate many to migrate to the US. Sánchez reported:

> Most undocumented immigrants have had to leave their economically ravaged towns in order to survive and assist their families. In the documentary *The Other Side of Immigration*,

filmmaker Roy Germano explored the causes of Mexican immigration to the United States by interviewing 700 men and women in the Mexican countryside. One of the major factors he found was the North American Free Trade Agreement (NAFTA) signed in 1994. . . . Many people were forced to leave their homes because there were no employment opportunities or because they lost their farms as a flood of cheaper corn came South from the United States.[17]

Fear of immigrants from Mexico and Central America has led the US government to undertake extreme measures in order to keep immigrants out of the US. The enormous wall that separates the US and Mexico is just one example of this. Both the wall's construction and the second-class status of the Mexican people parallel the situation between Palestinians and Israelis living in the occupied West Bank, East Jerusalem, Gaza, and throughout Israel. The walls that snake throughout these regions are made by the same manufacturers who helped construct the physical barriers along the US–Mexican border—with the same intent: to keep undesirable people out.[18]

Censored #20: Israel Counted Minimum Calorie Needs in Gaza Blockade, Documents Reveal

US corporate media regularly distort, and even censor, news reports about Israel–Palestine.[19] US corporate media systemically avoid stories on the Israel–Palestine conflict that portray Israel in critical terms, and when they do report on the conflict, that coverage employs double standards that favor Israel.[20] The "monumental cover-up" of news on Palestine, described by Alison Weir in 2004,[21] continues in 2013.

The Israeli human rights group Gisha fought a legal battle that led to the release, in October 2012, of government documents that exposed Israeli policy to permit Gazans just 2,279 calories of food each day.[22] The 2008 defense ministry study, titled "Food Consumption in the Gaza Strip—Red Lines," sought to determine the "minimal subsistence basket" that was "sufficient for subsistence without the development of malnutrition."[23] The evidence indicates that Israel decided hunger would be an effective means to coerce residents of Gaza to force out the Hamas government.

Since June 2007, Israel has imposed tightened restrictions as a form of collective punishment for Palestinians who democratically elected Hamas to lead the government in Gaza. From 2007 until 2010, Israel only allowed food into Gaza that it determined as vital for the survival of the civilian population. Furthermore, with limited exceptions, Israel has banned the export of virtually all goods from Gaza, creating additional hardships for Gazans attempting to earn a living and support their families.[24] In January 2011, WikiLeaks released a US diplomatic cable from 2008 in which Israel informed US officials of its intent to keep Gaza's economy "on the brink of collapse" while avoiding a humanitarian crisis, which would require an international response.[25] Despite its restrictions, Israel continues to allege that it does not control Gaza.

Censored #25: Israel Gave Birth Control to Ethiopian Immigrants Without Their Consent

In January 2013, Israel acknowledged that medical authorities have been giving Ethiopian immigrants long-term birth-control injections, often without their knowledge or consent. The Israeli government had previously denied the charges, which were first brought to light by investigative reporter Gal Gabbay in a broadcast of Israeli Educational Television's news program, *Vacuum*, on December 8, 2012. The following month, the Israeli Health Ministry's director-general, Roni Gamzo, ordered all gynecologists to stop administering the drugs.

Alistair Dawber reports for the UK's *Independent* that the Ethiopian women in question believed they had to accept medical treatment in order to be allowed to enter and stay in Israel; but medical personnel administering the injections—alleged to be Depo-Provera, a highly effective and long-lasting form of contraception—did not explain the injections' purpose.[26] *The Electronic Intifada*'s Ali Abunimah reported that the Israeli health ministry ran the convert contraception program in transit camps with the assistance of the American Jewish Joint Distribution Committee (JDC),[27] which describes itself as the "world's leading Jewish humanitarian assistance organization."[28]

In late January 2013, in a carefully framed article, the *Times of Israel* reported that health minister Roni Gamzo ordered new standards when renewing prescriptions of the birth-control drug Depo-Provera for new Ethiopian immigrants.[29] Gamzo did not admit wrongdoing and only acknowledged that the women had been given the shots without understanding their effects. The article provided further denials that Ethiopian women were singled out, and the JDC denied any involvement in procedures for Jewish immigrants to Israel.[30]

Nevertheless, these health policies raise concerns of government-sanctioned racism. If the shots were given without proper consent, with the intent to target Ethiopian women and reduce their birthrates, then the forced contraception program may fit the legal definition of genocide, in violation of Article II(d) of the Convention on the Prevention and Punishment of the Crime of Genocide.[31]

This story must be understood against the backdrop of anti-African sentiment, and even violence, in Israel. Israeli Prime Minister Benjamin Netanyahu has publically stated that African migrants threaten the existence of Israel as a Jewish and democratic state.[32] And, in May 2012, a thousand Jewish Israelis ran through the streets of Tel Aviv, looting and destroying African-operated businesses and physically assaulting any person of color they encountered.[33] As David Sheen reported, such racism has not been properly addressed or quashed by Israeli religious, economic, or political leaders; instead, that establishment has "ramped up their efforts to expel all non-Jewish African people from the country."[34]

CONCLUSION

Each of the stories in this news cluster demonstrates how those in power will go to great lengths to maintain social and political institutions that favor them. The conflicts that charge these underreported news stories involve a paradigm of white- and/or Jewish-supremacy and policies and practices aimed at maintaining status quo demographics in order to sustain hegemony over people who are not white and/or Jewish. Judged on the basis of their reluctance to cover such stories adequately, US corporate media appear to have an interest in maintaining such power structures. Therefore, it is urgent that we continue to report and reveal the truth.

SUSAN RAHMAN, MA, is a sociology instructor at Santa Rosa Junior College and the College of Marin. Her areas of interest include Palestinian self-determination, issues of privilege and inequality, and media literacy. Her current work focuses on the role of self-reflection in social transformation. She lives in Sebastopol, California, with her partner Carlos, daughter Jordan, and dogs, Rosie and Cody.

DONNA NASSOR is an adjunct United Nations Non-Governmental Organization (UNNGO) representative with the International Peace Research Association, a UNNGO Human Rights Committee Member, a restorative justice and business professional, a retired attorney, and a mediator. She is working on a PhD in nonclinical psychology at Saybrook University. Her current research project is titled "Palestinian Voices: Peace with Justice through the Eyes of Palestinians Living in Their Homeland."

Notes

1. Michelle Alexander, *The New Jim Crow: Mass Incarceration in the Age of Colorblindness* (New York: The New Press, 2010).
2. Ibid.
3. LaurieInQueens, "'Patriot' Groups At All-Time High, Hate Groups Up Again: Report," National Memo, March 7, 2013, http://www.nationalmemo.com/patriot-groups-at-all-time-high-hate-groups-up-again-report/. The National Memo story is based on the SPLC report itself. See Mark Potok, *Intelligence Report: The Year in Hate and Extremism*, Southern Poverty Law Center, Spring 2013, http://www.splcenter.org/home/2013/spring/the-year-in-hate-and-extremism.
4. Southern Poverty Law Center, "Hate Map," accessed June 4, 2013, http://www.splcenter.org/get-informed/hate-map.
5. Ibid.; quoted by LaurieInQueens, "'Patriot' Groups At All-Time High."
6. J. Richard Cohen, "SPLC Letter to DOJ & DHS," Southern Poverty Law Center, March 5, 2013, http://www.splcenter.org/home/splc-letter-to-DOJ-DHS - .Ua4kueCCKXs.
7. For example, on "major terrorist plots and racist rampages that have emerged from the American radical right in the years since Oklahoma City," see "Terror From the Right: Plots, Conspiracies and Racist Rampages Since Oklahoma City," Southern Poverty Law Center, no date, http://www.splcenter.org/get-informed/publications/terror-from-the-right.
8. Brian Levin, "U.S. Hate and Extremist Groups Hit Record Levels, New Record Says," *Huffington Post*, March 8, 2012, http://www.huffingtonpost.com/brian-levin-jd/hate-groups-splc_b_1331318.html.
9. Cohen, "SPLC Letter to DOJ & DHS."
10. "Hate and Extremism," Southern Poverty Law Center, no date, http://www.splcenter.org/what-we-do/hate-and-extremism.
11. See Potok, "Year of Hate and Extremism."
12. Juan Gonzales, *Harvest of Empire* (New York: Penguin, 2011).
13. Erika L. Sánchez, "Ripped Off by Smugglers, Groped by Border Patrol: The Nightmares Women Migrants Face," *AlterNet*, June 26, 2012, http://www.alternet.org/immigration/156035/ripped_off_by_smugglers,_groped_by_border_patrol%3A_the_nightmares_women_migrants_face?page=entire.
14. No More Deaths, "A Culture of Cruelty," September 21, 2011, http://www.nomoredeaths.org/cultureofcruelty.html.
15. Sánchez, "Ripped Off."
16. No More Deaths, "Culture of Cruelty."
17. Sánchez, "Ripped Off."
18. The Department of Homeland contracted Kollsman, Inc., the US subsidiary of Israeli-based Elbit Systems Ltd., to work on its Secure Borders Initiative. See, for example, "Israeli Firm Gets Mexico Border Wall Contract," *World War 4 Report*, November 8, 2006, http://www.ww4report.com/node/2743; "Boeing Team Awarded SBInet Contract by Department of Homeland Security," September 21, 2006, http://www.boeing.com/news/releases/2006/q3/060921a_nr.html.
19. Alison Weir, "American Media Distortion on Palestine," *Middle East Monitor*, May 1, 2013, http://www.middleeastmonitor.com/articles/guest-writers/5890-american-media-distortion-on-palestine.
20. See, for example, Peter Phillips, et al., "A Study of Bias in the Associated Press," *Censored 2007: The Top 25 Censored Stories*, ed. Peter Phillips and Project Censored (New York: Seven Stories, 2006), 348–349; Phillips, et al.'s analysis of AP bias in coverage of the Israel–Palestine conflict drew on "Deadly Distortion: Associated Press Coverage of Israeli and Palestinian Deaths," If Americans Only Knew, April 26, 2006, http://ifamericansknew.org/media/ap-report.html.
21. Alison Weir, "U.S. Media Coverage of Israel Palestine: Choosing Sides," *Censored 2005: The Top 25 Censored Stories*, ed. Peter Phillips and Project Censored (New York: Seven Stories, 2004), 285–300, quote at 285.

22. "Israel Forced to Release Study on Gaza Blockade," BBC News, October 17, 2012, http://www.bbc.co.uk/news/world-middle-east-19975211; John Glaser, "Israel Counted Minimum Calorie Needs in Gaza Blockade, Documents Reveal," Antiwar.com, October 17, 2012, http://news.antiwar.com/2012/10/17/israel-counted-minimum-calorie-needs-in-gaza-blockade-documents-reveal/.
23. Gisha, the Israeli human rights organization that secured the document, has published an English version of it online, http://www.gisha.org/UserFiles/File/publications/redlines/redlines-presentation-eng.pdf.
24. David Poort, "History of Israeli Blockade on Gaza," Al Jazeera, November 2, 1011, http://www.aljazeera.com/indepth/features/2011/10/2011103017235699380.html.
25. The Norwegian newspaper Aftenposten was the first to publish the leaked cable: http://www.aftenposten.no/spesial/wikileaksdokumenter/article3972840.ece.
26. Alistair Dawber, "Israel Gave Birth Control to Ethiopian Jews Without Their Consent," Independent, January 27, 2013, http://www.independent.co.uk/news/world/middle-east/israel-gave-birth-control-to-ethiopian-jews-without-their-consent-8468800.html.
27. Ali Abunimah, "Did Israel Violate the Genocide Convention by Forcing Contraceptives on Ethiopian Women?," Electronic Intifada, January 28, 2013, http://electronicintifada.net/blogs/ali-abunimah/did-israel-violate-genocide-convention-forcing-contraceptives-ethiopian-women.
28. "About JDC," American Jewish Joint Distribution Committee, http://www.jdc.org/about-jdc/.
29. Asher Zeiger, "Israel Changes Birth-control Policy for Ethiopian Immigrants," Times of Israel, January 29, 2013, http://www.timesofisrael.com/israel-changes-birth-control-policy-for-ethiopian-immigrants/.
30. Ibid.
31. Abunimah, "Did Israel Violate the Genocide Convention?"
32. Ibid.
33. David Sheen, "A Year in Review: Anti-African Racism and Asylum Seekers in Israel," Uruknet, May 29, 2013, http://www.uruknet.info/?p=m97985&hd&l=e.
34. Ibid.

CENSORED NEWS CLUSTER

Technologies and Ecologies of War

Targol Mesbah and Zara Zimbardo

Censored #7

Merchants of Death and Nuclear Weapons

Marc Pilisuk, "Occupying the Merchants of Death," Project Censored, November 22, 2012, http://www.projectcensored.org/top-stories/articles/occupying-the-merchants-of-death/.

Student Researcher: Jessica Eccles (Sonoma State University)

Faculty Evaluator: Peter Phillips (Sonoma State University)

Censored #11

Bush Blocked Iran Nuclear Deal

Gareth Porter, "Bush Blocked Iran Disarmament Deal," *Consortium News*, June 6, 2012, http://consortiumnews.com/2012/06/06/bush-blocked-iran-nuke-deal/.

Student Researcher: Seamus O'Herlihy (Santa Rosa Junior College)

Faculty Evaluator: Susan Rahman (Santa Rosa Junior College)

Censored #12

The US Has Left Iraq with an Epidemic of Cancers and Birth Defects

Sarah Morrison, "Iraq Records Huge Rise in Birth Defects," *Independent*, October 14, 2012, http://www.independent.co.uk/life-style/health-and-families/health-news/iraq-records-huge-rise-in-birth-defects-8210444.html.

Ross Caputi, "The Victims of Fallujah's Health Crisis are Stifled by Western Silence," *Guardian*, October 25, 2012, http://www.guardian.co.uk/commentisfree/2012/oct/25/fallujah-iraq-health-crisis-silence?INTCMP=SRCH.

Dahr Jamail, "Ten Years Later, U.S. Has Left Iraq with Mass Displacement & Epidemic of Birth Defects, Cancers," *Democracy Now!*, March 20, 2013, http://www.democracynow.org/2013/3/20/ten_years_later_us_has_left.

M. Al-Sabbak, S. Sadik Ali, O. Savabi, et al., "Metal Contamination and the Epidemic of Congenital Birth Defects in Iraqi Cities," *Bulletin of Environmental Contamination and Toxicology* 89, no. 5 (November 2012), http://www.springerlink.com/content/u35001451t13g645/fulltext.html.

Student Researchers: Ivan Konza (Florida Atlantic University); Marc David Prophete (Indian River State College)

Faculty Evaluators: James F. Tracy (Florida Atlantic University); Elliot D. Cohen (Indian River State College)

113

Oil and Fraud: Why We Went to Iraq

"Secret Pentagon Docs Reveal Pre-War Plans to Get Big Oil into Iraq," Institute for Public Accuracy, July 17, 2012, http://www.accuracy.org/release/secret-pentagon-docs-reveal-pre-war-plans-to-get-big-oil-into-iraq/.

"'Fuel on the Fire': Author Greg Muttitt on Oil and Politics in Occupied Iraq, Arab Spring," *Democracy Now!*, July 16, 2012, http://www.democracynow.org/2012/7/16/fuel_on_the_fire_author_greg.

Student Researcher: Jennifer Garza (Sonoma State University)

Faculty Evaluator: Barbara Widhalm (Sonoma State University)

INTRODUCTION

The tenth anniversary of the invasion of Iraq passed largely in silence in the corporate news media. Writing in the *Atlantic*, Ta-Nehisi Coates remarked that we "don't want to 'look back' on things that might demand onerous labor on our part." But, Coates observed, the failures of the Iraq War are likely to be repeated if the nation only "looks forward."[1]

Looking back to the beginnings of "endless war" in October 2001, United States Vice President Dick Cheney glibly declared, "It is different than the Gulf War was, in the sense that it may never end. At least, not in our lifetime."[2] Before considering some of the extant consequences of a perpetual war on terror, let us briefly reflect on the semantics of Cheney's statement. The uncertainty projected onto the open-ended war on terror, with its attendant incitement of fear, is presented here in contradistinction to the definitive end of the Gulf War. It replays the rhetoric of precision and speed that characterized the surgical language of the Gulf War: in Operation Desert Storm, precision-guided munitions and smart bombs were supposed to strategically take out military targets with minimal collateral cost. By most accounts, the Gulf War did end, once Saddam Hussein withdrew his troops from Kuwait in late February 1991, and US troops returned in March. Yet, the extent of the casualties from the use of depleted uranium is becoming more apparent—although not through US corporate media's reporting. Thus, for example, in a recent book on "slow violence" and the temporality and scale of ecological disasters, Rob Nixon brings attention to the "ecology of the aftermath" in his discussion of belated Gulf War victims who suffer from the long-term consequences of exposure to radioactive depleted uranium.[3]

To conceptualize the war event in terms of an ecology of war suggests an alternate temporality to normalized accounts of its duration. It also significantly shifts the spatial coordinates of war's logistics to make visible the range of violence, from the consequences of corporate oil extraction to reckless dumping of toxic metals.

These censored stories reveal critical glimpses into the breadth and depth of the cost of war in ways that we are not yet able to measure. Looking back again, *Censored 2009*'s #1 story was, "Over One Million Iraqi Deaths Caused by US Occupation."[4] As reported in the story, a study conducted by the prestigious British polling group Opinion Research Business (ORB) found casualty figures at least ten times greater than otherwise reported in corporate media. The same year, Joseph E. Stiglitz and Linda J. Bilmes published *The Three Trillion Dollar War*.[5] Their study's stark quantification of the war's human and economic costs challenges readers to weigh US interventionist policies in terms of the "opportunity costs" of the trillions spent, what the US has sacrificed domestically by pursuing wars in Iraq and Afghanistan. Among the wars' hidden costs, Stiglitz and Bilmes identified long-term physical and mental health care for veterans.[6] As this year's censored stories on war illustrate, we are now facing costs staggeringly far beyond even Bilmes and Stiglitz's calculations, uncountable and unaccountable.

In 2012, Hollywood offered frames within which to selectively understand US foreign policy, its military role, and the retroactive justification for targeted killing and torture, through feature films such as *Zero Dark Thirty* and *Argo*.[7] By contrast, the independent documentary films *Dirty Wars*, by Richard Rowley and investigative journalist Jeremy Scahill, and *The Invisible War*, by Kirby Dick, have exposed both America's covert and increasingly privatized wars and the extent of sexual assault in the United States military. The political lines drawn to understand war's officially recognized "end" and "beginning" are erased by the realities of suffocating sanctions imposed on Iran and the Iraq military campaign's continuing contamination epidemics. As the national gaze is focused on the apocalyptic vision of potential nuclear annihilation at Iran's hands, we are blinded to the actual slow apocalypse in poisoned areas of Iraq.

The independent news stories featured in this *Censored* News Cluster bring the ecologies of war into sharper focus.

Censored #7: Merchants of Death and Nuclear Weapons

With the coordinated production of fear and obsession around Iran's alleged nuclear threat, a commensurate assessment of our sprawling military-industrial complex's economic logic is arrested. Public debate is corralled into concern projected abroad, away from domestic scrutiny. Drawing on the National Nuclear Security Administration's 2012 report, Marc Pilisuk wrote,

> Despite a White House pledge to seek a world without nuclear weapons, the 2011 federal budget for nuclear weapons research and development exceeded $7 billion and could (if the Obama administration has its way) exceed $8 billion per year by the end of this decade. This steady and growing investment stands in stark contrast to the promising U.S. rhetoric of nuclear disarmament.[8]

The corporate players financing and profiting from the nuclear complex are backed with political support that contradicts official rhetoric. "The staggering budget for this dangerous drift is staunchly defended by corporate lobbyists and gigantic contracts are awarded out of public view."[9] This report names all the institutions most heavily involved in financing nuclear arms makers.

Pilisuk's report also analyzed the economic relationships that undergird the United States' increasing reliance on drones as weapons of war. As critics of the US drone strikes have noted, the Obama administration describes US drone policy in seductive and sanitized terms, as "targeted" killings that are "costless" to the US.[10] Writing for the *Guardian*, George Monbiot, for example, contrasted President Obama's sorrow for the child victims of the December 2012 Newtown school shooting with his silence regarding children murdered by drones:

> If the victims of Mr. Obama's drone strikes are mentioned by the state at all, they are discussed in terms which suggest

that they are less than human. The people who operate the drones, *Rolling Stone* magazine reports, describe their casualties as "bug splats" . . . since viewing the body through a grainy-green video image gives the sense of an insect being crushed.[11]

Elsewhere the victims of US drone strikes are linguistically reduced to the status of vegetation: Justifying drone strikes, former Central Intelligence Agency (CIA) analyst and Obama counterterrorism adviser Bruce Riedel likened drones to lawn mowers: "You've got to mow the lawn all the time. The minute you stop mowing, the grass is going to grow back."[12]

Pilisuk warned against a proliferating combination of nuclear weapons with remote weapons delivery systems, such as drones. Compared with the Cold War's large-scale nuclear delivery systems, today's drones are much more economical. Thus, in Pilisuk's view, "the world is quickly moving toward a matrix of surveillance vehicles of unknown origin and likely soon to include nuclear weapons. This is not the world that sane people wish to hand off to our children."[13]

The satirical newspaper the *Onion* ran the headline in February 2012, "Iran Worried U.S. Might Be Building 8,500th Nuclear Weapon." "Reporting" from Tehran, the *Onion*'s mock story continued, "Obviously, the prospect of this happening is very distressing to Iran and all countries like Iran. After all, the United States is a volatile nation that's proven it needs little provocation to attack anyone anywhere in the world whom it perceives to be a threat."[14] Although the *Onion* only slightly exaggerates the number of US nuclear warheads, the article's reversal makes absurdly explicit the doublespeak and double standards at play.

Censored #11: Bush Blocked Iran Nuclear Deal

Corporate media's recurrent narrative on nuclear weapons portrays the US as consistently doing everything in its power to prevent Iran's development of nuclear weapons, while Iran resolutely pursues that goal. Gareth Porter's report for *Consortium News* throws a wrench into the works of the Bush and Obama administrations' self-rationalizing and polarizing foreign policies toward Iran (e.g., "leave all options on the table"). The specter of a "nuclear Middle East," a persistent phrase in White House discourse regarding Iran, clearly aims to generate fear and anxiety in the US public. A highly effective spell, each time administration officials invoke this phrase it renders invisible the reality that the Middle East is already "nuclear," given Israel's possession of warheads. US government officials and corporate media emphasize the intolerable existential threat of Iran possibly acquiring nuclear weapons, while downplaying Israel's status as an existing nuclear power in the region. The echo chamber of "We can't wait for a smoking gun in the form of a mushroom cloud" is reanimated, from Iraq to Iran.

The formulaic and predictable steps to war are being followed in textbook (read: CIA handbook) fashion: demonize the enemy, exaggerate a threat, fake a diplomatic effort, and then establish a line that was supposedly crossed as a pretext for military intervention. The construction of simmering inevitability lays the psychic national backdrop against which allegedly imminent threats can be brought to boil in the public's imagination. Fear and selective amnesia never fail as the tandem tools of empire. Recognizable masks for war are donned and adjusted as Oceania begins another propaganda round of "We've always been at war with Eastasia."[15]

In another instance of the double standards and rhetorical distinctions that characterize the US promotion of its foreign policy, economic sanctions are presented as peaceful means to neutralize the nation's enemies.

Although India, Israel, and Pakistan possess nuclear arsenals, none are currently a signatory to the nuclear Non-Proliferation Treaty (NPT).[16] By contrast, Iran—which has been a NPT signatory since 1968—has been repeatedly targeted, most recently with sanctions that have had devastating effects on the Iranian people, despite the fact that the NPT's terms allow for uranium enrichment.

Against this backdrop, revelations in Seyed Hossein Mousavian's recent memoir, *The Iranian Nuclear Crisis*, deserve more widespread news coverage. Mousavian, one of Iran's top nuclear negotiators in 2004–05, offers new details about how President George W. Bush blocked a deal with Iran, despite a number of European Union members' support for the deal. By Mousavian's account, Iran had offered a deal to the United

States, France, Germany, and the United Kingdom that would have made it impossible for it to build nuclear weapons. The deal involved Iran shipping its uranium to an "agreed upon country" for enrichment in exchange for yellowcake, the raw material used to make fuel rods. As Gareth Porter reported, "Iran did not have the capability to fabricate fuel rods, so the implication was that the LEU [Low Enriched Uranium] would have to be shipped to another country for conversion or would have to be done under international auspices within Iran. Once the fuel rods were fabricated, it would be practically impossible for Iran to reconvert them for military purposes."[17]

As such, it is important to note that the current sanctions on Iran were not in fact inevitable, as the official Washington narrative insists. Moreover, these sanctions are not a "peaceful" or "humanitarian" means of negotiation given some of the more deadly consequences most vividly evidenced in the lack of access to medicine and medical equipment.

In June 2012, Hamid Dabashi offered a searing critique of Nicholas Kristof's report for the *New York Times* in which Kristof unequivocally declared that sanctions against Iran were working. Based on his much-hyped "1,700-mile drive around the country," Kristof offered his "blunt" claim that US-led "sanctions are succeeding as intended: They are inflicting prodigious economic pain on Iranians and are generating discontent."[18] Assessing Kristof's reportage, Dabashi wrote, "This is journalism at the *de facto* service of a bewildered empire, a journalism that does not only fail to raise very basic and simple questions about dangerous policies of the journalist's home country but that has in fact become the effective extension of imperial wars by other means."[19]

Censored #12: The US Has Left Iraq with an Epidemic of Cancers and Birth Defects

Depleted uranium is highly radioactive with a 4.5 billion year half-life. The United Nations Commission on Human Rights has classified it as a "weapon of indiscriminate effect," alongside nuclear, biological, and chemical weapons.[20] Yet, depleted uranium has been used in conventional warfare—particularly by US forces—since the Gulf War; more recently, its use has also been documented in Libya, Iraq, Afghanistan, the Balkans, and Lebanon.[21] By 2003, US Army training manuals advised personnel to use respiratory and skin protection when operating within seventy-five yards of destroyed tanks or spent shells, though Pentagon officials categorically denied any link between depleted uranium and the dramatic rise in cancers reported in areas known to have been densely bombarded.[22]

Acknowledging the severe health consequences of exposure to depleted uranium would also dramatically affect the US government's position on the vexed topic of Gulf War illness (also known as Gulf War syndrome). Indeed, the "slow violence" of environmental contamination has not discriminated against US veterans of the Gulf War.

While contemporary corporate media coverage of ongoing violence in postwar Iraq focuses superficially on "sectarian" conflict, the magnitude of the health crisis that permeates daily life due to the war remains effectively invisible. Nonetheless, epidemiological studies are beginning to register the extent of long-term health effects in

Basra and Fallujah, two known sites of intensive bombing during the war. At Al-Basra Maternity Hospital, a team of researchers reported that, from 2003 to 2011, "congenital birth defects increased by an astonishing seventeen-fold."[23]

In addition to depleted uranium, this study also found unhealthy levels of other heavy metals—including mercury and lead—among the affected populations. Reporting for the UK's *Independent*, Sarah Morrison quoted Dr. Mozhgan Savabieasfahani, an environmental toxicologist at the University of Michigan and one of the study's lead authors: the study's first documentation of a "footprint of metal in the population" is "compelling evidence linking the staggering increases in Iraqi birth defects to neuro-toxic metal contamination following the repeated bombardments of Iraqi cities." Dr. Savabieasfahani called the "epidemic" a "public health crisis."[24] She added: "We need extensive environmental sampling, of food, water and air to find out where this is coming from. Then we can clean it up. Now we are seeing 50 percent of children being born with malformations; in a few years it could be everyone."

The stark case of censorship in this instance pushes the question of media ethics and accountability to an extreme. Although new epidemiological studies demonstrate links between Iraq's current health crises and the US's past military activities and make plain the severity of this environmental disaster, US officials refuse to acknowledge responsibility and American corporate media ignore investigating the story. As Ross Caputi reports in the *Guardian*:

> Modern means of warfare may be inherently indiscriminate. This is a scientific finding worthy of discussion at the highest levels of academia, politics and international affairs. While it may yet get some attention outside the borders of the United States, its "controversial" nature (its implications of the US military's guilt in creating possibly the worst public health crisis in history) ensures that it will be ignored at all costs by the callous and corrupt US government and its subservient media establishment.[25]

To put the Fallujah birth defects in comparative perspective, Dahr Jamail noted: "From 2004 up to this day, we are seeing a rate of congenital malformations in the city of Fallujah that has surpassed even that in the wake of the Japanese cities of Hiroshima and Nagasaki," on which the US used nuclear bombs at the end of World War II.[26]

One of the most egregious aspects of coverage of the US war on terror has been and continues to be the systematic exclusion of the voices of victims of US violence, whose lives, suffering, deaths, and mourning are invisible to news spectators, dehumanized into nonexistence.

RELATED VALIDATED INDEPENDENT NEWS STORY

Oil and Fraud: Why We Went to Iraq

In efforts to forestall the US invasion of Iraq, antiwar protestors marched with signs that read "No Blood for Oil" and activists called for a "separation of oil and state." As Norman Solomon identified, advocates of the invasion of Iraq used the negative frame, "This is Not at All About Oil or Corporate Profits," to build the case for war.[27] Corporate news outlets acted as a verbatim megaphone for the government to sell a repeatedly rebranded war, from preemptive strike against nonexistent weapons of mass destruction (WMDs), Operation Iraqi Liberation, and dictatorial regime change, to installing democracy and freedom (better understood as free trade), to a necessary victory in the war against terror, to a refusal to "cut and run," to the rhetorical detergent of Operation New Dawn.

In 2007, the publication of former Federal Reserve chairman Alan Greenspan's memoir, *The Age of Turbulence*, caused a stir, in part because he wrote, "I'm saddened that it is politically inconvenient to acknowledge what everyone knows: The Iraq war is largely about oil."[28] Dominance of the world's second largest oil reserves was at the heart of British-backed US military policy toward Iraq. These recycled narratives of disavowal—the war was about oil but nonetheless it was not about oil—are continuously deployed.

Since even before the start of the US bombing and invasion in 2003, independent reporters and alternative media sources have worked tirelessly to expose the war effort's material motives. In 2013, on the tenth anniversary of war, the corporate media appear to remain convinced by the establishment line that anyone (besides Alan Greenspan, perhaps) who argues that oil motivated US military policy in Iraq is a conspiracy theorist. Indeed, this has been the fate of both Greg Muttitt, author of *Fuel on Fire: Oil and Politics in Occupied Iraq*; and Antonia Juhasz, author of *The Bush Agenda: Invading the World, One Economy at a Time* and *The Tyranny of Oil: The World's Most Powerful Industry—And What We Must Do to Stop It*, among other critics with expertise on the topic. Thus, in 2008, the *Washington Post's* energy correspondent, Steven Mufson wrote, "There is no single conspiracy theory about why the Bush administration allegedly waged this 'war for oil.'"[29] Then Mufson identified and described a variety of critical explanations—including those advanced by Juhasz and Muttitt—before concluding in terms that redefine his conception of "conspiracy," dismissing how private, corporate interests might have motivated Bush administration military policy toward Iraq in favor of collective complicity as the best explanation. "In a sense," Mufson concluded:

> All Americans are part of that conspiracy. We have built a society that is profligate with its energy and relies on petroleum that happens to be pooled under some unstable or unfriendly regimes. We have frittered away energy resources with little regard for the strategic consequences. And now it's hard and expensive to change our ways.[30]

Over the past decade, even as Juhasz's analysis of Big Oil in Iraq gained standing in the corporate media, editors consistently relegated her work to the opinion section. Thus, for example, in April 2013, CNN featured Juhasz's "Why The War in Iraq was Fought for Big Oil," as an opinion piece in its "complete coverage of the Iraq War anniversary."[31] In her article, Juhasz identified opening up Iraq to foreign oil companies as the "central goal" of the war, and she cited "top U.S. military and political figures" who had stated so in public, including General John Abizaid, former head of US Central Command in Iraq, in 2007; former Federal Reserve Chairman Alan Greenspan; and Chuck Hagel, who served as a senator in 2007.[32] "Big Oil" was the true winner of the war, Juhasz wrote. "Before the 2003 invasion, Iraq's domestic oil industry was fully nationalized and closed to Western oil companies. A decade of war later, it is largely privatized and utterly dominated by foreign firms."[33]

Of approximately 2,000 comments posted online in response to Juhasz's article, over 500 asked why it has taken ten years to say this; and many questioned CNN's decision to label Juhasz's piece as "opinion," rather than "news." When corporate outlets have filed "news" stories on contracts secured or lost in Iraq, these reports have typically failed to connect critical dots to examine the strategic relationships in the planning and execution of the war, thus serving to fragment understanding of the oil agenda beyond comprehension, coherence or concern.

As evidenced by the US attempt to overhaul the Iraqi economy at gunpoint, war is corporate globalization by other means.[34] Indeed, after the start of its "shock and awe" bombing campaign, the Bush administration announced its plans for a Middle East Free Trade Area initiative (MEFTA) by 2013. In 2013, years after former Bush officials publicly stated that securing access for Western oil companies in Iraq was central to the drive for war, "Oil and Fraud: Why We Went to Iraq" is still a censored story—a stunning indictment of the corporate media's failure to investigate war crimes in anything like a timely, independent manner. Any *mea culpas* from the corporate media, regarding their central role in promoting the Bush administration's case for the war to mobilize public support, have appeared in the opinion section, rather than as front-page news stories in their own right. To the extent that corporate media do look back on their own performance with a critical eye, they often give voice to government and military sources who, on looking back, identify and acknowledge "mistakes." But there should be no ambiguity: what they call "mistakes" are, in fact, crimes. And now our leaders ask us to look forward.

TARGOL MESBAH, PHD, is a member of interdisciplinary studies and anthropology & social change faculty at the California Institute of Integral Studies, where she teaches critical theory, postcolonial critique, global studies, and film and media studies. She received her BA in film studies from the University of California–Irvine and her PhD in History of Consciousness from the University of California–Santa Cruz. She is cocurator of MENA Experimental: Experimental Film and New Media from the Middle East, North Africa and their Diasporas. She is currently writing a book on the multiple temporalities of war and media.

ZARA ZIMBARDO, MA, is member of the interdisciplinary studies faculty at the California Institute of Integral Studies. She has a background in independent media as producer of an alternative current events television series highlighting grassroots movements for social and environmental justice, and has developed critical media literacy workshops, presentations, and curricula in collaboration with schools throughout the Bay Area. As a member of the National Council of the Fellowship of Reconciliation, she has worked in solidarity with nonviolent activists resisting militarism in the US, Palestine/Israel, and Colombia. She is an anti-oppression facilitator and consultant, and cofounder of the antiracist feminist resource and training group, the White Noise Collective. Her ongoing research interests include the politics of representation; Islamophobia; collective memory; US militarism; and nonviolent social movements.

Notes

1. Ta-Nehisi Coates, "The Iraq War and History as Self-Flattery," *Atlantic*, March 20, 2013, http://www.theatlantic.com/politics/archive/2013/03/the-iraq-war-and-history-as-self-flattery/274192/.

2. Bob Woodward, "CIA Told to Do 'Whatever Necessary' to Kill Bin Laden," *Washington Post*, October 21, 2001, http://www.washingtonpost.com/wp-dyn/content/article/2007/11/18/AR2007111800655.html.

3. Rob Nixon, *Slow Violence and the Environmentalism of the Poor* (Cambridge: Harvard University Press, 2011).

4. "Over One Million Iraqi Deaths Caused by US Occupation," *Censored 2009: The Top 25 Censored Stories of 2007–08*, ed. Peter Phillips and Andrew Roth with Project Censored (New York: Seven Stories, 2008), 20–25.

5. Joseph E. Stiglitz and Linda J. Bilmes, *The Three Trillion Dollar War: The True Cost of the Iraq Conflict* (New York: W. W. Norton, 2008).

6. Ibid., 61–90.

7. For analysis of these films, see Rob Williams, "Screening the Homeland," ch. 8 in this volume.

8. Marc Pilisuk, "Occupying the Merchants of Death," Project Censored, November 22, 2012, http://www.projectcensored.org/topstories/articles/occupying-the-merchants-of-death/. See also, National Nuclear Security Administration, "Budget," no date, http://www.nnsa.energy.gov/aboutus/budget.

9. Pilisuk, ibid.

10. For analysis of corporate news coverage of US drone policy, see Andy Lee Roth, "Framing Al-Awlaki: How Government Officials and Corporate Media Legitimized a Targeted Killing," *Censored 2013: Dispatches from the Media Revolution*, Mickey Huff and Andy Lee Roth with Project Censored (New York: Seven Stories, 2012), 345–373.

11. George Monbiot, "In the US, Mass Child Killings are Tragedies. In Pakistan, Mere Bug Splats," *Guardian*, December 17, 2012, http://www.guardian.co.uk/commentisfree/2012/dec/17/us-killings-tragedies-pakistan-bug-splats. Monbiot quotes Michael Hastings, "The Rise of the Killer Drones: How America Goes to War in Secret," *Rolling Stone*, April 16, 2012, http://www.rollingstone.com/politics/news/the-rise-of-the-killer-drones-how-america-goes-to-war-in-secret-20120416.

12. Greg Miller, "Plan for Hunting Terrorists Signals U.S. Intends to Keep Adding Names to Kill Lists," *Washington Post*, October 23, 2012, http://articles.washingtonpost.com/2012-10-23/world/35500278_1_drone-campaign-obama-administration-matrix.

13. Pilisuk, "Occupying."

14. "Iran Worried U.S. Might Be Building 8,500th Nuclear Weapon," *Onion*, February 9, 2012, http://www.theonion.com/articles/iran-worried-us-might-be-building-8500th-nuclear-w,27325/.

15. George Orwell, *Nineteen Eighty-Four* (New York: Harcourt, Brace & Co., 1949).

16. David Barsamian, *Targeting Iran* (San Francisco: City Lights, 2007), 20.

17. Gareth Porter, "Bush Blocked Iran Disarmament Deal," *Consortium News*, June 6, 2012, http://consortiumnews.com/2012/06/06/bush-blocked-iran-nuke-deal/.

18. Nicholas D. Kristof, "Pinched and Griping in Iran," *New York Times*, June 16, 2012, http://www.nytimes.com/2012/06/17/opinion/sunday/kristof-pinched-and-griping-in-iran.html.

19. Hamid Dabashi, "War by Other Means," Al Jazeera, June 27, 2012, http://www.aljazeera.com/indepth/opinion/2012/06/2012625113228557622.html.

20. Nixon, *Slow Violence*, 204–205.

21. For Project Censored's coverage, see, for example, *Censored* story #9, "US Troops Exposed to Depleted Uranium During Gulf War," *Censored 1997*, ed. Peter Phillips and Project Censored (New York: Seven Stories Press, 1997), 47–51; *Censored* story #5, "US Weapons of Mass Destruction Linked to the Deaths of a Half-Million Children," *Censored 1999*, ed. Peter Phillips and Project Censored (New York: Seven Stories Press, 1999), 43–46; *Censored* story #6, "NATO Defends Private Economic Interests in the Balkans," *Censored 2000*, ed. Peter Phillips and Project Censored (New York: Seven Stories Press, 2000), 40–43; *Censored* story #4, "High Uranium Levels Found in Troops and Civilians," *Censored 2005*, ed. Peter Phillips and Project Censored (New York: Seven Stories Press, 2004), 48–54; and *Censored* story #25, "Extension of DU to Libya," *Censored 2012*, ed. Mickey Huff and Project Censored (New York: Seven Stories Press, 2011), 45, 52–53.

22. Nixon, *Slow Violence*, 217–218.

23. M. Al-Sabbak et al., "Metal Contamination and the Epidemic of Congenital Birth Defects in Iraqi Cities," *Bulletin of Environmental Contamination and Toxicology* 89, no. 5 (November 2012), http://www.springerlink.com/content/u35001451113g645/fulltext.html.

24. Sarah Morrison, "Iraq Records Huge Rise in Birth Defects," *Independent*, October 14, 2012, http://www.independent.co.uk/life-style/health-and-famalies/health-news/iraq-records-huge-rise-in-birth-defects-8210444.html.

25. Ross Caputi, "The Victims of Fallujah's Health Crisis are Stifled by Western Silence," *Guardian*, October 25, 2012, http://www.guardianco.uk/commentisfree/2012/oct/25/fallujah-iraq-health-crisis-silence?INTCMP=SRCH.

26. Dahr Jamail, "Ten Years Later, U.S. Has Left Iraq with Mass Displacement & Epidemic of Birth Defects, Cancers," *Democracy Now!*, March 20, 2013, http://www.democracynow.org/2013/3/20/ten_years_later_us_has_left. In the *Democracy Now!* interview, Jamail attributes the comparison of Fallujah to Hiroshima and Nagasaki to Dr. Samira Alani, a pediatrician at Fallujah General Hospital, whose work he had previously covered. See, for example, Dahr Jamail, "Fallujah Babies: Under a New Kind of Siege," Al Jazeera, January 6, 2012, http://www.aljazeera.com/indepth/features/2012/01/2012126394859797.html.

27. Norman Solomon, *War Made Easy: How Presidents and Pundits Keep Spinning Us to Death* (New Jersey: John Wiley & Sons, 2005), 87ff.

28. Alan Greenspan, *The Age of Turbulence: Adventures in a New World* (New York: Penguin, 2008), 463. On immediate controversy over Greenspan's assessment, see, for example, Bob Woodward, "Greenspan: Ouster of Hussein Crucial for Oil Security," *Washington Post*, September 17, 2007, http://www.washingtonpost.com/wp-dyn/content/article/2007/09/16/AR2007091601287.html?nav=rss_business.

29. Steven Mufson, "A Crude Case for War?," *Washington Post*, March 16, 2008, http://articles.washingtonpost.com/2008-03-16/business/36886089_1_oil-revenues-oil-fields-cheap-oil.

30. Ibid.

31. Antonia Juhasz, "Why the War in Iraq Was Fought for Big Oil," CNN, April 15, 2013, http://www.cnn.com/2013/03/19/opinion/iraq-war-oil-juhasz.

32. Ibid.

33. Ibid.

34. See "Interview with Vandana Shiva," *In Motion Magazine*, August 27, 2003, http://www.inmotionmagazine.com/global/vshiva4_int.html, for the quote, "Globalization is war by other means and war is globalization by other means."

Health and the Environment

Susan Rahman and Liliana Valdez-Madera

Censored #14

Wireless Technology a Looming Health Crisis

James F. Tracy, "Looming Health Crisis: Wireless Technology and the Toxification of America," Global Research, July 8, 2012, http://www.globalresearch.ca/index.php?context=va&aid=31816.

Student Researcher: Lyndsey Casey (Sonoma State University)

Faculty Evaluator: Peter Phillips (Sonoma State University)

Censored #15

Food Riots: The New Normal?

Nafeez Mosaddeq Ahmed, "Why Food Riots Are Likely to Become the New Normal," Guardian, March 6, 2013, http://www.guardian.co.uk/environment/blog/2013/mar/06/food-riots-new-normal.

Paul R. Ehrlich and Anne H. Ehrlich, "Can a Collapse of Global Civilization Be Avoided?," Proceedings of the Royal Society 280, no. 1754 (March 7, 2013), http://rspb.royalsocietypublishing.org/content/280/1754/20122845.full.

Student Researcher: Julian Kuartei (College of Marin)

Faculty Evaluator: Andy Lee Roth (College of Marin)

Censored #18

Fracking Our Food Supply

Elizabeth Royte, "Fracking Our Food Supply," Nation, December 17, 2012, http://www.thenation.com/article/171504/fracking-our-food-supply.

Michelle Bamberger and Robert E. Oswald, "Impacts of Gas Drilling on Human and Animal Health," New Solutions 22, no. 1 (January 2012): 51–77, http://www.psehealthyenergy.org/Impacts_of_Gas_Drilling_on_Human_and_Animal_Health.

Student Researchers: Rayne Madison and Nayeli Castaneda (College of Marin)

Faculty Evaluators: Susan Rahman and Andy Lee Roth (College of Marin)

Censored #21

Monsanto and India's "Suicide Economy"

Belen Fernandez, "Dirty White Gold," Al Jazeera, December 8, 2012, http://www.aljazeera.com/indepth/opinion/2012/12/201212575935285501.html.

Jason Overdorf, "India: Gutting of India's Cotton Farmers," Global Post, October 8, 2012, http://www.globalpost.com/dispatches/globalpost-blogs/america-the-gutted/india-cotton-farmers-monsanto-suicides.

Student Researcher: Nicole Anacker (College of Marin)

Faculty Evaluator: Susan Rahman (College of Marin)

Censored #24

Widespread GMO Contamination: Did Monsanto Plant GMOs Before USDA Approval?

Cassandra Anderson and Anthony Gucciardi, "Widespread GMO Contamination: Did Monsanto Plant GMOs Before USDA Approval?" Global Research, May 4, 2012, http://www.globalresearch.ca/widespread-gmo-contamination-did-monsanto-plant-gmos-before-usda-approval/.

Student Researcher: Adam Hotchkiss (Sonoma State University)

Faculty Evaluator: Greg Hicks (Mendocino College)

RELATED VALIDATED INDEPENDENT NEWS STORIES

Hydraulic Fracturing: United States vs. United Kingdom

"Fracking Can be Undertaken Safely if Best Practice and Regulations are in Force," Royal Academy of Engineering, June 29, 2012, http://www.raeng.org.uk/news/releases/shownews.htm?NewsID=771.

Fiona Harvey, "Gas 'Fracking' Gets Green Light," Guardian, April 16, 2012, http://www.guardian.co.uk/environment/2012/apr/17/gas-fracking-gets-green-light.

Leigh Phillips, "UK Fracking Safe but US Operations Marred by Poor Practices," Nature, June 29, 2012, http://blogs.nature.com/news/2012/06/fracking-safe-in-uk-but-us-home-to-poor-practices.html.

Student Researchers: Brody Schoen, Hunter Leaman, and Ashley Conard (DePauw University)

Faculty Evaluators: James Mills and Kevin Howley (DePauw University)

Can Fracking and Carbon Sequestration Coexist?

Christa Marshall, "Can Fracking and Carbon Sequestration Coexist?," Scientific American, March 16, 2012, http://www.scientificamerican.com/article.cfm?id=can-fracking-and-carbon-sequestration-co-exist.

Student Researcher: Amanda McNulty (Sonoma State University)

Faculty Evaluator: Charles Thomsen (American River College)

Embracing Sustainability: Forsaking Meat and Chemical Agriculture

Colin Todhunter, "Embracing Sustainability: Forsaking Meat and Chemical Agriculture," Global Research, September 18, 2012, http://www.globalresearch.ca/embracing-sustainability-forsaking-meat-and-chemical-agriculture/5305093.

Student Researcher: Dave Lan Franco (College of Marin)

Faculty Evaluator: Susan Rahman (College of Marin)

Global Food Insecurity: Fisheries Are Being Destroyed

"Rising Ocean Acid Levels Are 'The Biggest Threat to Coral Reefs,'" Guardian, July 9, 2012, http://www.guardian.co.uk/environment/2012/jul/09/acid-threat-coral-reef.

Suzanne Goldenberg, "Report Warns of Global Food Insecurity as Climate Change Destroys Fisheries," *Guardian*, September 24, 2012, http://www.guardian.co.uk/environment/2012/sep/24/food-climate-change-fisheries.

Student Researchers: Paige Henry and Sarah Crandall (DePauw University)

Faculty Evaluators: Vanessa Fox and Kevin Howley (DePauw University)

Global Food Crisis in the Making

Richard Anderson, "Food Price Crisis: What Crisis?" BBC News, October 15, 2012, http://www.bbc.co.uk/news/business-19715504.

Eric Darier, "Is The World Heading Towards Another Food Crisis?" Greenpeace, November 15, 2012, http://www.greenpeace.org/international/en/news/Blogs/makingwaves/is-the-world-heading-towards-another-food-cri/blog/42999/.

Student Researcher: J. J. Sotomayor (Sonoma State University)

Faculty Evaluator: Rich Campbell (Sonoma State University)

Monsanto Changed Stance on GMO Labeling

Ethan A. Huff, "Monsanto Supported GMO Labeling in Europe, But Not in US," *Natural News*, September 16, 2012, http://www.naturalnews.com/037222_GMO_labeling_Monsanto_Europe.html.

James Corbett and Anthony Gucciardi, "GMO Foods: Science, PR, and Public Backlash," Global Research TV, October 29, 2012, http://tv.globalresearch.ca/2012/10/gmo-foods-science-pr-and-public-backlash.

Student Researcher: Skye Pinney (Frostburg State University)

Faculty Evaluator: Andy Duncan (Frostburg State University)

Pesticides May Lead to Cancer and Autism in Children

Viji Sundaram, "Pesticides Harm Kids' Health and Intelligence, Study Finds," *New American Media*, October 10, 2012, http://newamericamedia.org/2012/10/pesticides-harm-kids-health-and-intelligence-study-finds.php.

Student Researcher: Joe Raspolich (Florida Atlantic University)

Faculty Evaluator: James Tracy (Florida Atlantic University)

INTRODUCTION

For several years now, a set of familiar topics have featured in Project Censored's "Health and the Environment" news cluster. Radiation from wireless technology, hydraulic fracturing, and genetically modified food are big stories again this year. Independent journalists continue to research and report news on these topics beyond the boundaries of the corporate media's limited coverage.

It is instructive to ask why corporate media turn a blind eye to these stories—or, when they do cover them, why they frame their coverage in ways that minimize the risks—and, in some cases, even suggest benefits. Understanding the financial connections among corporate media and pharmaceutical companies, the gas and oil industry, and Big Agriculture helps to answer these questions. Corporate media ignore or manipulate these stories to serve the interest of those in power, often by attempting to sway public opinion in favor of those corporations and their interests.

Government, including our elected representatives, plays a role too. When the revolving door between government (including Congress, the Environmental Protection Agency [EPA], the United States Department of Agriculture [USDA], and the Food and Drug Administration [FDA]) and companies like Monsanto is in full swing, it is hard to develop and enforce policies that hold corporations accountable, that prevent them from putting profits before people. For example, Hillary Clinton, Donald Rumsfeld, and Clarence Thomas all have Monsanto connections, making it unlikely that they would ever hold the company to account when it violates environmental laws; in fact, they may use their political influence to cover up such offenses.[1]

A larger theme that Project Censored regularly covers is also evident in this cluster's stories: a small number of people make decisions about what is best for the entire globe. Although we in the US espouse democracy and freedom as foundations of our society, corporate capture of regulatory processes, governmental compliance, and misleading propaganda constantly threaten those foundations. It is easy to be oblivious to these threats because corporate media—which ought to inform the public about them—is increasingly a tool used to maintain the status quo.

This is a recipe for the demise of the earth: Eventually even human life will not be sustainable if we continue on our current path.[2] But this year's Project Censored stories show that, with real changes in how we relate to the earth, we can turn things around. To do so, however, we must stop treating the earth like our garbage can.

It is our duty as an informed citizenry to speak for the planet. The citizens of Iceland did so when they affirmed the commons in their proposed constitution.[3] As Dr. Seuss wrote, "I am the Lorax, I speak for the trees." The independent journalists and news organizations that Project Censored highlights in this news cluster do, too. We hope that the following reports encourage you to raise your voice on behalf of human health and the environment as our most fundamental commons.

"SMART GRIDS" AREN'T SO SMART AFTER ALL

Wireless technology has been linked to potentially dangerous radiation exposure. Phones are sold with warnings—albeit obscure ones—about not holding them too close to your head for too long, due to electromagnetic radiation's impact on the brain.[4] The increased use of these technologies in our environment creates cumulative exposure levels higher than we may imagine. As consumers, we ought to know what the potential risks are so we can make informed decisions. Instead, industry-sponsored studies often minimize the risks.[5]

Censored story #14, James F. Tracy's "Wireless Technology a Looming Health Crisis," examined "smart grids" and their potential risks. As a multitude of hazardous wireless technologies are deployed in homes, schools, and workplaces, government officials and industry representatives continue to insist on their safety despite growing evidence to the contrary. The deployment of "smart grid" technology hastens what Tracy describes as a "looming health crisis."[6]

By now, many residents in the US and Canada have smart meters installed on their dwellings. Each meter is equipped with an electronic cellular transmitter that uses powerful bursts of electromagnetic radio frequency (RF) radiation to communicate with nearby meters. Together they form an interlocking network that transfers detailed information on residents' electrical usage back to the utility. Smart grid technology is being sold to the public as a way to "empower" individual energy consumers by allowing them to access information on their energy usage. This way, consumers may eventually save money by programming "smart" (i.e., wireless-enabled) home appliances and equipment that will coordinate with the smart meter in order to run when electrical rates are lowest. However, the same technology may prepare the way for a tiered rate system for electricity consumption, set by utility companies, to which customers will have no choice but to conform.

Lack of choice for consumers in terms of from whom to buy is already prevalent. Increasingly, mergers make it harder to do business with companies that do business ethically. Opting out of smart grid technology requires the consumer to pay more per month on their bill—an option that is not possible for all consumers. For now, being informed and willing to pay a premium allows some people to opt out of this particular technology; but as smart grid technology becomes standardized, doing so will become increasingly difficult. In a time of fewer job opportunities, the resulting loss of meter reader jobs is also noteworthy.

WHAT THE FRACK?

Hydraulic fracturing is the controversial practice of injecting water, sand, and chemicals under extreme pressure into wells, which fractures shale so that previously inaccessible natural gas can flow to the surface. In the past six decades, this method has delivered 600 trillion cubic feet of natural gas to American consumers, but at a high cost. Operations in the United States seem risky at best. Practices in the United Kingdom call for mandatory risk assessment across the entire life cycle of gas extraction to prevent tremors and water contamination. Companies in the UK are required to disclose chemical mixtures put into the ground, whereas companies in the US claim this information is proprietary.[7]

Censored story #18 story, Elizabeth Royte's "Fracking Our Food Supply," revealed that chemicals used in the fracking process contaminate surrounding land, water, and air. As Royte reported, ranchers in Pennsylvania, North Dakota, Louisiana, and New Mexico report health problems, and incidents of dead and tainted livestock, due to elevated levels of contaminants from nearby wells.[8]

Although no long-term research on the effects of fracking on humans, livestock, or plants exists, a peer-reviewed study by Michelle Bamberger and Robert Oswald linked fracking to illness in animals.[9] They believe chemicals leaking from fracking sites could start appearing in human food supplies, due to lack of regulation and testing.

Along with the potential dangers to both animals and humans, fracking also releases greenhouse gases that have been shown to contribute to climate change. "Carbon sequestration" refers to the long-term storage of carbon dioxide or other forms of carbon in order to mitigate climate change. It has been proposed as a way to slow the atmospheric and marine accumulation of greenhouse gases, which are released by burning fossil fuels.[10] As Christa Marshall reported, natural gas production and carbon sequestration may be headed for an underground collision course: shale-gas extraction involves fracturing rock that could be needed as an impenetrable cover to hold CO_2 underground permanently, without it leaking back into the atmosphere. There is an obvious conflict between fracking and carbon sequestration.

OUR ENVIRONMENT, OUR FOOD SUPPLY

On a global scale, the world's food supply is fragile. *Censored* story #15, Nafeez Mosaddeq Ahmed's "Food Riots: The New Normal?," and a set of supporting validated independent news stories, address the connections between the world's food supply and our environment.[11]

Global food prices have been consistently higher than in preceding decades leading to dramatic price increases in staple foods and triggering food riots across the Middle East, North Africa, and South Asia, Ahmed reported. The crux of this global phenomenon is climate change: severe natural disasters including drought, flood, heat waves, and monsoons have affected major regional food baskets. By mid-century it is estimated that world crop yields could fall as much as 20 to 40 percent because of climate change alone.[12] Industrial agricultural methods that disrupt soil also contribute to impending food shortages. As a result, global land productivity has dropped significantly, from 2.1 percent, 1950–1990, to 1.2 percent, 1990–2007.[13]

To contrast this, corporate media coverage of food insecurity tends to treat it as a local and episodic problem. For example, an April 2008 story in the *Los Angeles Times* covered food riots in Haiti, which resulted in three deaths.[14] Similarly, a March 2013 *New York Times* piece addressed how loss of farmland and farm labor to urbanization contributes to rising food costs in China.[15] Corporate media have not connected the dots to analyze how intensifying inequality, debt, climate change, and consumption of fossil fuels contribute to the potential for a global food crisis in the near future.

Drawing on figures from the United Nations and the USDA, the BBC's Richard Anderson reported that we will need to produce 70 percent more food by 2050 to feed the world's expanding population; yet global corn stocks have dropped by 50 percent since 1998; more than 100 million more people across the world suffer from hunger due to recent increases in food price rises; and globally, one in eight people do not have enough food.[16]

One partial solution to the looming food crisis is to reduce food waste. The US alone wastes about 40 percent of the food it produces.[17] Consumers in rich countries waste almost as much food as the entire net food production of sub-Saharan Africa.[18] Jeremy Seifert's documentary film, *Dive!*, offers a personal perspective on the problem of food waste.[19]

Although cutting back on food waste is definitely part of the solution, we must also reevaluate different types of food production and their comparative effects on the environment and world hunger. Thus, in "Embracing Sustainability: Forsaking Meat and Chemical Agriculture," Colin Todhunter reported that, according to the United Nations' Food and Agriculture Organization, livestock accounts for nearly 18 percent of greenhouse gas emissions worldwide.[20] Since 1965, the number of animals slaughtered each year has increased from ten billion to fifty-five billion. This in turn means that 9 percent of total greenhouse gas emissions, 37 percent of methane emissions, and 65 percent of nitrous oxide emissions come from livestock alone. Livestock also occupy 26 percent of the earth's usable land.[21]

Livestock is not the only issue; modern food production techniques also harm the global environment. In the industrial age, farming relies heavily on fossil fuels, pesticides, and hormones, which not only harm consumers but also the earth's soils and atmosphere. A shift from these practices to more sustainable, organic farming is necessary to reduce the impacts of cars and industry on the global environmental.[22]

The human need for food impacts our oceans as well.[23] As the *Guardian* reported, rising acid levels in our oceans now threaten coral reefs to an extent that poses dangers for global food security.[24] Scientists claimed nearly one billion people in the world depend on seafood as their main source of protein. The high acidity levels are due to the oceans absorbing excess carbon dioxide from the atmosphere. Gradual climate change in conjunction with the increase in ocean acidification presents many problematic issues for marine life and the food supply.[25]

According to Jane Lubchenco, chief of the National Oceanic and Atmospheric Administration (NOAA), oceanic acid levels are increasing quicker than originally predicted, making acidification climate change's "equally evil twin."[26] For example, higher acid levels slow the growth rate of oyster shells and the formation of coral skeletons, and impairs the sense of smell of clown fish and salmon.[27]

As Suzanne Goldenberg reported, "The Gulf, Libya, and Pakistan are at high risk of food insecurity in the coming decades because climate change and ocean acidification are destroying fisheries."[28] In these and other countries characterized by high rates of population growth and malnutrition, Goldenberg reported, fisheries provide crucial sources of protein and economic livelihood. However, a report released by Oceana, titled *Ocean-Based Food Security Threatened in a High CO2 World*, indicated that many such countries will lose up to 40 percent of their fish catch by 2050, while the Gulf is estimated to lose over 50 percent of its fisheries.[29] The Oceana report predicted that the US will lose 12 percent of its catch by 2050.

Not only are our oceans in peril, but our freshwater sources are increasingly at risk. As Richard Anderson reported in his article, "Global Food Crisis in the Making," without water, crops cannot grow and the world cannot eat.[30] And in 2012, wasn't enough water. The US has seen its worst drought in more than fifty years, vast swathes of Russia have been left parched by lack of rain, India has had a dry monsoon season, while rainfall in South America early in the year fell well below expectations. As a direct result, harvests of many crops have been decimated, forcing the price of some cereals back up toward levels last seen four years ago—a time when high prices sparked riots in twelve countries across the world and forced the United Nations to call a food price crisis summit.[31] In May 2013, a global summit involving 500 of the world's leading water scientists concluded that without major reforms, within two generations a majority of the world's population will "be living under the handicap of severe pressure on fresh water."[32]

GENETICALLY MODIFIED CROPS TO THE RESCUE?

Advocates of genetically modified (GM) crops have touted them as a technological solution to the problem of food supplies in a world characterized by human growth and limited natural resources. However, as one of the most powerful producers of GM crops, Monsanto has been anything but a champion in terms of feeding the world's

hungry. As shown by *Censored* story #21, "Monsanto and India's 'Suicide Economy,'" and story #24, "Did Monsanto Plant GMOs Before USDA Approval?," Monsanto is focused on profits over people.

Jason Overdorf of the GlobalPost and Belen Fernandez of Al Jazeera reported on Monsanto's impact on farmers in India.[33] Since 1995, an estimated 250,000 Indian farmers have committed suicide due to massive debt.[34] Vandana Shiva and other critics have concluded that Monsanto's profit-driven policies have led to a "suicide economy" in India.[35] Monsanto has argued that these suicides have no single cause. But evidence involving the corporation's pest-resistant Bt cotton implicates Monsanto, according to Shiva. She noted, "The price per kilogram of cotton seeds [has gone] from 7 to 17,000 rupees. . . . Monsanto sells its GMO seeds on fraudulent claims of yields of 1500 kg/year when farmers harvest 300–400 kg/year on an average."[36] Although Overdorf avoided directly blaming Monsanto, he identified India's financial system, characterized by high interest rates and predatory lending practices, as a contributing factor to the despair of India's farmers.[37]

A new documentary film, *Dirty White Gold* by Leah Borromeo, goes beyond the issue of farmer suicides to explain how the global fashion industry and international consumer habits contribute to the lives and deaths of Indian farmers. *Dirty White Gold* examined the cotton supply chain, with the aim of generating support for legislation that will, in Borromeo's words, "make ethics and sustainability the norm in the fashion industry."[38] A previous documentary film, Micha X. Peled's *Bitter Seeds*, also illuminated Monsanto's negative impacts in India. *Bitter Seeds*, which followed a teenage girl whose father committed suicide due to debt, showed how Monsanto lies directly to Indian farmers, going as far as making up fictitious farmers who "have success" with the new Bt cotton. Monsanto has claimed that there has also been a 25 percent reduction in pesticide costs. In *Bitter Seeds*, both of these claims were proven false.[39]

The uniformity created by Monsanto's seeds, and by GM seeds more generally, has led to agricultural catastrophes because there is less seed diversity compared to earlier times. For example, today only four varieties of potatoes are widely grown, and one study indicated that we have lost about 97 percent of the varieties of vegetables grown before the twentieth century.[40] What's been done is done: we may not be able to recover seed lines lost in the process of our desperate desire to make all tomatoes look identical or "perfect." However, agricultural standards of uniformity are not the only issue. We may be able to survive with only a few varieties of vegetables, but GM crops have been shown to pose health risks.[41] Our faith in technology, coupled with our desire for perfection, comes at great cost, not only for farmers, such as those in India, but also for consumers.

One solution is to assure that consumers are better informed about the health risks of GM foods. If members of the public had better information about the potential risks of eating genetically modified food, then they could make informed decisions about whether or not to eat it. In California, Proposition 37 was an attempt to inform the public. If passed, it would have required labels indicating if a product contained any GM ingredients. In November 2012, the proposition failed to pass due to large donations from big corporations, including Monsanto.[42] Though consumers in California suffer less than farmers in India, both are victims of Monsanto's pursuit of money at the expense of public health.

Previous *Censored* reports have addressed the health risks associated with GM foods, as well as efforts by Big Ag and the US government to affect policy, both domestically and abroad, on their regulation.[43] In this year's *Censored* story #24, Cassandra Anderson and Anthony Gucciardi reported that Monsanto's GM alfalfa may have been set free in 2003—a full two years or more before it was deregulated in 2005.[44] In a letter obtained by health website NaturalSociety with permission to post for public viewing, it becomes clear that the USDA may have turned a blind eye to the entire situation, allowing the possibility of widespread GM contamination of GM-free crops.

The case is especially problematic because alfalfa is a perennial crop; it does not need replanting each year, like annual crops do. As a perennial, it is vulnerable to cross-pollination and, therefore, GM contamination. For this reason, genetically modified alfalfa could quickly spread to crops across the US, threatening the integrity of organic products—including organic meat and dairy products, if those animals are fed alfalfa believed to be GMO-free, but are in fact carrying Monsanto's patented genetically modified trait.[45]

The revolving door between Monsanto and the USDA—alluded to in the introduction of this news cluster—may be partly to blame. Thus, for example, Michael Taylor, the FDA's deputy commissioner for foods previously served as the vice president for public policy at Monsanto; Supreme Court Justice Clarence Thomas, whom Monsanto employed as a corporate lawyer in the 1970s, recently ruled in favor of Monsanto in a case pitting the corporation against a soybean farmer from Indiana; and Obama's chief agricultural negotiator in the Office of the US Trade Representative, Islam Siddiqui, previously worked as the vice president of CropLife America, a lobbying group that represents pesticide and genetic engineering companies, including Monsanto, Dow Chemical, and DuPont.[46]

The more the public learns about the potential hazards of GMOs, the stronger the opposition gets. The US may wish to follow the lead of other nations that have taken robust stands against GMO production. Peru placed a ten-year moratorium on GMO seeds, which otherwise threaten that country's diverse, abundant crops.[47] As Jonathan

Benson reported, "This embargo will help perpetuate the native bio-diversity practices that have sustained Peruvians since the days when the Incan Empire reigned supreme."[48]

Bans and boycotts are nonviolent forms of resistance to GMOs. When we put our money where our mouths are, change can happen. In Europe, Monsanto has halted the lobbying of GMO plants due to low demand from local farmers.[49] It is simply supply and demand. If we don't buy it, they'll stop making it.

CONCLUSION

The natural world sustains us. In pursuing technological advances, we often do great damage to our planet's natural processes. Technology can be wonderful, but we must use it with care and remember our duty to protect and preserve the planet that ultimately sustains us. Perhaps a return to what was once valued will be our salvation; the Suquamish leader Seattle (1780–1866) continues to remind us: "The Earth does not belong to us. We belong to the Earth."

SUSAN RAHMAN, MA, is a sociology instructor at Santa Rosa Junior College and the College of Marin. Her areas of interest include Palestinian self-determination, issues of privilege and inequality, and media literacy. Her current work focuses on the role of self-reflection in social transformation. She lives in Sebastopol, California, with her partner Carlos, daughter Jordan, and dogs, Rosie and Cody.

LILIANA VALDEZ-MADERA was the student researcher for *Censored* story #24, "Alabama Farmers Look to Replace Migrants with Prisoners," in *Censored 2013*, and for *Censored* story #20, "Israel Counted Minimum Calorie Needs in Gaza Blockade," in this volume. She recently graduated from Santa Rosa Junior College and will transfer to Dominican University of California this fall. A psychology major and aspiring poet, she plans to continue her involvement with Project Censored.

Notes

1. See, for example, Jeremy Bloom, "Monsanto Employees in the Halls of Government," Red, Green, and Blue, February 9, 2011, http://redgreenandblue.org/2011/02/09/monsanto-employees-in-the-halls-of-government/, and a supporting graphic, http://c1redgreenandblueorg.wpengine.netdna-cdn.com/files/2012/02/monsanto-employees-government-revolving-door.jpg.

2. "The world hasn't ended, but the world as we know it has—even if we don't quite know it yet," Bill McKibben, *Eaarth: Making a Life on a Tough New Planet* (New York: Henry Holt 2010), 2.

3. See the Censored News Cluster, "Iceland, the Power of Peaceful Revolution, and the Commons," in this volume.

4. See, for example, Devra Davis, "Cicadas and Cell Phones," *Huffington Post*, April 30, 2013, http://www.huffingtonpost.com/devra-davis-phd/cell-phones-cancer_b_3157171.html.

5. For example, "No Evidence Linking Cell Phone Use to Risk of Brain Tumors," US Food and Drug Administration, May 17, 2010, http://www.fda.gov/ForConsumers/ConsumerUpdates/ucm212273.htm.

6. James F. Tracy, "Looming Health Crisis: Wireless Technology and the Toxification of America," *Global Research*, July 8, 2012, http://www.globalresearch.ca/index.php?context=va&aid=31816.

7. "Fracking Can be Undertaken Safely if Best Practice and Regulations are in Force," Royal Academy of Engineering, June 29, 2012, http://www.raeng.org.uk/news/releases/shownews.htm?NewsID=771.

8. Elizabeth Royte, "Fracking Our Food Supply," *Nation*, December 17, 2012, http://www.thenation.com/article/171504/fracking-our-food-supply.

9. Michelle Bamberger and Robert E. Oswald, "Impacts of Gas Drilling on Human and Animal Health," *New Solutions* 22, no. 1 (January 2012), http://www.psehealthyenergy.org/Impacts_of_Gas_Drilling_on_Human_and_Animal_Health. Cited Royte, "Fracking Our Food Supply."

10. Christa Marshall, "Can Fracking and Carbon Sequestration Coexist?," *Scientific American*, March 16, 2012, http://www.scientificamerican.com/article.cfm?id=can-fracking-and-carbon-sequestration-co-exist.

11. Nafeez Mosaddeq Ahmed, "Why Food Riots Are Likely to Become the New Normal," *Guardian*, March 6, 2013, http://www.guardian.co.uk/environment/blog/2013/mar/06/food-riots-new-normal.

12. Ibid.

13. Ibid.

14. "3 Killed in Haiti Amid Food Riots, Clashes," *Los Angeles Times*, April 5, 2008, http://articles.latimes.com/2008/apr/05/world/fg-haiti5.

15. "Food Cost Threatens Rebound in China," *New York Times*, March 11, 2013, http://www.nytimes.com/2013/03/12/business/global/food-costs-threaten-rebound-in-china.html?ref=foodprices.

16. Richard Anderson, "Food Price Crisis: What Crisis?" BBC News, October 15, 2012, http://www.bbc.co.uk/news/business-19715504.

17. "Food Facts: Your Scraps Add Up," Natural Resources Defense Council, March 2013, http://www.nrdc.org/living/eatingwell/files/foodwaste_2pgr.pdf; "USDA and EPA Launch U.S. Food Waste Challenge," United States Department of Agriculture, June 4, 2013, http://www.usda.gov/wps/portal/usda/usdahome?contentid=2013/06/0112.xml.

18. Anderson, "Food Price Crisis."

19. *Dive!*, directed by Jeremy Seifert (2009; self-released), http://www.divethefilm.com.

20. Colin Todhunter, "Embracing Sustainability: Forsaking Meat and Chemical Agriculture," Global Research, September 18, 2012, http://www.globalresearch.ca/embracing-sustainability-forsaking-meat-and-chemical-agriculture/5305093.

21. Ibid.

22. Ibid.

23. See also, *Censored* story #2, "Oceans in Peril," in *Censored 2013: Dispatches from the Media Revolution*, Mickey Huff and Andy Lee Roth with Project Censored (New York: Seven Stories, 2012), 87–89.

24. "Rising Ocean Acid Levels Are 'The Biggest Threat to Coral Reefs,'" *Guardian*, July 9, 2012, http://www.guardian.co.uk/environment/2012/jul/09/acid-threat-coral-reef.

25. Ibid.

26. Ibid.

27. Ibid.

28. Suzanne Goldenberg, "Report Warns of Global Food Insecurity as Climate Change Destroys Fisheries," *Guardian*, September 24, 2012, http://www.guardian.co.uk/environment/2012/sep/24/food-climate-change-fisheries.

29. Matthew Huelsenbeck, *Ocean-Based Food Security Threatened in a High CO2 World*, report, Oceana, September 2012, http://oceana.org/sites/default/files/reports/Ocean-Based_Food_Security_Threatened_in_a_High_CO2_World.pdf; cited in Goldenberg, "Report Warns."

30. Richard Anderson, "Food Price Crisis: What Crisis?" BBC News, October 15, 2012, http://www.bbc.co.uk/news/business-19715504.

31. Ibid.

32. James A. Foley, "Humanity's Access to Fresh Water in Peril, Conference of 500 Water Scientists Says," Nature World News, May 25, 2013, http://www.natureworldnews.com/articles/2110/20130525/humanitys-access-fresh-water-peril-conference-500-wateer-scientits-s.htm.

33. Jason Overdorf, "India: Gutting of India's Cotton Farmers," GlobalPost, October 8, 2012, http://www.globalpost.com/dispatches/globalpost-blogs/america-the-gutted/india-cotton-farmers-monsanto-suicides; Belen Fernandez, "Dirty White Gold," Al Jazeera, December 8, 2012, http://www.aljazeera.com/indepth/opinion/2012/12/20121257593528550l.html.

34. Overdorf, "India."

35. Ibid.; Fernandez, "Dirty White Gold."

36. Vandana Shiva, "From Seeds of Suicide to Seeds of Hope: Why Are Indian Farmers Committing Suicide and How Can We Stop This Tragedy?," *Huffington Post*, April 28, 2009, http://www.huffingtonpost.com/vandana-shiva/from-seeds-of-suicide-to_b_192419.html; quoted in Fernandez, "Dirty White Gold."

37. Overdorf, "India."

38. Fernandez, "Dirty White Gold."

39. *Bitter Seeds*, directed by Micha X. Peled, 60 min., http://www.itvs.org/films/bitter-seeds.

40. A study by the Rural Advancement Fund International (RAFI) compared the number of varieties of different commercial crops known to the US Department of Agriculture in 1903 to the number of varieties of these crops for which seeds existed in the National Seed Storage Laboratory (NSSL) in 1983. Considering about seventy-five different vegetables together, the RAFI study found that approximately 97 percent of the varieties on the 1903 lists are now extinct. See Cary Fowler and Pat Mooney, *Shattering: Food Politics and the Loss of Genetic Diversity* (Tucson: University of Arizona Press, 1990), 63.

41. For example, James Corbett and Anthony Gucciardi, "GMO Foods: Science, PR, and Public Backlash," Global Research TV, October 29, 2012, http://tv.globalresearch.ca/2012/10/gmo-foods-science-pr-and-public-backlash.

42. Ronnie Cummins and Katherine Paul, "Did Monsanto Win Prop 37? Round One in the Food Fight of Our Lives," *AlterNet*, November 9, 2012,http://www.alternet.org/food/did-monsanto-win-prop-37-round-one-food-fight-our-lives.

43. On GM health risks, see Censored story #11, "Dangers of Genetically Modified Food Confirmed, *Censored 2007*, ed. Peter Phillips and Project Censored (New York: Seven Stories Press, 2006), 72–74; on industry and government efforts to avoid regulation and open markets, respectively, see Censored story #20, "US Agencies Trying to Outlaw GMO Food Labeling," *Censored 2012*, ed. Mickey Huff and Project Censored (New York: Seven Stories Press, 2011), 95–96, and Censored story #21, "Forcing a World Market for GMOs," *Censored 2005*, ed. Peter Phillips and Project Censored (New York: Seven Stories, 2004), 101–104.

44. Cassandra Anderson and Anthony Gucciardi, "Widespread GMO Contamination: Did Monsanto Plant GMOs Before USDA Approval?" Global Research, May 4, 2012, http://www.globalresearch.ca/widespread-gmo-contamination-did-monsanto-plant-gmos-before-usda-approval/.

45. Ibid.

46. Bloom, "Monsanto Employees in the Halls of Government"; Janie Boschma, "Monsanto: Big Guy on the Block When it Comes to Friends in Washington," Open Secrets, February 19, 2013, http://www.opensecrets.org/news/2013/02/monsanto.html; "USDA Watch: Which Side is

CENSORED 2014 **141**

Obama On?," Organic Consumers Association, no date, http://www.organicconsumers.org/usda_watch.cfm.

47. Annie Murphy, "Peru Says No to GMO," *Christian Science Monitor*, April 25, 2013, http://www.csmonitor.com/World/Americas/2013/0425/Peru-says-no-to-GMO.

48. Jonathan Benson, "Peru Bans All GMOs," Natural News, May 8, 2013, http://www.naturalnews.com/040245_GMO_ban_Peru_Monsanto.html#ixzz2SiRUtjON.

49. "Monsanto Set to Halt GMO Push in Europe," RT, May 31, 2013, http://rt.com/news/monsanto-stop-lobbying-eu-084/.

Iceland, the Power of Peaceful Revolution, and the Commons

Andy Lee Roth

Censored #9

Icelanders Vote to Include Commons in Their Constitution

Jessica Conrad, "Icelanders Vote to Include the Commons in Their Constitution," *Commons Magazine*, November 2012, http://onthecommons.org/magazine/icelanders-vote-include-commons-their-constitution.

Thorvaldur Gylfason, "Iceland: Direct Democracy in Action," *Open Democracy*, November 12, 2012, http://www.opendemocracy.net/thorvaldur-gylfason/iceland-direct-democracy-in-action.

Student Researcher: Pedro Martin Del Campo (Sonoma State University)

Faculty Evaluator: Andy Lee Roth (Sonoma State University)

Censored #17

The Creative Commons Celebrates Ten Years of Sharing and Cultural Creation

Paul M. Davis, "Creative Commons Celebrates 10 Years of Opening Culture," *Shareable*, December 7, 2012, http://www.shareable.net/blog/creative-commons-celebrates-10-years-of-opening-culture.

Jason Hibbets, "Celebrating 10 Years of Creative Commons," opensource.com, November 29, 2012, http://opensource.com/law/12/11/celebrating-ten-years-creative-commons.

Timothy Vollmer, "Pallante's Push for U.S. Copyright Reform," Creative Commons News, March 20, 2013, http://creativecommons.org/weblog/entry/37576.

Student Researcher: Nicholas Lanoil (San Francisco State University)

Faculty Evaluator: Kenn Burrows (San Francisco State University)

Censored #19

The Power of Peaceful Revolution in Iceland

Alex Pietrowski, "Iceland's Hördur Torfason—How to Beat the Banksters," *Waking Times*, December 11, 2012, http://www.wakingtimes.com/2012/12/11/icelands-hordur-torfason-how-to-beat-the-banksters.

Student Researcher: Pedro Martin Del Campo (Sonoma State University)

Faculty Evaluator: Ed Beebout (Sonoma State University)

Iceland's Modern Media Initiative Supports WikiLeaks Alternative

Lowana Veal, "Alternative to Wikileaks Arises in Iceland," Inter Press Service, September 24, 2012, http://www.ipsnews.net/2012/09/alternative-to-wikileaks-arises-in-iceland.

Student Researcher: Rory Scotland (Sonoma State University)

Faculty Evaluator: Peter Chamberlin (Sonoma State University)

Iceland Refuses to Aid FBI in WikiLeaks Investigation

"FBI Agents Flew to Iceland to Investigate WikiLeaks," *Democracy Now!*, February 1, 2013, http://www.democracynow.org/2013/2/1/headlines/report_fbi_agents_flew_to_iceland_to_investigate_wikileaks.

"Iceland Denies Aid to FBI in WikiLeaks Investigation," RT, February 2, 2013, http://rt.com/news/iceland-fbi-wikileaks-investigation-292.

Trisha Marczak, "Iceland Gives FBI the Boot," MPN (Mint Press News), February 4, 2013, http://www.mintpress.net/iceland-gives-fbi-the-boot.

"Eight FBI Agents Conduct Interrogation in Iceland in Relation to Ongoing U.S. Investigation of WikiLeaks," WikiLeaks, February 7, 2013, https://wikileaks.org/Eight-FBI-agents-conduct.html.

Student Researcher: Ariel Garcia (College of Marin)

Faculty Evaluator: Susan Rahman (College of Marin)

Norway's Economic Success: Managing Petroleum Wealth

Bruce Campbell, "Norway Imposes 78% Tax On All Gas and Oil Companies," *Monitor*, Canadian Center for Policy Alternatives, November 1, 2012, http://pdc-connection.ebscohost.com/c/articles/84309448/norway-imposes-taxes-78-all-oil-gas-companies.

Student Researcher: Paige Fischer (Sonoma State University)

Faculty Evaluator: Andy Deseran (Sonoma State University)

The revolutionary question becomes: Where do decisions that affect society as a whole get made? For this is where power resides. It is time we opened the doors of that house to everyone.

—Cindy Milstein[1]

OPENING THE DOORS

What conditions must hold for citizens to respond directly to systemic fiscal misconduct? In a globalized culture that increasingly deifies individual self-interest and capitalist markets, how to demonstrate that the choice between community and self-interest is a false one?

In 2012–13, the people of Iceland (*Censored* stories #9 and #19) and the tenth anniversary of the Creative Commons (*Censored* story #17) provided constructive answers to these crucial questions. At the complex intersection of political order and economic power, Iceland and the Creative Commons movement exemplify the transformative potentials of greater inclusivity in politics and popular resistance to economic hegemony.

Icelandic Reverb: Popular Constitution-Making and the Commons

The positive reverberations from Iceland's 2008 "kitchenware" revolution continued in 2012–2013, despite the dampening effects of limited corporate news coverage and setbacks in the nation's April 2013 parliamentary elections.

Triggered by unregulated banks "borrowing more than their country's gross domestic product from international wholesale money markets,"[2] Iceland's 2008 economic collapse inflicted terrible damage on foreign creditors and local residents alike. At the time, the *Economist* declared Iceland's banking collapse "the biggest, relative to the size of an economy, that any country has ever suffered."[3] In response, Iceland's populist, peaceful "kitchenware" revolution led to nationalization of the country's main bank, resignation of implicated government officials, and the dissolving of the ruling government.[4] In the elections of January 2009, "Icelanders leaned left," electing a coalition of social democrats and "red-greens," which subsequently "put the country's house in order."[5] Perhaps more importantly, about 200 high-level executives and bankers responsible for the economic crisis were arrested and charged with crimes; in a few notable cases, they were sentenced to jail.[6] In less than objective style, the *New York Times* reported on Iceland's "fervent prosecution" but "meager returns" in holding the banksters criminally accountable for the nation's economic collapse.[7]

In March 2010, 93 percent of Iceland's electorate voted to deny payment of the 3.5 billion euro debt (approximately US $5.4 billion) that Iceland's bankers had saddled on Iceland.[8] Iceland's voters rejected debt repayment a second time in April 2011.[9] And in January 2013, the court of the European Free Trade Association (EFTA) ruled that Iceland was justified in refusing to "compensate Britain for the state expense of bailing out depositors in Icesave," when the bank, which had offered high-interest-bearing online accounts, failed and lacked sufficient funds to compensate all its overseas depositors.[10]

Iceland's October 2012 affirmation of the nation's natural resources as a commons reflects the peoples' rejection of the global trend to privatize profits while socializing risks. In the 2012 referendum, 67 percent of the electorate expressed support for the constitutional draft, and 83 percent voted to protect natural resources not already privately owned as national property.[11] Analyzing the vote, Jessica Conrad of On the Commons observed, "It is clear that citizens are beginning to recognize the value of what they share together over the perceived wealth created by the market economy."[12] After the October vote, Iceland's Prime Minister Jóhanna Sigurðardóttir said, "The people have put the parliament on probation."[13]

The constitutional bill that led to the referendum was the product of genuine participatory democracy. A national assembly of 950 citizens, drawn at random from the national registry, drafted the initial resolutions, which a twenty-five–member Constitutional Council, elected by the nation and appointed by the Parliament, converted into a coherent draft constitution.[14] Its preamble established the core values that framed the document: "We, the people of Iceland, wish to create a just society where everyone has a seat at the same table."[15] An analysis by the Comparative Constitutions Project found that Iceland's draft constitution is "one of the most inclusive in history," measured by the degree to which it includes citizens in decision-making, notably through its provisions for referenda and initiatives.[16]

Thorvaldur Gylfason, a professor of economics at the University of Iceland, and one of the citizens who sought a position as a member of the Constitutional Council, described his election campaign in terms that would be startling to US citizens, by now used to multiyear, multi-million dollar campaigns for any election or important ballot proposition:

> Like other candidates, I was interviewed for three or four minutes on state radio . . . I posted a few short articles on the internet with websites that accept such contributions from candidates. Also, I opened a Facebook page where I posted a few short messages intended for my friends. The daily news-

paper in which I had published a weekly column since 2003 asked me to lay aside my pen from the announcement of my candidacy until after the election. Many if not most of the other candidates kept an equally low profile. . . . As I see it, this was the least expensive and most civilized election "campaign" in the history of the republic.[17]

Just because Gylfason's campaign was low-key does not mean that the stakes Constitutional Council members fought for were inconsequential. As he noted, the political opposition in Parliament fought the referendum "tooth and nail," resorting to "filibustering in an attempt to derail the promised referendum, an action that ultimately failed."[18] Instead, the understated campaign, involving direct participation by the nation's citizens, suggests a viable alternative to the big money, lobby-driven electoral campaigns to which the US electorate has become all too habituated.

The revised constitution affirmed by Iceland's electorate in October 2012 does not specifically require Parliament to adopt it. To go into effect, Parliament must approve the public's constitutional proposals.[19] The results of the April 2013 parliamentary elections make this less likely.

In April 2013, Iceland's center-right parties returned to parliamentary power in what the BBC reported as "a dramatic comeback for parties widely blamed for Iceland's economic meltdown in 2008."[20] The Social Democrats who came to power after the 2008 crisis mustered just a 13 percent share of the parliamentary vote, perhaps due to a backlash against programs deemed too austere and painful by the electorate, according to the BBC report. However, Iceland's electorate is by no means unanimous in supporting this reversal, as indicated by the gain of three parliamentary seats by Iceland's Pirate Party, which was founded partly to promote reform of the country's copyright and open content laws.[21]

As Gylfason indicated, the most recent parliamentary elections probably matter less, since the outgoing Parliament not only refused to bring the new constitution to a vote but also established more stringent standards for future constitutional changes, including the requirements of two-thirds of Parliament plus 40 percent of the popular vote, meaning that at least 80 percent voter turnout would be necessary for any constitutional reform to be accepted in Parliament's next session.[22]

Gylfason pragmatically observed, "We are back to square one as intended by the enemies of the new constitution" and concluded that there is "faint hope" that the new Parliament will "respect the will of the people."[23] Despite the resurgent old guard of political elites, experts observing from outside Iceland affirmed that its constitution-making process has been "tremendously innovative and participatory," putting it "at the cutting edge of ensuring public participation in ongoing governance."[24]

The corporate media reported the April 2013 election that resulted in the swing back to the center-right, but altogether ignored the earlier constitutional referendum.[25] Despite a constitution that is one of the most inclusive in history, a May 2013 *Washington Post* story identified Iceland as one of "12 countries where the government regulates what you can name your child."[26] More often, Iceland features in corporate media as an exotic vacation destination or the source of unconventional artists like Björk.

The corporate media is ignoring the real story—as Joel Bleifuss, editor of *In These Times*, observed: the Icelandic experience "demonstrates that an engaged and radicalized populace can challenge the orthodoxies of the technocrats—and avoid the false choice between the ballot box and the street protest by making savvy use of both."[27]

Iceland's Modern Media Initiative, Whistleblowing Protection, and Resistance to FBI Encroachment

Iceland is not only a global leader because of its direct, participatory constitution-making. Of equal note, spurred by the public, Iceland's government has created cutting-edge legislation to protect and strengthen modern freedom of expression.[28] As a result, the Icelandic Modern Media Initiative (IMMI) promises to establish Iceland at the global forefront of societies championing robust media freedoms, including new information technologies.[29] Indeed, as *Censored 2014* went to press, the *Guardian* was reporting that Edward Snowden, the whistleblower behind the biggest security leak in the US National Security Administration's history, considered Iceland his best hope for asylum.[30]

With strong bulwarks to protect journalists, their sources, and whistleblowers against retaliation, Iceland has become a stronghold for investigative journalism. Thus, Lowana Veal of Inter Press Service reported on the establishment of the Associated Whistle-Blowing Press (AWP) in Iceland.[31] Established in September 2012, AWP operates as a WikiLeaks alternative, "dedicated to bringing forth and analyzing leaked content" through "an international network of prominent journalists, researchers, lawyers and media activists based on local nodes and working together to provide society with a trustful and friendly source of analysis of information brought into light by whistle-blowers around the world."[32]

The IMMI could not stop eight Federal Bureau of Investigation (FBI) agents from secretly entering Iceland in August 2011 as part of their attempts to investigate WikiLeaks operations in Iceland and to track down WikiLeaks founder Julian Assange.[33] But, as was made public in February 2013, when Iceland's interior minister, Ögmundur Jónasson, learned that FBI agents had arrived in Iceland and were seeking cooperation from local police, he ordered the agents to leave the country. WikiLeaks subsequently reported that, despite the order to leave Iceland, FBI agents remained, continuing to interrogate one eighteen-year old individual over the course of at least five more days, without the presence of Icelandic police officers.[34] Iceland lodged a formal protest against the FBI actions with US officials; the US Department of Justice has refused to comment on the case.[35]

Despite US pressure on WikiLeaks and Iceland, in April 2013, Iceland's Supreme Court issued a landmark ruling in favor of WikiLeaks. The court held that Valitor (formerly VISA Iceland, and currently a Visa subcontractor) had unlawfully terminated its contract with WikiLeaks donations processor DataCell.[36] Since December 2010, Visa had effectively enforced an economic blockade by preventing the processing of WikiLeaks donations by credit card. The Icelandic Supreme Court ordered Visa's Valitor to reinstate payment processing for WikiLeaks donations within fifteen days or face a fine of 800,000 Icelandic króna ($6,830) per day. WikiLeaks publisher Julian Assange called the decision a "victory for free speech" and "against the rise of economic censorship to crack down against journalists and publishers."[37] Although it is still impossible to donate directly to WikiLeaks via credit card, the Freedom of the Press Foundation allows donors to make anonymous, tax-deductible donations by credit card.[38]

Corporate media have all but ignored IMMI. A search of the Pro-Quest Newsstand database on this topic returns just two stories from that period. An editorial in the *Christian Science Monitor* on the global state of free speech made passing reference to Iceland; the other article, published in the *Los Angeles Times*, noted that in crafting its "leading edge" legislation, Iceland's lawmakers had consulted with "WikiLeaks' controversial founder," Julian Assange, and pushed Iceland "into uncharted territory."[39]

Creative Commons Celebrates Ten Years of Sharing and Cultural Creation

It is our good fortune that all is not yet couched in terms of purchase and sale.

—Marcel Mauss, 1925[40]

Founded in 2001, Creative Commons announced its first copyright licenses in December 2002.[41] Part of a larger free culture movement, Creative Commons (CC) sought to show, in the words of the organization's executive director, Glenn Otis Brown, that "the choice between self-interest and community is a false choice. . . . Sharing, done properly, is both smart and right."[42]

Ten years later, Jason Hibbets of opensource.com reported that governments—including Austria and Italy—are using Creative Commons for their open data portals; the University of California–Santa Cruz library has adopted a CC license for all of its content; and YouTube now has over four million Creative Commons videos available.[43]

In corporate coverage of Creative Commons' ten-year anniversary, the *Wall Street Journal* ran an editorial by one of CC's founding board members, Lawrence Lessig, but otherwise CC received only fleeting notice, usually in association with the death of Aaron Swartz.[44] *The New York Times* did note the appointment of Joichi Ito—director of the Massachusetts Institute of Technology's Media Lab and a CC board member—to the board of the New York Times Company.[45]

In March 2013, CC's Timothy Vollmer reported that the United States Register of Copyright, Maria Pallante, testified to Congress's House Subcommittee on Courts, Intellectual Property, and the Internet that the US needs "bold adjustments" to US copyright law.[46] As

Vollmer reported, Pallante's remarks highlighted "the crucial need to expand and protect the public domain."[47] A search in the ProQuest Newsstand database returned no corporate news coverage of Pallante's congressional testimony.

Pallante's call for "bold adjustments" took place against the backdrop of a strong international push for copyright reform, as exemplified by the work of the World Intellectual Property Organization (WIPO).[48] However, through multinational treaties—including the Anti-Counterfeiting Trade Agreement (ACTA) and Trans-Pacific Partnership (TPP)—the US is "one of the leading nations advocating for stronger copyright protection."[49]

This is not an either/or situation. As Vollmer reported, "The existence of CC licenses does not limit the need for reform. Open licenses help forward-thinking people and institutions to live and thrive in the digital age now, and illuminate the roadmap for beneficial reform to come."[50]

CONCLUSION

From Marcel Mauss to Cindy Milstein, progressive thinkers have proposed alternatives to the pursuits of wealth and power as ends in themselves. In his 1925 classic, *The Gift*, Mauss deconstructed the assumption that all significant human interaction could be analyzed in market terms. Instead, he argued, gift economies not only predated markets but also provided a more robust basis for "group morality," because exchange of useful articles in gift economies connected not simply individuals but, more fundamentally, groups.[51] More recently, Milstein has championed a more horizontal, direct form of democracy—instead of its representative form—as the best means of "freedom making."[52]

The alternative visions of Mauss, Milstein, and many more call into question corporate power and hierarchical government. As 2012–13 independent news coverage of Iceland and the Creative Commons demonstrates, alternatives to top-down government and market-driven economies are not just viable but robust. Regardless of inattentive corporate media and their cursory, slanted coverage, Iceland and the Creative Commons show us that, regarding popular participation in the political and economic decisions that affect society as a whole, the doors of the house are increasingly open.

ANDY LEE ROTH, PHD, is associate director of Project Censored and teaches sociology at Sonoma State University and College of Marin.

Thanks to Elizabeth Boyd, Thorvaldur Gylfason, and Nick Wolfinger for suggestions on earlier versions of this text.

Notes

1. Cindy Milstein, "Democracy is Direct," in *Globalize Liberation: How to Uproot the System and Build a Better World*, ed. David Solnit (San Francisco: City Lights, 2004), 42.
2. Jessica Conrad, "Icelanders Vote to Include the Commons in Their Constitution," *Commons Magazine*, November 2012, http://onthecommons.org/magazine/icelanders-vote-include-commons-their-constitution.
3. "Cracks in the Crust," *Economist*, December 11, 2008, http://www.economist.com/node/12762027.
4. Alex Pietrowski, "Iceland's Hördur Torfason—How to Beat the Banksters," *Waking Times*, December 11, 2012, http://www.wakingtimes.com/2012/12/11/icelands-hordur-torfason-how-to-beat-the-banksters.
5. Joel Bleifuss, "Icelandic Lesson in Democracy," *In These Times*, May 2013, 5.
6. For instance, "Former Kaupthing Bank Boss Hreidar Mar Sigurdsson Arrested in Iceland," *Ice News*, May 6, 2010, http://www.icenews.is/2010/05/06/former-kaupthing-bank-boss-hreidar-mar-sigurdsson-arrested-in-iceland/. The first executives charged with responsibility for the collapse received jail sentences in December 2012, while approximately eighty cases brought by the special prosecutor remain to go to trial. See, for example, "Executives at Collapsed Iceland Bank Jailed for Fraud," Reuters, December 28, 2012, http://uk.reuters.com/article/2012/12/28/uk-iceland-crisis-idUKBRE8BR0EW20121228.
7. Andrew Higgins, "Iceland, Fervent Prosecutor of Bankers, Sees Meager Returns," *New York Times*, February 3, 2013:A6.
8. For example, "Icelandic People Refuse to Repay Internet Bank's Multi-Billion Debt," RT News, March 9, 2010, http://rt.com/news/iceland-icesave-bank-referendum/.
9. For example, "Icelandic Voters Reject Icesave Debt Repayment Plan," *Guardian*, April 10, 2011, http://www.guardian.co.uk/world/2011/apr/10/iceland-icesave-debt-repayment-no-vote.
10. Ben Chu, "'Total Victory' for Iceland over UK in Saga of Icesave Depositors," *Independent*, January 29, 2013, http://www.independent.co.uk/news/business/news/total-victory-for-iceland-over-uk-in-saga-of-icesave-depositors-8470714.html. The EFTA court decision received limited coverage in the *New York Times*: Andrew Higgins, "Iceland Wins a European Court Victory in a Banking Case," *New York Times*, January 29, 2013:B4.
11. The referendum read: "Would you want natural resources which are not in private ownership to be declared the property of the nation in a new Constitution?" Gylfason, "Iceland: Direct Democracy," and Conrad, "Icelanders Vote."
12. Conrad, ibid.
13. Ibid.
14. See Gylfason, "Iceland: Direct Democracy," and Thorvaldur Gylfason, "Putsch: Iceland's Crowd-Sourced Constitution Killed by Parliament," *Truthout*, April 1, 2013, http://truth-out.org/news/item/15462-putsch-icelands-crowd-sourced-constitution-killed-by-parliament.

15. "Constitutional Bill: A proposal for a new constitution for the Republic of Iceland delivered to the Althing by The Constitutional Council on 29 July 2011," http://stjornarskrarfelagid.is/wp-content/uploads/2011/09/Iceland_New_Constitutional_Bill.pdf.

16. The study compared Iceland's 2012 draft constitution with twenty-four other national constitutions, including Iceland's current constitution, drafted in 1944, and the US Constitution of 1789. In terms of inclusivity, Iceland's draft constitution ranked second only to Bolivia's 2009 constitution. (The US Constitution of 1789 ranked twenty-third, by comparison.) See Zachary Elkins, Tom Ginsburg, James Melton, "A Review of Iceland's Draft Constitution," Comparative Constitutions Project, October 14, 2012, 3–4, https://webspace.utexas.edu/elkinszs/web/CCP Iceland Report.pdf.

17. Gylfason, "Iceland: Direct Democracy in Action."

18. Ibid.

19. See Article 66 of the "Constitutional Bill."

20. "Iceland Vote: Centre-Right Opposition Wins Election," BBC News, April 28, 2013, http://www.bbc.co.uk/news/world-europe-22320282.

21. Ibid. See also "Pirate Party Makes History in Iceland Elections," RT News, April 29, 2013, http://rt.com/news/pirate-party-gains-iceland-587/.

22. Gylfason, "Putsch."

23. Ibid.

24. Elkins, Ginsburg, and Melton, "Iceland's Draft Constitution," 11.

25. See, for example, Sarah Lyall, "Iceland Ousts Government that Steered It Out of Crisis," New York Times, April 29, 2013:A4; Clemens Bomsdorf, "Iceland Votes for Power Change," Wall Street Journal, April 28, 2013:A14. A search in the ProQuest Newsstand database, using combinations of the terms "Iceland," "constitution" and "referendum," generated no instances of corporate news coverage on the electorates' overwhelming approval of a new constitution including the commons.

26. Caitlin Dewey, "12 Countries Where the Government Regulates What You Can Name Your Child," Washington Post, May 3, 2013: "In Iceland, for instance, parents must choose from a list of roughly 1,800 girls' names and 1,700 boys' names."

27. Bleifuss, "Icelandic Lesson." By contrast, the New York Times notes that "the lessons of Iceland's turnaround are not readily applicable to Europe's more complex economies;" see "Iceland's Mending Economy," New York Times, July 8, 2012: A6.

28. See Articles 14, 15 and 16, on "Freedom of Opinion and Expression," "Right to Information" and "Freedom of the Media," respectively, "Constitutional Bill."

29. "Icelandic Modern Media Initiative," International Modern Media Institute, https://immi.is/index.php/projects/immi.

30. Snowden: "My predisposition is to seek asylum in a country with shared values. The nation that most encompasses this is Iceland. They stood up for people over internet freedom," quoted in Ewen MacAskill, "Edward Snowden, NSA Files Source: 'If They Want to Get You, in Time They Will,'" Guardian, June 9, 2013, http://www.guardian.co.uk/world/2013/jun/09/nsa-whistleblower-edward-snowden-why. See also Owen Bowcott, Alexandra Topping, and Ed Pilkington, "Beyond Hong Kong: Edward Snowden's Best Options for Asylum," Guardian, June 10, 2013, http://www.guardian.co.uk/world/2013/jun/10/hong-kong-edward-snowden-asylum.

31. Lowana Veal, "Alternative to Wikileaks Arises in Iceland," Inter Press Service, September 24, 2012, http://www.ipsnews.net/2012/09/alternative-to-wikileaks-arises-in-iceland/.

32. Associated Whistle-Blowing Press, http://awp.is/.

33. Stuart Bramhall, "Wikileaks Reports FBI Banned from Iceland," Daily Censored, February 4, 2013, http://www.dailycensored.com/wikileaks-reports-fbi-banned-from-iceland/.

34. "Eight FBI Agents Conduct Interrogation in Iceland in Relation to Ongoing U.S. Investigation of WikiLeaks," WikiLeaks, February 7, 2013, https://wikileaks.org/Eight-FBI-agents-conduct.html.

35. "Iceland Denies Aid to FBI in WikiLeaks Investigation," RT, February 2, 2013, http://rt.com/news/iceland-fbi-wikileaks-investigation-292.

36. "Milestone Supreme Court Decision for WikiLeaks Case in Iceland," WikiLeaks, April 24, 2013, http://www.twitlonger.com/show/n_1rjulqn.

37. Ibid.

38. Freedom of the Press Foundation, https://pressfreedomfoundation.org/.

39. Mike Sacks, "Free Speech: What if Terry Jones Went to Sweden?," *Christian Science Monitor*, October 2, 2010:7; Henry Chu, "Iceland Seeks to Be a Free-Speech Sanctuary," *Los Angeles Times*, April 3, 2011: A3.

40. Marcel Mauss, *The Gift: Forms and Functions of Exchange in Archaic Societies*, trans. Ian Cunnison (New York: W.W. Norton, 1967[1925]), 80.

41. Glenn Otis Brown, "Creative Commons Unveils Machine-Readable Copyright Licenses," Creative Commons, December 16, 2002, http://creativecommons.org/press-releases/entry/3476.

42. Ibid.

43. Jason Hibbets, "Celebrating 10 Years of Creative Commons," opensource.com, November 29, 2012, http://opensource.com/law/12/11/celebrating-ten-years-creative-commons. See also, Jane Park, "Government and Library Open Data Using Creative Commons Tools," opensource.com, May 3, 2012, http://opensource.com/government/12/5/government-and-library-open-data-using-creative-commons-tools; Ruth Suehle, "UC Santa Cruz Library Chooses Creative Commons," opensource.com, February 6, 2012, http://opensource.com/life/12/2/uc-santa-cruz-library-chooses-creative-commons; and Casey Brown, "Creative Commons CEO Reflects on YouTube's Remixable Library," opensource.com, July 27, 2012, http://opensource.com/life/12/7/creative-commons-ceo-reflects-youtubes-creative-commons-library.

44. Lawrence Lessig, "Online Artists Share Work—Tyrants Would Prefer They Share a Cell," *Wall Street Journal*, January 8, 2013:A17. On the association of CC with Swartz, see for example, Noam Cohen, "A Data Crusader, a Defendant and Now, a Cause," *New York Times*, January 14, 2013:A1.

45. Christine Haughney, "Times Names 2 With Broad Technology Experience to Its Board," *New York Times*, June 22, 2012:B2.

46. Timothy Vollmer, "Pallante's Push for U.S. Copyright Reform," Creative Commons News, March 20, 2013, http://creativecommons.org/weblog/entry/37576. See also "Statement of Maria A. Pallante," Register of Copyrights of the United States Subcommittee on Courts, Intellectual Property and the Internet, Committee on the Judiciary, United States House of Representatives, 113th Congress, 1st Session, March 20, 2013, http://judiciary.house.gov/hearings/113th/03202013/Pallante 032013.pdf.

47. Vollmer, "Pallante's Push."

48. "The World Intellectual Property Organization (WIPO) is the United Nations agency dedicated to the use of intellectual property (patents, copyright, trademarks, designs, etc.) as a means of stimulating innovation and creativity." See http://www.wipo.int/portal/index.html.en.

49. Vollmer, "Pallante's Push." On TPP, see *Censored* story #3 and James F. Tracy's Censored News Cluster on "Plutocracy, Poverty & Prosperity" in this volume.

50. Vollmer, ibid.

51. "Our morality is not solely commercial," Mauss, *The Gift*, 63, 66. For a timely assessment of Mauss's work, see David Graeber, "Give It Away," Free Words, no date, http://www.freewords.org/graeber.html.

52. Milstein, "Democracy is Direct," 39: "Democracy's underlying logic is essentially the unceasing movement of freedom making."

CHAPTER 2

Déjà Vu
What Happened to Previous Top *Censored* Stories

Mickey Huff and Nolan Higdon, with research and writing from
Project Censored interns Andrew O'Connor-Watts, Jen Eiden,
Allen Kew, Emmie Ruhland, Aaron Hudson, Rex Yang, Sam Park,
Amitai Cohen, Michael Kolbe, and Matthew Carhart

*That men do not learn very much from the lessons of
history is the most important of all the lessons that history has to teach.*

—Aldous Huxley[1]

Each year, Project Censored reviews stories that were featured in previous years' Top 25 lists. These reviews focus on the stories' subsequent
corporate coverage and the extent to which they have become part of
broader public discourse, or whether they remain "censored" by corporate media and marginal in terms of public exposure and attention.

Too often, we find that *Censored* stories continue to suffer from neglect by the corporate media. In such cases, but for the original reports
by independent journalists, these stories would languish unknown to
any segment of the public. For instance, *Censored* story #1 for 2009,
"Over One Million Deaths Caused by US Occupation," remains unac-
knowledged by corporate media. Consequently, few Americans understand the extraordinary toll of US military operations in Iraq.[2]

For *Censored* stories that the big media outlets do eventually cover,
we have noticed a consistent lag of roughly one to two years between
the moment when independent journalists cover a particular story and
the time when the corporate news "breaks" it. This is the same lag that

Project Censored founder, Professor Carl Jensen, noted in analyzing press coverage of the Watergate scandal that led to United States President Richard Nixon's resignation in 1974. Stories about the scandal circulated in the independent press in early 1972, but corporate coverage lagged. Jensen wondered how the outcome of the 1972 election might have differed if Watergate had broken as a prominent news feature much sooner. That was the genesis of Project Censored.

Over thirty-seven years later, the trend of lagging corporate coverage continues. For instance, story #1 from *Censored 2012*, "More US Soldiers Committed Suicide than Died in Combat" has finally gained momentum in corporate news coverage.[3] And, as reported in this chapter, the devastating consequences of US drone strikes in Yemen, Somalia, and especially Pakistan—which featured in independent news coverage at least two years previously—have at last broken through to the attention of corporate media in a meaningful way in 2013. In addition to an update of *Censored* story #3 from 2012, "Obama Authorizes International Assassination Campaign," this year Project Censored reviews subsequent coverage of the following stories from *Censored 2013*: #1, "Signs of an Emerging Police State"; #4, "FBI Agents Responsible for Majority of Terrorist Plots in the United States"; #6, "Small Network of Corporations Run the Global Economy"; #12, "US Joins Forces with al-Qaeda in Syria"; and #16, "Sexual Violence Against Women Soldiers on the Rise and Under Wraps."[4]

As we try to learn lessons from our recent history, let us strive for these significant yet underreported stories to get a fair and broad hearing in the present, such that future people's historians can more accurately and assuredly learn and share their own.

Censored 2013 #1

Signs of an Emerging Police State

SUMMARY: In 2011 and 2012, the United States showed more signs of moving towards a police state. Some examples of such a shift include the National Defense Authorization Act (NDAA), which President Barack Obama signed into law on December 31, 2011. The NDAA's vague language gave the president the right to use military force to detain American citizens indefinitely without trial. In March 2012, passage of the National Defense Resources Preparedness Executive Order gave the federal government and military widespread control over the national economy and resources during "national emergencies" as well as "peacetime." Along with these laws came an increase in surveillance, including the National Security Agency's construction of a two-billion-dollar electronic intelligence compound in Utah. American citizens continue to have their civil liberties threatened more and more each day.

UPDATE: Until National Security Administration (NSA) whistleblower Edward Snowden galvanized the public's attention on the pervasive nature of domestic surveillance in the US, the continuation of NDAA and NSA policies had been almost completely ignored by the corporate media. The NDAA has received little corporate media coverage since *Censored 2013*.

In January 2012, journalist Chris Hedges filed a lawsuit to challenge section 1021 (b)(2) of the NDAA, which authorized indefinite detention for anyone who is "a part of or substantially supports al-Qaeda, the Taliban, or associated forces." Federal Judge Katherine B. Forrest issued a permanent injunction on September 11, 2012, blocking the government's use of NDAA to detain citizens indefinitely. The Obama administration responded with an emergency block and appeal.

As *Censored 2014* went to press, no decision had been made on the appeal. *Hedges v. Obama* received corporate media coverage, mostly in the *New York Times*. An editorial by the *Washington Post* offered support for the Obama administration's appeal, calling Judge Forrest's ruling an "overreaction." Originally signed into law with little fanfare on December 31, 2012, when Americans were busy celebrating the New Year's holiday, the NDAA remains law in 2013 while the appeal is decided. It was signed on for another year by the president in January 2013. Corporate media coverage focused on whether or not President Obama would sign the bill rather than the bill's specific implications, or Hedges's lawsuit.

However, also as *Censored 2014* went to press, three other major stories about government secrecy and police state power surfaced. One covered the revelations of the Obama justice department spying on

Associated Press (AP) and Fox News journalists. A *Democracy Now!* story with Chris Hedges on May 15, 2013, rightfully called it a terrifying step in the state assault on press freedom, and while the corporate media covered the story and even vilified the Obama administration over it, this faded from memory fairly quickly. After being declared legal by the Obama administration, there was little fanfare as if all this was simply the new normal—eerily, it is.[5] The second story, which involved Supreme Court case *Holder v. Humanitarian Law Project*, had arguably even broader civil rights implications than the NDAA or AP scandal and received almost no attention in the media. In this case, justices ruled that speech (and other forms of nonviolent advocacy) could be construed as material support for terrorist organizations.[6]

The last of these stories, however, did break, blowing up in the media even more than both of the preceding stories—in fact, overshadowing them. This involved Edward Snowden, a former NSA contractor who leaked information regarding an NSA program, PRISM, that collects data on all Americans, creating a massive spy database. Journalist Glenn Greenwald broke the story in the *Guardian* (out of London, so not a US media outlet).[7] The story was quickly pounced upon by the US press, but mostly to deny or downplay the claims of America's latest whistleblower. Many prominent liberals like Jeffrey Toobin attacked Snowden as a narcissist who should be in prison, a sentiment echoed by most Washington establishment politicians and the press.[8] For most in the corporate media, there was little interest in the specifics of what Snowden was revealing via Greenwald, and, rather, a great focus on spinning the information and how these programs are part of the war on terror, while framing Snowden as a traitor, not a hero exposing controversial and dubious government spy programs. This is a common theme, as we will see.

In what should be the high-profile legal case of the year, most US major media are absent from or locked out of the WikiLeaks whistleblower Bradley Manning trial that began in early June (see story #1 in chapter 1 of this volume). According to Rainey Reitman of Freedom of the Press Foundation, the Military District of Washington Media Desk, which issues press passes, only granted 70 out of 350 requests for media access. *Reader Supported News* filed a motion to intervene and secure media access, or at least a video feed of the proceedings, and the judge ruled against the motion even though many of the seventy people granted access were apparently not even showing up to the media operations room.[9]

Further, what corporate media coverage there was regarding the Manning trial seemed to miss the point, as was shown by Matt Taibbi of *Rolling Stone*. Taibbi wrote that "the government couldn't have scripted the headlines any better."[10] The government court marshal and compliant corporate media have tried to make the case about Pfc. Manning, a troubled young man with gender identity issues, and frame the case by posing the question of "Is he a hero or traitor?" Taibbi rightfully called out this distraction, saying, "In reality, this case does not have anything to do with who Bradley Manning is, or even, really, what his motives were. This case is entirely about the 'classified' materials Manning had access to, and whether or not they contained widespread evidence of war crimes."[11] Most in the corporate media have missed this point,[12] and it's likely that Pentagon public relations people couldn't be happier with the coverage (and they didn't have to dip into their five billion dollar budget specifically for Pentagon PR). Further proving Taibbi's point, *Time* magazine's cover story during the second week of June equated whistleblowers like Manning and Snowden with spies. Again, a government PR team couldn't do a better job disseminating such propaganda.[13]

This "shoot the messenger" *ad hominem*/red herring approach is standard fare in the US when dealing with those who dare to engage in fearless speech in fateful times, especially when revealing government secrecy and lies. From Daniel Ellsberg to Julian Assange, the US political establishment has sought to discredit, attack, and prosecute those who dare announce that the emperor has no clothes. The Obama administration has targeted whistleblowers more than all previous US administrations combined (see story #4 in chapter 1 of this volume), further evidenced by the legal proceedings involving Bradley Manning; the prosecution of CIA whistleblower John Kiriakou, the source exposing CIA torture program; and the federal prosecutorial overreach and legal haranguing[14] of Creative Commons tech prodigy and Internet freedom activist Aaron Swartz, which led to his suicide.[15] It is clear the Obama administration wants to make examples out of those who are strong advocates of freedom of information and the public's right to know. It appears that in failing to point out these attacks on the state of press freedom and public rights, corporate media is missing key elements of the story.

SOURCES:

"Detention Wars, Continued," *Washington Post*, September 16, 2012, http://www.washingtonpost.com/opinions/detention-wars-continued/2012/09/16/df1eacac-fea8-11e1-a31e-804fccb658f9_story.html.

Charlie Savage, "U.S. Appeals Judge Grants Stay of Ruling on Detention Law," *New York Times*, September 18, 2012, http://www.nytimes.com/2012/09/19/us/politics/us-appeals-judge-grants-stay-of-ruling-on-detention-law.html?_r=0.

Natasha Lennard, "Obama Signs NDAA Again, Disappoints on Gitmo and Civil Liberties Again," *Salon*, January 3, 2013, http://www.salon.com/2013/01/03/obama_signs_ndaa_again/.

Charlie Savage, "Obama Disputes Limits on Detainee Transfers Imposed in Defense Bill," *New York Times*, January 3, 2013, http://www.nytimes.com/2013/01/04/us/politics/obama-signs-defense-bill-with-conditions.html.

Peter Finn, "Defense Bill's Guantanamo Bay Provisions have Human Rights Groups Upset with Obama," *Washington Post*, January 3, 2013, http://www.washingtonpost.com/world/national-security/defense-bills-guantanamo-bay-provisions-have-human-rights-groups-upset-with-obama/2013/01/03/778be520-55e0-11e2-8b9e-dd8773594efc_story.html.

"2013 National Defense Authorization Act," American Civil Liberties Union, January 10, 2013, http://www.aclu.org/national-security-reproductive-freedom-womens-rights/2013-national-defense-bill-good-bad-and-ugly.

Chris Hedges, "The NDAA and the Death of the Democratic State," *Truthdig*, February 11, 2013, http://www.truthdig.com/report/item/the_ndaa_and_the_death_of_the_democratic_state_20130211/.

Kashmir Hill, "Surprise Visitors Are Unwelcome at the NSA's Unfinished Utah Spy Center (Especially When They Take Photos)," *Forbes*, March 4, 2013, http://www.forbes.com/sites/kashmirhill/2013/03/04/nsa-utah-data-center-visit/.

Glenn Greenwald, "NSA Collecting Phone Records of Millions of Verizon Customers Daily," *Guardian*, June 6, 2013, http://www.guardian.co.uk/world/2013/jun/06/nsa-phone-records-verizon-court-order.

Matt Taibbi, "As Bradley Manning Trial Begins, Press Predictably Misses the Point," *Rolling Stone*, June 6, 2013, http://www.rollingstone.com/politics/blogs/taibblog/as-bradley-manning-trial-begins-press-predictably-misses-the-point-20130605.

Kevin Gosztola, "*Time* Magazine Equates Whistleblowers with Spies in Cover Story on Snowden, Manning & Swartz," *Firedoglake*, June 13, 2013, http://dissenter.firedoglake.com/2013/06/13/time-magazine-equates-whistleblowers-with-spies-in-cover-story-on-snowden-manning-swartz/

Censored 2013 #4

FBI Agents Responsible for Majority of Terrorist Plots in the United States

SUMMARY: The Federal Bureau of Investigation has embarked on an unusual approach to ensure that the United States is secure from future terrorist attacks. The agency has developed a network of nearly 15,000 spies to infiltrate various communities in an attempt to uncover terrorist plots. However, these moles are actually assisting and encouraging people to commit crimes. Many informants receive cash rewards of up to $100,000 per case.

UPDATE: In November 2010, Mohamed Mohamud was arrested for attempting to detonate a car bomb at a Christmas tree-lighting ceremony in Portland, Oregon. Before his arrest, Mohamud had been under FBI surveillance for one year because he had written for a jihadi magazine and had been in email contact with two accused terrorists and a man who fought against coalition troops in Afghanistan. The FBI agents who established contact with Mohamud posed as al-Qaeda operatives and claimed that Mohamud had expressed an interest in car bombing. During his trial, Mohamud's lawyers argued that undercover FBI operatives entrapped the young Somali-American and coerced him. The jury determined that Mohamud was guilty as charged and found no fault with the FBI. He was sentenced to life in prison. Mohamud's case is one of at least eleven in which defendants have claimed entrapment in terrorism trials though none have been acquitted.

The FBI is accused of devising plots and then targeting operatives who are alienated loners or are easily manipulated. In the case of the Cleveland Five, who were accused of plotting to destroy a bridge outside Cleveland, friends and family members described them as "lost souls." As in Mohamud's case, the Cleveland Five involved an FBI-inspired plan. An FBI informant allegedly brought them to the bridge and argued that blowing it up would help the Occupy movement. He then connected them to another undercover FBI operative who provided them with C4 explosives.

The corporate media, at least in print, have picked up on these stories. David K. Shipler of the *New York Times* wrote in April of 2012 (note the one- to two-year lag mentioned in the introduction of this chapter), that while it may seem the FBI is thwarting terror plots at home, they are rather more intimately involved with the actual carrying out of these very incidents via under cover officers and informants. Shipler rightfully picked up on Trevor Aaronson's original story highlighted in *Censored 2013* as story #4.

The Cleveland scenario was repeated with Quazi Mohammad Nafis. Nafis, a Bangladeshi-born US visitor on a student visa, was described by acquaintances as unintelligent, flunking out of the university he attended in Bangladesh. Within six months of his arrival in the US, the FBI began investigating the twenty-one–year-old. According to public documents, in a phone call Nafis expressed admiration for Osama bin Laden and a desire to wage jihad in the US. In that conversation, Nafis's contact—who turned out to be an FBI informant—offered to put Nafis in contact with an al-Qaeda operative. Nafis told the informant that he wanted to bomb the New York Stock Exchange. The informant provided everything for Nafis, from the fake bomb and its detonator to the van used to contain the supposed explosives. He even drove with Nafis to the proposed bomb site—the Federal Reserve Bank in New York City—and parked the van outside. The two then went to a nearby hotel where Nafis proceeded to attempt a detonation by dialing a cell phone code. He tried several times before being arrested by FBI agents. Nafis awaits trial.

Several major news outlets like CBS and *Huffington Post* have covered the Nafis case, but neither mentions the FBI's heavy involvement with the planning and facilitation of the plot. Nafis and Mohamud and at least 150 others have been arrested as a result of FBI involvement in terror plots. These stings have involved 15,000 registered informants, some are paid up to $100,000 per assignment. The FBI is paying known criminals in order to prevent potential FBI encouraged criminals from executing terrorist acts. The largest portion of the FBI's budget is for counterterrorism, which receives three billion dollars annually, and which goes to fund these operations.

Often, however, coverage by corporate media about these plots frame the event as if the FBI simply prevented the attacks, with no other details given outside of sweeping statements about agency efforts or local cooperation. This was the case with the May 2013 incident in Minnesota as it was simply announced that the FBI prevented an attack. No other information was given by the prominent *US News and World Report* story by Steven Nelson, "FBI: 'Terror Attack' Plot Disrupted in Minnesota Raid in Rural America Prevented 'Potential Tragedy,' FBI Says." "The FBI says" . . . and no follow report was done by Nelson.

Given the FBI's past with its Counter Intelligence Program (COINTELPRO), it is astounding that more reporters don't do more probing. The public would be wise to pay more attention to domestic "terror" attacks (like the one in Boston this past spring, during which the FBI gave several conflicting stories about their knowledge of the suspects) and to begin pressuring the media and government to investigate these matters more fully, more transparently, and with more detail paid to FBI involvement.

SOURCES:

David K. Shipler, "Terrorist Plots, Hatched by the FBI," *New York Times*, April 28, 2012, http://www.nytimes.com/2012/04/29/opinion/sunday/terrorist-plots-helped-along-by-the-fbi.html?pagewanted=all&_r=0.

Arun Gupta, "Cleveland Occupy Arrests Are the Latest in FBI's Pattern of Manipulation," *Guardian*, May 28, 2012, http://www.guardian.co.uk/commentisfree/cifamerica/2012/may/28/cleveland-occupy-arrests-fbi-manipulation.

John Miller, "Officials Say Alleged Fed Bank Bomber Had Big Plans," *CBS*, October 21, 2012, http://www.cbsnews.com/8301-201_162-57536921/officials-say-alleged-fed-bank-bomber-had-big-plans/

Dina Temple Raston, "Lawyers Say Teenage Terror Suspect Was Entrapped by FBI 2013," National Public Radio, January 10, 2013, http://www.npr.org/2013/01/10/169077527/lawyers-say-teenage-terror-suspect-was-entrapped-by-fbi.

Trevor Aaronson, "Inside the Terror Factory," *Mother Jones*, January 11, 2013, http://www.motherjones.com/politics/2013/01/terror-factory-fbi-trevor-aaronson-book.

Nigel Duara. "Mohamed Mohamud GUILTY Verdict: Oregon Car-Bomb Suspect Convicted of Terrorism." *Huffington Post*, January 31, 2013, http://www.huffingtonpost.com/2013/01/31/mohamed-mohamud-verdict-guilty_n_2594134.html.

Bryan Denson, "Mohamed Mohamud Guilty Verdict: No Reaction from Defendant, Lawyers Plan to Appeal," *Oregonian*, January 31, 2013, http://www.oregonlive.com/portland/index.ssf/2013/01/mohamed_mohamud_guilty_verdict_2.html.

Censored 2013 #6

Small Network of Corporations Run the Global Economy

SUMMARY: A University of Zurich study reported that a small group of companies—mainly banks—wields huge power over the global economy. The study was the first to look at all 43,060 transnational corporations and the web of ownership among them. The researchers' network analysis identified 147 companies that form a "super entity," controlling 40 percent of the global economy's total wealth. The close connections mean that the network could be prone to "systemic risk" and vulnerable to collapse.

UPDATE: The corporate media continues to ignore growing evidence of the systematic dangers produced by increasing concentration of corporate wealth. Corporate coverage of the Zurich study has been lacking, but the London Interbank Offered Rate (Libor) scandal has resulted in corporate news coverage. Libor is an estimated average interest rate that the world's leading banks use to determine borrowing charges. Members of the press first documented the Libor scandal in 2007, when an employee at the British bank Barclays argued that Libor rates were "unrealistically low." In 2008, another Barclays employee admitted that they had been manipulating Libor since at least 2005. In July 2012, the *Financial Times* reported that the numbers had been fixed since 1991. *The Wall Street Journal* reported that during the economic collapse of 2007–08, the big banks used manipulated Libor scores to make their banks appear healthier, and to gain access to better loans. At least three banks and possibly as many as sixteen were involved in manipulating $500 trillion worth of assets.

Many major media outlets eventually covered the Libor scandal. News outlets including *USA Today, Washington Post, Huffington Post, New York Times*, Fox News, and *Financial Times* filed hundreds of reports on the topic in 2012 alone.

Andrew Gavin Marshall offered an analysis on Occupy.com that compared the global corporate network of financial elites to a "global supra-government." Marshall argued that the "super entity" of connected corporations provides a dangerous amount of power to few and creates a controlling global force on government policies and financial markets (see chapter 9 of this volume for more analysis and exposure of the global ruling elite, also referred to as the transnational capitalist class).

In April 2013, Matt Taibbi of *Rolling Stone* documented that economic price-fixing goes far beyond the banks implicated in the Libor scandal. His investigation found that the financial elite not only had a hand in fixing Libor, the interest rates of swaps, but also gold and silver prices, which together would compromise "60 percent of the nation's GDP." He argued that fixing continues because banks use "loopholes" that do not require verified data. Taibbi concluded that "the world's largest banks may be fixing the prices of . . . just about everything." He went on to note that Libor was the biggest financial scam in history of markets.

But it gets worse. Taibbi continued:

> Libor may have a twin brother. Word has leaked out that the London-based firm ICAP, the world's largest broker of interest-rate swaps, is being investigated by American authorities for behavior that sounds eerily reminiscent of the Libor mess. Regulators are looking into whether or not a small group of brokers at ICAP may have worked with up to 15 of the world's largest banks to manipulate ISDAfix, a benchmark number used around the world to calculate the prices of interest-rate swaps.[16]

That's right, a conspiracy from the top of the world's leading financial institutions to manipulate interest-rate swaps. The very companies that can manipulate these are the very ones who can profit, while potentially trashing other sectors of the global economy. Taibbi concluded grimly:

> The only reason this problem has not received the attention it deserves is because the scale of it is so enormous that ordinary people simply cannot see it. It's not just stealing by reaching a hand into your pocket and taking out money, but stealing in which banks can hit a few keystrokes and magically make whatever's in your pocket worth less. This is cor-

ruption at the molecular level of the economy, Space Age stealing—and it's only just coming into view.[17]

As *Censored 2014* went to press, Taibbi noted stories from the Bloomberg business press on a possible scandal that could dwarf Libor involving the currency market, or foreign exchange rates, where insiders once again were poised to rig the system.[18] A small network is still running the global economy.

SOURCES:

Carrick Mollenkamp and Mark Whitehouse, "Study Casts Doubt on Key Rate," *Wall Street Journal*, May 29, 2008, http://online.wsj.com/article/SB121200703762027135.html.
"New York Fed's Libor Documents Reveal Cozy Relationship Between Regulators, Banks," *Huffington Post*, July 13, 2012, http://www.huffingtonpost.com/2012/07/13/new-york-fed-libor-documents_n_1671524.html.
"Libor Review: Wheatley Says System Must Change," BBC News, August 10, 2012, http://www.bbc.co.uk/news/business-19203103.
Michelle Williams, "Timeline of the Libor Scandal," *Washington Post*, December 19, 2012, http://www.washingtonpost.com/wp-srv/business/libor-timeline.html/.
Elizabeth Warren, "Libor Fraud Exposes Wall Street's Rotten Core," *Washington Post*, July 19, 2012, http://articles.washingtonpost.com/2012-07-19/opinions/35489555_1_libor-rates-barclays-traders-interest-rates/.
Andrew Gavin Marshall, "Welcome to the Network of Global Corporate Control," January 29, 2013, Occupy.com, http://www.occupy.com/article/welcome-network-global-corporate-control.
Matt Taibbi, "Everything Is Rigged: The Biggest Price-Fixing Scandal Ever," *Rolling Stone*, April 25, 2013, http://www.rollingstone.com/politics/news/everything-is-rigged-the-biggest-financial-scandal-yet-20130425.

Censored 2013 #12

US Joins Forces with al-Qaeda in Syria

SUMMARY: The US, Britain, France, and some conservative Arab allies have funded and armed the Syrian rebellion from its start in 2011. In fact, the US has been funding groups against the administration of Syrian president Bashar al-Assad since the mid-1990s. However, the anti-Assad ranks include members of al-Qaeda, Hamas, and other groups that the United States lists as terrorist organizations.

UPDATE: Since the beginning of Syria's civil war in 2011, the US and other international powers have considered intervening on behalf of opposition forces that seek to unseat President Bashar al-Assad, whose family has held the presidency since 1971. Trade agreements and other interests led to a bloc against United Nations intervention. Russia, which supplies the regime with weapons, led the blockade. The US has officially claimed it will support Syria unless they cross a "red line" by using chemical weapons. However, according to WikiLeaks, emails from the private intelligence firm Stratfor indicate that, as of 2012, Special Operations Forces (SOF) teams—presumably from US, UK, France, Jordan, and Turkey—"are already on the ground focused on recce (reconnaissance), missions . . . and training opposition forces."

Independent news sources found that the CIA is operating on the Turkish border, attempting to organize and train Syrian opposition forces. The CIA has also reportedly given fourteen stinger missiles to the opposition. In March 2013, the *New York Times* revealed that arms were being supplied from Saudi Arabia, Qatar, and Jordan, to Syria, and that supplies for the opposition, brought into Syria through Turkey, came from dummy corporations run by the CIA. In addition, the United Kingdom's *Daily Star* reported that "British MI6, US CIA, and both French and American soldiers" were operating in Syria, seeking Assad's chemical weapons. Israeli Special Forces were also implicated.

In 2012, the US government began to give public indications of support for the opposition. On February 28, 2013, the US government announced its pledge of sixty million dollars to the Syrian opposition. The BBC reported that the "US would provide direct support to rebel forces in the form of medical and food supplies." When the *New York Times* inquired into the covert program of training opposition forces, the State Department refused to answer. However a private source informed the *Times* that the CIA "has been training groups of Syrian rebels in Jordan" since the previous year.

Groups deemed terror organizations by the US operate among the Syrian opposition. In November 2012, many of the opposition forces united under the National Coalition for Syrian Revolutionary and Opposition Forces. Several groups, most notably Jabhat al-Nusra or the al-Nusra Front, joined the coalition. Al-Nusra is designated a terrorist organization by the US because of its pledges of allegiance to al-Qaeda. Al Jazeera reported that the UN Security Council has blacklisted al-Nusra, claiming it is an alias for al-Qaeda. Al-Nusra has claimed responsibility for bombings that have racked Syria for the past year, targeting Assad's regime and supporters. In April 2013, al-Nusra and al-Qaeda publicly announced support of each other.

Corporate reporting follows a well-worn Western narrative, emphasizing the dilemmas posed by humanitarian intervention—a frame much favored by officials in the Obama administration, and likely to become more pronounced since the appointments of Samantha Power and Susan Rice, to serve as US ambassador to the United Nations and as the president's national security advisor, respectively. The only corporate publication to offer a differing perspective was the *New York Times*, which investigated the claims of CIA involvement in Syria's civil war. All other major corporate news outlets have primarily focused on terror attacks in the region, the invisible "red line," John McCain's secret trip to Syria, and the true humanitarian crisis.

That stated, as *Censored 2014* went to press, the US officially announced it would arm and train the Syrian rebels via a CIA-run program.

SOURCES:

John Glaser, "Stratfor Emails: Covert Special Ops Inside Syria Since December," *Antiwar.com*, March 7, 2012, http://news.antiwar.com/2012/03/07/stratfor-emails-covert-special-ops-inside-syria-since-december/.

Eric Schmitt, "CIA Said to Aid in Steering Arms to Syrian Opposition," *New York Times*, June 21, 2012, http://www.nytimes.com/2012/06/21/world/middleeast/cia-said-to-aid-in-steering-arms-to-syrian-rebels.html.

"Obama Gives the 'Secret' Order for CIA to Help Syrian Rebels Dispose of Assad's Brutal Regime," *Daily Mail*, August 1, 2012, http://www.dailymail.co.uk/news/article-2182427/Obama-authorizes-secret-support-Syrian-rebels.html.

Chris Hughes, "CIA Spies 'Smuggle 14 Stinger Missiles into Syria So Rebels Can Take Out Regime Warplanes,'" *Mirror News*, August 18, 2012, http://www.mirror.co.uk/news/world-news/cia-spies-smuggle-14-stinger-1266487.

Marc Ginsberg, "Obama's Syrian 'Red Line' Is No Red Light to Hezbollah or Iran," *Huffington Post*, August 21, 2012, http://www.huffingtonpost.com/amb-marc-ginsberg/obamas-syrian-red-line-is_b_1819351.html.

Tony Cartalucci, "MI6, SAS, CIA: Western Troops in Syria," Global Research, September 1, 2012, http://www.globalresearch.ca/mi6-sas-cia-western-troops-in-syria/5302879.

"U.S. Intervention in Syria Appears Unlikely, Say Officials," *Washington Post*, September 2, 2012, http://www.washingtonpost.com/world/national-security/us-intervention-in-syria-appears-unlikely-say-officials/2012/09/02/c1cd4e9a-f2bb-11e1-a612-3cfc842a6d89_story_1.html.

Bill Van Auken, "US Escalates CIA Intervention on Syrian-Turkish Border," *World Socialist Web Site*, September 8, 2012, http://www.wsws.org/en/articles/2012/09/syri-s08.html.

Anne Gearan, "U.S. Yanks Support for Syrian Opposition Group, Warns of Extremist Takeover of Uprising," *Washington Post*, October 31, 2012, http://articles.washingtonpost.com/2012-10-31/world/35499721_1_syrian-national-council-opposition-group-snc.

Arthur Bright, "What is the National Coalition for Syrian Revolutionary and Opposition Forces?," *Christian Science Monitor*, November 12, 2012, http://www.csmonitor.com/World/terrorism-security/2012/1112/What-is-The-National-Coalition-for-Syrian-Revolutionary-and-Opposition-Forces-video.

Schlomi Diaz, Daniel Siryoti, Eli Leion, "Israeli Special Forces Tracking Chemical Weapons inside Syria," *Israel Hayom*, December 9, 2012, http://www.israelhayom.com/site/newsletter_article.php?id=6668.

Michael R. Gordon and Anne Barnard, "U.S. Places Militant Syrian Rebel Group on List of Terrorist Organizations," *New York Times*, December 10, 2012, http://www.nytimes.com/2012/12/11/world/middleeast/us-designates-syrian-al-nusra-front-as-terrorist-group.html.

"US Officially Designates Key Syrian Opposition Group as al-Qaeda Affiliate," Russia Today, December 11, 2012, http://rt.com/usa/us-opposition-group-al-nusra-853/.

Jamie Dettmer, "Jihadists Are Creeping Into Syria's Rebel Factions," *Daily Beast*, January 4, 2013, http://www.thedailybeast.com/articles/2013/01/04/jihadists-are-creeping-into-syria-s-rebel-factions.html.

Vladimir Isachenkov, "Russian Arms Trade With Syria Will Continue, State Arms Trader Says," *Huffington Post*, February 13, 2013, http://www.huffingtonpost.com/2013/02/13/russian-arms-syria_n_2677279.html.

Michael R. Gordon, "U.S. Steps Up Aid to Syrian Opposition, Pledging $60 Million," *New York Times*, February 28, 2013, http://www.nytimes.com/2013/03/01/world/middleeast/us-pledges-60-million-to-syrian-opposition.html.

C.J. Chivers and Eric Schmitt, "Arms Airlift to Syrian Rebels Expands, With Aid From C.I.A.," *New York Times*, March 24, 2013, http://www.nytimes.com/2013/03/25/world/middleeast/arms-airlift-to-syrian-rebels-expands-with-cia-aid.html.

Jim Muir, "Syria Crisis: Al-Nusra Pledges Allegiance to al-Qaeda," BBC News, April 10, 2013, http://www.bbc.co.uk/news/world-middle-east-22095099.

"McCain Sneaks across Border, Visits Syrian Rebels," Fox News, May 27, 2013, http://www.foxnews.com/politics/2013/05/27/mccain-sneaks-across-border-visits-syrian-rebels.

"UN Blacklists Syria's al-Nusra Front," Al Jazeera, May 31, 2013, http://www.aljazeera.com/news/americas/2013/05/201353021594299298.html

"CIA Will Lead US Effort to Arm, Train Syrian Rebel Forces," Fox News, June 15, 2103, http://www.foxnews.com/politics/2013/06/15/cia-will-lead-us-effort-to-arm-train-syrian-rebel-forces-fox-confirms/.

Censored 2013 #16

Sexual Violence Against Women Soldiers On The Rise and Under Wraps

SUMMARY: The 2005 death of US Army Private LaVena Johnson, officially ruled suicide by the Department of Defense, in fact exemplifies the sexual violence that female soldiers encounter while serving their country. Johnson's autopsy revealed wounds inconsistent with suicide, including chemical burns that many believe were intended to destroy DNA evidence of rape. The Pentagon has tried to intimidate reporters and editors working on stories about Johnson. Johnson's case is among at least twenty in which female soldiers have died under suspicious circumstances. The mysterious deaths are coinciding with an increase in sexual violence against women in the military. According to the Department of Defense, in 2010, there were 3,158 total reports of sexual assault in the military. The DOD estimates that this number represents only 13.5 percent of the actual assaults, making the total number of military rapes and sexual assaults over 19,000 for the year.

UPDATE: The near-epidemic of rape in the military has been covered heavily by the corporate media since its release in *Censored 2013*. For example, NBC News covered Secretary of Defense Chuck Hagel's decision to strip the authority of commanding generals to void military court convictions. This prevents generals from overturning sexual assault sentences. The defense department launched a "public relations campaign to show they're serious about cracking down on sexual assault in the military." The department "expanded its victim-assistance programs, sought help from outside advocacy groups, and required sexual assault to receive attention higher up the chain of command." Much attention was brought to this previously underreported issue of rape inside the military by the documentary *The Invisible War*. Directed by Kirby Dick and produced by Amy Ziering, *The Invisible War* received nominations for numerous awards including Best Documentary Feature at the Academy Awards. The Chicago Film Critics Association named it the Best Documentary of 2012. It appeared on numerous year-end best lists, including those published by the *New York Times* and the National Board of Review of Motion Pictures.

Although media attention on sexual assault in the military has increased, statistics do not reveal an improvement on the situation. Independent news center Common Dreams reported that, despite the changes in oversight championed by Hagel, issues persist. Abby Zimet reported, "The military's annual report shows sexual assaults are in fact on the rise, with at least 26,000 a year. That's about 70 a day." *Foreign Policy* reported that the Air Force's attempt focused on giving servicemen and women "a box of breath mints, which has a bold sticker on the cover that says 'NO MEANS NO!'" and a "2.5-ounce hand sanitizer bottle shaped like an open palm. Printed on the bottle: 'KEEP UR HANDS 2 YOURSELF,' along with the telephone number for the Sexual Assault Response Coordinators 24-hour hotline."

Another problem for victims is that those tasked with policing assaults are themselves assaulting victims. In 2013, Lieutenant Colonel Jeffrey Krusinski was charged with sexual battery against a woman in a parking lot. Krusinski's job until the charge was chief of the US Air Force's Sexual Assault Prevention and Response Program. Officially the program "reinforces the Air Force's commitment to eliminate incidents of sexual assault." Krusinki's arrest occurred the day before the Pentagon released its annual report on the epidemic of sexual assaults in the military. "How many more reasons do we need to take cases of rape and sexual assault out of the chain of command?" questioned Representative Jackie Speier (D-CA).

That is an excellent question. And given that this issue has become a much more high-profile one, deservedly so, this is one question the corporate media should press to have answered. The Senate's Committee on Armed Services was meeting to take action on this important issue in June as *Censored 2014* went to press, but at that time, there was very little coverage in the corporate media about this crucial hearing.[19]

SOURCES:

Ann Jones, "The War Against Women, at Home and Abroad," *Nation*, March 21, 2013, http://www.thenation.com/article/173463/war-against-women-home-and-abroad.

R. Clifton Spargo, "The Illuminator: Helen Benedict and the Journalistic Investigation that Inspired *The Invisible War*," *Huffington Post*, April 3, 2013, http://www.huffingtonpost.com/r-clifton-spargo/the-illuminator-helen-ben_b_3001042.html.

Bill Briggs, Jim Miklaszewski, and Courtney Kube, "Defense Secretary Hagel Demands Rape Reform in Military," NBC News, April 8, 2013, http://usnews.nbcnews.com/_news/2013/04/08/17658388-defense-secretary-hagel-demands-rape-reform-in-military.

Liesl Gerntholtz, "It's Not Just About Sexual Violence," *Huffington Post*, April 9, 2013, http://www.huffingtonpost.com/liesl-gerntholtz/its-not-just-about-sexual_b_3045633.html.

Abby Zimet, "Air Force Sexual Assault Prevention Chief Arrested for . . . Sexual Assault," Common Dreams, May 6, 2013, http://www.commondreams.org/further/2013/05/06-3.

Kevin Baron, "Air Force Fights Sexual Assault with Lip Balm, Hand Sanitizer, Breath Mints," *Foreign Policy*, April 24, 2013, http://e-ring.foreignpolicy.com/posts/2013/04/24/air_force_fights_sexual_assault_with_lip_balm_hand_sanitizer_breath_mints

Kumar Ramanathan , "What The Military Is Doing To Address Its Sexual Assault Crisis," *ThinkProgress*, June 14, 2013, http://thinkprogress.org/security/2013/06/14/2150351/military-address-sexual-assault.

Censored 2012 #3

Obama Authorizes International Assassination Campaign

SUMMARY: Advancing a policy set forth by the George W. Bush administration, the Obama administration created an "international assassination program" to carry out "targeted killings" of suspected terrorists. Under this program, the president has authorized the high-profile killing of Osama bin Laden, as well as the killings of US citizens, such as Anwar al-Awlaki. The Obama administration has gone even further by leading covert drone wars in Pakistan, Yemen, and Somalia.

UPDATE: Despite coverage from both corporate and independent media outlets, the Obama administration's targeted killing program remains shrouded in secrecy. In January 2013, a federal judge dismissed a parallel Freedom of Information Act (FOIA) lawsuit, by the

American Civil Liberties Union (ACLU) and the *New York Times*, that would have required the government to disclose documents that justify with evidence the targeted killing of US citizen Anwar al-Awlaki. Judge Colleen McMahon stated in response to her ruling, "I can find no way around the thicket of laws and precedents that effectively allow the executive branch of our government to proclaim as perfectly lawful certain actions that seem on their face incompatible with our Constitution and laws while keeping the reasons for their conclusion a secret." Both the ACLU and *New York Times* appealed this decision, while the ACLU filed another FOIA lawsuit requesting information to be released on who and how many people have been killed in targeted drone strikes. The number is currently estimated to be around 4,000 casualties.

On February 4, 2013, NBC News published a "white paper" leaked by the Department of Justice, which meant to give legal justification for the US government to carry out the extrajudicial killing of a US citizen. The document, which is not an official legal memo, offers the broad explanation that a citizen can be targeted if "an informed, high-level official" determines the person to be "an imminent threat," "capture is infeasible," and the killing is carried out within "applicable law of war principles." More examples of the white paper's vague language include the targeted individual being a part of al-Qaeda or "associated forces," with little definition of what an associated force is.

As a journalist whose sources include members of groups such as the Taliban, Chris Hedges is concerned that, under the guidelines of the DOJ white paper, the US might consider him included among those "associated" who could be targeted. The memo offers no geographical restrictions as to where these killings can occur. Furthermore, it effectively eliminates due process by stating there is no court that can evaluate the constitutional issues because "matters intimately related to foreign policy and national security are rarely proper subjects for judicial intervention." As a response to the overly broad language, *Mother Jones* reported that members of the House sent a letter to President Obama requesting further clarification on several points of the white paper.

On March 6, 2013, Senator Rand Paul of Kentucky performed a thirteen-hour filibuster during the nomination hearings on John

Brennan's appointment to become director of the CIA. Paul sought to encourage the Obama administration to release information concerning its drone program. The next day, Paul stated that he had received the desired information from the White House. On Fox News, he read a brief letter of response from Attorney General Eric Holder, which stated, "It has come to my attention that you have now asked an additional question: 'Does the President have the authority to use a weaponized drone to kill an American not engaged in combat on American soil?' The answer to that question is no." Attorney General Holder's response in effect further stalled the corporate media's coverage of the topic.

Then, on March 10, 2013, a lengthy *New York Times* article chronicled the events leading to the Obama administration's decision to kill Anwar al-Awlaki. Citing interviews with legal and counterterrorism officials, the report described a decade of investigation of al-Awlaki by the FBI, alleging that he "was clearly a direct plotter, no longer just a dangerous propagandist," and which concluded by declaring that al-Awlaki posed sufficient threat to US security that "his constitutional rights did not bar the government from killing him without a trial."

The Times came under criticism for its coverage from multiple outlets, with Glenn Greenwald in the *Guardian* stating that the article only "summarizes the unverified justifications" of officials, and expressing concern that the *Times*' account allowed government officials to present evidence after the fact without having "done the same thing in a court of law prior to killing him." The ACLU and Center for Constitutional Rights called the report "the latest in a series of one-sided, selective disclosures that prevent meaningful public debate and legal or even political accountability for the government's killing program, including its use against citizens."

While the issue of drone strikes is now covered by the corporate media, the issue has still oft been framed in ways that do not highlight the many civilian deaths associated with the program, or what appear to be clear violations of due process. In President Obama's national security speech on May 23, 2013, which corporate media covered extensively, he stated that America could not be on a permanent war footing, and that the government needed to close Guantánamo, curtail drone strikes, and have more oversight of such matters. Conservatives decried the talk as a "victory for terrorists," while many liberals tried to support the president's strong reformist rhetoric. Meanwhile, ACLU executive director Anthony Romero's remarks were covered in some independent online sources, but not much was covered elsewhere besides cursory mentions on the *Washington Post* blog and in *USA Today*. Romero remained skeptical of Obama's claims and added,

> To the extent the speech signals an end to signature strikes, recognizes the need for congressional oversight, and restricts the use of drones to threats against the American people, the developments on targeted killings are promising. Yet the president still claims broad authority to carry out targeted killings far from any battlefield, and there is still insufficient transparency. We continue to disagree fundamentally with the idea that due process requirements can be satisfied without any form of judicial oversight by regular federal courts.

SOURCES:

"Court Dismisses Most of FOIA Lawsuit on Targeted Killings of U.S. Citizens," American Civil Liberties Union, January 2, 2013, http://www.aclu.org/national-security/court-dismisses-most-foia-lawsuit-targeted-killings-us-citizens.

Adam Liptak, "Secrecy of Memo on Drone Killing is Upheld," *New York Times*, January 2, 2013, http://www.nytimes.com/2013/01/03/us/judge-rules-memo-on-targeted-killing-can-remain-secret.html.

Martin Michael, "Obama Signs 2013 NDAA into Law, Preventing Gitmo Closure," *Mint Press News*, January 5, 2013, http://www.mintpressnews.com/federal-judge-permanently-strikes-down-ndaa-provision-upholds-previous-rulings/.

Michael Isikoff, "Justice Department Memo Reveals Legal Case for Drone Strikes on Americans," NBC News, February 4, 2013, http://openchannel.nbcnews.com/_news/2013/02/04/16843014-justice-department-memo-reveals-legal-case-for-drone-strikes-on-americans?lite.

Jameel Jaffer, interview with Amy Goodman, "Kill List Exposed: Leaked Obama Memo Show Assassination of U.S. Citizens 'Has No Geographic Limit,'" *Democracy Now!*, February 5, 2013, http://www.democracynow.org/2013/2/5/kill_list_exposed_leaked_obama_memo.

Adam Serwer, "Obama Targeted Killing Document: If We Do It, It's Not Illegal," *Mother Jones*, February 5, 2013, http://www.motherjones.com/mojo/2013/02/obama-targeted-killing-white-paper-drone-strikes.

Carrie Dan, "Rand Paul Gets His Answer," NBC News, March 7, 2013, http://firstread.nbcnews.com/_news/2013/03/07/17226153-rand-paul-gets-his-answer.

Department of Justice White Paper, "Lawfulness of a Lethal Operation Directed Against a U.S. Citizen who is a Senior Operational Leader of Al-Qa'ida or an Associated Force," NBC News, http://msnbcmedia.msn.com/i/msnbc/sections/news/020413_DOJ_White_Paper.pdf.

Mark Mazetti, Charlie Savage, and Scott Shane, "How a U.S. Citizen Came to Be in America's Cross Hairs," *New York Times*, March 9, 2013, http://www.nytimes.com/2013/03/10/world/middleeast/anwar-al-awlaki-a-us-citizen-in-americas-cross-hairs.html.

"ACLU and CCR Comment on New York Times Article on Killing of Anwar al-Aulaqi", American Civil Liberties Union, March 10, 2013, http://www.aclu.org/national-security/aclu-and-ccr-comment-new-york-times-article-killing-anwar-al-aulaqi.

Glenn Greenwald, "The NYT and Obama Officials Collaborate to Prosecute Awlaki After He's Executed," *Guardian*, March 11, 2013, http://www.guardian.co.uk/commentisfree/2013/mar/11/nyt-obama-awlaki.

Jon Queally, "House Democrats Demand Answers from Obama about Drone Killings," Common Dreams, March 12, 2013, https://www.commondreams.org/headline/2013/03/12-3.

Peter Hart, "Killing a Citizen, NYT, Awlaki, and 'Muddying the Moral Clarity,'" Fairness and Accuracy in Reporting, March 12, 2013, http://www.fair.org/blog/2013/03/12/killing-a-citizen-nyt-awlaki-and-muddying-the-moral-clarity/.

Anthony D. Romero, "ACLU Comment on President's National Security Speech," America Civil Liberties Union, May 23, 2013, http://www.aclu.org/national-security/aclu-comment-presidents-national-security-speech.

Greg Sargent, "Obama's Speech: An Imperfect Effort to Reconcile National Security with American Values," *Washington Post*, Plum Line blog, May 23, 2013, http://www.washingtonpost.com/blogs/plum-line/wp/2013/05/23/obamas-speech-an-imperfect-effort-to-reconcile-national-security-with-american-values/.

David Jackson, "Obama Outlines Counterterrorism Policy," *USA Today*, May 23, 2013, http://www.usatoday.com/story/news/nation/2013/05/23/obama-counter-terrorism-speech-drones-guantanamo-bay/2354001/.

Notes

1. Aldous Huxley, "A Case of Voluntary Ignorance," *Esquire Magazine*, October 1956.
2. See Peter Phillips and Andrew Roth, eds., *Censored 2009*, (New York: Seven Stories, 2008), 20–25; and Peter Phillips and Mickey Huff, eds., *Censored 2010* (New York: Seven Stores, 2009), 121–122. For more on this theme, see the Censored News Cluster, "Technologies and Ecologies of War," in this volume. In fact, not only has the corporate media not addressed the significance of Iraqi casualty rates, organizations like the Associated Press have repeated grossly undercounted figures of 87,000, which dips well below even the most conservative counts of academic studies on the matter. So in this case, it's not just under reporting, it's willful ignorance coupled with misinformation at best, if not outright disinformation to mislead the American public.
3. Mickey Huff and Project Censored, *Censored 2012* (New York: Seven Stories, 2011), 46–48.
4. All previous Project Censored stories, and their original sources, are available online at http://www.projectcensored.org.
5. Bethania Palma Markus, "Welcome to the Freakshow: Media Gets Targeted by Obama, Discovers No One Cares Except the Media," *Counterpunch*, May 29, 2013, http://www.counterpunch.org/2013/05/29/media-gets-targeted-by-obama-administration-discovers-no-one-cares-except-the-media/.
6. Ken Klippenstein, "Holder's Justice: Worse than The AP Phone Scandal," *Counterpunch*, May 17, 2013, http://www.counterpunch.org/2013/05/17/worse-than-the-ap-phone-scandal/.
7. Glenn Greenwald, "NSA Collecting Phone Records of Millions of Verizon Customers Daily," *Guardian*, June 5, 2013, http://www.guardian.co.uk/world/2013/jun/06/nsa-phone-records-verizon-court-order. See also Glenn Greenwald, et al., "Edward Snowden: The Whistleblower behind the NSA Surveillance Revelations," *Guardian*, June 9, 2013, http://www.guardian.co.uk/world/2013/jun/09/edward-snowden-nsa-whistleblower-surveillance.
8. Jeffery Toobin, "Edward Snowden Is No Hero," *New Yorker*, June 10, 2013, http://www.newyorker.com/online/blogs/comment/2013/06/edward-snowden-nsa-leaker-is-no-hero.html.
9. Rainey Reitman, "Day One of the Manning Trial: How Public Will This Court Martial Be?" *Huffington Post*, June 4, 2013, http://www.huffingtonpost.com/rainey-reitman/; and James Bamford, "Manning Judge Rules Against RSN, Media Access," *Reader Supported News*, June 13, 2012, http://readersupportednews.org/news-section2/317-65/17913-focus-manning-judge-rules-against-rsn-media-access.

10. Matt Taibbi, "As Bradley Manning Trial Begins, Press Predictably Misses the Point," *Rolling Stone*, June 6, 2013, http://www.rollingstone.com/politics/blogs/taibblog/as-bradley-manning-trial-begins-press-predictably-misses-the-point-20130605. See also story #1 in ch. 1 of this volume.

11. Ibid.

12. One notable exception, it could be argued, is Denver Nicks, "Bradley Manning and Our Real Secrecy Problem," *Time*, June 5, 2013, http://ideas.time.com/2013/06/05/viewpoint-our-real-secrecy-problem/#ixzz2VNWKyjq8. Taibbi attacked Nicks's article in his article criticizing the corporate press, though it seems Nicks and Taibbi agree that the Manning case is about excessive government secrecy at the very least. However, a week later, the publication in question, *Time*, ran a cover story equating whistleblowers with spies. Taibbi's overall claim seems to stand up at least in terms of corporate media missing the point, and showing their bias, even if Nicks's piece had a different angle. See Kevin Gosztola, "*Time* Magazine Equates Whistleblowers with Spies in Cover Story on Snowden, Manning & Swartz," *FireDogLake*, June 13, 2013, http://dissenter.firedoglake.com/2013/06/13/time-magazine-equates-whistleblowers-with-spies-in-cover-story-on-snowden-manning-swartz/.

13. Gosztola, "TIME Magazine Equates Whistleblowers with Spies." See also story #1 in ch. 1 of this volume, as well as Brian Covert, "Censored News Cluster: Whistleblowers and Gag Laws."

14. Iain Thompson, "Anger Grows over the Death of Aaron Swartz," *Register*, January 13, 2013, http://www.theregister.co.uk/2013/01/13/anger_death_aaron_swartz.

15. See Andy Lee Roth, "Censored News Cluster: Iceland, the Power of Peaceful Revolution, and the Commons," and Brian Covert, "Censored News Cluster: Whistleblowers and Gag Laws," in ch. 1 of this volume.

16. Matt Taibbi, "Everything Is Rigged: The Biggest Price-Fixing Scandal Ever," *Rolling Stone*, April 25, 2013, http://www.rollingstone.com/politics/news/everything-is-rigged-the-biggest-financial-scandal-yet-20130425.

17. Ibid.

18. Matt Taibbi, "Everything is Rigged, Vol. 9,713: This Time, It's Currencies," *Rolling Stone*, Taibblog, June 13, 2013, http://www.rollingstone.com/politics/blogs/taibblog/everything-is-rigged-vol-9-713-this-time-its-currencies-20130613.

19. Samantha Wyatt, "Fox News Spent 4 Hours Covering IRS Hearing, 14 Minutes On Military Sexual Assault Hearing," Media Matters, June 5, 2013, http://mediamatters.org/research/2013/06/05/fox-news-spent-4-hours-covering-irs-hearing-14/194353.

CHAPTER 3

U Can't Touch This
Junk Food News, News Abuse Are
Off the Infotainment Charts!

Mickey Huff, Michael Kolbe, Nolan Higdon, Sam Park, Jennifer
Eiden, and Kimberly Soiero

*The waters are rising while we are dreaming of dancing
with the stars.*

—Walter Mosley[1]

*I do not mean to imply that television news deliberately
aims to deprive Americans of a coherent, contextual
understanding of their world. I mean to say that when
news is packaged as entertainment, that is the inevitable
result. And in saying that the television news show en-
tertains but does not inform, I am saying something far
more serious than that we are being deprived of authen-
tic information. I am saying we are losing our sense of
what it means to be well informed.*

—Neil Postman, *Amusing Ourselves to Death: Public Discourse in the Age of Show Business* (1985)

Thirty years ago, Project Censored founder, Dr. Carl Jensen, coined the
term Junk Food News. Jensen referred to the increased coverage of ut-
ter inanity as serious news as Junk Food, like Twinkies for the brain.
Around that same time, New York University media ecologist Neil
Postman published a seminal work—*Amusing Ourselves to Death: Pub-*

lic Discourse in the Age of Show Business.[2] In the book, Postman perhaps unwittingly yet presciently warned about what has grown to become our current bread and circus sideshow, made-for-reality TV faux news culture—comprised of deleterious distractions and distortions that produce dazed, disgruntled, and dismayed civic dilettantes in delirious denial about key issues of our time, about where we are heading as a society, and the eventual decline of American civilization.[3]

Since the 1980s, Project Censored has covered the growing and now normalized trend of Junk Food News, which Jensen began analyzing after news editors took umbrage at his critiques of the failures and possible censorship concerns related to the so-called "mainstream" press dating back to 1976. They claimed his cries of censorship were too harsh, that they had to use news judgment when deciding what to report.

Jensen thought that was a fair response. Therefore, during the early 1980s, he focused more on what the news media *were* covering, rather than what they may have been left out or censored. What he discovered was that the major news media were in fact systematically failing to report important stories to the public, not because they didn't have time, but because they exercised poor news judgment. They chose infotainment. This is especially the case on TV (to which well over half of Americans still turn for news, as we'll note in a moment). The fixation on the inane and titillating over the relevant and substantive has grown to dominate news coverage so much so, that this entire volume could be an expanded version of this chapter—chock-full of example after example.

These problems have not completely escaped public notice. The American public seems to be aware there is a problem with the news, but to mixed degrees. A recent Pew Research Center's Project for Excellence in Journalism's study, *State of the News Media 2013*, sheds some light on the news media landscape.[4] On one hand, the number of Americans who do not trust the major news sources, especially on TV, has risen.[5] Interestingly, at the same time, these same news outlets, especially on cable, are broadcasting more and more opinion journalism, not straight, factual reporting. MSNBC leads the way with an astonishing 85 percent of its airtime filled with opinion programming, with Fox and CNN trailing, but CNN was the only network of the three to have slightly more news reporting than opinion (54 to 46 percent). These studies suggest a possible factor in why nearly one-third of American news consumers are tuning out—they are not getting the quality of hard news in the quantity they once did.[6]

With a slightly different focus, another study by Public Policy Polling (PPP) found that among American voters, "there's only one source more Americans trust than distrust: PBS," in which 52 percent reported their trust.[7] This included all major TV network and cable news outlets. Furthermore, another Pew poll from 2011 found that "fully 66% say news stories often are inaccurate, 77% think that news organizations tend to favor one side, and 80% say news organizations are often influenced by powerful people and organizations."[8] Despite these figures, well over half of Americans still listed TV news as their main news source, and most claimed that while they distrusted news sources in general, the ones that *they* chose to view were somehow more accurate, exempt from their related broader criticism (as pointed out in the PPP study above).[9]

That said, it should be hard to ignore the link between Junk Food News and News Abuse and the erosion of public trust in news media. Our purpose is not to dwell on this problem, but to call attention to it in an intelligent and clever way, and to show readers not only how corporate news media are entertaining rather than informing us, but also how corporate media could be devoting time to covering issues published by independent news sources. In other words, the very type of news story Project Censored highlights in its Top 25 each year could be reported instead of the faux news of celebrity births and deaths, fad dances, and the outcomes of popular shows like *American Idol* or *The Voice*. We can be well informed by our news, or we can be well entertained. The choice is ours. We should choose wisely.

JUNK FOOD NEWS[10]

When a population becomes distracted by trivia, when cultural life is redefined as a perpetual round of entertainments, when serious public conversation becomes a form of baby-talk, when, in short, a people become an audience, and their public business a vaudeville act, then a nation finds itself at risk; culture-death is a clear possibility.

—Neil Postman, *Amusing Ourselves to Death: Public Discourse in the Age of Show Business* (1985)

Junk Food News: The Next Generation

The arrival of celebrity babies once again led the corporate media to hand out imaginary cigars for the superfluous entertainment class. Kim Kardashian, Drew Barrymore, Kate Middleton, and Snooki added to the cacophony of inane and useless information by bearing the next generation of junk food news spawn. However, none gained more media attention than the future heir to the Royal throne. CBS News, *The Huffington Post*, and Fox News devoted their energies to speculating over possible baby names, even consulting baby naming "experts." Internet traffic after news of the royal pregnancy crashed the royal couple's website.[11] The Junk Food News media frenzy even tragically led to the suicide of a nurse after shock jocks Mel Greig and Michael Christian of 2Day FM, masquerading as Queen Elizabeth II and Prince Charles, tricked her into divulging Kate Middleton's treatment for morning sickness.[12]

While the corporate media focused on celebrity births, the alternative media outlet Common Dreams reported that civilian deaths connected to terrorism are on the rise. Their account is based upon the findings of the Global Terrorism Index (GTI), produced by the Institute for Economics and Peace (IEP), located at the University of Maryland. In its attempt to analyze the economic and social dimensions of terrorism in countries, the GTI found that the areas where the United States military has most actively engaged terrorists have experienced an increase in terrorist activity and civilian deaths. According to IEP founder and executive chairman Steve Killelea, "Iraq accounts for about a third of all terrorist deaths over the last decade, and Iraq, Pakistan and Afghanistan account for over 50 percent of fatalities." Critics of the report argue that it contains a narrow definition of terrorism, and fails to include state-supported violence against civilians. The GTI report defines terrorism as the "threatened or actual use of illegal force and violence by a non-state actor to attain a political, economic, religious, or social goal through fear, coercion, or intimidation."[13] However, linguist, political activist, and longtime critic of American foreign policy Noam Chomsky offered an alternative definition suggesting that the "wanton killing of innocent civilians is terrorism, not a war against terrorism."[14]

This is certainly a far more newsworthy topic for discussion, one we as a free people ought to be having. Instead, we get celebrity birth reporting and related shenanigans around the clock, which literally are driving some people to death. That said, we likely won't see purveyors of such junk food news up on terrorism charges any time soon.

Daze of Plunder

The corporate media love a messy celebrity split. This past year, Katy Perry and Russell Brand, Arnold Schwarzenegger and Maria Shriver, Jennifer Lopez and Marc Anthony, Justin Bieber and Selena Gomez, Al and Tipper Gore, and Kris Humphries and Kim Kardashian, ended their relationships. After five years of marriage, actor Tom Cruise and actress Katie Holmes divorced. Celebrity reporters and gossip columnists flooded the media with an overabundance of rumors and speculation to explain the breakup.[15] Despite media speculation, Holmes did not publicly charge the couple's religion—Scientology—as the cause of the divorce. Nevertheless, the media invented a bevy of stories in relation to the Cruise-Holmes split spanning over seven months that included "Katie's Escape Plan," Scientology's influence on the couple's child, the divorce settlement, or gossip over Cruise's latest romantic exploits. *Days of Thunder* star Cruise couldn't get a reprieve from the media storm.

While breakups dominated many corporate media headlines even outside of entertainment news programs, a story concerning the London Interbank Offered Rate (Libor), which impacts billions of consumers of financial products and taxpayers, went underreported. Among those bothering to cover the Libor scandal, instead of celebrity divorces, there is a consensus that the situation is the largest financial scandal of recent years. Libor refers to the interest rate for which international banks may borrow from one another. It has a direct effect upon the borrowing costs for a wide array of financial products, including home mortgages, car loans, credit cards, and student loans among others. Additionally, it sets prices on the derivative market, totaling over $750 trillion.[16]

The scandal began when investigators discovered that banks were understating borrowing costs. This resulted in higher prices for consumers and greater profits for banks. However, regulators at the Federal Reserve Bank and the Bank of England suspected the underreporting as early as 2007.[17] In the end, the British banking giant Barclays settled for $450 million in a plea bargain with British and American authorities for their manipulation of Libor rates and the resignations of top bank officials, including the chief executive of Barclays, Robert E. Diamond. In an effort to recover costs to the city due to Libor manipulation, Baltimore, Maryland, has filed a law suit against sixteen banks, including Charles Schwab, Barclays, Royal Bank of Scotland Group, HSBC, Bank of America, Citigroup, JPMorgan Chase, UBS, and Deutsche Bank.[18]

The corporate media presented some coverage via the Internet, but not much more at the time the scandal was really breaking (even though Bloomberg reported that Barclays announced LIBOR misstatements some four years earlier). Ben Dimiero and Rob Savillo of Media Matters for America reported that during the period between June 27 through July 12, 2012, television networks ABC, NBC, CNN, Fox News, and MSNBC spent nearly ninety-one minutes reporting on the Tom-Kat divorce, while the Libor scandal received only a miniscule twelve minutes of coverage.[19] As Wall Street and Washington sloganeer that the banks are "too big to fail, too big to jail," maybe we need some celebrity big bank breakups for financial scandals the magnitude of Libor to attract the big media attention they truly deserve.

"Kill the Gays Law?" Corporate Media Coverage Won't Touch This!

South Korean songwriter, rapper, dancer, and producer Park Jae-Sang, or, as he is known on stage, "Psy," became a junk news sensation over the past year. He is best known for his international hit song "Gangnam Style," which became the most-watched video in the history of YouTube with nearly one trillion views.[20] The video's success even earned the singer a trip to the White House to meet President Obama.[21] Corporate media–induced controversy struck Psy when health officials in England issued a warning to middle-aged men to avoid overexerting themselves, after a forty-six-year-old Psy fan with a heart condition collapsed while performing the equally popular signature dance that accompanies Psy's hit song.[22]

After the tragedy, the singer issued an apology to the family "for any pain caused."[23]

Corporate media pundits previously took offense to Psy's 2004 performance of "Dear American," which expressed criticism of the "war on terror" and the murder of two Korean schoolgirls by US artillery. Just as conservative media pundits had objected to the White House invitation extended by the Obama administration to rapper and poet Common, they also petitioned to bar the Korean rapper from performing there, prompting Psy to issue an apology for the nearly ten-year-old performance criticizing US actions.[24] Despite the controversy, Psy became a media darling and performed with former rap/pop sensation MC Hammer at the American Music Awards. They performed Hammer's 1990 mega-hit "U Can't Touch This," which dominated the airwaves and was part of the New Year's celebration in New York's Times Square.

While the corporate media fretted over Psy and celebrated the return of MC Hammer, Equality Matters reported that between October 31 and December 5, 2012, corporate news outlets CNN and Fox News devoted more time to "Gangnam Style" than the renewal of Uganda's "Kill the Gays" law.[25] The law bans intercourse with same-sex, underaged, or disabled persons, and allows the death penalty as punishment for offenders. The law found little attention in the American corporate press, but plenty of coverage in alternative and foreign media.[26] Regarding the bill, Ugandan speaker of parliament Rebecca Kadaga said that the country had "no space for gays." In a ghastly interpretation of the holiday spirit, she vowed to push the bill into law "as a Christmas gift."[27] For those looking for more egregiously open and hostile, murderously intolerant, in-your-face, homophobic policies by governments around the world—U Can't Touch This (though sadly, there are several other countries trying).

Triumph of the Swill: Sailing the Seas for Junk Food News

The overabundance of corporate news media coverage surrounding a cruise ship that was stranded without power adrift in the Gulf of Mexico left many angry, shocked, and even . . . rudderless. The 102,000-ton Carnival Cruise ship, aptly named "Triumph," lost power after an engine room fire.[28] There were no injuries reported from the 3,143 passengers and 1,086 crew members. The liner was ultimately towed by tugboat to Mobile, Alabama.[29]

Corporate media outlets, and CNN in particular, offered in-depth and lengthy coverage of the inconveniences and less than luxurious conditions the passengers and crew endured. Most notably, they had to do without air conditioning, elevators, toilets, and kitchen equipment to prepare hot meals. The luxury liner was temporarily unable to provide fresh water. Passengers dealt with the privations by defecating in plastic bags, eating cold meals, and sleeping upon the deck of the ship. Sewage swill sloshed along Triumph's hallways and passengers had to wait in long lines for meals. CNN provided a forum for passengers to recount their own personal horrors of the experience.[30] CNN posted over fourteen stories and videos on their website and dedicated five reporters to the story.[31] They even ran uninterrupted coverage, something previously reserved for events like 9/11. Understandably, CNN drew the ire of more serious reporters as well as *The Daily Show*'s Jon Stewart, who charged that the absurd amount of coverage was an attempt to boost the network's sinking ratings. Maybe the joke was on Stewart as the endless (and mostly uneventful) coverage of the so-called "Cruise from Hell" doubled CNN's rating for the week.[32]

While passengers facing "first world problems" received an abundance of coverage, poor Americans found themselves shipwrecked. Compromises between the Obama administration and Republicans under the rubric of the Budget Control Act of 2011 received little coverage. The backroom agreement called for infinitesimal cuts in military spending while calling for a whopping $500 billion cut in domestic spending (which is about two-thirds of the Pentagon's annual budget). The proposed cuts will lead to the loss of food stamps for an estimated 600,000 women and children; the loss of government-financed housing for some 100,000 formerly homeless people; the elimination of early education slots for as many as 70,000 poor children; the elimination of federal support for 7,200 school employees who serve special-needs children, and who inspect for job or food safety, forcing unpaid furloughs; and finally, the reduction by $500 million of federal loans to small businesses.[33] There are plenty of real castaways in America who deserve our attention and concern, not the ones being towed on a luxury cruise liner, to the unblinking eyes and misplaced gasps of corporate media's self-proclaimed "Most Trusted Name in News."

NEWS ABUSE

[M]ost of our daily news is inert, consisting of information that gives us something to talk about but cannot lead to any meaningful action.

—Neil Postman, *Amusing Ourselves to Death: Public Discourse in the Age of Show Business* (1985)

Former Project Censored director Dr. Peter Phillips created the category of News Abuse over a decade ago. Phillips differentiated between Junk Food News, stating that News Abuse was distorted reporting about otherwise serious issues. Phillips suggested that many stories that ended up taking on the veneer of a Junk Food News story in fact began as legitimate topics for news coverage. The news media can lose sight of the original thesis of a story, miss or distort important facts that alter the meaning of a report, or give far too much attention to a story than the subject's overall societal significance merits. What is lacking most often in News Abuse stories is a substantive topic or subject context and history. Because they address serious, newsworthy issues, News Abuse stories linger in the public mind, but in a skewed or erroneous form. News Abuse stories can also take a turn into the sensational, the irrelevant, the trivial, the mundane, or worse—they become a form of propaganda.[34]

Phillips's message was most underscored whenever news media coverage missed the point of newsworthy issues. This year, our examples include how Sesame Street again became part of our national political discourse as a major party candidate used a fictitious character to wage ideological conflict in an election. The election and candidate were clearly newsworthy, but the media's focus on Big Bird rather than on more substantive issues in the election was News Abuse. And so it goes. From sex scandals in the CIA distracted from their arming the al-Qaeda-linked Libyan (and Syrian) opposition; Americans pleaded to save Twinkies (real junk food) instead of real people's pensions and jobs—here are this year's examples of News Abuse in action.

Saint Elmo's Fire: Sesame Street Under Attack . . . Again

In 2012, PBS and *Sesame Street* found themselves in the conservative crosshairs yet again. During the electoral debates, Republican candidate Mitt Romney targeted Big Bird when he suggested the elimination of the subsidy to PBS as a means to reduce government spending. The statement caused a flurry of activity within social media as people attempted to rally support for Big Bird and PBS. The incident gathered even more momentum when mainstream media outlets reprinted a letter by eight-year-old Alabama resident Cecelia Crawford, who wrote: "When I grow up I'm going to get married and I want my kids to watch it so do not cut it off. . . . You find something else to cut off!"[35] In response, media pundits suggested the letter was a forgery, while the Obama campaign capitalized on it by posting on the web: "Save Big Bird! Vote Democratic."

While Big Bird and Sesame Street served as a bloody shirt to rally the respective Republican and Democratic bases, the corporate media became transfixed upon sex allegations surrounding Kevin Clash. Clash was the voice and puppeteer for Elmo on *Sesame Street*. He testified before congress as Elmo in support of children's music programs. Clash, who is gay, was accused by a former lover of having sexual intercourse with him while he was a minor. The accuser ultimately recanted and the charges were deemed false. However, three additional accusations surfaced from former lovers seeking financial compensation.[36] Clash's accusers admitted that the sex was consensual, though they had been underage. They are currently seeking damages ranging from $75,000 to $5 million.[37] The allegations ended Clash's twenty-four-year run with *Sesame Street*.

The story became a corporate media distraction from stories that matter to a nation that claims to support democratic ideals. Conservatives argued that Clash was proof that the Democratic–supported PBS undermined "American Values."[38] News outlets such as *TMZ*, Fox News, CBS News, the *New York Daily News*, as well as the *Huffington Post*, immediately fixated upon the story. It was ranked by the *Huffington Post* as one of the top crime stories for 2012—although no criminal charges had actually been filed by the time of this writing.[39]

Meanwhile, stories of environmental importance went unnoticed by the corporate media during the Elmo fire, but not in the alternative press. Independent media outlet Common Dreams reported that, in return for a waiver of future prosecution, British Petroleum (BP) agreed to pay $4.5 billion in fines and pled guilty to fourteen felony and misdemeanor charges as a result of the Deep Water Horizon oil rig disaster in the Gulf of Mexico. The "spill," as it was erroneously dubbed by the corporate media, gushed 4.9 million barrels of oil into the Gulf over a three-month period (some argue even more, not to mention the damage of the chemical Corexit that was dumped to "clean up" the mess in violation of Environmental Protection Agency rules).[40] The incident also killed eleven workers and has seriously damaged the Gulf region over the long term, impacting the thousands—and possibly millions—that relied on the Gulf to make a living, or were simply unfortunate enough to be living on the coast where toxins linger. The Department of Justice found the company guilty of one misdemeanor count under the Clean Water Act and another under the Migratory Bird Treaty Act. Finally, BP was found guilty of one felony count for obstruction of Congress for misleading Congress about the amount of oil that had surged into the Gulf.[41]

Another story ignored during the Elmo fallout was the release of scientific findings that waters around the Fukushima Daiichi Nuclear Power Plant continue to remain toxic. The water around the plant contains levels of caesium-137 at around 1,000 becquerels. Caesium-137 is a radioactive isotope commonly used in nuclear reactors and weaponry. It is a highly problematic and virulent substance because it is easily soluble in water. These findings were presented at the Fukushima Ocean Impacts Symposium at the University of Tokyo.[42]

It's too bad that, like Sesame Street, the corporate news is often literally brought to us by the letters B and P, as in BP, who like many in the oil and energy sector are major advertising clients (read: revenue source) for corporate media, which in turn played down BP's role in the Gulf oil ecocide for which they were responsible. Corporate media also failed to emphasize that the amount BP was fined was actually less than the corporation's profits for one quarter of one year. As for Fukushima—a lingering disaster that may have an epic and growing legacy as trouble still mounts—the corporate media in the US can't be bothered. For most Americans, it's Fuku who? They've moved on to the next distraction.

From Benghazi with Love: The Scandal of Making a Scandal

The year's most widely covered sex scandal involved former director of the Central Intelligence Agency (CIA), General David Petraeus, and his biographer Paula Broadwell. As commander of forces in Iraq, supporters of General Petraeus, including the media, hailed him as an innovator and the "best general since Eisenhower."[43] (And yes, Petraeus was the head of a spy and secret-keeping agency and couldn't keep a secret about his own affairs—maybe that is news after all.) Petraeus's resignation came upon the heels of the September 11 and 12, 2012, attacks upon the American consulate and the CIA annex in Benghazi, Libya, in which four people were killed, including US Ambassador J. Christopher Stevens. According to noncorporate sources, Stevens was, in fact, the US liaison to the al-Qaeda-linked Libyan opposition.[44] Moreover, Stevens allegedly facilitated the shipment of arms to the insurgents fighting against the government in Syria.[45]

Media outlets reported that the affair was uncovered by the Federal Bureau of Investigation (FBI) while investigating complaints that Broadwell had sent threatening e-mails to socialite and military groupie Jill Kelley, whom she suspected of having an affair with Petraeus as well. Kelley, who has been dubbed "The Tampa Kardashian," was also implicated in charges of sexual misconduct involving former Afghanistan commander General John Allen.[46] In addition, there have been allegations that Broadwell attempted to gain access to Petraeus's e-mails and may have been privy to other classified information.[47] It appears as though Broadwell has confirmed these suspicions herself; during a speech at the University of Denver, she claimed that the attack upon the CIA annex was an attempt to rescue captured Libyan militia members.[48]

At the outset of the September 11 and 12, 2012, attacks, the Obama administration stumbled to find explanations, falsely claiming that the attacks were a protest against an anti-Islamic video made in the United States and posted on the Internet; an explanation initially signed off on by Petraeus. Eventually, however, the Obama administration, the CIA, and Petraeus concluded that the attacks were indeed perpetrated by an element related to al-Qaeda. Republicans quickly seized upon the administration's lies in an attempt to derail Obama's re-election campaign. Only later was it revealed that the attacks were carried out by Ansar al-Shariam, a militia group that is sympathetic to al-Qaeda, and allegedly materially funded by the United States.[49]

In a half-hearted effort to investigate the causes and failures surrounding the Benghazi attacks, the Accountability Review Board (ARB) issued a report that placed the preponderance of the blame upon the State Department for the security lapses that preceded the attacks upon the American consulate. National security officials failed to properly assess the escalation of violence and disorder in eastern Libya that witnessed "a string of assassinations, an attack upon a British envoy's motorcade and the explosion of a bomb outside the American Mission."[50] The inquiry found that the State Department had relied too heavily upon inadequately trained personal and local militias. Moreover, the ARB report found that State Department officials had appallingly denied requests for more security by personnel stationed at the American Embassy in Tripoli.[51] The report concluded by charging "systemic failures and leadership and management deficiencies at senior levels within . . ." the bureaus of Diplomatic Security and Near Eastern Affairs within the State Department, which led to a security environment "that was inadequate for Benghazi and grossly inadequate to deal with the attack that took place."[52] A critic of the ARB report, Ronda Hauben of Global Research, charged that it failed to shed light on the Benghazi attacks.[53] First, she argued the division of the report into "classified" and "unclassified" versions could only serve to obfuscate any attempt to discover the truth. Second, the ARB report did not mention the CIA's role, which she contended was "the crucial question that any legitimate investigation into the situation must explore."[54]

The corporate press focused on the subsequent political firestorm surrounding Petraeus's resignation, and thereby created a media environment that failed to cover the real story of the Benghazi attacks. Barry Grey of the World Socialist Web Site explained: "The attack on the US consulate and the CIA annex exposed the fact that Washington had financed and helped arm al-Qaeda–linked Islamist and jihadist forces in its bloody 2011 war to overthrow Muammar Gaddafi and install a more pliant regime."[55] The government and media cover-up of the CIA's role in the Benghazi attacks has screened the agency's actions from the eyes of US citizens and the aided overthrow of sovereign leaders. This no doubt diminishes the standing of the Unites States in the global community and erodes fundamental American ideals. This is also further evidence of the scandal of manufacturing a scandal in order to distract from another scandal at work in Washington DC. One might also say this is obfuscation writ large.

While the "mainstream" corporate media inflated the Petraeus affair beyond all comprehension, avoiding more crucial issues at hand in Libya, it also ultimately obscured the ongoing and deplorable treatment of women in the military (see *Censored* story #16 in this volume), which has eventually found some coverage due to a congressional inquiry into allegations of sexual assault at Joint Base San Antonio–Lackland. The scandal has been labeled "the largest sex scandal in military history" and drew comparisons to the "Tail-hook Scandal." As a result of an Air Force inquiry into the allegations, six instructors have been court martialed for adultery, rape, and conducting unprofessional relationships and nine others and are awaiting court martial. Moreover, the Air Force found thirty-two military training instructors allegedly engaged in inappropriate or coercive sexual relationships with fifty-nine recruits and airmen at Lackland. The Pentagon estimates that 19,000 cases of sexual assault occur each year with only a few thousand actually reported. Out of the incidents reported, only 200 resulted in court martial.[56]

A recent article by the Associated Press reported that 30 percent of military commanders who have lost their jobs in the last eight years have been due to various charges of sexual misconduct that range from harassment to adultery to improper relationships.[57] News Abuse stories don't only function as obfuscators regarding their own subject matter, they also can function as broader distractions from breaking news developments and revelations about other very important issues.

Corporate Media Ignore Worker Rights . . . Claim Twinkie Defense

Some notable celebrity deaths of the last year included Michael Clarke Duncan, Neil Armstrong, Phyllis Diller, Gore Vidal, Sherman Helmsley, Ernest Borgnine, and Andy Griffith. However, the corporate media demonstrated considerably more *grief* reporting regarding the bankruptcy of Hostess and the subsequent loss of a beloved snack icon—the Twinkie. Television pundits on *Good Morning America* anticipated the "Chocodile" tears of millions of school children, and mourned while they stuffed their faces with their last memorial Twinkies. Jesse Thomas, a contributor to *Forbes Magazine* online, echoed similar sentiments, lamenting: "This announcement is a travesty for pre-packaged desserts and kindergarten lunch-boxes across America."[58]

Yet, not all media outlets grieve in the same fashion. Those with a pro-corporate bias such as Fox News (News Corp.) and ABC News (Disney) vented their rage at labor, suggesting that disputes between management and labor ultimately contributed to the company's bankruptcy. Fox's *America's Newsroom*, and ABC News repeated statements issued by Hostess that placed "[blame upon] a worker's strike for crippling their ability to make and deliver their products."[59] Some in the corporate media noted Hostess's inability to adapt to a changing marketplace, yet did so with a hint of derision; though acknowledging that Americans have been attempting to be more conscious of the nutritional content of foods they eat, *Forbes Magazine* labeled the trend a "health food craze."[60] And the *Huffington Post* speculated that "even a repackaged Twinkie would be hard to sell to the current generation of health-obsessed parents."[61]

Preposterously, some angry bloggers bitterly remarked, "The Twinkie was Michelle Obama's Osama bin laden," in a thinly veiled jab at the first lady's unveiling of the new United States Department of Agriculture's (USDA) nutritional guide titled "My Plate."[62] Few in the corporate media reported that Hostess initially filed for bankruptcy in 2004. At that time, the company had cited "declining sales, high food costs, excess capacity and worker benefit expenses," as contributing factors to its difficulties. In response, the company closed some bakeries and restructured union contracts; however, this did not mitigate the problem of its debt, which totaled nearly $800 million. Members of the Bakery, Confectionary, Tobacco Workers, and Grain Millers International Union, expressed little surprise (unlike those in the press) by the company's second bankruptcy filing and even "accused the company of having 'frittered away' union concessions, wasting money on a corporate headquarters move, according to court papers."[63]

The Huffington Post reported that panic-stricken Hostess-philes desperately bought up remaining supplies of various Hostess products on eBay, while other more enterprising individuals sold cartons of unopened Twinkies as a vanishing piece of Americana for as much as five hundred dollars.[64] As it turned out, the panic surrounding the Hostess bankruptcy and the beloved filling-stuffed polystyrene snack was premature. The judge hearing the bankruptcy proceeding urged both the union and Hostess into mediation, a measure that may yet lengthen the companies' shelf life. Moreover, Hostess has claimed that several other companies have expressed interest in the brand.[65]

While the corporate media offered coverage of overpaid television pundits stuffing their faces with Twinkies, poorly paid and mistreated Walmart employees attempted a strike against the world's largest retailer. Employees at several locations including: Chicago, Milwaukee, Washington DC, Dallas, Los Angeles, Sacramento, San Francisco, and Seattle walked off the job for the first time in Walmart's fifty-year history.[66] While the strike *has* received coverage in the corporate press, there has been a noticeable bias toward covering the management's perspective along with profits—all while the retailer logged record Black Friday sales.

According to their website, Walmart employs over two million employees in twenty-seven countries. Walmart has supported the unionization of its employees in foreign countries such as China, yet has fought unionization within the United States. In the past, Walmart's relationships with its labor force have been strained, to say the least. Former abuses against employees have included violation of child labor laws, failure to pay back wages and overtime, and the employment of undocumented workers. Walmart has been the focus of many studies, books, and documentaries that have all attempted to expose the unethical business practices of the company as well as its negative impacts on communities. Walmart has attempted to silence the most recent push to hold the company accountable for its treatment of its employees. And, as outlined by Paddy Ryan on *Daily Kos*,

> Walmart, one of the richest corporations in the world, refuses to pay its employees a livable wage or provide any form of decent healthcare, increasing reliance on government as-

sistance, and the need for a social safety net. . . . Walmart's poverty wages force employees to rely on $2.66 billion in government help every year, or about $420,000 per store. In state after state, Walmart employees are the top recipients of Medicaid. As many as 80 percent of workers in Walmart stores use food stamps.[67]

Possibly further driving the ire of workers is the fact that Walmart's CEO makes $16,826 an hour, while the typical Walmart worker makes $13,650 a year. But at least that's not quite a full-blown two-to-one/year-to-hour wage ratio like in the late nineteenth century under the Rockefeller monopoly, so, it's an obvious improvement for workers, right?[68]

The fight for unionization at Walmart is long-standing and complex. Lawyers for Walmart filed an injunction against the United Food and Commercial Workers International Union (UFCW) in response to the striking workers. UFCW aided the creation of the 2010 Organization United for Respect at Walmart, or OUR Walmart. The fledgling organization has called for protests at one thousand Walmart stores during the Black Friday shopping weekend.[69] Striking employees charge that the company not only manipulates hours and benefits, leading to low wages and part-time status, but they allege that it also discriminates against women and minorities. OUR Walmart filed a claim with the National Labor Relations Board "that Walmart's human resources department violated the National Labor Relations Act by instructing store managers to threaten workers with termination and disciplinary actions if they participate in the strikes."[70] Nonetheless, in spite of the controversy it has generated, Walmart has been ranked by *Forbes Magazine* as the twenty-fourth most powerful brand. Its annual sales exceed over $450 billion.[71]

Corporate media has demonstrated a noticeable bias toward management in their coverage; Fox News questioned Walmart's ability to control its striking workers. Moreover, Fox News expressed worry that this latest labor dispute (notice it isn't referred to as a management dispute) would interrupt sales in what has become a traditional post-Thanksgiving rush for unnecessary consumer goods. Nonetheless, Fox praised Walmart for "taking on" unions and even ran a segment sponsored by Walmart that defended the company against striking workers.[72] Regardless of the publicity surrounding the desperate situation of Walmart employees, fewer than 1 percent of the company's workforce participated in the strike. Unfortunately, very few shoppers were informed enough, or cared enough, to be able to stand up for impoverished workers and resist the lure of cheap consumer goods.[73] Meanwhile, in the US, CEO pay and compensation packages can go as high as 1,795 to 1 compared to average workers at companies like J. C. Penney. Abercrombie and Fitch's CEO made 1,640 to 1 compared to the average retail worker in the company. All of this indicates that there is some money to go around that could pay more wages and benefits, and could lead to more full-time employment, but the corporate media often fail to come to that conclusion.[74]

With All Eyes on Marriage Equality, Monsanto Slips Under the Radar

Two same-sex marriage Supreme Court cases began on March 26, 2013. The first case was *Hollingsworth v. Perry*, which challenges the constitutionality of California's 2008 ballot initiative Proposition 8. Proposition 8 defines marriage to be between a man and a woman and does not allow same-sex couples to legally marry. Opponents of Proposition 8 argue it to be unconstitutional on the basis that it violates the Equal Protection Clause of the Fourteenth Amendment. The next day, the Supreme Court heard arguments for *United States v. Windsor*, disputing the Defense of Marriage Act (DOMA). This case claims DOMA to be unconstitutional because it allows legally married same-sex couples to be treated differently under federal law than opposite-sex couples, such as denying them federal benefits.[75] Both cases are very significant, have been a long time coming, and have the potential to be a big step towards equal rights for same-sex couples.

Coverage of these cases is key, and there has certainly been media coverage from most major news outlets. Many devoted extensive amounts of time to the court proceedings, including live coverage, numerous reports, and transcripts after the fact. However, with the time given to this issue, some reports deteriorated to News Abuse, including the usual partisan battles and "who just came out supporting/opposing gay marriage" focus. The *Los Angeles Times* kept the public up to date on the latest celebrity "tweeting" about the Supreme Court cases,[76] while CNN chronicled the most interesting signs and costumes seen outside the courtroom.[77]

With so much focus on the Proposition 8 and DOMA Supreme Court cases, little attention was given to President Obama signing spending bill HR 933, which included the "Monsanto Protection Act." Hidden in the Agricultural Appropriations bill under the modest title of "Farmer Assurance Provision," the Monsanto Protection Act "strips federal courts of the authority to immediately halt the planting and sale of genetically modified seed crops regardless of any consumer health concerns."[78] With neither certainty over the safety of genetically modified crops nor a labeling system in place, it is one more step backward for food safety and justice. And with the public's eyes on the Supreme Court, directed by the corporate media's infatuation with culture war issues, the act was hardly even noticed. While the public should be informed about marriage equality, they should be just as concerned about the quality and safety of the food they are eating, and about which big corporations are literally writing themselves into the law so they can be shielded from any future liability.

As Censored 2014 went to press, the Supreme Court of the United States ruled on DOMA, setting the stage for marital equality. While this is a major step forward for civil rights, people should also pay very close attention to the independent press to see what else may be missed, from the court's rulings on voting rights and the US prosecution resting their case against Bradley Manning to the protests going on in Turkey and the military coup overthrowing the Morsi government in Egypt. Bait and switch is an old game, and the major news media should be able to cover more than just a few stories at a time in detail, with context and clarity, and for the betterment of the public.

(Lack of) Election Coverage 2012

The year 2012 marked the spectacle of another US presidential election season. Corporate media coverage of the entire election process was akin to political theater: dripping with pageantry, oozing with canned patriotism, lacking any real objectivity or critical perspective. All major news media outlets were on board to cover former Massachusetts governor and Republican candidate Mitt Romney, and current president and Democratic candidate Barack Obama throughout the campaign trail, cataloguing and remarking upon their every move, however irrelevant.

The country watched three presidential debates—which are controlled by a private corporation run by Democrats and Republicans, called the Commission on Presidential Debates—between the Republican and Democratic candidates only, along with one debate between the two vice presidential candidates, as they discussed topics including the economy, healthcare, and the role of the federal government, among others. While the public focused on coverage of two candidates arguing two sides of an official narrative, along the way providing entertainment with oddities from "Big Bird" to "binders full of women," something very important was missing from their news reports on the 2012 election: actual democracy. So-called "mainstream" corporate media offered no coverage of third party presidential candidates, who were actually bringing forth many alternatives to the views espoused by the two major, corporate-backed, political party candidates.

While corporate media offered extensive coverage of Barack Obama and Mitt Romney, only *Democracy Now!* and the *Huffington Post* provided any time to third party candidates during the 2012 presidential election. *Democracy Now!* aired "expanding the debate" segments for each of the presidential and vice presidential debates. These broadcasts showed each of the debates in real time and paused to allow third party candidates—such as Green Party candidate Jill Stein, Justice Party candidate Rocky Anderson, and Constitution Party candidate Virgil Goode—the same amount of time to answer the same questions. *The Huffington Post* offered similar coverage, giving Reform Party candidate Andre Barnett and Libertarian Party candidate Gary Johnson the opportunity to participate in the debate as well.

If there had been corporate media coverage of these third-party candidates during the debates, the public would have had a broader range of ideas to consider, and a more representative pool of candidates from which to choose. While Obama and Romney presented and argued about the exact same ideas for health care, both Jill Stein and Rocky Anderson criticized "insurance company care" and advocated for single-payer universal health care, which was totally absent from the presidential debate.[79] Many of the third party candidates talked about ending all wars, bringing troops home now, and cutting the defense budget, instead of offering arbitrary timelines and refusing to cut from defense in the name of "national security."[80] They even addressed the emerging police state, with some candidates promoting the repeal of the National Defense Authorization Act (NDAA) and the USA PATRIOT Act, following due process, and ending warrantless spying.[81] With proper mainstream news coverage, the country could have been more informed about their actual choices beyond the two major party candidates.

Democracy Now! also reported on the secret debate contract for the 2012 election. This twenty-one-page document, drawn up by the Democratic and Republican candidates, excluded all third party candidates from the presidential debates, prohibited these two candidates from participating in any other debates, and restricted the moderator in the debates from asking any follow-up questions.[82] In response to the exclusion, Green Party candidate Jill Stein and vice presidential candidate Cheri Honkala tried to simply gain access to one of the debates at Hofstra University and were arrested. They were then literally bound and tied in custody for eight hours. Yes, in the United States of America, land of the free, these official candidates on the national Green Party ticket for president and vice president, two women on the ballot in most states from a legally registered political party, were arrested trying to access a public debate at an institution of higher learning, and bound by authorities, like in a third world dictatorship. But hey, at least they weren't shot, they were only tied up—this is America, after all. Of course, how this type of corporatist collusion with a police state can even exist let alone be tolerated in the US should be quite a mystery.

One would think this merited serious news coverage, even investigating. Not in America. Before being taken away, Dr. Stein offered a statement that encompassed the presidential elections of 2012: "This is what democracy looks like in the twenty-first century."[83] And a grim look it is at that.

Thatcher vs. Chávez: Celebrity Death Match of Political Grief Porn Propaganda

The first few months of 2013 saw the deaths of two significant global political figures. On March 5, 2013, Venezuelan President Hugo Chávez died of cancer at the age of fifty-eight. Chávez held power for fourteen years in Venezuela, and was known for transforming the country through a socialist revolution. One month later, on April 8, 2013, former prime minister of Great Britain Margaret Thatcher died of a stroke at the age of eighty-seven. As Britain's first female prime minister, Thatcher led the country for twelve years and ushered in a wave of capitalism heavily focused on Milton Friedman–inspired free market economics. Both were important and controversial leaders in their respective countries, and both of their deaths received substantial amounts of corporate media coverage in the US. Reports following their deaths showed a clear bias regarding their political legacies.

Americans love their grief porn, their infatuation with deaths of well-known people, and the fact that some celebrities are political figures sometimes even exaggerates attention. The deaths of Michael Jackson and Whitney Houston were certainly big news, and the deaths of Thatcher and Chávez also garnered considerable attention, but for different reasons.

Corporate news reports on the death of Margaret Thatcher tended to have a very positive view on her life and politics. For a leader considered to be controversial, there was no shortage of praise when it came to Thatcher's time as prime minister. Hailed for being the "Iron Lady" and "uncompromising," many news reports focused on her success in the financial sector of the country. By pushing for deregulation and privatization, the *Wall Street Journal* stated she "helped turn London from an increasingly obsolete financial center into a rival to Wall Street."[84] The "patriot prime minister" had "taken a country that was on its knees and made it stand tall again" according to BBC News.[85] The US admired her patriotism as well. Fox News reported "she never faltered, in word or deed, in her support of the United States," while NBC News quoted President Barack Obama calling Thatcher "an exemplar of British strength" and a "role model for young women."[86]

Whenever a report offered a negative statement, it quickly switched back to something positive, while reminders of respecting the deceased became a common refrain. This kind of coverage paid little attention to the drawbacks of Thatcher's economic policies, such as the detrimental effects they had on the average working person while continuing to make the rich richer. Anything truly controversial was left out of corporate media coverage, such as her support for Chilean dictator Augusto Pinochet, her support of the apartheid regime, or her use of police and the secret service to defeat powerful unions.[87] With a leader whose political values closely mirrored those of the US establishment, there was not much room for unfavorable facts to be mentioned. Yet no such restraint was shown to Chávez in the US.

While corporate media coverage for Margaret Thatcher was mostly fawning and kept in a tone of respect for the recently deceased, the same respect was not given when it came to coverage of the death of Hugo Chavez. Corporate outlets mentioned some of the good Chávez did with redirecting Venezuela's oil profits toward social programs for the poor, along with some affirmative statistics such as a stark decrease in poverty, child mortality, and malnutrition deaths.[88] But for every one of these statements, there were numerous that promptly followed, representing an opposing, belittling comment. Common criticisms included the country's high inflation, high crime rates, and Venezuela being left with an unsustainable economic model, all of which had a tendency to be exaggerated. Some, like Pamela Sampson of Associated Press went so far as to say that Chávez wasted money on the poor and could have built lavish cities like in Dubai. Jim Naureckas, of the media watchdog group Fairness and Accuracy In Reporting (FAIR), quoted Sampson,

> Chávez invested Venezuela's oil wealth into social programs including state-run food markets, cash benefits for poor families, free health clinics and education programs. But those gains were meager compared with the spectacular construction projects that oil riches spurred in glittering Middle Eastern cities, including the world's tallest building in Dubai and plans for branches of the Louvre and Guggenheim museums in Abu Dhabi.[89]

Naureckas remarked:

> That's right: Chávez squandered his nation's oil money on healthcare, education and nutrition when he could have been building the world's tallest building or his own branch of the Louvre. What kind of monster has priorities like that?[90]

Furthermore, reporting became exceptionally poor when it came to personal attacks on Chávez. Descriptions ranged from CBS referring to him as a "bully" to USA Today quoting that he ran "the Venezuelan economy and political system into the ground," with the worst being Fox News calling him a "dictator" and "thug," stating that "many rejoiced" upon his death.[91] So much for extending respect to the dead, as was the rallying cry around any criticism of Margaret Thatcher. American comedian turned cultural critic George Carlin once said—let's not have a double standard here, one standard will do just fine. Indeed.[92]

US corporate media coverage of the deaths of Margaret Thatcher and Hugo Chávez were skewed and misrepresented in many respects, and primarily positive reporting only went to the leader that more closely represented the policies of the US. The corporate press in America never gave the public a fair or balanced accounting in the matter. And that degree of framing and spin is clearly News Abuse.

EPITAPH AS EPILOGUE, AND THE REBIRTH OF MEDIA FREEDOM

It is not necessary to conceal anything from a public insensible to contradiction and narcotized by technological diversions.

—Neil Postman, *Amusing Ourselves to Death: Public Discourse in the Age of Show Business* (1985)

Over the years, the research for these Junk Food News and News Abuse chapters amounts to a cultural epitaph for the American public. Cultural historian Morris Berman, in his last book *Why America Failed: The Roots of Imperial Decline*, painstakingly points out that America has become a land victimized by its own illusions of progress, crass materialism, and anti-intellectual furor, all heralded as the "American way" by corporate media.[93] But there are more Americans and more global citizens born every day, and through education, media literacy, critical thinking, community building, and the fostering of increased awareness and solidarity, we can build a movement to navigate these troubled waters history has given us.

While this chapter closes on bleak notes, we must be ever alerted to the fact that across the US and the world, millions of people yearn for a better life, more transparent governments, and broader possibilities of who we can become as a global village. Part of the Junk Food and News Abuse chapter "snarkily" calls out the chicanery of corporate media failures, but it does so to also illustrate that we the people are in on the game and can transcend it.

While we certainly want to pressure big media to keep the public informed given the size and potential significance of their megaphone, we can't merely wait for change to come. We must also be that change. Together, working with each other on more independent and grassroots levels, we can more accurately inform each other and become the media. By what we do and how we act, we make irrelevant the once towering but now gatekeeping institutions of the corporate press—ones now teetering, faltering, built on houses of cards and lies, waiting for their own epitaph to be scribed. It is one that we the people, the independent and citizen journalists of tomorrow, will happily write in our own headlines of a people's history in the making. Count on it. Be the media. Free the press. Via, veritas, vita.

MICKEY HUFF is the director of Project Censored, and professor of social science and history at Diablo Valley College.

NOLAN HIGDON is adjunct faculty in history at Diablo Valley College, and an affiliate researcher with Project Censored.

MICHAEL KOLBE, SAM PARK, JENNIFER EIDEN, AND KIMBERLY SOIERO are past or present Project Censored interns, undergraduates and college graduates alike, who contributed to this chapter.

Notes

1. "By the Book: Walter Mosely," *New York Times Book Review,* June 2, 2013, 10.
2. Neil Postman, *Amusing Ourselves to Death: Public Discourse in the Age of Show Business,* (New York: Penguin, 1985). This chapter has been guided by Postman's work for some time, and also informed by other like-minded scholars including Chris Hedges, Mark Crispin Miller, Daniel J. Boorstin, Marshall McLuhan, Jean Baudrillard, and Morris Berman, to name a few.
3. The decline of American civilization has been the serious subject of numerous scholars for the better part of half a century. For more on this thesis, and some of the latest scholarly work on the matter, see Morris Berman, *Why America Failed: The Roots of Imperial Decline* (Hoboken: John Wiley & Sons, 2012).
4. Mark Jurkowitz, et al., "The Changing TV News Landscape," *State of the News Media 2013: An Annual Report on American Journalism,* Pew Research Center's Project for Excellence in Journalism (2013), http://stateofthemedia.org/2013/the-changing-tv-news-landscape/. For more on the state of the news media studies by Pew, see http://stateofthemedia.org/.
5. Jodi Enda and Amy Mitchell, "Americans Show Signs of Leaving a News Outlet, Citing Less Information," *State of the News Media 2013: An Annual Report on American Journalism,* Pew Research Center's Project for Excellence in Journalism (2013), http:// stateofthemedia.org/2013/specia-reports-landing-page/citing-reduced-quality-many-americans-abandon-news-outlets. Other issues impacting media credibility and public trust include serious news blunders by major corporate media outlets, like this past year when CNN and Fox both reported that the Obama health care law was overturned by the Supreme Court, while it was not, but both networks rushed to broadcast before getting all the facts and were slow to reverse course. See Steve Myers, "Were CNN & Fox News' Mistakes on Supreme Court Ruling Part of 'Process Journalism'?" Poynter.org, June 29, 2012, http://www.poynter.org/latest-news/top-stories/179341/were-cnn-fox-news-mistakes-on-supreme-court-ruling-part-of-process-journalism.
6. Ibid.
7. "Fox News Credibility Declines," Public Policy Polling, February 6, 2013, http://www.publicpolicypolling.com/pdf/2011/PPP_Release_National_206.pdf. On voters' views on news sources: "We continue to find that Democrats trust most TV news sources other than Fox, while Republicans don't trust anything except Fox," said Dean Debnam, president of Public Policy Polling. "News preferences are very polarizing along party lines." In other words, people believe *their* sources of news are okay, and that all the rest of them are bunk.
8. "Press Widely Criticized, But Trusted More than Other Information Sources," Pew Research Center for the People & the Press, September 22, 2011, http://www.people-press.org/2011/09/22/press-widely-criticized-but-trusted-more-than-other-institutions.
9. Ibid.
10. A recounting of the development of Junk Food News and News Abuse research is published in Peter Phillips and Mickey Huff, eds., *Censored 2010* (New York: Seven Stories Press, 2009), ch. 3, "Infotainment Society: Junk Food News and News Abuse for 2008–09"; Mickey Huff and Peter Phillips, eds., *Censored 2011* (New York: Seven Stories Press, 2010), ch. 3, "Manufacturing Distraction: Junk Food News and New Abuse on a Feed to Know Basis"; Mickey Huff and Project Censored, *Censored 2012* (New York: Seven Stories Press, 2011), ch. 3, "Framing the Messengers: Junk Food News and News Abuse for Dummies"; and Mickey Huff, Andy Lee Roth, and Project Censored, *Censored 2013: Dispatches from the Media Revolution* (New York: Seven Stories Press, 2012), ch. 3, "American Idle: Junk Food News, News Abuse, and the Voice of Freedumb." Also see Carl Jensen and Project Censored, *Censored 1994* (New York: Four Walls Eight Windows, 1994), 142–143. Further, Jensen added to this sentiment in "Junk Food News 1877–2000," ch. 5 in Peter Phillips, ed., *Censored 2001* (New York: Seven Stories Press, 2001), 251–264.
11. Mark Saunders, "Royal Baby Announcement Marks Dramatic Break with Tradition," CNN, December 4, 2012, http://www.cnn.com/2012/12/04/world/europe/royal-baby-announcement-saunders/index.html.

12. Fox News, "Nurse Radio Hosts Pranked to Get Royal Baby Details Commits Suicide," December 7, 2012, http://www.foxnews.com/world/2012/12/07/royal-prank-call-nurse-reportedly-commits-suicide/#ixzz2Feolx8mO.

13. Jon Queally, "Decade of US 'War on Terror' Yields More 'Terrorism,'" Common Dreams, December 4, 2012, https://www.commondreams.org/headline/2012/12/04.

14. Noam Chomsky, 9-11 (New York: Seven Stories Press, 2001), 76.

15. Nancy Dillon, Taylor Dungjen, and Tina Moore, "Katie Holmes' Secret Escape Plan: Actress Rented Her Own New York City Apartment before Ditching Tom," New York Daily News, July 1, 2012, http://www.nydailynews.com/new-york/katie-holmes-secret-escape-plan-actress-rented-new-york-city-apartment-ditching-tom-article-1.1105652#ixzz2KqhXbCm4.

16. "Libor (Barclays Interest Rate Manipulation Case)," New York Times, December 19, 2012, http://topics.nytimes.com/top/reference/timestopics/subjects/l/london_interbank_offered_rate_libor/index.html.

17. Immanual Wallerstein, "The LIBOR Scandal: Why is it Scandalous?" Iwallerstein.com, Commentary 334, August 1, 2012, http://www.iwallerstein.com/libor-scandal-scandalous.

18. "Here Are the 16 Banks Under Investigation over the Libor Scandal," Huffington Post, Reuters, July 11, 2012, http://www.huffingtonpost.com/2012/07/11/libor-rate-scandal_n_1664737.html.

19. Ben Dimiero and Rob Savillo, "Media Prioritize Animal Attacks, Tom Cruise over Huge Bank Scandal, Media Matters for America," Media Matters, July 19, 2012, http://mediamatters.org/blog/2012/07/19/report-media-prioritize-animal-attacks-tom-crui/187238.

20. "Gangnam Style YouTube Views: Psy's Viral Hit Beats Bieber to Become Most-Viewed YouTube Video Ever," Huffington Post, November 24, 2012, ttp://www.huffingtonpost.com/2012/11/24/gangnam-style-youtube-views_n_2185280.html.

21. Jordan Zakarin, "Man Collapses, Dies After Dancing 'Gangnam Style,'" Hollywood Reporter, December 13, 2012, http://www.hollywoodreporter.com/earshot/man-dies-dancing-gangnam-style-402032.

22. "Man Dies of Heart Attack after Dancing to 'Gangnam Style,'" Sun, December 13, 2012, http://www.foxnews.com/health/2012/12/13/man-dies-heart-attack-after-dancing-to-gangnam-style/#ixzz2FfGTqN9S.

23. Jordan Zakarin, "Man Collapses, Dies After Dancing 'Gangnam Style,'" Hollywood Reporter, December 13, 2012, http://www.hollywoodreporter.com/earshot/man-dies-dancing-gangnam-style-402032.

24. Glenn Greenwald, "The PSY Scandal: Singing about Killing People v. Constantly Doing It," Guardian, December 10, 2012, http://www.commondreams.org/view/2012/12/10-3.

25. Carlos Maza, "Gangnam Style Overshadows Uganda's 'Kill The Gays' Bill In Cable News Coverage," Media Matters, December 12, 2012, http://mediamatters.org/research/2012/12/12/gangnam-style-overshadows-ugandas-kill-the-gays/191814.

26. Henry Wasswa, "Uganda's 'Kill the Gays' Bill Spreads Fear," Al Jazeera, January 3, 2013, http://www.aljazeera.com/indepth/features/2013/01/2013121392698654.html.

27. Ibid.

28. Gene Sloan, "Fire-Damaged Carnival Ship Stuck at Sea Another Day," USA Today, February 12, 2013, http://www.usatoday.com/story/travel/cruises/2013/02/11/carnival-cruise-ship-fire/191057.

29. Ibid.

30. Parisa Safarzadeh, "My Celebration Trip on the Carnival Triumph: From Joy to Misery," CNN, February 15, 2013, http://www.cnn.com/2013/02/15/opinion/safarzadeh-cruise-passenger-story/index.html?iid=article_sidebar.

31. Jordan Zackerin, "CNN's Cruise Ship Coverage Roundly Mocked by Jon Stewart, Media Snarkers," Hollywood Reporter, February 15, 2013, http://www.hollywoodreporter.com/live-feed/cnns-cruise-ship-coverage-roundly-421856.

32. Ibid. See also, Phyllis Fine, "CNN More than Doubles Ratings With Cruise-From-Hell Coverage," MediaPost, February 19, 2013, http://www.mediapost.com/publications/article/193842/cnn-more-than-doubles-ratings-with-cruise-from-hel.html#ixzz2W8yjCpUa.

33. Patrick Martin, "Obama Pushes Austerity in the Guise of Defending the 'Middle Class,'" Global Research, February 12, 2013, http://www.globalresearch.ca/obama-pushes-austerity-in-the-guise-of-defending-the-middle-class/5322673.

34. For the original and more detailed definition and explanation of News Abuse, see Peter Phillips, ed., *Censored 2003* (New York: Seven Stories Press, 2002), 196.

35. Melissa Knowles, "8-Year-Old's Letter to Romney Urges Him to Not Fire Big Bird," Yahoo News, October 5, 2012, http://news.yahoo.com/blogs/trending-now/8-old-letter-romney-urges-him-not-fire-173139170.html.

36. Associated Press, "Man Who Accused Elmo Puppeteer of Teen Sex Recants," Fox News, November 13, 2012, http://www.foxnews.com/entertainment/2012/11/13/man-who-accused-elmo-puppeteer-teen-sex-recants.

37. Justin George, "Claims Mount Against Kevin Clash, the Voice of Elmo," *Baltimore Sun*, December 26, 2012, http://articles.baltimoresun.com/2012-12-26/news/bs-md-kevin-clash-elmo-20121226_1_cecil-singleton-clash-s-new-york-inappropriate-relationship.

38. Andrew Kirell, "Limbaugh: Liberals Seek to Normalize Pedophilia, Just Like They Did with Gay Marriage," *Mediaite*, January 8, 2013, http://www.mediaite.com/online/limbaugh-liberals-seek-to-normalize-pedophilia-just-like-they-did-with-gay-marriage.

39. David Moye, "Muppet Scandals through the Years," *Huffington Post*, November 20, 2012, http://www.huffingtonpost.com/2012/11/20/muppet-scandals_n_2167209.html.

40. Mickey Huff, Frances A. Capell, and Adam Bessie, "Manufacturing Distraction: Junk Food News and New Abuse on a Feed to Know Basis" in *Censored 2011*, eds. Mickey Huff and Peter Phillips (New York: Seven Stories Press, 2010), ch. 3, 176–181. See also Kate Sheppard, "BP's Bad Breakup: How Toxic is Corexit?," *Mother Jones*, September/October 2010, http://www.motherjones.com/environment/2010/09/bp-ocean-dospersant-corexit; and Farron Cousins, "EPA Accused of Violating Clean Water Act Through Approval of Corexit in BP Gulf Oil Cleanup," *EcoNews*, March 7, 2013, http://ecowatch.com/2013/epa-corexit-bp-oil-spill.

41. "Crime, No Punishment: BP Gulf Settlement Deal 'Pathetic' Say Groups 'Fine Amounts to a Rounding Error for a Corporation the Size of BP,'" Common Dreams, November 15, 2012, http://www.commondreams.org/headline/2012/11/15-5.

42. "Radiation Still High in Seas Around Fukushima, Scientists Look to Sea Floor," Common Dreams, November 15, 2012, http://www.commondreams.org/headline/2012/11/15-6.

43. Peter Bergen, "How Petraeus Changed the U.S. military," CNN, November 11, 2012, http://www.cnn.com/2012/11/10/opinion/bergen-petraeus-legacy.

44. Vicky Nissen, "Was Stevens Murdered to Cover Up US Gun Running from Libya to AlQaeda in Syria?," *Examiner.com*, October 29, 2012, http://www.examiner.com/article/was-stevens-murdered-to-coverup-u-s-gun-running-from-libya-to-alqaeda-syria.

45. Ibid.

46. Shashank Bengali, David S. Cloud, and Joseph Tanfani, "Jill Kelley, Key Figure in David Petraeus Scandal, Led Lavish Life," *Los Angeles Times*, November 14, 2012, http://www.latimes.com/news/nationworld/nation/la-na-cia-scandal-20121115,0,5234898.story.

47. Glenn Greenwald, "Petraeus Scandal Is Reported with Compelled Veneration of All Things Military," *Guardian*, November 10, 2012, https://www.commondreams.org/view/2012/11/10-5.

48. RT News, "Petraeus Mistress Reveals Real Motive behind Benghazi Attack," RT News, 12 November 2012, http://rt.com/usa/news/petraeus-benghazi-attack-cia-535.

49. Vicky Nissen, "Was Stevens Murdered?"

50. Eric Schmitt And Michael R. Gordon, "Panel Assails Role of State Department in Benghazi Attack," *New York Times*, December 18, 2012, http://www.nytimes.com/2012/12/19/us/politics/inquiry-into-libya-attack-is-sharply-critical-of-state-department.html?_r=0.

51. Ibid.

52. Ibid.

53. Ronda Hauben, "The Benghazi Affair: Uncovering the Mystery of the Benghazi CIA Annex," Global Research, January 28, 2013, http://www.globalresearch.ca/the-benghazi-affair-uncovering-the-mystery-of-the-benghazi-cia-annex/5320872.

54. Ibid.

55. Barry Grey, "Petraeus Resignation Fuels Political Warfare over Benghazi Attack," Global Research, November 19, 2013, http://www.globalresearch.ca/petraeus-resignation-fuels-political-warfare-over-benghazi-attack/5312324.
56. Kristina Wong, "Air Force Sex-Scandal Hearing Set," *Washington Times*, January 22, 2013, http://www.washingtontimes.com/news/2013/jan/22/air-force-sex-scandal-hearing-set-first-open-testi/?page=all.
57. Lolita C. Baldor, "Sex Is Major Reason Military Commanders Are Fired," Associated Press, January 20, 2012, http://news.yahoo.com/sex-major-reason-military-commanders-fired-123720150.html.
58. Jesse Thomas, "A Tribute to Twinkie," *Forbes Magazine*, November 16, 2012, http://www.forbes.com/sites/jessethomas/2012/11/16/a-tribute-to-twinkie.
59. "Fox Ignores Hostess' Array of Troubles to Scapegoat Union For Liquidation," Media Matters, November 16, 2012, http://mediamatters.org/research/2012/11/16/fox-ignores-hostess-array-of-troubles-to-scapeg/191440.
60. Jesse Thomas, "A Tribute to Twinkie."
61. Alice Hines, "Twinkie Shortage Shows Hostess Fans Went a Little Crazy over Bankruptcy," *Huffington Post*, November 16, 2012, http://www.huffingtonpost.com/2012/11/16/twinkie-shortage-hostess-bankruptcy_n_2147012.html.
62. "USDA Replaces Food Pyramid with 'MyPlate' in Hopes to Promote Healthier Eating," *Washington Post*, June 3, 2012, http://articles.washingtonpost.com/2011-06-03/national/35236118_1_myplate-food-pyramid-usda-headquarters.
63. Caroline Hummer, "Companies Turn to Bankruptcy Again—and Again," Reuters, March 6, 2012, http://www.reuters.com/article/2012/03/06/us-bankruptcy-repeats-idUSTRE8251N120120306.
64. Alice Hines, "Twinkie Shortage."
65. Associated Press, "Twinkies Saved? Hostess, Union Agree to Mediation," CNBC, November 19, 2012, http://www.cnbc.com/id/49889974/.
66. "Walmart Strike Goes Nationwide on Black Friday," RT News, November 23, 2012, http://rt.com/usa/news/walmart-strike-black-friday-436.
67. Paddy Ryan, "Walmart: America's Real 'Welfare Queen,'" *Daily Kos*, October 10, 2012, http://www.dailykos.com/story/2012/10/10/1141724/-Walmart-fuels-inequality-epidemic-taking-advantage-of-our-safety-net#.
68. Alice Gomstyn, "Walmart CEO Pay: More in an Hour Than Workers Get All Year?," ABC News, July 2, 2010,http://abcnews.go.com/Buisness/walmart-ceo-pay-hour-workers-year/story?id=11067470#.Ubquc-ulNQp.
69. Susan Berfield, "Walmart vs. Union-Backed OUR Walmart," Bloomberg Business Week, December 13, 2012, http://www.businessweek.com/articles/2012-12-13/walmart-vs-dot-union-backed-our-walmart#p2.
70. "Walmart Strike Goes Nationwide on Black Friday."
71. "The World's Most Powerful Brands," *Forbes Magazine*, October 2012, http://www.forbes.com/companies/wal-mart-stores.
72. Matt Gertz, "Fox's Fawning Pro-Walmart Segment 'Brought To You By Walmart'" Media Matters, November 19, 2012, http://mediamatters.org/blog/2012/11/19/foxs-fawning-pro-walmart-segment-brought-to-you/191459.
73. Susan Berfield, "Walmart vs. Union-Backed OUR Walmart."
74. Elliot Blair Smith and Phil Kuntz, "CEO Pay 1,795-to-1 Multiple of Wages Skirts U.S. Law," Bloomberg, April 29, 2013, http://www.bloomberg.com/news/2013-04-30/ceo-pay-1-795-to-1-multiple-of-workers-skirts-law-as-sec-delays.html.
75. Lauren McCauley, "DOMA Challenge Reaches Supreme Court," Common Dreams, March 27, 2013, www.commondreams.org/headline/2013/03/27-1.
76. Kate Mather, "Prop 8: Celebrities Sound Off on Twitter on Supreme Court Hearing," *Los Angeles Times*, March 26, 2013, www.latimes.com/local/lanow/la-me-ln-prop-8-celebrities-20130326,0,3435484.story.
77. Dorrine Mendoza, "16 Brave and Humorous Signs on Same-Sex Marriage," CNN, March 28, 2013, www.cnn.com/2013/03/27/tech/16-brave-and-humorous-signs-on-same-sex-marriage.

78. Joe Klamar, "'Monsanto Protection Act' Slips Silently through US Congress," RT, March 26, 2013, rt.com/usa/Monsanto-congress-silently-slips-830.

79. Amy Goodman, "Expanding the Debate Exclusive: Third-Party Candidates Break the Sound Barrier as Obama-Romney Spar," Democracy Now!, October 4, 2012, http://www.democracynow.org/2012/10/4/expanding_the_debate_exclusive_third_party.

80. Marc Lamont Hill and Alicia Menendez, "Third Party Debate: The Candidates Discuss Governing," Huffington Post, October 4, 2012, http://www.huffingtonpost.com/2012/10/04/third-party-debate-the-ca_n_1940500.html.

81. Amy Goodman, "Expanding the Debate Exclusive."

82. George Farah, interview with Amy Goodman, "Secret Debate Contract Reveals Obama and Romney Campaigns Exclude Third Parties, Control Questions," Democracy Now!, October 16, 2012, http://www.democracynow.org/2012/10/16/secret_debate_contract_reveals_obama_and.

83. Dr. Jill Stein, interview with Amy Goodman, "Green Party Candidates Arrested, Shackled to Chairs for 8 Hours After Trying to Enter Hofstra Debate," Democracy Now!, October 17, 2012, http://www.democracynow.org/2012/10/17/green_partys_jill_stein_cheri_honkala.

84. Alistair Macdonald, "Former British Prime Minister Margaret Thatcher Dies," Wall Street Journal, April 8, 2013, http://online.wsj.com/article/SB10001424052527023054107045755628830 77035078.

85. "Ex-Prime Minister Baroness Thatcher Dies Aged 87," BBC News, April 8, 2013, www.bbc.co/uk/news/uk-politics-22067155.

86. "Former British Prime Minister Margaret Thatcher Dies After Suffering Stroke," Fox News, April 8, 2013, www.foxnews.com/world/2013/04/08/britian-margaret-thatcher-at-age-87-dies-after-suffering-stroke.

87. Erin McClam, "Margaret Thatcher, 'Iron Lady' Who Led Conservative Resurgence in Britain, Dies at 87," NBC News, April 8, 2013, worldnews.nbcnews.com/_news/2013/04/08/17653388-margaret-thatcher-iron-lady-who-led-conservative-resurgence-in-britain-dies-at-87?lite.

88. Tariq Ali, interview with Amy Goodman, "Margaret Thatcher (1925–2013): Tariq Ali on Late British PM's Legacy From Austerity to Apartheid," Democracy Now!, April 8, 2013, www.democracynow.org/2013/4/8/margaret_thatcher_1925_2013_Tariq_ali.

89. Tracy Connor, "Venezuela's 'Comandante' Hugo Chavez Dies," NBC News, March 6, 2013, worldnews.nbcnews.com/_news/2013/03/05/17135772-venezuelas-comandante-hugo-chavez-dies?lite.

90. Jim Naureckes, "AP: Chavez Wasted His Money on Healthcare When He Could Have Built Gigantic Skyscrapers," Fairness and Accuracy in Reporting, March 6, 2013, http://www.fair.org/blog/2013/03/06/ap-chavez-wasted-his-money-on-healthcare-when-he-could-have-built-gigantic-skyscrapers.

91. Ibid.

92. "Chavez Death Echoes With Leftists Worldwide," CBS News, March 5, 2013, www.cbsnews.com/8301-202_162-57572735/chavez-death-echoes-with-leftists-worldwide/; Girish Gupta, "Venezuelan Leader Hugo Chavez Dies," USA Today, March 5, 2013, www.usatoday.com/story/news/world/2013/03/05/hugo-chavez-obit/1956067/; and Rich Lowry, "Bias Bash: Hugo Chavez Dies, Liberal Media Pays Tribute," Fox News, March 7, 2013, video.foxnews.com/v/2209817103001.

93. For more on the double standards of coverage in the US corporate media on this issue, see Alan MacLeod, "Two Deaths: Hugo Chavez And Margaret Thatcher," Before It's News, April 15, 2013, http://beforeitsnews.com/eu/2013/04/two-deaths-hugo-chavez-and-margaret-thatcher-251684.html. See also Don Wooten, "Chavez and Thatcher: A Tale of Two Dead Leaders," Quad-Cities Online, April 20, 2013, http://www.qconline.com/archives/qco/display.php?id=635396.

94. Berman, Why America Failed. See also, Chris Hedges, Empire of Illusion: The End of Literacy and the Triumph of Spectacle (New York: Nation Books, 2009).

CHAPTER 4

Media Democracy in Action
Free Press and Free Speech Advocates Who Make a Difference

Compiled by Mickey Huff, with contributions by Daniel Ellsberg, On Civil Courage; Josh Wolf, Journalism that Matters; William Creely, Foundation for Individual Rights in Education; Christopher M. Finan, American Booksellers Foundation for Free Expression; Acacia O'Connor, National Coalition Against Censorship and Kids' Right to Read; Tony Diaz, Librotraficante; Beau Hodai, DBA Press; Sunsara Taylor, Stop Patriarchy; John Collins, *The Weave*; and Ken Walden, What the World Could Be

I'm for truth, no matter who tells it. I'm for justice, no matter who it's for or against. I'm a human being first and foremost, and as such I'm for whoever and whatever benefits humanity as a whole.

—Malcolm X

Never doubt that a small group of thoughtful, committed citizens can change the world. Indeed, it is the only thing that ever has.

—Margaret Mead

Each year, Project Censored invites committed activists, scholars, and organizations to share their common mission and work with our readers. Arguably now more than ever, We the People must band together in the struggle to wrest the promises of freedom and liberty from forces so eager to take them away. From government overreach to corporate influence and control of our economy and legislative and legal process, we must be ever vigilant to protect the right of a free press, to exercise our right of free speech and expression, and to demand the right to know what our government—and the powerful forces in our society that so strongly influence them—are doing in the public interest.

As this year's contributors illustrate, we live in an era of corporatism, of constant surveillance, of perpetual war, where civil rights and human lives are parsed and whittled away with a collective societal shrug. But we also live in an era of civil courage and the growing possibilities of citizen journalism in its many guises. The following individuals, organizations, and projects—whistleblowers, independent journalists, lawyers, teachers, publishers, filmmakers, and activists among them—are the antidote to such colossal indifference, to the destructive forces responsible for the decaying state of our current affairs. We would all do well to pitch in, join hands, and help any way we can with these exemplary global citizens. If knowing is half the battle, this chapter is dedicated not only to that end, but also to the other half of our struggle: the encouragement to act in an informed, critical, and conscious manner. Our future depends upon it.[1]

ON CIVIL COURAGE AND ITS PUNISHMENTS[2]

Daniel Ellsberg

Both civil and battlefield risk-taking for the benefit of others involves real courage; but one is far more rare than the other. Why?

Battlefield courage is expected to (and does) lead to the respect and thanks of those closest to you, your team and your superiors, immediately. (As we'll discuss below, courage off the battlefield commonly does the opposite). The respect is from some of the people you most respect, and whose respect you most value. It's good for your career, though that's not ordinarily a consideration in the immediate circumstances. And it's not only immediate—it can be ongoing.

To the very common extent that it involves saving the lives of others, those others are your teammates—"us," known to you, some of them friends—who could be expected to risk their own lives to save yours in comparable circumstances. And the saving of their lives is immediate and often visible to others; they are under imminent risk. Parallels in civilian life include rescuing a child who has wandered into traffic, or dangerously swerving a car in order to avoid hitting a pedestrian or animal. Both the risk and the benefit are immediate and usually visible—i.e., likely to evoke thanks or praise. You will not only feel you have done the right thing, but your community, your "we" group will agree, applaud, thank you, and perhaps even reward you.

Thus, it is not only possible—and universally done—but also relatively *easy* to *train* ordinary people, chosen at random (for example, by draft) to behave bravely on the battlefield: to inculcate a spirit of team loyalty in them, and (in military circumstances) to impress obedience to orders and to a "mission." Extreme physical courage becomes almost routine. As Admiral Chester Nimitz said of the Marines on Iwo Jima: "Uncommon valor was a common virtue."

Civil courage is almost the opposite in all these respects. Especially whistleblowing, which involves the exposure to outsiders of wrongdoing or reckless behavior by one's own team, superiors, organization—thus exposing one's own team members, superiors, and organization to risk of sanctions. For this you should expect not only a lack of thanks from your superiors and teammates but condemnation, contempt, ostracism, lost chances of promotion, risk of firing, and denial of respect from those you most respect and from whom you want respect.

And all this is not only from those whose misguided, dangerous behavior or wrongdoing has been exposed, but from their—and your—teammates and superiors, who feel you have endangered or stigmatized their prized organization and shown "disloyalty" (to it and to them), even when they are not personally involved in the behavior you have exposed. (Some of them may have strongly opposed it themselves, *inside* the group or organization—no "airing of dirty laundry" to outsiders—usually to no effect, but such internal critiques seldom result in either sanctions or, more importantly, changes in the wrongful behavior.)

In all cases, you may have acted to save lives, physically, or to safeguard indirectly the welfare of others. But while in the battlefield case, the lives you have saved (at the risk of your own) are your friends, your teammates, "us," in the civil case, the lives are likely to be those of "outsiders" and "others"—who may well be foreign, distant, or personally unknown to you and your group. Nothing is more human than to value, or to show concern for and readiness to take personal risks for, the lives or welfare of "others" who are "not-'us'" much less "one of us."

Moreover, the dangers (perhaps from "us," or some of us) from which these others have been saved may or may not be immediate or easily traceable to their cause. These harms are "conjectural," "speculative," or "uncertain." They may appear to be highly likely or virtually certain to the risk-taking whistleblower—who may possess special knowledge of these dangers. That knowledge may be widely known to other insiders, who take no action on it. But to other members of your group or organization, the alleged danger to these outsiders, especially in the future and especially from "us," may be irrelevant, invisible, or nonexistent.

For this latter group, the future (or immediate) danger to the lives or physical well-being of these "others" weighs less, in effect, than the immediate harm (from protecting those "others") to the careers and reputations of one's in-group. Such priorities of concern—for "us" rather than "them" (even when "they" are not enemies)—are virtually universal, and perhaps an attribute of humanity in general.

If whistleblowing involves holding one's own team, superiors, or organization accountable for causing harm to others on the battlefield, these others will typically be foreigners and are likely to be understood as "the enemy" who threatens the lives or well-being of your own "side." In the civil case, where the stakes of whistleblowing are more likely to involve damage to prestige, career, budget, and promotion, rather than life or death, you are seen as harming "your own friends," "us," those to whom you are expected (or even pledged) to show "loyalty." Loyalty may encompass the hiding of wrongdoing from outsiders, as is true not only in the mafia, but in all collectivities that establish unyielding boundaries to distinguish "we" from "them."

Battlefield courage ensures continued membership in a highly valued group admired by society: "battlefield brothers," and "our brave soldiers, our best." Civil courage commonly risks—and almost ensures—ostracism, not only from an immediate group but also from one's own society.

In these terms, is there much uncertainty left as to why battlefield bravery (while not universal) is so common, whereas civil courage is so very rare? Battlefield courage is not only trained for but also generally rewarded (if the risk-taker lives). By contrast, civil courage is often punished: Whistleblowers and others who display civil courage do not necessarily risk their lives, but often their actions entail sacrifice of their freedom for years or life in prison! Moreover, those who display civil courage are sanctioned in terms that many regard as "worse than death": exclusion and ostracism.

Thus the answer to what may seem paradoxical: the same individuals who have risked their bodies and lives in combat prove unwilling, in civilian life—see: General Colin Powell—to take any significant risk of their clearances, their access to power, their job or career, even when vast numbers of lives (of "others") are at stake! Even Socrates chose death over exile, even when he regarded either punishment as unjust.

Where does this leave us? Might we train people for civil courage, as we do for battlefield courage?

Current training, in schools and on the job, encourages conformity and obedience: training for obedience to authority, loyalty to the group, adherence to promises (in particular, of secrecy, silence, and obedience)—even when these endanger many others outside one's group. Whether explicitly or not, such training produces a mindset along the lines of the unofficial congressional motto, "to get along, go along"— in other words, the very opposite of standing at odds from the crowd, dissenting from the organization's policies or a superior's directive, or warning against and exposing misconduct within one's own group.

Could both the training and the expectations be changed, or at least added to? Might we realistically change people's expectations regarding the consequences of their actions in the eyes of those they respect? In this sense, any award for whistleblowing or other types of civil courage demonstrates that such actions do not necessarily lead to the loss of *all* social respect. (Think, for example, of John F. Kennedy's Pulitzer Prize–winning *Profiles in Courage*, which featured a number of congressional "representatives" who went against the desires or beliefs of their constituents.)

One challenge for anyone who faces ostracism for displaying civil courage is that newly earned and demonstrated respect may come from groups that the individual has long been taught to despise and disregard. You lose (perhaps all) your old friends, but you do gain new ones, whose values you discover correspond to those that came to separate you from your former relationships. For example, Sibel Edmonds found that Federal Bureau of Investigation whistleblowers (including, initially, herself) were extremely uneasy at being applauded by, or even associated with, members of the American Civil Liberties Union. General Lee Butler, who denounced the nuclear weapons that he had previously been in charge of, found that he couldn't lunch any more with other generals, but was acclaimed by antiwar and antinuclear crowds, whom he had previously found, at best, simplistic, wrongheaded, or unpatriotic. (He backed away from his public stand, though he didn't repudiate it.)

Still, the Ridenhour Prizes for journalistic courage and whistleblowing (presented by the Fertel Foundation and the Nation Institute) and Yoko Ono's recent Courage Award to Julian Assange, are steps in the direction of honoring civil courage. They make potential whistleblowers or other insider dissenters aware, at least, that while they lose membership and respect from groups they have long belonged to and valued (and this sense of loss, including the loss of multiple personal friendships, may be long felt and never fully compensated for), they will not be outcasts from the larger society, and will even earn extreme respect from groups they themselves come to respect and value. In addition to high-profile awards, organizations like Edmonds's National Security Whistleblowers Coalition and Ray McGovern's Veteran Intelligence Professionals for Sanity provide valuable reassurance of this.

Observers have noted that the Iraq and Afghanistan wars have provided us with virtually no nationally known heroes for battlefield courage, though a number have earned high decorations. But Bradley Manning is a war hero from those conflicts whose name will ring for a long time—even, and perhaps especially, if he spends his life in prison.

DANIEL ELLSBERG, the former American military analyst who in 1971 released the Pentagon Papers, a top-secret study of government decision-making during the Vietnam War, to the *New York Times* and other newspapers, is the author of three books: *Papers on the War* (1971), *Secrets: A Memoir of Vietnam and the Pentagon Papers* (2002), and *Risk, Ambiguity and Decision* (2001). Since the end of the Vietnam War, he has been a lecturer, writer, and activist on the dangers of the nuclear era, wrongful US interventions, and the urgent need for patriotic whistleblowing. In 2006, the Right Livelihood Award Foundation awarded Ellsberg its prize, known as the "Alternative Nobel," for "putting peace and truth first, at considerable personal risk, and dedicating his life to inspiring others to follow his example."

WHAT'S POSSIBLE? JOURNALISM THAT MATTERS

Josh Wolf

For two short days in Denver this past spring, I momentarily forgot that the news business is barreling down a collision course with democracy.

At a journalism conference, ironically titled "Journalism Is Dead, Long Live Journalism," about one hundred journalists huddled together in small groups to explore what journalism might look like over the next century. Although everyone in attendance was well aware of the industry's uncertain prognosis, no one dwelled on what isn't working. Instead, every participant at the conference was focused on what's possible and on how to turn possibilities into reality.

Since 2001, the nonprofit organization Journalism that Matters (JTM) has been bringing together journalism professionals, student journalists, and anyone else invested in the future of news to both ask and answer the questions that are central to practicing journalism in the twenty-first century.

One month after 9/11, JTM convened its first gathering within the Associated Press Managing Editor's board conference to discuss "Journalism that Matters in a World Gone Mad." The reaction among participants was powerful; more than one said they got more ideas out of the experience than out of the rest of the conference.

While most conferences set clear agendas and designate certain people as panelists, moderators, and attendees, JTM instead uses "Open-Space Technology," an approach for hosting conferences and other types of meetings that was "discovered" in the mid-1980s by Harrison

Owen, after he grew tired of planning and preparing for his annual organizational management conference and had an epiphany at the bar:

> The following year, he sent out a simple, one-paragraph invitation, and more than 100 people showed up to discuss Organization Transformation. In his main meeting room he set the chairs in one large circle and proceeded to explain that what participants could see in the room was the extent of his organizing work. If they had an issue or opportunity that they felt passionate about and wanted to discuss with other participants, they should come to the center of the circle, get a marker and paper, write their issue and their name, read that out, and post it on the wall. It took about 90 minutes for the 100+ people to organize a 3-day agenda of conference sessions, each one titled, hosted, and scheduled by somebody in the group.[3]

Over the past twelve years, JTM has hosted more than fifteen gatherings with well over 1,000 journalists participating in the process of crafting the agenda and igniting the future for news. In 2008, I attended my first JTM conference at the Yahoo! campus in Sunnyvale, California.

The topic for this gathering was NewsTools, and one of the tools that came out of the conference was Spot.Us, an online crowdfunding platform developed a year before Kickstarter was launched. David Cohn, the founder of the innovative nonprofit, described it as Kiva for journalism, in reference to the Kiva microfinance lending website. Cohn went on to receive a $340,000 grant from the Knight Foundation, and in 2011 his organization was acquired by American Public Media after successfully financing hundreds of stories.

The next month, JTM hosted another event in Minneapolis in conjunction with the National Conference for Media Reform (NCMR), a semiannual event organized by the group Free Press. While my entire experience in the Twin Cities that week was amazing, I found the traditional conference structure of the media reform conference jarring and alienating in comparison to the JTM unconference that had immediately preceded it.

While the JTM gathering had been about discussing new solutions, my experience at the NCMR centered on listening to people talk about old problems. In fact, the only speech I can remember from the conference was an incendiary keynote delivered by Van Jones less than a year before he was appointed by President Barack Obama as Special Advisor for Green Jobs. Mysteriously, the complete version of Jones's speech was taken down from the Free Press YouTube channel shortly after it was posted and is no longer available, though the rest of the keynotes appear to remain online.

Just as Owen had discovered before creating Open-Space Technology, the best part of the NCMR were the coffee breaks, the sole opportunity to actually engage people in a dialogue. These coffee breaks quickly crept further and further into the lectures and I soon felt like a grad student cutting class.

A few years later, when the NCMR hosted their 2013 conference in Denver, I had decided that I would participate in the JTM preconference and then avoid the lectures at the NCMR entirely.

I don't think I attended a single session of the conference, but the conversations I had just outside were more valuable than any lecture. I can only imagine the solutions we might find if the thousands of people at the conference simply stopped listening to what's wrong with the media and started creating what's possible.

JOSH WOLF is a freelance journalist and documentary filmmaker who is best known for his fight for the reporter's privilege that landed him in a federal prison for more than six months. A visionary writer and producer, he was recognized in 2006 as Journalist of the Year by the Northern California chapter of the Society of Professional Journalists "for upholding the principles of a free and independent press." A 2011 graduate from the University of California–Berkeley Graduate School of Journalism, Wolf has been a staff member, since 2013, at Journalism that Matters, a nonprofit that convenes diverse communities in conversations fostering collaboration, innovation, and action to develop thriving news and information ecologies.

THE FIRE: ACADEMIC FREEDOM UNDER THREAT

William Creely

The Foundation for Individual Rights in Education (FIRE) is a nonpartisan, nonprofit organization dedicated to defending core civil liberties at our nation's colleges and universities—and since our founding in 1999, we have stayed very busy. FIRE's work on behalf of student and faculty rights demonstrates, with depressing clarity, that academic freedom and freedom of expression remain under threat on far too many campuses nationwide.

Two recent faculty cases provide ample demonstration of the continuing disregard for academic freedom and free speech.

In March of 2012, North Carolina's Appalachian State University placed tenured sociology professor Jammie Price on administrative leave following complaints from students in her "Introduction to Sociology" course. Professor Price's offense? Offending students. According to the suspension letter Price received from Appalachian State's vice provost, four of her students objected to her in-class criticism of the university administration for its response to student allegations of sexual assault and its treatment of student athletes. According to the letter, the students also complained about Price's screening of a documentary that critically examined the adult film industry without "introduc[ing] the film or explain[ing] that the material may be objectionable or upsetting to students."

Shockingly, Price was investigated and found guilty of creating a "hostile environment," despite the fact that the allegedly harassing behavior did not remotely approach the standard for hostile environment harassment in the educational context and should have been protected by any reasonable conception of academic freedom. The university's disciplinary response included imposing a development plan that required "corrective actions," such as specific requirements for how to teach "sensitive topics" and "controversial materials." Both the Faculty Due Process Committee and the Faculty Grievance Committee issued reports objecting to Price's punishment, and FIRE sent letters of protest to Appalachian State administrators. Nevertheless, the university chancellor and the board of trustees each rejected Price's appeals. The lesson for Appalachian State faculty could not have been clearer: have the temerity to criticize the university or offend your students' delicate sensibilities, and you will be subject to sanction, academic freedom be damned.

Like Price, Professor Arthur Gilbert of the University of Denver was disciplined for the content of his classroom lectures in contravention of long-established understandings of academic freedom. Gilbert, a fifty-year teaching veteran, was teaching a spring 2011 graduate-level course titled "The Domestic and International Consequences of the Drug War." Course texts for a portion of the syllabus concerning "Drugs and Sin in American Life: From Masturbation and Prostitution to Alcohol and Drugs" included readings concerning "purity crusades" and a screening of the film *Requiem for a Dream*, which includes graphic depictions of the consequences of heroin use. In April 2011, two graduate students submitted anonymous complaints concerning in-class comments from Gilbert about course materials regarding shifting societal attitudes about masturbation.

Following an investigation, human resources administrators from the university's Office of Diversity and Equal Opportunity concluded, that "absent an academic justification, you created a hostile sexual environment in your class. *Whether this is justified by the academic integrity of your teaching of the subject matter is beyond the scope of this investigation and will be determined by the appropriate academic decision makers.*" (Emphasis added.) But such a determination on the academic merit of Gilbert's allegedly harassing speech was never solicited from faculty. Instead, the dean of the university's Josef Korbel School of International Studies simply suspended Gilbert. The suspension prompted sharp protest from the university's faculty review committee, which found the suspension of a veteran professor on the basis of two anonymous complaints about in-class speech to be "outrageous and in variance with time-honored tradition in academe."

Both FIRE and the American Association of University Professors (AAUP) agreed, writing letters of protest. Undeterred, the university provost upheld the suspension, signaling a chilling disregard for academic freedom. As the University of Denver's AAUP chapter president told the *Chronicle of Higher Education*, "Given how Professor Gilbert was treated, I'm not inclined to teach my course on human-evolved psychology and sexuality—a course whose subject matter significantly overlaps with that taught by Gilbert and whose academic content inevitably creates student discomfort—until the institution establishes better policies respecting academic freedom and due process. The risk to professional career and reputation, in my opinion, is too great."

Unfortunately, these are just two of an untold number of examples of faculty silenced by misguided administrators seeking to protect students from encountering challenging or disagreeable ideas. There are many more: Professor James Miller of the University of Wisconsin–Stout, threatened with criminal charges for posting a quote from the popular science-fiction show *Firefly* outside of his office; Professor Hyung-il Jung of the University of Central Florida, suspended for asking his accounting class, "Am I on a killing spree or what?" after a series of particularly hard exam review questions; Professor Donald Hindley of Brandeis University, found guilty of racial harassment for explaining and criticizing the use of the slur "wetbacks" in his Latin American politics course.

Of course, the censorship of students is equally widespread—and equally shameful. For a more complete picture of the problem on campus, I recommend visiting FIRE's website, TheFIRE.org, and reading FIRE President Greg Lukianoff's recent book, *Unlearning Liberty: Campus Censorship and the End of American Debate*.

Instead of providing students and faculty with unfettered access to what Justice William Brennan once memorably deemed the "marketplace of ideas," today's colleges too often answer dissenting, provocative, challenging, or simply inconvenient student and faculty expression with censorship. By choosing to silence opposing viewpoints instead of responding with still more speech, administrators teach their students precisely the wrong lesson about life in our modern liberal democracy. Properly conceived, the American campus must be where no idea is beyond challenge, where truth wins out through reasoned debate, and where we explore in dialogue with one another the social, moral, legal, artistic, and political challenges of our time.

WILLIAM CREELY is director of legal and public advocacy for the Foundation for Individual Rights in Education (FIRE), and a 2006 graduate of New York University School of Law. Defending student and faculty rights for FIRE since 2006, William has spoken to students, faculty, attorneys, and administrators at events across the country and online, and has led FIRE's continuing legal education programs in New York and Pennsylvania, and on LawLine.com. William has coauthored *amicus curiae* briefs submitted to a number of courts, including the Supreme Court of the United States and the United States Courts of Appeals for the Third, Ninth, and Eleventh Circuits. William has appeared on national cable television and radio to discuss student rights, and his writing has been published by the *Chronicle of Higher Education, Jurist, Inside Higher Ed,* the *Huffington Post, Daily Journal,* the *Charleston Law Review,* the *Providence Journal,* the *Boston Phoenix, Free Inquiry,* the *Legal Satyricon,* and others. William is a member of the New York State Bar and the First Amendment Lawyers Association.

BOOKSELLERS AND THE FIGHT FOR FREE SPEECH

Christopher M. Finan

Last year comedian Joan Rivers handcuffed herself to a shopping cart at a Costco store in Burbank, California, and began shouting through a megaphone that she was the victim of censorship.

She was unhappy that Costco had decided not to sell her new book, *I Hate Everyone . . . Starting With Me.* She charged that the book had been banned because of its racy content. "Costco should not be like Nazi Germany," she said. "Next thing they'll be burning the Bible." As TV news crews watched, she was escorted from the store by security personnel and Burbank police.

Costco is not a bookstore. But when booksellers heard about the Rivers's protest, they shook their heads in weary recognition. Almost all of them have been criticized for "censoring" authors. Particularly during election years, they hear frequent complaints that they are not selling enough books by one side or the other.

In the din of a bullhorn, it is easy to become confused about the meaning of "censorship." Governments censor, applying the full force of the state to deprive citizens of ideas that their rulers consider dangerous. Booksellers select books that they think their customers will want to buy. If a customer can't find a particular book, booksellers are almost always delighted to order it.

Not only do booksellers not censor, they are deeply committed to defending the First Amendment rights of their customers. They have rejected efforts to force them to remove controversial works from their stores, lobbied against censorship legislation in Congress and the state legislatures, and become plaintiffs in lawsuits challenging laws that restrict free speech. They support free expression through groups like the American Civil Liberties Union and Media Coalition, and in 1990 they created their own organization, the American Booksellers Foundation for Free Expression (ABFFE), the bookseller's voice in the fight against censorship.

It wasn't always so. In the early twentieth century, booksellers were part of a literary establishment that looked down on the growing Modernist movement with its emphasis on realistic depictions of life, including sex. In Boston during the early 1920s, booksellers collaborated with a local decency group, the Watch and Ward Society, in suppressing as many as seventy-five books. Then Boston police got in on the act, banning a long list of titles that would become classics, including Sinclair Lewis's *Elmer Gantry*, Theodore Dreiser's *American Tragedy*, and D. H. Lawrence's *Lady Chatterley's Lover*.

The threat of government censorship led booksellers and others in the publishing world to rethink their role. They had seen themselves as cultural arbiters responsible for selling works with a strong moral tone. Increasingly, they came to believe their main job was to protect their customers' right to make their own decisions about which books were immoral. Some even joined the battle to repeal the obscenity laws that made it a crime to sell those books. In 1957, Lawrence Ferlinghetti, a poet and painter who had opened the City Lights Bookstore in San Francisco, was arrested with one of his clerks for selling Allen Ginsberg's poem *Howl*, which Ferlinghetti had also published. Their acquittal on obscenity charges encouraged others to challenge censorship laws.

By 1980 many of those laws had been repealed or narrowed by Supreme Court decisions. But advocates of censorship never gave up, and following the election of Ronald Reagan they launched a counterattack. Conservatives who had long championed a return to "decency" persuaded Reagan to create a "pornography" commission to recommend new restrictions. The conservatives were joined by a small group of feminists who argued that sexually explicit material violated the civil rights of women. The city of Indianapolis approved legislation, authorizing the victims of sexual crimes to sue booksellers who sold books or magazines that allegedly inspired the attacks by depicting or describing "the sexually explicit subordination of women."

Booksellers played an important role in preventing the counterattack from seriously undermining First Amendment rights. In Michigan, a bookseller helped organize a coalition that prevented the passage of bills that provided drastic penalties for selling material with sexual content that is not obscene and therefore protected by the First Amendment. Booksellers joined in the legal battle that struck down the Indianapolis law. A Colorado bookseller led a campaign that persuaded 60 percent of voters in a referendum to reject a constitutional amendment broadening the state's obscenity definition.

In recent years, booksellers have been active in defending reader privacy. In 1998, Kenneth Starr, a special prosecutor investigating possible crimes by President Bill Clinton, subpoenaed two Washington bookstores in an effort to identify books purchased by Monica Lewinsky, a White House intern. Booksellers believed that complying with the subpoena would have a chilling effect on their customers' right to read whatever they want, including books that the government might disapprove. They challenged the subpoena on First Amendment grounds, and a judge acknowledged the free speech issue, ruling that Starr was not entitled to everything he was demanding. The case was dismissed after Lewinsky herself turned over her records in exchange for immunity.

The issue of reader privacy surfaced again in Colorado in 2000, when police used a search warrant in an effort to obtain the reading records of someone suspected of manufacturing methamphetamine. The Tattered Cover Book Store in Denver waged a two-year legal battle to keep the records secret. The Colorado Supreme Court voted unanimously to quash the search warrant.

Today the reader privacy issue is being fought at the national level. The USA PATRIOT Act gives the government the power to demand any records it needs to investigate a terrorist threat or espionage by a foreign government. The FBI must apply for a court order, but it does not need to demonstrate that there is probable cause to believe that the person whose records are sought is engaged in illegal acts.

Booksellers were deeply distressed when they learned of the government's power under the Patriot Act. Without a requirement to show probable cause, the government could get any record that is "relevant" to an investigation. In addition, the government was authorized to permanently gag recipients of its orders, raising the question of whether a bookseller could challenge the order in court or even consult an attorney.

In an effort to restore the safeguards for reader privacy, booksellers joined librarians, publishers, and authors in launching a Campaign for Reader Privacy in 2004. Although there was some fear that they might alienate customers, booksellers around the country circulated petitions calling on their members of Congress to amend the law. Within three months, 120,000 signatures were collected by more than 400 booksellers in 38 states.

In 2005, the House finally approved a Freedom to Read Protection Act, which had been introduced by Rep. Bernie Sanders (I-VT). Although the bill did not become law, public pressure did force Congress to make it clear that PATRIOT Act orders and their accompanying gags could be challenged in court. The Campaign for Reader Privacy will renew its efforts to restore the safeguards for reader privacy when Congress considers renewing the PATRIOT Act in 2015.

These examples of bookseller activism are highlights from what is now a long history of fighting censorship. The fight continues today at the local level as booksellers confront complaints about books on their shelves, efforts to ban titles that they sell in schools, and protests against authors who express controversial views during bookstore appearances.

No bookstore can offer every book. But booksellers are proud of their role in protecting the freedom to read.

CHRISTOPHER M. FINAN is president of American Booksellers Foundation for Free Expression (ABFFE.org), the bookseller's voice in the fight against censorship. He has been involved in the fight for free speech since 1982. Prior to joining ABFFE, he was executive director of Media Coalition, a trade association that defends the First Amendment rights of businesses. He is a trustee of the Freedom to Read Foundation. After working as a newspaper reporter, he studied American history at Columbia University, where he received his PhD. His latest book is *From the Palmer Raids to the Patriot Act: A History of the Fight for Free Speech in America* (Beacon Press). It won the 2008 Eli M. Oboler Award of the American Library Association. Finan received the 2011 Freedom to Read Foundation's Roll of Honor Award.

NATIONAL COALITION AGAINST CENSORSHIP

Acacia O'Connor

In just a few months, the National Coalition Against Censorship (NCAC), the oldest civil liberties coalition in the US, will celebrate its fortieth year. NCAC opposes censorship locally and nationally regardless of the likelihood of success in a court of law. We take action both when the censor is a public institution and when it is a private company. In its wide reach, NCAC is unique among First Amendment organizations and provides a service increasingly valuable at a time when spaces for communication are increasingly privatized and when litigation can be a long and expensive process.

NCAC was founded in 1974, in the aftermath of *Miller v. California*, a landmark Supreme Court decision that established "community standards" as a test for what the law could consider obscene. The organizations that came to comprise NCAC shared a commitment to free speech and a concern that the new "community standards" test would lead to an increase in obscenity prosecutions and more censorship. In the digital age, the concept of community is even more nebulous, and concerns over the chilling effect of "community standards" are especially relevant.

Over the years, NCAC has worked on issues relating to sexuality and sex education, government control of information, science censorship, video games, books, art, online speech, academic freedom, and more. Fighting censorship is an ongoing battle; there is no last stand. While its targets change, the desire to resolve problems (imagined or real) by speech restrictions and censorship remains a persistent human impulse.

Today, we're a coalition of over fifty organizations including literary, artistic, religious, educational, professional, labor, and civil liberties groups, who support NCAC's mission to protect freedom of thought and expression and oppose censorship in all its forms. In addition to our current signature initiatives—the Arts Advocacy Project, Youth Free Expression Project, and Kids' Right to Read Project—NCAC maintains an overview of the full range of debates around freedom of speech in America. We do so through our coalition of allied organizations as well as through our work as a convener of the Free Expression Network (an information-exchange structure including all the key US First Amendment organizations). Our newly launched wiki, Censorpedia (wiki.ncac.org), is a rapidly expanding repository of information about censorship cases around the world.

Many Americans today are dismissive of claims of censorship, preferring to relegate it to a bygone era or to see it as something that happens in other, "undemocratic" countries. Whenever a book is removed from a school library or an app is barred from the iTunes marketplace because its content violates the terms of service, someone will predictably respond: "They can still get it elsewhere, at a store or on Amazon. They can go to the library. It's not censorship." The myth that censorship is a single, easily identifiable beast is a useful fantasy for those who would control information.

That myth will not convince an artist faced with losing a grant because a work offends some congressman's religious sensibilities, or a librarian facing pressure to remove a particular book. Those facing censorship feel the nagging suspicion that something is wrong, but often don't know what to do next: their jobs are at stake, and the loudest, most fanatical voices are against them.

NCAC helps communities resist censorship in their work, their schools, their universities, their libraries. We're there to offer insight and guidance and raise awareness of where a specific case fits into the bigger picture. We can advise on best practices and connect people with national organizations equipped to take up their fight.

As the landscape of media has changed, so have the threats to free speech. In some cases, the change is more superficial: where adults panicked that comic books are destroying the nation's youth, today they raise the alarm about video games. Other changes are real: we have the Internet, Twitter, and multiplying platforms of communication that simultaneously make it possible for everyone to share ideas yet very hard for any one authority figure to control access to information. But will the Internet deliver on this promising development in terms of media democracy, or will the private companies that serve as intermediaries impose their own terms of service on our new public square? And might not governments use social media as a tool for surveillance?

The privatization of the Internet, just like the privatization of exhibition spaces and educational institutions, makes First Amendment protections largely irrelevant, leaving free speech to the whims of private entities. NCAC has the organizational flexibility to confront such challenges as they come along, and we are determined to continue doing so. One thing we have realized in our forty years of existence is that we can never take our right to free expression for granted—to forget is to risk losing it altogether.

KIDS' RIGHT TO READ

Acacia O'Connor

In March 2013, someone in the Chicago Public Schools sent around a directive to remove any and all copies of the graphic novel *Persepolis* from classrooms and libraries. It was unclear where the mandate had come from, who it applied to, and above all, why, after many years in Chicago classrooms, the beloved memoir about a young woman growing up during the Iranian Revolution should suddenly be banned, without explanation.

Months later, and despite every effort by the Kids' Right to Read Project (KRRP), CPS has refused to divulge what exactly happened. All we know is that someone wanted *Persepolis* removed without conducting a formal review process and without consulting with educators or anyone else. The district deftly, if slowly, spun the removal as a legitimate and apolitical "curriculum change" and only superficially responded to Freedom of Information Act and other requests for clarification.

As the *Persepolis* controversy was unfolding, the district announced it would be closing fifty-four schools, mostly in African-American and Hispanic neighborhoods. As part of KRRP's work on *Persepolis*, I spoke to a high school language arts teacher not long after the closings were announced. I said I realized that, compared to the school closings, the *Persepolis* controversy might be small beans.

"It's not a small beans issue," the teacher replied, distressed. To her, it is all part of the same problem. The school board officials and administrators—who are appointed, not elected—aren't accountable to anyone and they know it. "My kids' school is going to be closed. What can I do? I can't vote them out, I can't do anything."

The Kids' Right to Read project combats book challenges and bans on a grassroots level: it holds public officials accountable and alerts them to the First Amendment implications of book banning, works with the media to expand the conversation around free speech, and advises local activists and those embroiled in censorship controversies. Cofounded by the National Coalition Against Censorship and the American Booksellers Foundation for Free Expression, it is also supported by the Comic Book Legal Defense Fund and Association of American Publishers. We intervene whenever there's a book challenge, urging schools to protect students' freedom to read.

Even the smallest of censorship incidents—those which affect a single classroom of middle school students or a modest public library branch—is a flash point for the most combustible issues in our culture and society today.

Last year, as the tide continued to turn on the debate over gay marriage, a number of children's books were censored because they spoke matter-of-factly about nontraditional families. Ironically, one of these books—*In Our Mothers' House* by Patricia Polacco—was selected for a school library specifically because some students in the school came from nontraditional families. In Erie, Illinois, another censored book, *The Family Book* by Todd Parr, was being used for a course on Tolerance, Diversity and Anti-Bullying. *And Then Came Tango*, a play about two male penguins raising an egg together, based on the frequently challenged children's book *And Tango Makes Three*, was set to be performed in Austin Public Schools, until a principal complained. The performance was canceled. "Elementary schools typically . . . do not delve into human sexuality, religion, or other politically hot topics," the district's director of fine arts wrote by way of an explanation.

The written word is deeply affecting and enduringly powerful. That same power, which makes books like *Persepolis* or *The Absolutely True Diary of a Part-Time Indian* so beloved, scares others. For a lonely student in a small town, grappling with physical abuse, or questioning his or her sexuality, books like *Bastard Out of Carolina*, *The Perks of Being a Wallflower*, or *Looking for Alaska* can be lifesaving. Many have tried to keep these books out of the hands of students, for the sake of that abstract concept: innocence. Yet ignorance is not innocence: the real damage is done by keeping students from getting the information they need and by indicating they should be ashamed to explore subjects like sex, depression, drugs and abuse.

In the firm belief that intellectual freedom is crucial to our development as well-rounded, socially engaged and empathetic human beings, the Kids' Right to Read project fights for young people's right to explore and grow by reading good books.

ACACIA O'CONNOR is coordinator of the Kids' Right to Read Project, a coalition project of the National Coalition Against Censorship (NCAC.org). Her position with KRRP combines many of her passions, including but not limited to literature, libraries, language, and freedom of speech. Also an Italian translator, Acacia received her master's degree in literary translation studies from the University of Rochester.

THE LIBROTRAFICANTE OPPRESSION DETECTION KIT

Tony Diaz, El Librotraficante

When Arizona legislators tried to erase our history, we decided to make more. When Arizona House Bill 2281 was used to ban Mexican American studies, we decided to take a stand. What started as the Librotraficante Caravan to smuggle banned books back to Tucson has blossomed into a movement. In March of 2012, we organized six cities, smuggled over 1,000 books donated from all over the country, and opened four underground libraries.

The Librotraficante movement is the tip of the pyramid. It stands on the base created by its parent organization, Nuestra Palabra: Latino Writers Having Their Say, which I founded, to promote Latino literature and literacy in Houston, Texas, in 1998. In that time, we have worked with most of the authors whose work was banned by the Tucson Unified School District (TUSD). The writings of our most beloved authors form the base of our movement.

Currently, Arizona HB 2281 has been used to make only our history illegal; however, these anti-intellectual laws, like Arizona's anti-immigration laws, will also spread. Although right now only Mexican American studies is outlawed, Arizona HB 2281 will pave the way to outlaw Asian studies and African American studies, not just in Arizona, but in other states. The end result would be disastrous: the dismantling of ethnic studies courses that have stemmed the drop out rate, an attack on critical thinking, and a trampling of the intellectual landscape of America.

We must not allow that to happen, and we are making some progress.

Texas Republican Senator Dan Patrick introduced Senate Bill 1128, and Texas Republican House of Representative Giovanni Capriglione introduced House Bill 1938 in spring of 2013. Last year we organized the Librotraficante Caravan to smuggle books banned in Arizona, back to Arizona, and this year we defended ethnic studies in our own back yard.

We formed a Texas-wide coalition that fought against HB 1938 and SB 1128, which would discredit ethnic studies at Texas state colleges and universities and effectively eliminate Mexican American, African American, and women's studies programs among others. Both bills are now dead.[4] We leave records of these struggles posted online as a testament to this stage of the civil rights movement of which we, and many others, are a part. Look for it sooner than later before the hackers strike, as the Librotraficante.com website regularly gets attacked.

In terms of the legacy of the current civil rights movement, I have no doubt that our brothers and sisters in Arizona will be victorious. The Librotraficante movement believes it would be a powerful example of poetic justice in democracy if the only Latina Supreme Court justice Sonia Sotomayor could sign the majority opinion overturning Arizona HB 2811 signed into law by Arizona Governor Jan Brewer, and used as the legal trigger to prohibit Mexican American studies in Arizona.[5]

These tactics are straight out of the Arizona Republican Playbook. The far right's anti-immigrant movement is well known, and even addressed in the Republican Party's Growth and Opportunity Project.[6] However, they have not openly discussed, admitted to, or renounced the far right attack on ethnic studies. Here is an overview of some of the strategies used to attack ethnic studies indirectly.

1. Vague Laws
2. Code Words
3. Micromanaging Classrooms
4. Doughnut Hole Legislation
5. Bogus Reports
6. Denial

Vague Laws

The anti–ethnic studies bill is vague, successfully hiding that the target is Mexican American studies. Even as the Arizona Supreme Court condoned HB 2281, it was pointed out by one of the judges on the case, A. Wallace Tashima, that the part of the law was so vague that it was unconstitutional. HB 2281 never even mentions Mexican American studies. Of course, once we are out of the way and our programs are terminated, the other ethnic studies shall fall, too, for the rules will be set to eliminate all other ethnic and women's studies, or to never implement them. This is also part of an attack on "critical thinking," which the Texas 2012 Republican platform is very honest about.[7]

Code Words

Here are some direct quotations taken from the 2012 Texas Republican platform that appear again and again and again in anti–ethnic studies legislation or are used to justify such bills.

"We believe the current teaching of a multicultural curriculum is *divisive*. We favor *strengthening our common American identity* and loyalty instead of political correctness that nurtures *alienation* among racial and ethnic groups. . . .

"We oppose the teaching of Higher Order Thinking Skills (HOTS) (values clarification), critical thinking skills and similar programs . . ." (Emphasis added.)[8]

Micromanaging Classrooms

Anti–ethnic studies policies strive to legislate the books we can put into students' hands. This was the case in Arizona and in Texas.

An editorial against HB 1938 and SB 1128 by the *San Antonio Express-News* put it best:

> The Legislature should leave the content of Texas college courses alone. Micromanaging education from the peanut gallery is hazardous. Repeated attempts over the years by some members of the State Board of Education to impose their ideologies into the textbooks being used in Texas classrooms made the state a laughingstock of the nation on more than one occasion.[9]

Doughnut Hole Legislation

Arizona Republicans fine-tuned the tactic of creating "doughnut hole legislation" to attack ethnic studies.[10] Teachers are the targets of the attack; rather than attacking them directly, though, laws are enacted to surround them and pressure them into compliance. Dan Patrick's SB 1128 is doughnut hole legislation, and the National Association of Scholars (NAS) report, *Recasting History: Are Race, Class, and Gender Dominating American History?*, revealed that professors are, indeed, the target.

The report stated: "We looked at the assigned readings for each course and the research interests of the forty-six faculty members who taught them. We also compared faculty members' research interests with the readings they chose to assign. . . . We classified faculty members assigning primarily high RCG [race, class, and gender] readings as 'high assigners' of RCG materials."[11]

Bogus Reports

House Bill 2811 was created to prohibit courses that promote the overthrow of the government? Who even worries about that? Besides, we already have a Sedition Act that prevents individuals from promoting the overthrow of the government. Why do we need a Sedition Act for academic courses? How do you even put a school course on trial? Oh, I guess you can't. Thus, the US Supreme Court will throw out that law, even though it might take another three to five years, and half a million to a million dollars.

Just as illogical, Texas's HB 1938 and SB 1128 were based on the aforementioned National Association of Scholars *Recasting History* report, which slammed professors for talking too much about race, class, and gender when discussing the following American classics like *Narrative of the Life of Frederick Douglass* and *César Chávez and La Causa* among others.[12]

Denial

To this day, the far right Republican regime denies that books have been banned in Arizona. It will be up to the Supreme Court to convince them of that. A press release from the Tucson Unified School District, posted on their website on January 17, 2012, denied that it had banned books, though it does admit that enforcers walked into classrooms during class time and, in front of our young, boxed up books by our most beloved authors.[13]

And here is just one quote that is a testament to the doublespeak that George Orwell warned us about: "NONE of the above books have been banned by TUSD. Each book has been boxed and stored as part of the process of suspending the classes. The books listed above were cited in the ruling that found the classes out of compliance with state law."[14]

Likewise, in Texas, the Republican legislators who proposed HB 1938 and SB 1128 deny that they wanted to attack ethnic studies. I can't tell you what is in these legislators' hearts, but I can tell you what was in their bills. These bills would have led to the demise of ethnic studies. We must nip these oppressive laws in the bud, for it's much harder for them to be taken off the books once they're in place.

When asked what brought this issue to his attention, Rep. Capriglione did not refer to the NAS report, although the author and champions of the bill were sitting behind him and about to testify—authors who had so twisted their definition of censorship that they could so easily write a denial of our history into their report: "The kinds of courses that Librotraficante is concerned about will most likely, if the bill is passed, still continue to be offered at Texas public universities as electives. The only change would be that they would not count toward the state US history requirement in general education."[15]

Rep. Capriglione did, however, cite Jay Leno's "Jaywalking" segment as proof that Texas college students did not know enough about US history. If discrediting our history is not a big deal, then I suggest that Rep. Capriglione's Jaywalking comprehensive history course be an elective. We would at least get to see the content of the course, and could then get a better idea of what is in the minds, hearts, and imaginations of the far right.

During this whole period, no one ever showed us the "comprehensive American history course" that the Texan bills and the Republican legislators were advocating. However, they would have gone into effect in just four months, if the law had been passed.

HB 1938 would have taken US history back to 1938, before ethnic studies existed. I'm so proud of everyone who stood up for critical thinking, ethnic studies, and intellectual freedom. We look forward to uniting with the broader community to protect intellectual freedom for all.

TONY DIAZ, "El Librotraficante," is a novelist and holds a master of fine arts in creative writing. He brings together contemporary Latino arts, culture, and business in ways that have transformed Houston, Texas, and the nation. He made national and international news in 2012 in his role as a leader of the Librotraficante movement, championing freedom of speech. Diaz is also cofounder of Protectors of the Dream, which awards grants and free legal representation to youth of the Dream Act movement. See more at TonyDiaz.net.

THE SPIN GAME: POLICE ATTEMPT TO HIDE INFILTRATION OF ACTIVIST GROUPS[16]

Beau Hodai

Infiltrate: verb [with object]
1. enter or gain access to (an organization, place, etc.) surreptitiously and gradually, especially in order to acquire secret information: other areas of the establishment were infiltrated by fascists; permeate or become a part of (something) by infiltration: computing has infiltrated most professions now. Medicine (of a tumor, cells, etc.) spread into or invade (a tissue or organ).
2. (of a liquid) permeate (something) by filtration: virtually no water infiltrates deserts such as the Sahara; introduce (a liquid) into something by filtration: lignocaine was infiltrated into the wound.

—Oxford American English Dictionary

On May 22, 2013, *Democracy Now!* interviewed Matthew Rothschild, editor of the *Progressive*, about his cover story for the June edition entitled "Spying on Occupy Activists." This story was based on a report I authored that was issued on May 20 by DBA Press and the Center for Media and Democracy, titled *Dissent or Terror: How the Nation's Counter Terrorism Apparatus, in Partnership with Corporate America, Turned on Occupy Wall Street.*

The report details how counterterrorism personnel employed at many of the nation's "fusion centers" monitored and surveilled citizens engaged in the Occupy Wall Street movement nationwide. While a number of related issues are discussed in "Dissent or Terror," its central narrative explores the actions of counterterrorism/ law enforcement personnel engaged in the Arizona Counter Terrorism Information Center (ACTIC, commonly known as the "Arizona Fusion Center") directed toward members of Occupy Phoenix, as well as other Arizona activist groups. Such counterterrorism/law enforcement entities engaged in ACTIC include the US Department of Homeland Security (DHS) offices of Infrastructure Protection and Intelligence and Analysis, Transportation Security Administration (a DHS component agency), Federal Bureau of Investigation, Arizona Department of Public Safety's Intelligence Bureau, and numerous "homeland defense/counterterrorism" units of Phoenix metropolitan area police departments—such as the Phoenix Police Department Homeland Defense Bureau (HDB).

Among the key findings discussed in "Dissent or Terror," as well as the *Progressive's* cover story, is the fact that the Phoenix Police Department (PPD) had dispatched an undercover officer to gather intelligence on the activities of both the Occupy Phoenix movement and activist groups planning protest actions in relation to the American Legislative Exchange Council's (ALEC) 2011 States and Nation Policy Summit, which was held in the upscale Phoenix suburb of Scottsdale in late November and early December of that year. This undercover officer, most likely a PPD detective from the Major Offender Bureau by the name of Saul Ayala, had been infiltrating activist groups as early as July 2011 (according to activist accounts) and had been asked to attend and report on activist plans for the launch of Occupy Phoenix (which officially launched over a two-day event held on October 14 and 15) as early as October 2, 2011. In order to execute this infiltration, the undercover detective presented himself to activists as a homeless Mexican national by the name of "Saul DeLara." Saul attempted to support this false identity and his social networking throughout the Phoenix activist community be establishing a Facebook page under his false name and by gathering numerous activist Facebook "friends."

Interestingly, according to activist accounts, toward the end of

Saul's infiltration of the Phoenix activist community, he claimed to have ties to certain "anarchist" actions in Mexico. This appears to have been an oblique reference to a group in Mexico calling themselves the Conspiracy of Cells of Fire/Informal Anarchist Federation, which, through a number of anarchist online forums, had claimed responsibility for a fire at Las Torres shopping mall in Juarez on November 2, 2011.

As detailed in "Dissent or Terror," records obtained by DBA Press and the Center for Media and Democracy show that intelligence gathered by Saul through his infiltration of the Phoenix activist community was reported—via his superior, Career Criminal Squad Sgt. Tom Van Dorn—to Phoenix police entities, including HDB, and that this intelligence was likely used in the creation of intelligence products that were delivered via ACTIC personnel to private corporations, banks, and security personnel employed by private entities that were subject of Occupy Phoenix protests. Furthermore, records indicate that Ayala and Van Dorn attended a number of meetings at ACTIC, held for the purpose of discussing activist protest plans for the ALEC conference. Records indicate that Michael Rohme, a terrorism liaison officer with the ACTIC and a detective with the police Intelligence Unit, had invited Phil Black, director of security of the Westin Kierland Resort and Spa (the Scottsdale resort at which the ALEC conference was held), to attend at least one of these meetings. Black was the de facto head of ALEC's private security detail in Arizona (a security detail that was largely comprised of off-duty Phoenix police officers earning thirty-five dollars per hour). Records indicate that Rohme had been a regular recipient of intelligence provided by Saul and was the chief point of ACTIC/HDB contact with both ALEC personnel and other private entities working on behalf of ALEC—including Mark Davis, head of corporate security for then-ALEC member corporation Bayer HealthCare.

In preparation for the May 22 Rothschild interview, *Democracy Now!* requested comment from PPD Public Information Officer (PIO) Trent Crump on a number of the report's findings. Crump declined to be interviewed on the show, but did respond to a number of questions submitted in writing by the show.

One question posed to Crump asked whether Phoenix "law enforcement infiltrate[d] Occupy meetings," and if they had, why?

In response, Crump wrote: "Infiltrate? no, attend open meetings, yes." [sic]

Democracy Now!, relaying Crump's response, read this nonsense on television. Given the fact that earlier that day of May 22, the Facebook page utilized by "Saul DeLara" had been removed from Facebook, I thought this response on Crump's part was very interesting, especially since Crump had been unable to discuss the specifics of Saul's activity with me on several past occasions. On May 23, I wrote to Crump with a few follow-up questions.

First I asked how Crump would define the practice of "infiltration." The second question was as follows:

> From what I've gathered, a PPD Major Offender Bureau (PP-DMOB) undercover officer named Saul (most likely then-PPDMOB undercover detective Saul Ayala) posed as an activist, or person interested in becoming involved in activism, under the assumed name of "Saul DeLara." This individual presented a false identity to activists he approached and attempted to befriend, or otherwise gain the confidence of. Specifically, according to the accounts of activists who interacted with this officer, Saul reportedly stated that he was a homeless Mexican national who had just been released from prison and who had family/friends active in activism/anarchist groups in Mexico. Some activist accounts state that this activity on the part of this undercover officer began as early as July 2011.
>
> Evidence of the undercover officer's deliberate use of a false identity in order to gain the confidence of activists is contained on a Facebook page made by this undercover officer to support this false identity. Further supportive of the assertion that this undercover officer used this false identity to gain the trust/friendship of activists is the fact that this Facebook page was used to gather "friends." Interestingly enough, the page in question was removed from Facebook yesterday.
>
> I have reconstituted the page from screenshots taken in November 2012 here (for reference: http://dbapress.com/

source-materials-archive/dissent-or-terror-source-materials-archive/saul-delara-facebook-page). Furthermore, through the months of October and November 2011, this undercover officer did not merely attend open meetings held by activists, but also—utilizing his deliberately established false persona—regularly "hung out" with specific individuals in Cesar Chavez Plaza for the express purpose of intelligence gathering. Records indicate that the purpose of this undercover officer's attendance at meetings, as well as his days spent in Cesar Chavez Plaza "hanging out" with specific individuals, was to gather intelligence. This intelligence was delivered to then-PPDMOB Career Criminal Squad Sgt. Tom Van Dorn. Van Dorn would then pass this intelligence along to other personnel, including those employed at PPD Bureau of Homeland Defense, PPD Community Relations Bureau, other personnel engaged at ACTIC. . . .

While other records, namely various records associated with [Occupy Phoenix protest] Incident Action Plans, do reflect the more passive use of undercover officers through the placement of such plainclothes officers in activist marches, it seems to me that there is a much greater depth to the activities carried out by this PPDMOB undercover officer. How would this above-detailed activity compare/contrast with your definition of "infiltrate"?

Rather than supporting the claim he made for a *Democracy Now!* national audience—that PPD had not "infiltrated" activist groups, but had simply "attended open meetings"—Crump responded to my line of questioning with the following:

Beau, I am not a dictionary so I do not need to define it. This was your choice of words not mine and maybe that is why we differ. In fact, I believe I read another version in your article, something to the effect of, "Dispatched an undercover to attend activist planning meetings." If I were asked what we did in this case I would say, we used lawful techniques to gather information.

So there you have it: because, in one instance, I did not explicitly use the word "infiltrate" in describing the activities of this undercover detective, and because Crump is "not a dictionary," the Phoenix Police Department public information officer thinks he has *carte blanche* to twist his response to a simple question, delivered to a nationwide audience, to the point of mendacity—while, on the same day, someone attempted to scrub the Internet of evidence of PPD's infiltration of Phoenix activist groups by deleting the Facebook profile dedicated to the false persona of the undercover detective who, without a doubt, infiltrated the Phoenix activist community.

This is the amount of respect these public servants have for the public.

BEAU HODAI is the author of *Dissent or Terror: How the Nation's Counter Terrorism Apparatus, in Partnership with Corporate America, Turned on Occupy Wall Street.* The report was published jointly by the Center for Media and Democracy and DBA Press. Hodai is a regular contributor to the Center for Media and Democracy and is publisher of DBA Press.

STOP PATRIARCHY: SOCIAL JUSTICE CONFERENCE USES POLICE AND THREAT OF ARREST TO SUPPRESS AND CENSOR ANTIPORN VIEWS

Sunsara Taylor

On April 12, 2013, eight members of End Pornography and Patriarchy: The Enslavement and Degradation of Women (StopPatriarchy.org) were evicted, under threat of arrest, from the annual conference "From Abortion Rights to Social Justice, Building the Movement for Reproductive Freedom," sponsored by Hampshire College's program for Civil Liberties and Public Policy (CLPP).

Our alleged crime? Peacefully advocating antipornography and anti–sex industry views at our own officially registered organizational table.

According to Mia Sullivan, director of CLPP, our political opposition to the sex industry had made a few pro-porn conference-goers feel that the conference was no longer a "safe space."

However, just this single, uninvestigated complaint is all it took for Ms. Sullivan to bring police and insist that we leave immediately or be arrested for trespassing. And, to be very clear: the police were with Ms. Sullivan from the very first time she or anyone else from CLPP approached us.

This outrageous act of political suppression is a dangerous escalation in an overall growing trend toward a pro-porn, pro-"sex work" hegemony within academia as well as large sections of the so-called "women's movement." Not only is there an increasing embrace of pornography and the sex industry, but critiques focusing on the violence and degradation, the dehumanization and commodification of women's bodies and destruction of millions upon millions of real women's and young girls' lives through these industries is being shut down as "beyond the pale"—and in this case, even criminal.

Reversing this growing political suppression is essential. It is always wrong to call in agents of the highly oppressive and reactionary state to suppress the political views of fighters for liberation. It is also critical to women everywhere that the debate over, and opposition to, the truly monstrous crimes against women in the global sex industry deepen and spread.

What Exactly Happened at Our Table that Merited the Police?

A group of vociferous pro-porn people approached our table to argue in favor of porn and the sex industry, citing their personal experiences with the "sex industry," with sexual violence, and with bondage, domination, and sadomasochism (BDSM). As we are not in favor of intruding into people's consensual sexual behavior, we argued the larger point: sexuality is not formed for anyone in a vacuum. In a world that is saturated with violence against women, a world that sexualizes degradation and humiliation, it is not surprising that those ideas get reflected in people's genuinely felt sexual desires, including by victims of sexual violence.

But, the "right" to market yourself as a sexual commodity has no meaning outside of a world that gives rise to the idea of women's bodies as commodities, as things to be used, tortured, degraded, and hurt for the sexual pleasure of men. And in that kind of world, this real world is littered with the bodies of millions of women and very young girls who have been kidnapped, pimped, beaten, tortured, sold by starving families, drugged and tricked, and repeatedly raped and sold and then discarded as nothing more than unthinking flesh.

While this debate was passionate, we were calm, substantive and *principled*. We repeatedly refocused things on the need to look at all these phenomena from the vantage of the liberation of women, not from one's own narrow experience, and on the possibility and necessity of opening up space for truly liberating personal and sexual relations, based on equality, mutual respect, and a shared desire. We also drew attention to our call to action, which explicitly states that we are not seeking to enact laws to ban pornography, and that we oppose the criminalization of women in the sex industry; rather, we are challenging individuals to reject this culture of degradation and commodification of women.

For this the police were called, and we were escorted off campus grounds under threat of arrest.

A Little Background

Stop Patriarchy attended the CLPP conference due to our opposition to the war on women, especially as a result of the extreme escalation of attacks on abortion rights across the country. Today, abortion is more difficult to access, more stigmatized, and more dangerous to provide than at any time since *Roe v. Wade*.

StopPatriarchy.org sees this as the "mirror opposite" of the increasingly degrading, cruel, brutal, humiliating, and mainstream nature of pornography, and was eager to get into all this with conference participants. Within this, some members were bringing the view of all-the-way revolution and communism as it has been reenvisioned by Bob Avakian.[17]

It came as no surprise that people had strong reactions—positive and negative—to our politics. Some loved that we challenged the feelings of shame and guilt many women are made to feel about their abortions, while others claimed it was wrong to "tell women how to feel." Some appreciated that we called out President Barack Obama for conciliating with restrictions on abortion, for his drone program, for assassinating US citizens, and for continuing torture at Guantá-namo. Others insisted that Obama is "our friend." Some loved our opposition to porn and began wearing our stickers ("If you can't imagine sex without porn, you're fucked!"), others got into thoughtful discussion, and still others strongly disagreed.

We welcomed this. Isn't one of the purposes of a conference on social justice to make opportunities for people to hear different ap-proaches as they are put forward by those who share a commitment to defending the lives and rights of oppressed people?

However, we cannot dismiss that these political differences may have played a role in the CLPP organizers' eagerness to seize on the opportunity to remove us from their conference.

One Final Irony

We sent an open letter to the CLPP organizers and the Hampshire community:

> Finally, it is a bitter irony that your conference included nu-merous workshops on "state violence," "racial justice," and the "prison–industrial complex" yet one of the people you called the police on is a young Black man who has been Stopped & Frisked growing up in Brooklyn more times than he can re-member. This young man decided to put his body on the line and face up to a year in jail when he joined in the campaign of mass civil disobedience against Stop & Frisk last year to-gether with Carl Dix, Cornel West, and dozens of others. It is a further bitter irony that your conference held workshops and gave voice extensively to concerns about making the con-ference welcoming and safe for LGBT people, yet one of the people you called the police on is a transgender person who (owing to the obvious dangers which face transgender people particularly at the hands of police and in jail) has judiciously calculated which political activities to take part in specifically to avoid the risk of arrest. *Neither of these people imagined that a conference on "Abortion Rights" and "Social Justice" would be the place where they faced the greatest threat of being imprisoned!*

For more information about this use of police by Hampshire College's program for Civil Liberties and Public Policy, visit our website at StopPatriarchy.org/opposesuppression.

SUNSARA TAYLOR is a writer for *Revolution Newspaper* (revcom.us) and the initiator of the movement to End Pornography and Patriarchy: The Enslavement and Degradation of Women (StopPatriarchy.org).

THE WEAVE

John Collins

The Weave: Mediocracy Unspun (WeaveNews.org) emerged out of a seminar on global news analysis that I have designed and taught since 2000 in St. Lawrence University's Global Studies Department, one of the first degree-granting undergraduate global studies programs in the United States. The seminar sought to use analytical tools associated with political economy, ideology critique, and discourse analysis to help students engage critically with mainstream news media texts while also examining the mass media's broader social role. In keeping with the intellectual orientation of global studies, the course placed significant emphasis on how news media help create and reproduce power/knowledge regimes that are grounded in pervasive global hierarchies. As the course evolved to take into account the rise of the Internet and the proliferation of web-based independent and alternative media outlets, however, students decided that rather than simply engaging in the detached analysis of CNN and the *New York Times*, they wanted to be part of the solution.

Discussions around these concerns became the catalyst for the transformation of the seminar into a more praxis-oriented course. Students in the 2006 seminar developed the idea of creating a blog-based website that would attempt to provide the kind of context that is often lacking in mainstream news reports. One student came up with the project's name after researching the etymology of the word "context": from the Latin *contextus*, meaning "to weave together." Another student built the initial *Weave* website, and each member of the seminar worked on researching and blogging about a particular underreported story. Some of the topics covered during the project's early stages included the US practice of so-called "extraordinary rendition," threats to the world's oceans, and the rise of private military companies.

The current *Weave* website, launched in 2011, continues to feature blogs focusing on underreported stories. Many of these are created by students who take the news analysis seminar now titled "Blogging the Globe: News Analysis and Investigative Journalism." In the seminar, students are trained in basic media analysis, investigative journalism, and blog-style writing. Some notable topics in recent years include the global politics of trash, internally displaced persons (IDPs) in Colombia, legal and jurisdictional politics on Native American reservations, and underreported aspects of the environmental movement.

According to its mission statement, the *Weave*

> seeks to contribute to positive social change and the cultivation of an informed citizenry by providing critical perspectives on important stories, voices, and processes that are not receiving sufficient public attention . . . [T]he *Weave* is a small but determined response to media consolidation (the concentration of more and more media power in fewer and fewer hands) and the failures of the mainstream media to provide the depth of information and the breadth of perspectives that are crucial to a healthy democratic culture.

This core mission is supplemented by a series of five overlapping commitments to public intellectual work, responsible representation, citizen journalism, democratic dialogue, and social justice.

A second type of content found on the *Weave* website is the Big Questions project inspired by the example of Dropping Knowledge (DroppingKnowledge.org). *Weave* staffers have developed a series of broad questions that concern people in all parts of the world (e.g., "What comes after capitalism?" or "What is today's most underreported story?") and have developed a growing archive of video responses to these questions. The responses are gleaned from interviews conducted both on the SLU campus and beyond, such as on study trips or at national conferences. Examples of interviewees who have responded to the Big Questions include prominent scholars (e.g. Dr. Linda Alcoff), journalists (e.g. Amy Goodman, the late Anthony Shadid), public intellectuals (e.g. Dr. Vandana Shiva, Bill McKibben), community activists (e.g. Ruben García), and artists (e.g. Staceyann Chin). Participation in the Big Questions project helps students gain valuable training in techniques of basic media production as they work to record, edit, and upload videos, and circulate them through social media.

A notable recent addition to the *Weave* project was the creation of a credit-bearing internship course in 2011. *Weave* interns study the history of independent and alternative media, read about and discuss some of the particular dilemmas confronting such efforts, and work on collaborative projects designed to move the *Weave* forward. The projects help them develop a range of practical skills—fundraising, public relations, community outreach, media production, grant writing, event planning, professional presentations—that will serve them well in a variety of post-graduation career paths.

Lukasz Niparko, a global studies major from Poznan, Poland, was a *Weave* intern in 2011 and subsequently created a blog titled *Solidarity Avenue*. "When I heard about the *Weave*, I decided to make it my 'little solution' to the world's problems," he recalled. "After all, the *Weave* embraces Gramsci's idea of organic intellectualism, understands the ideological apparatuses of Althusser, promotes the self-empowerment and social organizing found in Freire, and is a form of praxis that comes from Marx. *The Weave* became my ultimate answer to 'what I can do as a student,' but also to what can I do as a citizen who is striving to understand this globalizing world."

Given the ongoing realities of media consolidation and the erosion of the core investigative role of professional journalism, there is an urgent need to develop opportunities for the next generation to fill in the informational gaps left by the mainstream media—and to build new alternatives that can contribute to positive social change. With this in mind, the *Weave* is looking to expand its reach and impact by creating collaborative relationships with other colleges and universities, working with professors to build investigative blogging into their courses, providing more in-depth training to its staff members, networking with other independent journalists throughout the United States and beyond, and expanding its roster of bloggers and videographers.

JOHN COLLINS, PHD, is professor and chair of the Global Studies Department at St. Lawrence University, and director of *The Weave*.

IT'S TIME TO FIX THIS MESS: WHAT THE WORLD COULD BE

Ken Walden

What the World Could Be is a series of short movies meant to empower people by helping them access and understand often difficult information regarding the problems we face, to help transcend these problems with achievable solutions in effort to make the world, well, more of what it could be—a better place for all. *What the World Could Be* focuses not just on problems, but how to work through them in creative, often simple ways. So, I want to talk about more than problems, something that will make you smile: solutions.

We face many problems as a species, but since that is a pretty large topic I'm going to start with one example we deal with in our film shorts: global warming. The best part is that the solutions are really easy to implement, they will save you tons of money, and improve your health. Yes, it sounds like and cheesy sales pitch . . . but it's very true. Read on!

First, if you want to know more after reading here, please watch videos we produced about these troubling issues by visiting our site at WhatTheWorldCouldBe.com. Our goal is to provide assistance through learning about these complex issues and then show how you can become an active part of solving these issues. This article is an example of how our series of film projects works, and all of the resources for this article and our project are listed on our website.

Problems vs. Solutions

Most people get a knot in their stomach just hearing the word "news."

Have you ever noticed how a lot of "journalism" or "news" is based on reporting a problem and then leaving you at this point?

You are left to figure out what, if anything, to do about what you just read or saw, and that can be a very difficult task. In fact, after going through this process ourselves for years, we can tell you that it is. Feeling ill about reading news is a major reason why 30 to 40 percent don't read news at all. Our goal is to make that easy. Let's get to our example, the key issue of global warming.

Global Warming and Climate Change

For many, the discovery of the very problems we face as a society is the scary part. But once we understand a problem, we must move to the solutions, and that doesn't have to be an immobilizing process.

Yes, global warming is real and it's very dangerous, as in "extinction-level" dangerous.

In short, we are putting too much carbon into our environment, and most of it is from coal power plants and transportation. Let's look at a few main areas of concern with doing this.

Melting Ice Caps = Rising Seas

One problem is that this carbon is heating up the planet's oceans and atmosphere, which in turn melts our ice caps and glaciers. According to National Aeronautics and Space Administration (NASA) satellite photos, roughly one-third of our ice caps have melted since around 1980. When we melt too much ice, the oceans rise, which makes a mess of our coastal cities . . . and most of our major cities are on the coasts. The result would be like a disaster movie—or worse, like a *real* disaster, like Hurricane Sandy.

Crazy Weather and Droughts

The other tricky thing to understand is that this slight increase in temperature makes the weather more erratic and unpredictable. We have bigger big storms, colder cold weather, hotter hot weather, and bad droughts. Droughts interfere with our ability to grow food. Yes, food . . . that yummy stuff we eat every day. We're already having major drought problems.

Also, water from glacial runoff supplies water to hundreds of millions of people. So if we melt the ice caps, there goes the water supply.

Carbon in Oceans Kills off Food & Oxygen

Now hang tight because this is the super scary part, but then we get into the fun "fix it and save you money" part, so please keep on reading.

Much of this excessive carbon gets absorbed into our oceans, making the oceans more acidic. This is the kind of acidity that burns the coral reefs and kills shellfish and shell-like life-forms. Coral reefs and planktons are the bottom of the food chain so if you fry them, you fry our fishes' food supply and that's not good . . . at all. Fish are a major part of the world's food supply.

Here is yet another piece of the puzzle. As we mentioned, ocean acidity also kills plankton. Who cares? Well if you breathe oxygen, you care. Phytoplankton creates around two-thirds of our oxygen. We're killing off roughly 1 percent a year. Between that and rapid deforestation, which is the other major contributor to our oxygen supply, we're wiping out our oxygen supply. Not good.

In the last 200 to 250 years we've increased the acidity of the oceans roughly 30 percent. If you're thinking "Yikes," then you are comprehending this correctly.

How Long Do We Have?

You know in a horror/thriller movie where things are really bad, and then they get worse? This is that part.

As of May 2013, it is estimated that we have some eighteen months to turn this around before we hit a very undesirable tipping point on climate change. We can do it, but we need to act *now*. If not, it will be irreversible, and over the next ten to sixty years, things will start to *really* unravel.

Congratulations! You've made it through the yucky part. Now the fun part.

The Solutions!

First, an estimated 40 percent of greenhouse gas comes from industrialized farming and shipping products all over the world. So buying locally produced organic food and goods has a *big* impact. Plus, your health will improve by not eating food laced with pesticides. Simple! On our site, we've listed simple ways to increase the efficiency of your driving by 20 to 25 percent, which saves you money and helps reduce carbon output.

Did you know that putting solar on your home—or even your apartment—is free, and you start saving money while helping reduce carbon output? These are just a few easy ways to address this major problem and there are far more on our site. Yes, we need our government to get moving on this too, and we cover that as well.

That Was Easy. See, that wasn't so bad, and this is what our site is about. We want you to be part of the solution and make it easier to do. Please check out our site and share it. The more people understand the problems, and that they can be part of the solution, the more chance we have to make the world what it could be. Visit What-TheWorldCouldBe.com for more information about the challenges we face, what is already being done about them, and where you can plug in.[18]

Remember, you are the solution!

KEN WALDEN is the director and founder of What the World Could Be. He has an extensive background in audio and video production, and he has run his own business for over nine years. Ken feels strongly that the best possible application of those skills is to make the issues facing humanity more accessible for understanding and present solutions on which everyone can act.

Notes

1. The phrase Media Democracy in Action has been a tagline used by Project Censored for over a decade. Even though this theme runs throughout our books every year, since 2011 we have included a specific chapter highlighting activists, scholars, independent journalists, and others dedicated to issues of media democracy and media freedom. We continue that tradition here. See Mickey Huff and Project Censored, *Censored 2012: Sourcebook for the Media Revolution* (New York: Seven Stories Press), ch. 5; and Mickey Huff, Andy Lee Roth, and Project Censored, *Censored 2013: Dispatches from the Media Revolution* (New York: Seven Stories Press), ch. 4. for previous installments, or visit our website at http://www.projectcensored.org.

2. Thoughts inspired by an interview with Project Censored's Mickey Huff and Peter Phillips on KPFA, Pacifica Free Speech Radio, *The Morning Mix: The Project Censored* Show, February 15, 2013.
3. See "Open-space Technology," http://en.wikipedia.org/wiki/Open-space_technology.
4. Find out more about Librotraficante's work and strategies by visiting http://www.stoptxhb1938.org.
5. HB 2281, 49th legis., 2nd reg. sess. (2010), http://www.azleg.gov/legtext/49leg/2r/bills/hb2281s.pdf.
6. Republican National Committee, *Growth and Opportunity Project* (2013), http://growthopp.gop.com/RNC_Growth_Opportunity_Book_2013.pdf.
7. Alison Sacriponte, "Federal judge upholds Arizona ethnic studies," *Jurist*, March 13, 2013, prohibitionhttp://jurist.org/paperchase/2013/03/federal-judge-upholds-arizona-ethnic-studies-prohibition.php; 2012 Republican Party of Texas, *Report of Platform Committee* (2012), http://s3.amazonaws.com/texasgop_pre/assets/original/2012Platform_Final.pdf. See also Tony Diaz, "Texas GOP Platform Would Discourage Multiculturalism," July 11, 2012, http://www.chron.com/opinion/outlook/article/Texas-GOP-platform-would-discourage-3700653.php.
8. Ibid., 8.
9. "Lawmakers Should Stop Micromanaging Classes," *San Antonio Express-News*, March 15, 2013, http://www.mysanantonio.com/opinion/editorials/article/Lawmakers-should-stop-micromanaging-classes-4358374.php.
10. Tony Diaz, "Plan to Play Down Ethnic Studies Is Bad for Texas," *Houston Chronicle*, April 5, 2013, http://www.chron.com/opinion/outlook/article/Plan-to-play-down-ethnic-studies-is-bad-for-Texas-4412967.php.
11. Richard W. Fonte, Peter W. Wood, and Ashley Thorne, *Recasting History: Are Race, Class, and Gender Dominating American History?*, report, National Association of Scholars (January 2013), http://www.nas.org/images/documents/Recasting_History.pdf.
12. Ashley Thorne, "Texas Legislature Hears Arguments on Comprehensive Survey' Bill," National Association of Scholars, April 19, 2013, http://www.nas.org/articles/texas_legislature_hears_arguments_on_comprehensive_survey_bill.
13. "Reports of TUSD Book Ban Completely False and Misleading," Tucson Unified School District, January 17, 2012, http://www.tusd.k12.az.us/contents/news/press1112/01-17-12.html.
14. Ibid.
15. Ashley Thorne, "Why 'Comprehensive' History is Controversial," March 19, 2013, National Association of Scholars, http://www.nas.org/articles/why_comprehensive_history_is_controversial.
16. Beau Hodai, *Dissent or Terror: How the Nation's Counter Terrorism Apparatus, in Partnership with Corporate America, Turned on Occupy Wall Street*, PR Watch, May 20, 2013, http://www.prwatch.org/files/Dissent%20or%20Terror%20FINAL_0.pdf. See also Beau Hodai, "Government Surveillance of Occupy Movement," http://www.sourcewatch.org/index.php/Government_Surveillance_of_Occupy_Movement.
17. For more on Revcom, see http://revcom.us/avakian/index.html.
18. For a detailed list of sources used for this portion of the chapter, and for the series of films in the project What the World Could Be, see the website http://www.whattheworldcouldbe.com; for more sources on solutions in this section by Ken Walden, see http://www.whattheworldcouldbe.com/WWCB/Solutions.html. To read more on solutions-oriented journalism in this volume, see the foreword by Sarah van Gelder, and ch. 13 by Michael Nagler, "The New Story: Why We Need One and How to Create It." Also see past Project Censored books *Censored 2011*, ch. 4; *Censored 2012*, ch. 4; and *Censored 2013*, ch. 10, for the work of Kenn Burrows. The Media Freedom Foundation/Project Censored is a nonprofit fiscal sponsor of this project.

CRITICAL THINKING, MEDIA LITERACY, AND NARRATIVES OF POWER

Free speech is necessary to democracy; without it, the people cannot truly participate in government. For example, Ronald Dworkin has argued,

> Free speech is a condition of legitimate government. Laws and policies are not legitimate unless they have been adopted through a democratic process, and a process is not democratic if government has prevented anyone from expressing his convictions about what those laws and policies should be.[1]

But by itself, free speech is not sufficient to guarantee legitimate democratic government. As Herbert Marcuse argued, if those who control the media have sufficiently indoctrinated the public and manipulated popular opinion, then free speech may actually serve the interests of those in power more effectively than censorship in a totalitarian society.[2] As Foucault observed in his lectures on free speech, at least since Plato, anyone interested in promoting free speech must contend with the possibility that some will abuse their license to it by making unthinking or dangerous remarks that could weaken or demolish democracy.[3]

Thus, though a necessary condition for democracy, free speech is a not sufficient for it. Free speech requires the support of critical thinking and, in our contemporary context, media literacy, or else the laws and policies that undergird democratic societies will lack legitimacy.

The chapters in Section II of *Censored 2014* address the crucial skills of critical thinking and media literacy. More than that, they demonstrate these skills in action.

In Chapter 5, "Digging Deeper," Elliot D. Cohen contrasts systematic forms of manipulation—including, for example, fear mongering, propagation of prejudice, and jingoistic appeals—with six specific critical thinking skills necessary to forestall the "human gullibility and unreason" on which the despotic exercise of power depends.

In Chapter 6, "Diffusing Conspiracy Panics," James F. Tracy distinguishes "human reason from the surface rationality of bureaucratic and technological systems" and argues for the importance of the former in challenging "official accounts of public events" and embracing our "own intrinsic social and historical agency."

In Chapter 7, "Censorship That Dares Not Speak Its Name," John Pilger documents his experience in unwittingly overstepping what he describes as the "invisible boundaries" of American liberalism. His account is a cautionary tale for any who believe that censorship is absent from the liberal foundations that seemingly support progressive politics and free speech.

Finally, in Chapter 8, "Screening the Homeland," Rob Williams addresses two recent and popular narratives of American power, the films *Argo* and *Zero Dark Thirty*. Employing the critical thinking skills and reason advocated in Cohen's and Tracy's chapters, Williams deconstructs each film's narrative to expose them as propaganda on behalf of American empire.

Notes

1. Ronald Dworkin, "The Right to Ridicule," *New York Review of Books*, March 23, 2006, http://www.nybooks.com/articles/archives/2006/mar/23/the-right-to-ridicule/. Of course, in addition to government, the mass media and other institutions can act to prevent the public expression of convictions necessary to legitimate democratic government.
2. Herbert Marcuse, "Repressive Tolerance," in *A Critique of Pure Tolerance*, eds. Robert Paul Wolff, Barrington Moore Jr., and Herbert Marcuse (Boston: Beacon Press, 1969), 95–137; http://ada.evergreen.edu/~arunc/texts/frankfurt/marcuse/tolerance.pdf.
3. Michel Foucault, *Fearless Speech*, ed. Joseph Pearson (Los Angeles: Semiotext(e), 2001), 13–14. See also the editors' introduction to this volume.

CHAPTER 5

Digging Deeper
Politico-Corporate Media Manipulation, Critical Thinking, and Democracy

Elliot D. Cohen

THE MYTH OF THE LEMMINGS

In 1958, the Disney Corporation, which now owns ABC, produced a film, *White Wilderness,* as part of its "True Life Adventure" series. The film showed lemmings, small mouse-like rodents, supposedly committing mass suicide by leaping into the sea. According to Disney's narrator, "a kind of compulsion seizes each tiny rodent and, carried along by an unreasoning hysteria, each falls into step for a march that will take them to a strange destiny." The Disney documentary is the source of the common belief that lemmings voluntarily march to their deaths.

Disney filmmakers faked the lemming scene, throwing them off the cliff. There is no evidence that blind compulsion ever moves lemmings in their natural habitats to commit suicide en masse.[1]

But we cannot blame the motion picture industry for such deceptions unless we are prepared to confront our own complicity in deceit. Mass deception by corporate media is possible because we, the "masses," are deceiv*able*. It is difficult but necessary to recognize our own collusion.

Democracy depends on an informed populace. The power of corporate media to propagate myth and present it as reality is a major factor in the evisceration of American democracy. American corporate media and government have done their utmost to propagate and

sustain an image of America as a beacon of freedom, the world's leading democracy and a majority of Americans have, in turn, embraced
this comfortable, mythic view as their own. The truth about America—both its past and present—is less palatable and more inconvenient than the popular myth.[2]

It is important to note that the primary motivation of gigantic media conglomerates like Disney is the amassing of profit, not truth. As
a general rule, only if truth pays will they report it. Likewise, a government seeking power and control over its citizens (which is what
all governments do to one extent or another) is likely to censor and
whitewash the information it provides to its citizens, and even worse,
to propagate disinformation, especially when the facts get in the way
of implementing its own agenda. For example, the latter was the case
in the lead-up to the Iraq War when the George W. Bush administration attempted to "make the facts fit the policy" in order to justify the
war.[3]

So it would be naïve to expect a government that seeks power and
control over its citizens *not* to use its influence over the corporate
media in order to spread self-serving propaganda. Inasmuch as the
corporate media need government to maximize their bottom line—
through tax breaks, military contracts, relaxed media ownership rules,
access to its officials and spokespersons, as well as other incentives
and kickbacks—government has incredible power and leverage over
the corporate media. Thus, instead of blaming the government for
having lied to and deceived its citizens, better not to allow ourselves to
be suckered into believing such propaganda in the first place. As this
chapter argues, our liberties are most vulnerable to faulty thinking
and best defended by sound logic.

AN ETHICS OF BELIEF FOR A FREE AMERICA

We Americans are not *helpless* victims of the politico-corporate media
establishment. Victims, yes: helpless, no. We largely permit ourselves
to be duped and manipulated. If you think otherwise, then you are
subscribing to a view of human nature that makes lemmings of us
all, for no rodent has the uniquely *human* ability of complex rational
thought. This includes the ability to doubt that for which one lacks

sufficient evidence, and to investigate a claim before believing it. As W. K. Clifford remarked in his famous essay of 1877, *The Ethics of Belief*, "It is wrong in all cases to believe on insufficient evidence; and where it is presumption to doubt and to investigate, there it is worse than presumption to believe."[4]

In fact, Clifford maintained that each and every one of us (and not just politicians, lawyers, journalists, and others who bear a fiduciary relationship to us) has a duty to question things before we commit them to belief. "It is not only the leader of men, statesmen, philosopher, or poet that owes this bounden duty to mankind," stated Clifford. "No simplicity of mind, no obscurity of station, can escape the universal duty of questioning all that we believe."[5]

So, in the sociopolitical context of mass media manipulation, how can we manage to avoid being deceived? The short answer is the one that Clifford has given—namely, by executing our duty to believe only on sufficient evidence.

However, this assumes that we are able, in the first place, to distinguish fact from fiction, and sufficient evidence from pseudo-evi-

dence. We must have a sense of what constitutes rational criteria for belief before we can even begin to determine if we have a good reason to commit something to belief. But this is possible only if we are privy to the sophistical mechanisms that the politico-corporate media establishment uses to manipulate and garner our support.

For example, the Downing Street memos document that, prior to the invasion of Iraq, Bush did not truly believe that Saddam Hussein posed a serious threat to national security.[6] Nevertheless, the Bush administration sought public support for invading Iraq and rightly believed that we, the American people, were feeling insecure enough after the attacks of September 11, 2001, to support the invasion if we were told it was necessary to prevent another terrorist attack. So the Bush administration used our vulnerability to manipulate our support.

HOW POLITICO-CORPORATE MEDIA MANIPULATION WORKS

Unfortunately, we based our commitment to Bush's war on faulty thinking. The Bush administration dug the hole, exhorted us to jump in, and we listened. This same destructive pattern has repeated itself ad nauseam. The politico-corporate establishment has indeed attempted to manipulate Americans, but we have repeatedly permitted ourselves to be duped. This is because we have relied on faulty thinking rather than on sound logic.

Government and corporate media have encouraged the masses to engage in faulty thinking, in an effort to gain public support for self-serving agendas that typically cannot be justified rationally; the only way to get them through is by sophistical means. For example, the Bush administration resorted to the systematic use of manipulation including:

- ▸ fearmongering (raising and lowering the terrorism alert level),
- ▸ well-poisoning (calling people who oppose the war "un-American"),
- ▸ making threats (threatening to jail journalists who publish "classified" government leaks),

- propagation of prejudice (media stereotypes of Arabs as terrorists and suicide bombers),
- claiming a divine right (as Bush did in waging war in Iraq),
- jingoistic appeals (positioning the American flag behind news anchors on Fox News),

and a host of other manipulative devices aimed at short circuiting rational argument. All such manipulation works by appealing to Americans' interests and values. For example, many Americans were willing to surrender their right to privacy when government officials framed such compromises in civil liberties as a means to prevent another attack on the homeland. Similarly, the movement to pass a constitutional amendment defining marriage as between a man and a woman gained support when presented as a way of preventing the desecration of what is holy. The attempt by right-wing Republicans to get women to relinquish their legal rights to birth control and abortion—such as during the 2012 Mitt Romney–Paul Ryan presidential campaign—has been orchestrated by systematic intimidation through use of such language as "baby killer," "murderer," and "slut," even though birth control prevents the need for abortions, and even though there are rational arguments on both sides of the abortion controversy. Americans were intimidated against protesting the war in Iraq because media presented such dissent as a refusal to "support the troops." Those who had the courage to stand up to the politico-corporate machine were branded "traitors" and were accused of sabotaging the effort to "win the war on terror."

From the USA PATRIOT Act of 2001 to the Clear Skies Act of 2003, legislation adverse to Americans' common interests was euphonized (and euphemized) with names that implied support for the very causes that the acts flaunted. Thus, provisions of the PATRIOT Act, such as the notorious "sneak and peek" provisions, were arguably unconstitutional and therefore markedly *un*patriotic, while the Clear Skies Act actually permitted widespread air pollution instead of cleaning it up. Yet the corporate media soft-peddled the legalization of such "unitary executive authority" while the average American citizen quietly acquiesced—some for want of knowledge, and others for failure to appreciate the potential of such legislation to undermine democracy.

Here then lies the crux of the problem: the corporate media do not ask the tough questions, and the people do not hold their feet to the fire. And public complacency reinforces government authority. We have tacitly condoned the demise of Fourth Amendment protections by not speaking up, and have passively sat by as the information portals have been dumbed down, controlled, and manipulated.

Nevertheless, we are a civilization governed by laws, and laws are supposed to ensure that the transfer of power preserves our civil liberties and democratic principles enshrined in the United States Constitution. Protection against encroachment on fundamental rights such as due process is not supposed to be based on faith that a government will not abuse its power. Thus, all Americans should care about the prospect that Barack Obama's administration (or a subsequent government administration) might, without judicial oversight, evoke the dubious provisions of the National Defense Authorization Act to destroy the life, liberty, and pursuit of happiness of anyone it perceives to stand in its way.[7]

To take back America, we must arm ourselves with reason. This means identifying and abandoning the self-defeating, anti-empirical, inauthentic, conformist styles of thinking that have made us gullible pawns, and substituting them for more rational, critical, and independent thinking.

While many Americans believe that the answer to stopping government oppression is to arm all Americans with guns, or at least to prevent government from placing any restrictions on our Second Amendment rights, neither proposal will achieve the desired end of protecting liberty and freedom if we are still uninformed, misinformed, or not thinking rationally. As our first priority, therefore, it is far better to "arm ourselves with the power which knowledge gives," as James Madison once wrote—to arm ourselves with reason and understanding.

HOW TO THINK FOR YOURSELF

A single article cannot cover all the rational thought processes that can help to promote democracy and protect us against totalitarianism's creep.[8] Nevertheless, the remainder of this article presents an overview of six practices that are crucial to thinking for ourselves in order to defend our nation against its most formidable enemies, human gullibility and unreason:

1. Ask for explanations.
2. Look for consistency.
3. Question the status quo; don't just believe it.
4. Believe only credible authorities.
5. Watch out for fear mongering and demagoguery.
6. Beware of media-supported stereotypes.

Taken together, these six instructions provide a useful heuristic for determining whether you are justified in accepting any media claim. In what follows, each is considered in its turn.

1. Ask for explanations.

Constant 24/7 news feeds on cable television networks such as Fox and CNN would suggest that Americans are kept well-informed; however, by any reasonable standard of what it means to be informed, this assumption is false.

What we really get when we tune into corporate network news is a stream of reports about disconnected events in the world with little or no attempt to explain them. This happenstance rendition of reality as depicted by corporate news media is an important part of herding Americans into blind conformity.

Political scientist Michael Parenti astutely observed, "We are left to see the world as do mainstream pundits, as a scatter of events and personalities propelled by happenstance, circumstance, confused intentions, bungled operations, and individual ambitions—rarely by powerful class interests."[9] However, being adequately informed requires understanding these events, even though the underpinnings that support such knowledge have been removed. Thus, "we read or hear that 'fighting broke out in the region,' or 'many people were killed in the disturbances,' or 'famine is on the increase.' Recessions apparently just happen like some natural phenomenon ('our economy is in a slump'), having little to do with the constant war of capital against labor and the contradictions between productive power and earning power."[10]

Decontexualized news reports enable corporate media to spin reality to serve specific political agendas. Thus, being told that the "insurgents killed ten American troops" leaves out the fact that the so-called "insurgents" were motivated to defend their homeland against invaders—not unlike what motivated the Americans themselves to attack British invaders during the Revolutionary War. Here, emotionally charged pejorative language ("insurgent") fortifies the absolutistic notion that there is only one side to a story—the American side. The combination manipulates rather than informs.

So, as consumers of information, we must dig deeper beneath the surface by looking for explanations. We can't simply expect the corporate media to provide them for us. We must conduct our own investigations and seek out investigative journalism that provides context and deeper understanding. This means gathering evidence from multiple sources, not just corporate media but also independent and foreign sources.[11]

For example, in the past decade, thousands have been killed by Unmanned Aerial Vehicles (UAVs)—commonly called drones—in Pakistan. According to the Bureau of Investigative Journalism, since 2004 there have been 2,541 to 3,533 casualties estimated; 411 to 884 of these were civilians, and 168 to 197 were children. In addition, there were between 1,173 and 1,472 injured.[12] But the corporate media has given only lip service to these atrocities. The inadequate coverage by the corporate media is itself a story.

Digging deeper means finding out why these atrocities were not adequately covered, and taking a look at who owns the corporate media can help to uncover hidden motivation. The reality is less shocking when one learns that General Electric (GE) is a major drone and weapons manufacturer.[13] Prior to 2011, at the height of the Afghanistan War, GE owned NBC Universal, one of the largest media corporations on earth. Identifying and verifying connections among the media and telecommunication conglomerates and the US government help form the framework necessary to understand why the corporate media has been remiss in its First Amendment duty to keep the American people informed about questionable government activities, especially inside the military-industrial complex.[14]

Finding an explanation for something is not good enough, though. The explanation must not be based on speculation; it must instead be based on facts that make it *probable*. In other words, an explanation is probable to the extent that it is supported by known facts. Thus, the explanation that the US went to war in Iraq to free the Iraqi people from oppression does not adequately comprise enough known facts to be probable. For instance, it does not explain why the US invaded Iraq rather than some other nation such as Sudan, where the genocide in Darfur took place. Similarly, the explanation that the US went to war in Iraq because Saddam Hussein's regime posed a threat to the US does not take into account why the weapons inspectors were never able to find any such weapons, or why Bush ignored Hussein's open invitation for United Nations weapons inspectors to come to Iraq to look for weapons of mass destruction (WMD) and interview Iraqi scientists and engineers.[15]

On the other hand, the explanation that the motive for the war was to advance US influence in the Middle East is based on many verifiable facts: For example, the Bush administration was largely composed of members of the Project for the New American Century (PNAC), a politically influential group of far right ("neoconservative") ideologues whose professed goal was to advance the US's influence in the Middle East, especially Iraq, through military action. Also, according to the Downing Street memos, the Bush administration had already made up its mind to invade Iraq even though it admitted that the case for WMD was weak and that it was necessary to "make the facts fit the policy."[16]

2. Look for consistency.

Facts must be consistent. To the extent that an explanation is inconsistent with the facts, the explanation is not probable. Reality is important in that it is consistent; if a claim is false it will sooner or later have to reckon with reality. One falsehood may be heaped on top of another in order to avoid reality's indictment, but sooner or later the false belief will run up against a consistent network of truth.

A false media claim is no different. This is why you need to check several independent sources before accepting something as fact. For example, in 2005, when the *New York Times* "broke" the story that Bush was spying on Americans without warrants,[17] this contradicted Bush's prior claim that he was first obtaining warrants. So why did Bush lie to the American people?

One possible explanation is that he did not want the American people to know that they were being spied on because they would protest and try to put an end to it. As it turned out, the *New York Times* did not quite tell the truth (or at least not the whole truth) either, for it claimed that Bush was only wiretapping American citizens' international calls and not their domestic calls. However, Mark Klein, an AT&T whistleblower, refuted this claim by providing design documents of the equipment used to tap all calls (both domestic and international) and to route their contents to National Security Agency (NSA) computers hidden deeply within AT&T centers.[18] So, it appeared that neither the corporate media (in particular, the *New York Times*) nor the government cared to broker the truth; and this was evident by the inconsistency of their claims with verifiable facts.

3. Question the status quo; don't just believe it.

This leads to another important standard of rationality. Don't believe something just because it's popular. Indeed, some of the most popular beliefs are the biggest myths, as the Disney lemming story illustrated.

For example, federal law requires all telecommunication companies (such as Comcast and AT&T) to provide facilities for government surveillance equipment. How likely is it that these companies would divulge their roles in helping the government to spy on American citizens? Not very, and as a result, most Americans believe that their personal phone messages are private. But sometimes an unexpected comment by an invited guest can breach even the corporate media's veil of secrecy. Here is one telling example:

After the authorities released pictures of Tamerlan Tsarnaev, the deceased Boston bomber, his wife Katherine Russell placed a phone call to him. Corporate media, including the *New York Times*, downplayed any possibility that the phone conversation could be retrieved. Thus, the candor of Tim Clemente, a former Federal Bureau of Investigation (FBI) counterterrorism agent, caught CNN's Erin Burnett off guard when she interviewed him. "There's no way they actually can find out what happened, right, unless she tells them?" asked Burnett, attempting to lead Clemente to the status quo response. But here is the transcript of the dialog that followed:

> CLEMENTE: No, there is a way. We certainly have ways in national security investigations to find out exactly what was said in that conversation. It's not necessarily something that the FBI is going to want to present in court, but it may help lead the investigation and/or lead to questioning of her. We certainly can find that out.
>
> BURNETT: So they can actually get that? People are saying, look, that is incredible.
>
> CLEMENTE: No, welcome to America. All of that stuff is being captured as we speak whether we know it or like it or not.[19]

Burnett's quip about what people are saying was obviously an attempt to discredit Clemente's claim; for if that is what people are saying, then they must be right. Right?

Wrong. And Clemente's bluntness about the truth resonates with the importance of not believing something just because it is popularly believed.

A popular antiwar slogan during the 1960s and '70s in the US—"What would happen if they made a war and no one came?"—underscores the very serious truth that unnecessary and immoral wars (such as the Iraq War) and other forms of needless aggression are possible only because masses of people are willing to unquestioningly support them instead of thinking for themselves. For many, it is heresy to question the authority of the commander in chief. These are people who say, "The president said there are WMD [weapons of mass destruction] in Iraq, so he must know. After all, he's the president." This is blind trust in authority, the type of trust that made it possible for power-grabbing "authorities" like Bush to cancel the great writ of habeas corpus, operate prison camps that mercilessly tortured prisoners of war, contravene the Geneva Conventions, issue signing statements that nullified and trivialized the power of Congress, ignore congressional subpoenas, fire federal prosecutors for political reasons not relevant to their performances, stack the Supreme Court with political ideologues calculated to rubber stamp the neoconservative political agenda, deprive citizens of their First Amendment rights to free speech and peaceful assembly, contravene the American citizen's Fourth Amendment right against warrantless searches and seizures, and a host of other illegal and unconstitutional actions and policies.

And it is the same blind trust that presently allows the Obama administration to operate illegal assassination squads, launch robotic drone attacks that kill innocent civilians and children, continue to operate the infamous Abu Ghraib prison, hold detainees indefinitely without due process, pass laws that permit government to conduct mass warrantless dragnets of millions of American citizens, and involuntarily detain and rendition American citizens without judicial oversight or protection. These and many other policies now operating under the Obama administration are a continuation—in some cases an expansion—of the Bush administration's illegal policies, except that they have now been made part of the legal fabric of our nation. In other words, many of the policies that were illegal under the Bush administration are now "legal" under the Obama administration.

And the majority of Americans do not even question "the law." After all, these previously unlawful practices are now (officially) legal. Never mind that the First Amendment is supposed to protect peaceful assembly to protest government breaches of civil liberties, especially ones it alleges are "legal." Unfortunately, the Obama administration made it clear how intolerant it was of the exercise of this fundamental constitutional right when it classified the Occupy movement as a "domestic terrorist threat" complete with FBI monitoring despite the fact that the only violence perpetrated was against the demonstrators by local authorities.[20]

But there is still another, even more insidious form of blind acceptance of authority that works through intimidation, and to which many have been party. Psychologist Erich Fromm referred to this form as *anonymous authoritarianism*.[21] Anonymous authoritarianism contrasts with blind acceptance of authority (in which there is an identifiable person/s—for example, the president) by having no identifiable individual authority. In anonymous authoritarianism, claimed Fromm, "nobody makes a demand, neither a person nor an idea nor a moral law. Yet we all conform as much or more than people in an intensely authoritarian society would." Here the authority is a vacuous "It." And what is "It"? It is "profit, economic necessity, the market, common sense, public opinion, what 'one' does, thinks, or feels." Since this "authority" is not overtly identifiable, it is nearly unassailable. "Who can attack the invisible? Who can rebel against Nobody?"[22]

According to Fromm, the mechanism by which this form of authority works is that of *conformity*: "I ought to do what everybody does, hence, I must conform, not be different, not 'stick out' . . . The only thing which is permanent in me is just this readiness for change. Nobody has power over me, except the herd of which I am a part, yet to which I am subjected."[23]

A clear antidote to this malignant form of thinking is that stressed by W. K. Clifford, as cited earlier: "It is wrong in all cases to believe on insufficient evidence; and where it is presumption to doubt and to investigate, there it is worse than presumption to believe."[24] Whether the claim in question is popular or not, whether you will be loved or hated for not believing (or disbelieving) it, and whether it makes you stand out or fit in, all these things are irrelevant but for the need—no, the *urgency*—to commit yourself only to that which has rational merit.

4. Believe only credible authorities.

Of course, we are not always in a position to assess for ourselves whether a claim has rational merit. To the extent that we are not experts or "authorities" on given matters, we must rely on the testimony of others who are indeed experts in their respective fields.

In this regard, Clemente's testimony refuting the status quo belief that Americans still enjoy a right to privacy in their personal telephone conversations was credible for two reasons. First, he was a former *FBI* counterterrorism agent. If anyone knows about such matters, it is someone with his background and credentials. Second, he is presently a *former* FBI counterterrorism agent, so that he is less likely to be taking his marching orders from his superior officers. The key term here is "less likely," but this does not mean "necessarily." For example, some so-called "military analysts" are really former government officials hired by the government to appear on talk shows to spread government propaganda.[25]

This is one reason why it is always preferable to rely on several independent authorities (where possible) rather than just one. Again, while this does not yield certainty, to the extent that credible experts agree, you have greater assurance that you have gotten hold of the truth.

5. Watch out for fearmongering and demagoguery.

This is an ancient admonition. As Plato observed, democracies are typically destroyed from within rather than from without when a self-aggrandizing demagogue stirs up the passions of a gullible populace by falsely promising to keep them safe. Blaming others for the woes of state, this self-styled "protector" brings the alleged culprits to justice, winning the trust of the people, and eventually seizing power and becoming a tyrant.[26]

Saddam Hussein appears to have been such a scapegoat used by the Bush administration to justify the invasion of Iraq. The underlying strategy was classic. Want to support the invasion of a sovereign nation that poses no threat to the homeland? Just get average citizens to think they might be the next victims of al-Qaeda if they fail to jump on the war bandwagon.

This mechanism of fearmongering typically works by exaggerating the consequences of something untoward happening. For example, Georgia Republican Chairperson Sue Everhart warned that allowing gay marriage would create serious potential for fraud. "You may be as straight as an arrow," she warned, "and you may have a friend that is as straight as an arrow. Say you had a great job with the government where you had this wonderful health plan. I mean, what would prohibit you from saying that you're gay, and y'all get married."[27]

But the truth is that there is no evidence to support the claimed trend toward the commission of fraud within the nine states and the District of Columbia in which gay marriage has been legalized. Nor is there any evidence that gay parents turn their children gay or that married gays are destroying traditional marriage. Yet these are views popularly espoused in the media—most often by the fringe of the Republican Party—with little or no attempt to debunk them; in some cases, such as on Fox News, pundits defend the views.[28]

And it is not just gays who are the objects of groundless distortions of reality and fear mongering. "The feminist agenda is not about equal rights for women," said televangelist Pat Robertson on the *700 Club* television show. "It is about a socialist, antifamily political movement that encourages women to leave their husbands, kill their children, practice witchcraft, destroy capitalism, and become lesbians."[29]

But it is just not clear how the "feminist agenda" (whatever exactly that is) is "socialist" and "antifamily," much less that it will lead to witchcraft, capitalism's destruction, or conversion of heterosexual women into lesbians. Frightening though such claims may sound to some, there is simply no evidence to support them. Such fear- and hatemongering works only if we are gullible and do not ask for evidence. Don't be gullible. Ask for evidence before committing something to belief.

6. Beware of stereotypes.

Asking for evidence can also defuse dangerous stereotypes, which are the coin of demagogues and hatemongers like Robertson. These are half-baked generalizations that rate, often in very unflattering terms, a class of people—like a race or a gender—without regard to individual differences among class members.[30]

It is small wonder that the simplistic portrayals of reality offered by corporate media reinforce stereotypes. An instructive example is the TV show *24*, which premiered on Fox in November 2001, just after 9/11, and aired through May 2010, during the height of the Iraq War. This show portrayed Arabs as terrorists, and encouraged dangerous, bandwagon thinking by depicting anti-American sentiments and hate crimes targeting Arabs.[31]

Of course, this is not a new trend. Indeed, the media have historically underwritten popular racial stereotypes. Consider, for example, the degrading portrayals of blacks and women in the popular 1950s CBS shows *Amos 'n' Andy* and *Father Knows Best*. Far from helping to liberate the socially oppressed, the corporate media have helped to legitimize such oppression in order to turn a profit.

Sadly, the price paid for this failure of media and culture to reject degrading stereotypes has been enormous, making it so much easier to exploit or even destroy them. Thus slavery was possible because slave owners told themselves that their slaves were not full-fledged human beings who were even capable of living freely. The oppressors of women thought the same of them. Unfortunately, though the victims of such exploitation have changed, the tendency to exploit is still very much alive.

Stereotypes rely on inadequate evidence; they are culturally transmitted, taught through the socialization we receive as children and through the popular images portrayed in the media.[32] For example, when 9/11 occurred, many Americans already had a stereotype of Arabs as terrorists, which they could use to justify their hatred of all Arabs. In fact, the stereotype of Arabs as terrorists arose in the late twentieth century, and earlier, they were popularly portrayed as villains, seducers, hustlers, and thieves.[33]

Stereotypes are driven by mindsets—the tendency to believe something even in the face of evidence to the contrary.[34] In an evidence-driven culture, stereotypes would not be accepted. Unfortunately, because all of us harbor stereotypes of one sort or another, it is important for us all to exercise willpower to resist pervasive, popular media images that support our preconceived, mindset-driven portrayals of human beings. Instead of acquiescing to belief in these images, we should make concerted efforts to be aware of our own stereotypes; to refute them by realizing that human beings need to be judged as individuals, as you yourself would wish to be judged; and to refuse to act on such simplistic, anti-empirical characterizations.

A NEW AGE OF CITIZEN JOURNALISTS

The corporate media treat news consumers as means to the end of maximizing profits. Its commitment is not to democratic principles, even though many reporters who work for the corporate media are committed to these principles. What is finally aired or published by these companies is sanitized and whitewashed to the beat of what is most conducive to its bottom line, which includes rolling over for government if it is profitable to do so.

The people cannot afford to be the puppets of the politico-corporate media establishment, for the cost is the evisceration of the most precious asset of all: our freedom. Fighting back is the only recourse we have; and this means arming ourselves with the most powerful weapon known to humankind: rational thinking. Presently, there is a sea of veridical information floating in cyberspace amid the sludge of false-to-fact claims. As consumers of knowledge and information we must surf this massive data sea, separating falsehoods from truths, testing the claims of corporate media against those of the cyber world. We must look for evidence and consistency, and we must challenge popular media images, stereotypes, and explanations, rather than believing things just because they are asserted by government officials or their media spokespersons. We must challenge what these "authorities" claim with the evidence gleaned from independent, credentialed authorities. Instead of allowing ourselves to be manipulated by anti-empirical fearmongering and demagoguery, we must defeat them with the facts.

In short, we must all be deputized as citizen investigative journalists, digging deeper beneath the surface of the corporate media façade. We must anchor our beliefs firmly in reality, not the myth. We must cease the outsourcing of our free press principles to private, for-profit entities and we must do more than attempt to hold journalistic institutions to account. We must also take on the responsibility of disseminating fact-based, people's narratives ourselves—in our communities person to person, and using whatever broader reaching communications technologies we have—as the corporate media become increasingly irrelevant in terms of accurately and meaningfully informing the public.

This means meeting our duty to think for ourselves head on. Democracy without responsible, vigilant media is not possible:

We must *be* this media!

ELLIOT D. COHEN, PHD, is a freelance journalist, director of the Institute of Critical Thinking: National Center for Logic-Based Therapy, and executive director of the National Philosophical Counseling Association (NPCA). He is also editor and founder of the *International Journal of Applied Philosophy* and the *International Journal of Philosophical Practice*, the ethics editor for *Free Inquiry* magazine, and a blogger for *Psychology Today*. His recent books include *Mass Surveillance and State Control* (Palgrave Macmillan, 2010) and *Critical Thinking Unleashed* (Rowman and Littlefield, 2009), and *The Dutiful Worrier: How to Stop Compulsive Worry without Feeling Guilty* (New Harbinger, 2011).

Notes

1. Riley Woodford, "Lemming Suicide Myth Disney Film Faked Bogus Suicide," Alaska Department of Fish and Game, September 2003, http://www.adfg.alaska.gov/index.cfm>adfg=wildlifenews.view_article&articles_id=56.

2. See, for example, Elizabeth (Betita) Martínez, "The U.S. Creation Myth and Its Premise Keepers," in *Globalize Liberation: How to Uproot the System and Build a Better World*, ed. David Solnit (San Francisco: City Lights, 2004), 51–60.

3. Text of the original Downing Street memos, http://downingstreetmemo.com/memos.html.

4. W. K. Clifford, "The Ethics of Belief," *Contemporary Review*, 1877, http://www.infidels.org/library/historical/w_k_clifford/ethics_of_belief.html.

5. Ibid.

6. See Downing Street memos, http://downingstreetmemo.com/memos.html.

7. "NDAA Signed Into Law By Obama Despite Guantanamo Veto Threat, Indefinite Detention Provisions," *Huffington Post*, January 3, 2013, http://www.huffingtonpost.com/2013/01/03/ndaa-obama-indefinite-detention_n_2402601.html. See also, Elliot D. Cohen, *Mass Surveillance and State Control: The Total Information Awareness Act* (New York: Palgrave Macmillan, 2010), 200.

8. For a detailed account of reasoning processes that promote free and rational thought, see Elliot D. Cohen, *Critical Thinking Unleashed* (Lanham, MD: Rowman and Littlefield, 2009).

9. Michael Parenti, "Monopoly Media Manipulation," May 2001, Michael Parenti Political Archive, http://www.michaelparenti.org/MonopolyMedia.html.

10. Ibid.

11. Project Censored, for example, publishes a list of reputable independent and foreign news organizations and the addresses of their websites. See http://www.projectcensored.org/news-sources.

12. Bureau of Investigative Journalism, "Obama 2013 Pakistan Drone Strikes," January 3, 2013, http://www.thebureauinvestigates.com/2013/01/03/obama-2013-pakistan-drone-strikes/. See also Mickey Huff et al., "Déja Vu: What Happened to Previous Censored Stories," ch. 2 in this volume.

13. See, for example, Seamus Milne, "America's murderous drone campaign is fuelling terror," *Guardian*, May 29, 2012, http://www.guardian.co.uk/commentisfree/2012/may/29/americas-drone-campaign-terror.

14. For analysis of additional economic and bureaucratic factors that have limited corporate news coverage of the US drone campaign, see Andy Lee Roth, "Framing Al-Awlaki: How Government Officials and Corporate Media Legitimized a Targeted Killing," *Censored 2013: Dispatches from the Media Revolution*, Mickey Huff and Andy Lee Roth with Project Censored (New York: Seven Stories Press, 2012), 353–355, 364–367. For more on the general theme of the military-industrial complex and media, see Robert Jensen, "Thinking Critically about Mass Media," in *The Military Industrial Complex at 50*, ed. David Swanson (Charlottesville, VA: MIC50.org, 2011), 152–160.

15. Saul Landau, "When Will the Media Ask Important Questions?" *Progresso*, April 10, 2013, http://progreso-weekly.com/ini/index.php/home/in-the-united-states/3876-when-will-the-media-ask-important-questions.

16. Downing Street memos.

17. James Risen and Eric Lichtblau, "Bush Lets US Spy on Callers without Courts," *New York Times*, December 16, 2005, http://www.nytimes.com/2005/12/16/politics/16program. html?pagewanted=all&_r=0.

18. Ryan Singel, "Spying in the Death Star: The AT&T Whistle-Blower Tells His Story," *Wired*, May 10, 2007, http://www.wired.com/politics/onlinerights/news/2007/05/kleininterview.

19. "Erin Burnett Out Front," CNN, May 1, 2013, http://transcripts.cnn.com/TRAN-SCRIPTS/1305/5/01/ebo.01.html. [Editor's Note: After this chapter was written and submitted for publication, the NSA, PRISM, and Edward Snowden whistleblower story broke, confirming pervasive government surveillance and spying working with private sector communications companies like Verizon and others. See ch. 1 and ch. 2 in this volume for more details. See also Glenn Greenwald, "NSA Collecting Phone Records of Millions of Verizon Customers Daily," *Guardian*, June 5, 2013, http://www.guardian.co.uk/world/2013/jun/06/nsa-phone-records-verizon-court-order.

20. Dennis Bernstein, "How FBI Monitored Occupy Movement," *Consortium News*, December 31, 2012, http://consortiumnews.com/2012/12/31/how-fbi-monitored-occupy-movement. See also Beau Hodai in "Media Democracy in Action," ch. 4 in this volume, as well as the full report online, *Dissent or Terror: How the Nation's Counter Terrorism Apparatus, in Partnership with Corporate America, Turned on Occupy Wall Street* (DBA Press and the Center for Media and Democracy, May 2013), http://www.prwatch.org/news/2013/05/11924/operation-tripwire-fbi-private-sector-and-monitoring-occupy-wall-street.

21. Erich Fromm, *The Sane Society* (New York: Henry Holt & Co., 1990).

22. Ibid., 152–153.

23. Ibid., 153–154.

24. Clifford, "Ethics of Belief."

25. David Barstow, "Beyond TV Analysts, Pentagon's Hidden Hand," *New York Times*, April 20, 2008, http://www.nytimes.com/2008/04/20/us/20generals.html?pagewanted=all. For another recent piece examining how corporate media advocate the public to "believe only credible authorities, " see Russ Baker, "New York Times Warning: Trust Authorities on Boston Bombing, or You're Nuts, " WhoWhatWhy.com, May 31, 2013. http://whowhatwhy.com/2013/05/31/new-york-times-warning-trust-authorities-on-boston-bombing-or-you're-nuts.

26. Plato, *The Republic*, Book VIII, trans. Benjamin Jowett, http://classics.mit.edi/Plato/republic.9.vii.html.

27. Luke Johnson, "Sue Everhart, Georgia GOP Chairwoman, Warns Of 'Free Ride' Gay Marriage Fraud," *Huffington Post*, April 1, 2013, http://www.huffingtonpost.com/2013/04/01/sue-everhart-gay-marriage_n_2991860.html.

28. Ben Dimiero and Eric Hananoki, "Ben Carson: Marriage Equality Could Destroy America Like The 'Fall Of The Roman Empire,'" Media Matters, March 29, 2013, http://mediamatters.org/blog/2013/03/29/ben-carson-marriage-equality-could-destory-amer/193345.

29. Anomaly, "Pat Robertson: God Will Destroy America Because of Gay Marriage," FreakOutNation, June 28, 2011, http://freakoutnation.com/2011/06/28/pat-robertson-god-will-destory-america-because-of-gay-marriage/.

30. Cohen, *Critical Thinking Unleashed*, 163.

31. See, for example, Deepa Kumar, *Islamophobia and the Politics of Empire* (Chicago: Haymarket Books, 2012), 152.

32. Cohen, *Critical Thinking Unleashed*.

33. Kumar, *Islamophobia*. See also http://arabface.us/. For further background, see the film, *Reel Bad Arabs* as it addresses the rise of Arab stereotypes in the US, http://www.reelbadarabs.com/. Rob Williams further addresses the issue of Islamophobia in "Screening the Homeland: How Hollywood Fantasy Mediates State Fascism in the US of Empire," ch. 8 in this volume.

34. Elliot D. Cohen, *Caution: Faulty Thinking Can Be Harmful to Your Happiness* (Fort Pierce, FL: Trace-Wilco, Inc., 2004).

CHAPTER 6

Diffusing Conspiracy Panics
On the Public Use of Reason in the Twenty-First Century Truth Emergency[1]

James F. Tracy

The most unpardonable sin in society is independence of thought.

—Emma Goldman

INTRODUCTION

Several years ago Project Censored's former and current directors Peter Phillips and Mickey Huff identified and explained the "truth emergency" that is among the greatest threats to human existence. This crisis of civil society is manifest in flawed (or nonexistent) investigations into 9/11 and other potential false-flag terrorism, fraudulent elections, and illegal wars, all of which are perpetuated by a corporate-controlled news media that fail to adequately inform the public on such matters.[2]

While obscuring inquiry into such events and phenomena, big media go a step further by disparaging independent journalists and researchers as "conspiracy theorists" or, more revealingly, "truthers."

As the truth emergency becomes more serious, social engineers, taking their cue from deeply antidemocratic minds such as Edward Bernays, have long understood the significance of undermining the use of reason, for it is only through reason that truth may be ascertained and evaluated. "Propaganda," on the other hand, must be unabashedly employed to guide the masses toward certain predetermined ends. Aided through the burgeoning field of mass psychology, Bernays wrote in 1928 how propaganda "is now scientific in the sense that it seeks to base its operations upon definite knowledge drawn from direct observation of the group mind, and upon the application of principles which have been demonstrated to be consistent and relatively constant."[3]

Today, a far greater technological sophistication involving the Internet, social media, and "smart" devices has brought about the conflation of propaganda with advertising and mass consumption. The preoccupation with, and ubiquity of, such media and message-making give the false impression of personal autonomy and free will, while actual political and economic power remains largely unchallenged. "We are no longer appealed to as thinking citizens," a commentary in the *Guardian* observed:

> We are simply flawed units to be prompted into spending more and costing the state less. The propaganda lies not only in the political-corporate manipulation of the public but also—most insidiously—in the way this is cloaked in the language of ideology-free empiricism and the semblance of autonomy: the idea that people are being nudged "to make better decisions for themselves" . . . Behaviour change— the "new science of irrationality," "neuro-economics," or "nudge"—claims that since people often fail to act rationally and in their best interests, their decisions and behaviour should be guided subconsciously by (rational) experts.[4]

In the years leading up to this microcosmic effort to harness reason, individuals and institutions achieving legitimacy in the public mind have long been recognized as holding a monopoly on the capacity to reason and are thus perceived as the foremost bearers of truth and knowledge. Through the endorsement of "experts"—figures perceived as authoritative in their field—the public is still easily persuaded on many matters, from genetically modified foods and water fluoridation, to terrorist attacks at home and military intervention abroad.

THE PUBLIC USES OF REASON

To a significant degree, reason is defined one-dimensionally, its relationship to truth largely taken-for-granted. Yet, as Enlightenment philosopher Gottfried Wilhelm Leibniz observed, reason marks our humanity, suggesting a portion of the soul capable of *a priori* recognition of truth. "Only reason can complete the happiness of the other virtues," political philosopher J. S. McClelland similarly remarked, "and reason does this partly through its relationship with the other faculties and partly through the pursuit of the true knowledge which is its own."[5]

With this in mind, the modern individual in the mass has been rendered at least partially soulless—devoid of self-knowledge—through her everyday deferral to the powerfully persuasive notion and representation of expertise that now extends to the subtle and voluntary dynamic of new media "interactivity." However narrowly focused, under the guise of objectivity, the institutionally affiliated journalist, academic, bureaucrat, and corporate spokesperson have in many instances become the portals of reason through which the public is summoned to observe "truth."

The human capacity to exercise reason and seek truth is further sidetracked and rerouted through a routine parade of news stories that are almost entirely divorced from political processes bearing upon the human condition and its historical trajectory. For example, the extensive media coverage afforded the trials of Jodi Arias or O. J. Simpson are platforms for applying human reason to events that have little bearing on truly critical affairs of the day. The news media's censorial tendency may be illustrated along these lines by noting how comparatively little news centers on significant trials that may allow the public to fathom the plausible cloak-and-dagger tactics of the US military–industrial–intelligence complex—specifically the legal proceedings for apparent Tucson Arizona shooter Jared Lee Loughner, alleged Aurora Colorado assassin James Holmes, the would-be Boston Marathon bomber Dzhokhar Tsarnaev, or especially Pfc. Bradley Manning in the case of WikiLeaks. The fallout from such momentous and highly questionable public events are repeatedly deemed unworthy for public consideration, while the myths fabricated to define their official meaning and significance are uniformly accepted through corporate media's carefully coordinated repetition and omission of select facts.

The understanding and application of reason is also crucial not only as a basis for assessing facts and recognizing these from the narrative and visual forms presenting themselves as news, but also to distinguish human reason from the surface rationality of bureaucratic and technological systems imposed on human activity. This is a fundamental problem of modern social relations that finds its firmament in late nineteenth- and twentieth-century social theories of the press, continuing through to the present as new media technologies further strengthen the social and political myths invented for the masses.[6]

The prevailing myth of terrorism as an existential threat to the Western world suggests the continued abandonment of reason and moves toward what Erich Fromm called the automaton, what C. Wright Mills referred to as "cheerful robots," and what David Riesman termed the "other-directed" impulse. Dissent—the desire to exert one's humanity and freedom through the application of reason to available facts—is often an unacceptable violation of the prevailing political rationality where fear and terror are prime motivators.[7]

The pressures to conform and restrain the use of reason are today often reinforced through a turn to scientific inquiry—particularly psychiatry and psychology—to rationalize and defend official accounts of public events. For example, some psychologists contend that "a conspiracy theory isn't so much a response to a single event as it is an expression of an overarching worldview," a New York Times opinion piece argued. "While psychologists can't know exactly what goes on inside our heads, they have, through surveys and laboratory studies, come up with a set of traits that correlate well with conspiracy belief."[8]

Such social science seeks to deny the individual's inherent possibility for apprehending truth and exercising intellectual agency by locating the causes of unorthodox thought and expression in presumed biological aberrations. This is readily apparent in the news media's quest to label forbidden political thought not conforming with official accounts as "conspiracy theory," with the attendant suggestion that consideration of unofficial accounts of important public events may indicate mental illness.[9]

This is an explicit move to not only augment the perceived rationality of corporate and state institutions that undergird civil society, but also to short circuit the effort to apprehend reality and assert the very human impulse toward the exercise of reason that affirms one's own freedom and being.[10] As Erich Fromm noted, in terms of evolutionary advances humanity has traveled a long biological road to arrive at *objectivity*—"that is, to acquire the faculty to see the world, nature, other persons and oneself as they are, and not distorted by desires and fears. The more man develops this objectivity, the more he is in touch with reality, the more he matures, the better can he create a human world in which he is at home."

For Fromm, the underlying element to apprehend in the rediscovery and expansion of a truly sane society has much more to do with the cultivation and exercise of reason than intelligence since the former distinguishes the human being's inclination toward truth. Fromm continued,

> Reason is man's faculty for grasping the world by thought, in contradiction to intelligence, which is man's ability to manipulate the world with the help of thought. Reason is man's instrument for arriving at the truth, intelligence is man's instrument for manipulating the world more successfully; the former is essentially human, the latter belongs to the animal part of man.[11]

Along these lines, Immanuel Kant infers how, aside from property ownership the ability to publicly exercise one's reason is a cornerstone of citizenship. In a well-known political essay, "An Answer to the Question: What is Enlightenment?," he argues that human beings can overcome their intellectual immaturity only through the "public use of reason" whereby they may reach further insight through the guidance of other reasoning minds. Without the public display of ideas the truth will likely remain obscure.[12]

Indeed, at no point in modern Western society is there a greater need for the public application of reason to current affairs than today, although the ability to publicly exercise reason is often confused with the notion of doing as one wishes or deciding between a preset array of options. C. Wright Mills argued:

> Freedom is, first of all, the chance to formulate the available choices, to argue over them—and then, the opportunity to choose. . . . That is why freedom cannot exist without an enlarged role of human reason in human affairs. Within an individual's biography and within a society's history, the social task of reason is to formulate choices, to enlarge the scope of human decisions in the making of history. The future of human affairs is not merely some set of variables to be predicted. The future is what is to be decided—within the limits, to be sure, of historical possibility. But this possibility is not fixed; in our time the limits seem very broad indeed.[13]

With this in mind, corporate news media's de facto safeguarding of the public sphere against nonconformist thought and expression seeks to demarcate the nature and style of acceptable deliberation, and in so doing shape and define the trajectory of history itself. Along these lines, journalists and academics—civil society's ostensible representatives and guardians of reason—are often complicit in reason's negation.

As instruments of state-sanctioned rationality, such agents are largely bereft of emotion, moderate in temperament, and speak or write in predictably formulaic tones. The narratives they relate and play out present tragedy and strife with the expectation of certain closure. And with a century of commercial media programming, the mass mind has come to not only accept but anticipate such regulation and control under the regime of institutionally sanctioned expertise.

This preservation of what passes for reason and truth cannot be sustained without a frequent dialectical struggle with unreason and falsity. Since many individuals have unconsciously placed their true reasoning faculties in abeyance and often lack a valid knowledge of politics and history, their unspoken faith in government and the broader political economy to protect and further their interests is unjustified. Against this milieu, those genuinely capable of utilizing their reasoning capacities in the pursuit of truth are often held up as heretical for their failure to accept what is presented as reality inside existing sociohistorical horizons, with the requisite "conspiracy theory" label wielded in Orwellian fashion to denote such nonconforming intellectual activity.

When lacking the autonomous use of reason to recognize truth, as well as a historical consciousness to render existing phenomena meaningful, form often trumps substance. For example, a seemingly obscure news website with unconventional graphics or an emotional news presenter purporting to discuss the day's affairs is typically perceived as untrustworthy and illegitimate by a public conditioned to accept forms of news and information where the appearance of objectivity and professionalism often camouflage disinformation.

CONSPIRACY PANICS: REASON VERSUS POLITICAL RATIONALITY

An important way of understanding the corporate media's broad domination of the public's sociopolitical consciousness and enforcement of established political rationalities is the invocation of conspiracy and what cultural historian Jack Bratich terms "conspiracy panics." Based on the sociocultural phenomenon of "moral panics," the conspiracy panic model suggests how the public use of reason is disallowed from examining deep events, such as how the assassination of President John F. Kennedy or 9/11 are downplayed, manipulated, or wholly suppressed by mainstream channels of communication and culture.[14]

Potentially fostered by the coordinated actions of government officials or agencies and major news organs to generate public suspicion and uncertainty,[15] a conspiracy panic is a demonstrable immediate or long-term reactive thrust against rational queries toward unusual and poorly understood events. To be sure, they are also intertwined with how the given society acknowledges and preserves its own identity—through "the management and expulsion of deviance." Along these lines, the concept further suggests how the public use of reason typically succumbs to the prevailing political rationality, thereby upholding the myths and beliefs that perpetuate the given political status quo.

Consider how positing that one's government may be partially composed of unaccountable criminal elements is cause for serious censure. Labeled "conspiracy theories" by a corporate media that prompt and channel emotionally laden mass consent, such perspectives are quickly dispatched to the memory hole lest they prompt meaningful discussion of the political prerogatives and designs held by a global power elite coordinating governments and broader geopolitical configurations.[16]

In the mythos of American exceptionalism, government intelligence and military operations are largely seen as being directed almost solely toward manipulation or coercion of unfortunate souls in foreign lands. To suggest otherwise, as independent researchers and commentators have done with the assassination of President John F. Kennedy, the Central Intelligence Agency (CIA)–Contra–crack cocaine connection, and 9/11, has been cause for sustained conspiracy panics that act to suppress inquiry into such events by professional and credentialed opinion leaders, particularly journalists and academics.

At the same time, a conspiracy panic serves a subtle yet important doctrinal function of manifesting and reproducing the ideational status quo of the "war on terror" era. "The scapegoating of conspiracy theories provides the conditions for social integration and political rationality," Bratich observed. "Conspiracy panics help to define the normal modes of dissent. Politically it is predicated on a consensus of 'us' over against a subversive and threatening 'them.'"[17] These days especially, the public suggestion that an official narrative may be amiss almost invariably puts one in the enemy camp.

CHALLENGING GOVERNMENT CONSPIRACY NARRATIVES

The time for a conspiracy panic to develop has decreased commensurately with the heightened spread and availability of information and communication technology that allows for the dissemination of news and research formerly suppressed by the perpetual data overload of corporate media. Before the wide access to information technology and the Internet, independent investigations into events including the JFK assassination took place over the course of many years, materializing in book-length treatments that could be dismissed by intelligence assets in news media and academe as the collective activity of "conspiracy buffs"—amateurish researchers who lack a government- or privately funded sinecure to overlook or obscure inquiry into deep events. The CIA directed media outlets and some key individuals to employ the term "conspiracy theorist" specifically to discredit publications and deter future inquiries into controversial, historical events.[18]

Not until Oliver Stone's 1991 blockbuster film *JFK*, essentially an adoption of works by author Jim Marrs, Colonel L. Fletcher Prouty, and New Orleans District Attorney Jim Garrison, did a substantial conspiracy panic take shape as a response to such analysis thrust upon the public in popular narrative form. This panic arose from and centered around Hollywood's challenge to traditional journalism's turf alongside commercial news outlets' typically deceptive interpretation of the event and almost wholly uncritical treatment of the Warren Commission Report.[19]

Shortly thereafter, investigative journalist Gary Webb's "Dark Alliance" series for the *San Jose Mercury News* demonstrated the Internet's capacity to explain and document a government conspiracy. With Webb's painstaking examination of the CIA's role in the illicit drug trade hyperlinked to a bevy of documentation and freely distributed online, the professional journalistic community and its intelligence penumbra fell silent for months.

In the interim, the story picked up steam in the nontraditional outlets of talk radio and tabloid television, with African Americans especially intrigued by the potential government role in the crack cocaine epidemic. Then suddenly major news outlets spewed forth a vitriolic attack on Webb and the *Mercury News* that amazingly resulted in the *Mercury*'s retraction of the story and Webb's eventual departure from the paper. Years later, Webb apparently committed suicide.[20]

Criticism of Webb's work predictably focused on petty misgivings toward his alleged poor judgment—specifically his intimation that the CIA intentionally caused the crack epidemic in African American communities, an observation that many blacks found logical and compelling. So not only did Webb find himself at the center of a conspiracy panic because of his assessment of the CIA's role in the drug trade; he was also causing mass "paranoia" within the African Ameri-

can community that major news media suggested were predisposed toward such thinking. Not incidentally, the CIA not only no longer denies Webb's assertions, they have admitted, though obfuscated, the degree of their involvement.[21]

Since the mid-1990s conspiracy panics have increasingly revolved around an effort by mainstream news media to link unorthodox political ideas and inquiry with violent acts. This dynamic was crystallized in Timothy McVeigh, the principal suspect in the April 19, 1995, Oklahoma City Alfred P. Murrah Federal Building bombing, who through the propaganda-like efforts of government and major news media was constructed to symbolize the dangers of "extremist" conspiratorial thought (his purported fascination with white supremacism and *The Turner Diaries*) and violent terrorist action (the bombing itself). Conveniently overlooked is the fact that McVeigh was trained as a black ops technician and still in US Army employ at the time of his 2001 execution according to his death certificate.[22]

Through a broad array of media coverage and subsequent book-length treatments by the left intelligentsia on the "radical right," the alleged lone wolf McVeigh and the Oklahoma City bombing became forever coupled in the national memory. The image and event seemingly attested to how certain modes of thought can bring about violence—even though McVeigh's role in what took place on April 19 was without question one part of an intricate web painstakingly examined by the Oklahoma Bombing Investigation Committee[23] and in the 2011 documentary *A Noble Lie: Oklahoma City 1995*.[24]

Independent researchers and alternative media utilizing the Internet have necessitated the rapid deployment of conspiracy panic-like reactions that appear far less natural and spontaneous than their predecessors to neutralize public debate and bolster often questionable official narratives of momentous and unusual events. For example, wide-scale skepticism surrounding the May 1, 2011, assault on Osama bin Laden's alleged lair in Pakistan was met with efforts to cultivate a conspiracy panic evident in editorials appearing across mainstream print, broadcast, and online news platforms. The untenable event, supported only by President Obama's pronouncement of the operation, was unquestioningly accepted by corporate media that shouted down calls for further evidence and alternative explanations of bin Laden's demise as "conspiracy theories."

Indeed, a LexisNexis search for "bin Laden" and "conspiracy theories" yields over 500 such stories and opinion pieces appearing across Western print and broadcast media outlets for the week of May 2, 2011.[25] "While much of America celebrated the dramatic killing of Osama bin Laden," the *Washington Post* opined, "the Sept. 11 conspiracy theorists still had questions. For them and a growing number of skeptics, the plot only thickened."[26]

Along these lines, retired General Mark Kimmitt remarked on CNN, "Well, I'm sure the conspiracy theorists will have a field day with this, about why it was done? Was it done? Is he still alive?"[27] "The conspiracy theorists are not going to be satisfied," Glenn Beck asserted. "Next thing you know, Trump is going to ask for the death certificate. And is it the real death certificate? And then all hell breaks loose."[28]

Like the Gulf of Tonkin incident that escalated the Vietnam War and the events of 9/11 used to justify the invasion of Iraq,[29] the narrative has since become a part of official history, disingenuously repeated in subsequent news accounts and elementary school history books—a history handed down from on high and amplified by corporate news outlets continually perpetuating nightmare fictions to a poorly informed and intellectually idle public.

This psycho-symbolic template is simultaneously evident in the Sandy Hook Elementary School shooting on December 14, 2012, and in the Boston Marathon bombing events and their aftermaths on April 15, 2013. Indeed, the brief yet intense Sandy Hook conspiracy panic, and to a lesser degree that of the Boston bombing, revolved at least partially around the "conspiracy theory professor,"[30] who, as a credentialed member of the intellectual class, overstepped his bounds by suggesting how there are many unanswered questions related to the tragedies that might lead one to conclude that the events did not take place in the way official pronouncements and major media have represented them. It is telling that critical assessments of domestic events and their relatedness to a corrupt media and governing apparatus are so vigorously assailed.

Yet to suggest that the news and information Americans accept as sound and factual on a routine basis is in fact a central means for manipulating their worldviews is not a matter for debate. Rather, it is an empirically verifiable assertion substantiated in a century of public relations and psychological warfare research and practice. Such propaganda efforts once reserved for foreign locales are now freely practiced in the US to keep the population increasingly on edge and disinclined to voice valid questions and concerns.

As a disciplinary mechanism against the public use of reason directed toward political leaders and the status quo, conspiracy panics serve to reinforce the myths and thought processes sustained by the corporate media's typically wholehearted advocacy of official narratives and deference to the dominant political rationality. Despite (or possibly because of) the immense technological sophistication at the dawn of the twenty-first century, a majority of the population remains bound and shackled in the bowels of Plato's cave, forever doomed to watch the shadows projected before them.

CONCLUSION

In 2013, the truth emergency remains a major concern, and in an era of seemingly never-ending pseudo-events and Potemkin villages presented as the reality with which we must contend,[31] the application of independent reason in pursuit of truth has all too frequently been replaced with an unthinking obeisance toward the smoke screen of expertise disguising corporate power and control.

Addressing the present truth emergency that began with the complex and still largely inexplicable set of events surrounding 9/11 requires a broad rekindling of the reasoning faculties so critical to further apprehending the objective reality Fromm pointed to almost sixty years ago. With this in mind we must ask whether modern educational institutions themselves are up to such a task. Project Censored is incorporated into scores of college classrooms each year, and is exemplary in pursuing the broader goal of an authentically liberal (liberating) education. Yet much of what passes for education today increasingly involves the conditioning of a docile yet efficient workforce and citizenry. Such a populace is far removed from seriously understanding or questioning the overall order of things, much less recognizing their own intrinsic social and historical agency.

In fact, the university environment actually makes one less inclined to voice opinions generally regarded as unpopular. This is reflected in a 2010 study by Association of American Colleges and Universities revealing that less than 20 percent of 9,000 faculty members surveyed believe it is safe to hold "unpopular views" on campus. Along these lines, the research also suggested how the longer students are enrolled at university the less open-minded they become. Of 25,000 students polled, only 40 percent of first-year students feel safe expressing unpopular positions versus 31 percent of seniors. Thus, ironically, the modern university tends to diminish the capacities it was originally established to cultivate—namely an appreciation of and proficiency in reasoning and informed inquiry.[32]

In a vein similar to Fromm's, Mills observed how the liberal educator's responsibility to the student and public revolves around two central aims:

> What he ought to do for the individual is to turn personal troubles and concerns into social issues and problems open to reason—his aim is to help the individual become a self-educating man, who only then would be reasonable and free. What he ought to do for the society is to combat all those

forces which are destroying genuine publics and creating a mass society—or put as a positive goal, his aim is to help build and strengthen self-cultivating publics. Only then might society be reasonable and free.[33]

Moving forward with such an orientation toward the intersections of history, biography, and society can only aid in addressing the ongoing truth emergency. And so is it also a central underlying theme guiding the endeavors of Project Censored—namely the undaunted use of reason toward the identification and reaffirmation of truth as a fundamental tenet in public deliberation, to authentically inform and sustain the human condition.

JAMES F. TRACY, PHD, is associate professor of media studies at Florida Atlantic University. His scholarly and critical writings have appeared in a wide variety of academic journals, edited volumes, and alternative news and analysis outlets. Tracy is editor of the Union for Democratic Communications' journal *Democratic Communiqué*. He is also a regular contributor to the Center for Research on Globalization's website GlobalResearch.ca, and a contributor to Project Censored's previous publication, *Censored 2013: Dispatches From the Media Revolution*.

Notes

1. This chapter draws in part on two previously published essays I have authored. "Social Engineering and the 21st Century Truth Emergency," Global Research, March 19, 2013, http://www.globalresearch.ca/false-flags-fake-media-reporting-deceiving-the-public-social-engineering-and-the-21st-century-truth-emergency/5325982; and "Media Disinformation and the Conspiracy Panic Phenomenon," Global Research, May 24, 2013, http://globalresearch.ca/media-disinformation-and-the-conspiracy-panic-phenomenon/5336221. Thanks to Project Censored director Mickey Huff for additional edits and sourcing for publication in this volume.
2. Peter Phillips and Mickey Huff, "Truth Emergency and Media Reform," *Daily Censored*, March 31, 2009, http://www.dailycensored.com/truth-emergency-and-media-reform/. For more on the Truth Emergency, see Peter Phillips, Mickey Huff, et al., "Truth Emergency Meets Media Reform," in eds. Peter Phillips and Andrew Roth, *Censored 2009* (New York: Seven Stories Press, 2008), 281–295; Peter Phillips and Mickey Huff, "Truth Emergency: Inside the Military Industrial Media Empire," in eds. Peter Phillips and Mickey Huff, *Censored 2010* (New York: Seven Stories Press, 2009), 197–220; and Mickey Huff and Peter Phillips, eds., *Censored 2011*, (New York: Seven Stories Press, 2010), sec. 2, "Truth Emergency," 221–352; Mickey Huff, Andy Lee Roth, and Project Censored, eds., *Censored 2013: Dispatches From the Media Revolution* (New York: Seven Stories Press, 2012), sec. 2 , "Truth Emergency," 213–331; and the Truth Emergency conference website from 2008 at http://truthemergency.us.
3. Edward Bernays, *Propaganda* (New York: Ig Publishing, 2005 [1928]), 48, 71, 72.
4. Eliane Glaser, "The West's Hidden Propaganda Machine," *Guardian*, May 17, 2013, http://www.guardian.co.uk/commentisfree/2013/may/17/west-hidden-propaganda-machine-social-media.

5. J. S. McClelland, *A History of Western Political Thought* (New York: Routledge, 1996), 25.
6. The tentative transition from community to society examined by Ferdinand Tönnies, Max Weber, Georg Simmel, and their contemporaries suggests the basis for such myths as the individual's faith in religion and collective ties was eclipsed by acceptance of the narratives from those representing civil society's apparent rationality. This faith, however, is groundless and devoid of the moral dimension accompanying the myths arising from communal existence. For Tönnies, "community is the true and lasting common life; society is only temporary." In other words, the community provides the concrete basis for human existence and involvement while society is characterized by a tentative expression arising from an industrial-metropolitan milieu. Julien Freund, "German Sociology in the Time of Max Weber," in Tom Bottomore and Robert Nisbet, eds., *A History of Sociological Analysis* (New York: Basic Books, 1978), 154.
7. David Riesman with Nathan Glazer and Reuel Denney, *The Lonely Crowd*, abridged ed. (New Haven CT: Yale University Press, 1961 [1950]), 192–197; C. Wright Mills, *The Sociological Imagination* (New York: Oxford University Press, 1959), 171–173.
8. Maggie Koerth-Baker, "Why Rational People Buy Into Conspiracy Theories," *New York Times*, May 21, 2013, http://www.nytimes.com/2013/05/26/magazine/why-rational-people-buy-into-conspiracy-theories.html?pagewanted=all&_r=0.
9. For some of the latest research on this subject, read Lance deHaven-Smith, *Conspiracy Theory in America* (Austin: University of Texas Press, 2013), 1–52.
10. Georg Simmel, "The Metropolis and Mental Life," in *Georg Simmel: On Individuality and Social Forms*, ed. Donald N. Levine (Chicago: University of Chicago Press, 1971), 335. "That we follow the laws of our inner nature—and this is what freedom is—becomes perceptible and convincing to us and to others only when the expression of this nature distinguish themselves from others; it is our irreplaceability by others which shows that our mode of existence is not imposed upon us from the outside."
11. Erich Fromm, *The Sane Society* (New York: Rinehart & Company, 1955), 63. On issues relating to objectivity in previous Project Censored publications, see Mickey Huff, Andy Lee Roth, and Project Censored, *Censored 2013: Dispatches From the Media Revolution* (New York: Seven Stories Press, 2012), sec. 2, "Truth Emergency," 214–15.
12. Slavko Splichal, *Principles of Publicity and Press Freedom* (Lanham MD: Rowman and Littlefield, 2002), 98, 102.
13. C. Wright Mills, *The Sociological Imagination* (New York: Oxford University Press, 2000[1959]), 174. Hans-Georg Gadamer similarly analogizes such a psycho-social "situation" in terms of the "standpoint that limits the possibility of vision. Hence an essential part of the concept of situation is the concept of 'horizon' . . . A person who has no horizon is a man who does not see far enough and hence overvalues what is nearest to him. Contrariwise, to have an horizon means not to be limited to what is nearest, but to be able to see beyond it." The rule similarly persists "[i]n the sphere of historical understanding." Hans-Georg Gadamer, "The Historicity of Understanding," in Paul Connerton, ed., *Critical Sociology* (New York: Penguin Books, 1976), 118.
14. Jack Z. Bratich, *Conspiracy Panics: Political Rationality and Popular Culture* (Albany NY: State University of New York Press, 2008).
15. See CIA Document 1035-960, "Concerning Criticism of the Warren Commission Report," JFK Lancer, n.d. http://www.jfklancer.com/CIA.html.
16. See deHaven-Smith, *Conspiracy Theory in America*.
17. Bratich, *Conspiracy Panics*, 11.
18. See the work of deHaven Smith, *Conspiracy Theory in America*, especially 1–52, and the works of Peter Dale Scott.
19. This despite some of the findings of the "Report of the Select Committee on Assassinations of the US House of Representatives" (1979) that admitted problems with the earlier government reports on JKF's death, as did the previous Church Committee (1976). Oliver Stone's new book and Showtime series with Peter Kuznick, *Untold History of the United States*, continues to challenge conventional interpretations and official narratives of US history in the twentieth century.
20. That was the coroner's official report. Some have argued it was a possible murder by elements within the US government, but that evidence is not conclusive. For example, Charlene Fassa,

"Gary Webb: More Pieces in the Suicide Puzzle, Pt. 1," Rense.com, December 11, 2005, http://rense.com/general69/webb1.htm.

21. Robert Parry, "CIA Admits Tolerating Contra- Cocaine Trafficking in 1980s," *Consortium News*, June 8, 2000, http://www.consortiumnews.com/2000/060800a.html.

22. Death Certificate of Timothy James McVeigh, June 11, 2001, http://www.autopsyfiles.org/reports/deathcert/mcveigh,%20timothy.pdf.

23. Oklahoma Bombing Investigation Committee, *Final Report on the Bombing of the Alfred P. Murrah Federal Building, April 19, 1995*, 2001. See also *Oklahoma City: What Really Happened?* Chuck Allen, dir., 1995, https://www.youtube.com/watch?v=nmBrMpcd_2k.

24. The film, *A Noble Lie*, argues the April 19, 1995 bombing that destroyed much of the Alfred P. Murrah Federal Building involved far more revealing evidence than the Federal Bureau of Investigation maintains, http://www.anoblelie.com/articles/the-noble-lie-in-oklahoma-city. For more on historical issues regarding controversial and potentially dubious dealings of the FBI and the post 9/11 war on terror, see Trevor Aaronson, *The Terror Factory: Inside the FBI's Manufactured War on Terrorism* (New York: Ig Publishing, 2013), which is based on Aaronson's article, "The Informants," *Mother Jones*, September/October 2011, http://motherjones.com/politics/2011/08/fbi-terrorist-informants. Aaronson's story was #4 in *Censored 2013*.

25. See James F. Tracy, "State Propaganda, Historical Revisionism, and Perpetuation of the 911 Myth," Global Research, May 6, 2012, http://www.globalresearch.ca/the-9-11-myth-state-propaganda-historical-revisionism-and-the-perpetuation-of-the-9-11-myth/30721.

26. Emily Wax, "Report of bin Laden's Death Spurs Questions From Conspiracy Theorists," *Washington Post*, May 2, 2011, http://www.washingtonpost.com/lifestyle/style/report-of-bin-ladens-death-spurs-questions-from-conspiracy-theorists/2011/05/02/AF90ZjbF_story.html. For an academic review and analysis on previous reports of the death of Osama bin Laden, see David Ray Griffin, *Osama bin Laden: Dead or Alive?* (Northampton: Olive Branch Press, 2009).

27. Gen. Mark Kimmitt on CNN Breaking News, "Osama bin Laden is Dead," CNN, May 2, 2011.

28. Glenn Beck, "Beck for May 2, 2011," Fox News, May 2, 2011.

29. See Norman Soloman, *War Made Easy: How Presidents and Pundits Keep Spinning Us to Death* (Hoboken: Wiley, 2006). See the film online at http://www.warmadeeasythemovie.org.

30. "Florida Conspiracy Theory Professor Who Said that the Sandy Hook Shooting May Not Have Happened Now Argues that the Government Was behind the Boston Marathon Bombing," *Daily Mail*, April 24, 2013, http://www.dailymail.co.uk/news/article-2314370/James-Tracy-Florida-conspiracy-theory-professor-said-Sandy-Hook-shooting-happened-argues-government-Boston-Marathon-bombing.html. [Editors' note: the professor in question is the author of this chapter. Also, it should be noted that Tracy has been quoted out of context often and attacked both in and by the media. That is one of the main focal points of this chapter—how corporate media work to discredit unpopular views and play "shoot the messenger" rather than report factually and transparently about controversial matters and how the press often fail to question the very people in power who craft official historical narratives.]

31. For more on the notion of pseudo-events, see Daniel J. Boorstin, *The Image: A Guide to Pseudo-Events in America* (New York: Athenum, 1962); and for analysis on how this phenomenon impacts news reporting and public consciousness in the present, see Mickey Huff, Andy Lee Roth, et al., "American Idle: Junk Food News, News Abuse, and the Voice of Freedumb," in *Censored 2013*, 151–176.

32. Eric L. Dey, Molly C. Ott, Mary Antonaros, and Matthew A. Holsapple, *Engaging Diverse Viewpoints: What is the Campus Climate for Perspective Taking?* (Washington DC: American Association of Colleges and Universities, 2010), 7, http://www.aacu.org/core_commitments/documents/Engaging_Diverse_Viewpoints.pdf.

33. Mills, *The Sociological Imagination*, 186.

CHAPTER 7

Censorship That Dares Not Speak its Name

The Strange Silencing of Liberal America[1]

John Pilger

Note: The chapter that follows, John Pilger's "Censorship That Dares Not Speak Its Name: The Strange Silencing of Liberal America," is an honest and heartfelt account of the frustration on the part of a distinguished journalist when faced with censorship from within our community. We include it here because to do otherwise would be to join in the silencing of a necessary voice. As the publishers of Gary Webb, Noam Chomsky, Kurt Vonnegut, the Boston Women's Health Book Collective and, indeed, Project Censored, we could not do otherwise. At the same time it pains us to do so, since in it John writes critically of friends of ours, and because we do not want to be part of the long-standing habit of the Left of disparaging its own. Nonetheless, in the end, our clear choice, our responsibility, is to include it here. We hope that readers will understand that in doing so we are placing our vote squarely on the side of openness and of free speech.

—Dan Simon and Veronica Liu, for Seven Stories Press; and Mickey Huff and Andy Lee Roth, for Project Censored

How does censorship work in liberal societies? When my film, *Year Zero: The Silent Death of Cambodia*, was banned in the United States in 1980, the broadcaster PBS cut all contact. Negotiations were ended abruptly; phone calls were not returned. Something had happened, but what? *Year Zero* had already alerted much of the world to the horrors of Pol Pot, but it also investigated the critical role of the Nixon administration in the tyrant's rise to power and the devastation of Cambodia.

Six months later, a PBS official denied this was censorship. "We're into difficult political days in Washington," he said. "Your film would have given us problems with the Reagan administration. Sorry."[2]

In Britain, the long war in Northern Ireland spawned a similar, deniable censorship. The investigative journalist Liz Curtis compiled a list of forty-eight television films in Britain that were never shown or indefinitely delayed. The word "ban" was rarely used, and those responsible would invariably insist they believed in free speech.[3]

The Lannan Foundation in Santa Fe, New Mexico, believes in free speech. The Foundation's website (Lannan.org) says it is "dedicated to cultural freedom, diversity and creativity." Authors, filmmakers, and poets make their way to a sanctum of liberalism bankrolled by the billionaire Patrick Lannan in the tradition of Carnegie, Rockefeller, and Ford. Lannan also awards "grants" to America's liberal media, such as Free Speech TV, the Foundation for National Progress (which publishes *Mother Jones* magazine), the Nation Institute, and the TV and radio program *Democracy Now!* In Britain, until 2011, Lannan was a supporter of the Martha Gellhorn Prize for Journalism.

The Lannan Foundation was set up in 1960 by J. Patrick Lannan, who amassed a fortune, much of it in art, while he was majority shareholder of the International Telephone and Telegraph Corporation (ITT). Founded in the 1920s, ITT had extensive interests in Europe. In the 1930s, ITT's companies in Germany expanded; an ITT subsidiary owned 25 percent of the aircraft company Focke-Wulf, which supplied the Luftwaffe; at the height of the Second World War, this was a majority holding.

During the American invasion of Vietnam in the 1960s, ITT produced navigation systems for laser-guided bombs and developed surveillance systems for what the Pentagon calls the "automated battlefield." In 1971, President Salvador Allende nationalized ITT's 70 percent interest in the Chilean Telephone Company. As declassified Central Intelligence Agency (CIA) files show, ITT's response was an eighteen-point covert "action plan" to overthrow Allende. According to *The CIA's Greatest Hits* by Mark Zepezauer, the CIA "sponsored demonstrations and strikes, funded by ITT and other US corporations with Chilean holdings," prior to General Augusto Pinochet's September 1973 military coup. ITT funded *El Mercurio*, the Chilean daily that opposed Allende and backed Pinochet.[4]

J. Patrick Lannan died in 1983. On the Lannan Foundation's website, he is described as a "liberal thinker." His son, Patrick, runs the Foundation today.

On June 15, 2011, I was due in Santa Fe, having been invited to share a platform with David Barsamian, whose interviews for his *Alternative Radio* program have brought him acclaim, notably those with Noam Chomsky. The subject of my talk was the role of American liberalism in a permanent state of war and in the demise of freedoms, such as the right to call government to account. I intended to make the case that Barack Obama, a liberal, was as much a warmonger as George W. Bush and had prosecuted more whistle-blowers than any US president, and that his singular achievement had been to seduce, co-opt, and silence much of liberal opinion in the United States.

The Lannan Foundation was also to host the US premiere of my new film, *The War You Don't See*, which investigates the role of the media in war-making, especially liberal media such as the *New York Times* and the BBC. It is a film about censorship that does not speak its name.

The organizer of my visit was Barbara Ventrello, Lannan's director of Cultural Freedom Public Events, with whom I had been in frequent contact. "We're all looking forward to seeing you here," she said. "Your events are proving very popular." On June 9, as I was about to leave for Santa Fe, I received this email:

> Dear John,
> I have just received a call from Patrick Lannan. . . . Something has come up and he has asked me to cancel all your events next week. He did not go into details so I have no idea what this is about, and I apologize. . . . We thank you for your understanding.
> With best regards,
> Barbara

David Barsamian was driving down from Boulder, Colorado, when he was reached and advised to turn back. He, too, was given no explanation. A frequent guest at Lannan events, he said he had never known anything like it. "I was there a couple of weeks ago," he told the *Santa Fe New Mexican*, "and Patrick said, 'Wow, looking forward to this. It's going to be great.' I didn't have a hint of any unease."[5]

I replied to Barbara Ventrello that Lannan was committed to staging the US premiere of my film at The Screen cinema in Santa Fe, and such an abrupt cancellation left me with no alternatives; the film's national promotion was linked to the Santa Fe premiere. I asked that the screening go ahead. I received this reply:

> Dear John,
> I am very sorry, but as stated in my email to you yesterday, _all_ events related to your visit to Santa Fe are cancelled. This includes the screening of your film.
> Regards,
> Barbara

"All" was in italics and underlined. Again, no reason was given. Patrick Lannan had phoned her from California, she said, without explanation.

I emailed Lannan himself several times and got no reply. I phoned him and left messages. A strange, unsettling silence followed. I phoned the manager of The Screen cinema in Santa Fe. "I'm baffled," he said. "I was expecting a sellout, then late on the night before the online advertising was due to go up, I had a call from a Lannan person telling me to stop everything. She gave no explanation."

I suggested to the cinema manager that I come to Santa Fe anyway, but when I tried to buy the plane ticket Lannan had arranged for me, I was told by the travel agent: "I've contacted the Foundation, and they won't allow you to buy it, even though this ticket, when cancelled, will be worthless. I don't understand it."

On the Lannan website, "Cancelled" appeared across a picture of me. There was no explanation. Not one of my phone calls and emails was returned. A Kafkaesque world of not-knowing descended. Of the 195 events staged by the Lannan Foundation, only one has been banned.

Like the cinema manager, the *Santa Fe New Mexican* had been called late on the night that a full-page interview with me by its arts reporter was about to go to press. "We had less than an hour to pull it," said the arts editor. "They wouldn't say why." The *New Mexican*'s weekly arts supplement, *Pasatiempo*, in which the interview would appear, is a primary source of local interest and ticket sales for all Lannan events.

The silence from Lannan lasted a week until, under pressure from local media, the Foundation put out a brief statement that too few tickets had been sold to make my visit "viable" and that "the Foundation regrets that the reason for the cancellation was not explained to Mr. Pilger or to the public at the time the decision was made."[6] The statement said that the film had been "secondary" and that I had "asked" for it to be shown. This was specious. With arrangements for a US premiere already under way, I *offered* an exclusive screening to Lannan. In March 2011, Barbara Ventrello had emailed me: "We would very much like to show your film. . . . We could possibly even schedule two showings. . . . We are sure there would be great interest in Santa Fe."

According to Patrick Lannan's belated statement, there was little interest in any of my events. A Foundation spokesperson, Christie Mazuera Davis, told the *Santa Fe New Mexican*: "This doesn't reflect that great on John, whom we were trying to protect, but he's turned it into this situation . . . he could have very graciously taken his check and said, 'I'm sorry it didn't work out.'"[7]

In other words, it was I who should have apologized for having my event and the premiere of my film cancelled summarily without consultation or explanation.

A robust editorial in the *Santa Fe New Mexican* had this to say:

> On Tuesday, Lannan issued a statement to the effect that only 152 tickets to the Lensic presentation had been sold; that he simply sought to spare Pilger the embarrassment of a mostly empty house. Lannan's explanation is bogus, and it serves only to further sully Lannan and his foundation's reputation for advancing freedom of expression: He cancelled before the popular and closely followed *Pasatiempo* came out. Not to beat our breasts about its influence, but that magazine has a long history of prompting attendance at our community's many cultural events—and of faithfully covering the foundation's events, on their merits. Pilger and Barsamian could

have expected closer to a packed 820-seat Lensic [Performing Arts Center].[8]

The manager of The Screen cinema told me that no one from the Foundation had contacted him to ask how ticket sales were going. Had they done so, he would have told them that, once the advertising had gotten under way, he expected a full house. At my suggestion, he rescheduled the film for June 23. This was a sellout, with a line around the block and many people turned away. Lannan's reason for the cancellation was demonstrably bogus.

"Something is going to surface," said David Barsamian. "They can't keep the lid on this."[9]

I am not so sure.

When I made the banning known, many in the US offered their support. Project Censored showed *The War You Don't See* in Berkeley, CA and organized an audience conversation with me via Skype. Dennis Bernstein invited me on his KPFA/Pacifica Radio program, *Flashpoints*. Hundreds of people contacted me, suggesting the episode was symptomatic of a wider, insidious suppression. The great whistle-blower Daniel Ellsberg called the ban "poisonous." He wrote to me: "Please count on me to participate in any way I can help out. This really needs to be investigated, publicized and resisted: seems especially ominous (though not exactly surprising). It's an uphill, long, long struggle."

However, other distinguished liberal voices remained silent or, when I sought their support, were all but affronted that I had dared whisper the word "censorship" in association with such a beacon of "cultural freedom" as the Lannan Foundation. What was striking was how readily they expressed deference to Lannan, as if evidence was irrelevant. The tone was sometimes resentful, even angry, as though I had embarrassed their patron, and them. I emailed a friend in New York, who had published my work and whose various endeavors were backed by Patrick Lannan. "I shall appreciate whatever solidarity you can give," I wrote, expecting no more than a gesture. When I suggested to him that Lannan's action might be political, I was reminded of all the progressive people Lannan had invited to Santa Fe; my friend wrote that, anyway, Lannan "is not a liberal, but has much better politics." He was concerned not with Lannan's action but with puncturing various theories as to why Lannan had stopped my events. There was no solidarity. Defending Lannan was clearly a priority. The last message I received was in lawyer-speak. "Until I know the full story," he wrote, "I am withholding any conclusive judgment." At least, I began to understand the tentacular power of patronage.

Around this time, I was due in New York to appear on Amy Goodman's *Democracy Now!* to show clips of *The War You Don't See*. I had sent a copy of the film ahead and agreed to dates with a producer. Amy Goodman had often interviewed me in New York and down the line in London. Once, she had devoted most of her show to my work.[10] I admired what Amy Goodman did, and had presented her with a Lannan award in Santa Fe in 2002. On June 13, I emailed the producer and asked when the interview would take place. He replied: "Will discuss with other producers and Amy and get back to you."

That was the last I heard from *Democracy Now!* None of my phone calls and emails to Amy Goodman and her staff were returned. A longstanding relationship evaporated without a word. *Democracy Now!* is backed by the Lannan Foundation.[11]

"The elites and their courtiers in the liberal class," wrote Chris Hedges in his book *Death of the Liberal Class*, "always condemn the rebel as impractical. They dismiss the stance of the rebel as counterproductive. They chastise the rebel for being angry. The elites and their apologists call for reason, and patience. They use the hypocritical language of compromise, generosity, and understanding to accept that we must accept and work with the systems of power. The rebel, however . . . refuses to be bought off with foundation grants, invitations to the White House, television appearances, book contracts, academic appointments, or empty rhetoric."[12]

Such is the stirring prose of a celebrated liberal foe of censorship. I had written to Chris Hedges on June 13, 2011, quoting one of his pieces on censorship, entitled "Kafka's America." I explained what had happened and sought his support. He wrote back, "Dear John, I heard about this and am as mystified as you are . . . Chris."

Some eighteen months later when Hedges was promoting his book on liberal America, I wrote again. He replied, "Until I see evidence otherwise, I have to take Patrick at his word."

I provided the evidence otherwise. He said only that it was "out of character" for Lannan to censor otherwise. He added that Patrick Lannan and Amy Goodman were "two of the very few allies I have left. It is pretty bleak over here." Chris Hedges is a Lannan Foundation "Fellow" frequently hosted in Santa Fe. His book is published by Nation Books, supported by Lannan.

Such are the ties that bind often-beleaguered liberal opinion in the United States to powerful foundations like Ford, Carnegie, Rockefeller, and Lannan. The annual "Socialism" conference in Chicago—at which I have spoken—is funded by the billionaire of Santa Fe. This is not to suggest powerful individuals like Lannan do not promote exceptional cultural and political work; Patrick Lannan has been unstinting in his support for Palestinian writers, such as the late Edward Said. Neither am I implying that the dependents of Lannan-style largesse perform to any agenda. But there are always invisible boundaries: that is the nature of liberalism. Overstep these unwittingly, and the reaction can be swift, as it would be in any royal court. In his ruthless behavior toward me, my film, and David Barsamian, Patrick Lannan merely demonstrated his capricious license to do what he wanted, when and how he wanted, and without having to justify his action. It is this wielding of a power based entirely on wealth—*not* any theory of why he behaved the way he did—that is the essence of this episode. It is the power, in microcosm, of imperial America.

In a 2011 article in the *Santa Fe New Mexican*, Robert M. Christie, professor emeritus of sociology at California State University–Dominguez Hills, wrote:

> When a community, or a nation for that matter, must depend upon the largess of a wealthy individual, or his foundation, or a few large corporations . . . for the free speech of renowned public intellectuals such as John Pilger, we are all in very deep trouble to begin with.
>
> I do not know Mr. Lannan, the sources of his wealth, nor how "connected" it and/or may be to "the powers that be," but it seems likely that either (1) he and his foundation suddenly had an epic epiphany of fascistic proportion, or (2) someone

rather high up in what I prefer to call the "petro-mil-corp-dys-infotainment" elite has somehow gotten to him . . .

A key cultural failure attending the privatization of public functions is that people, including many "liberals," have been persuaded that whoever runs such private foundations has the right to act privately with no responsibility to the public for the public consequences of their actions. Wrong! Any institution, public or private, the operations of which affect the public good, does owe the public an explanation for any action that appears contrary to the public interest. That is a moral, not legal, principle . . .

We live in dangerous times. Many resist admitting that, especially when such danger emanates from our own increasingly corporate-controlled, anti-public institutions . . .

What does Patrick Lannan fear? Civic-minded persons should want to know and he should tell us. [The public has a] right to seek the identity of any sources of political censorship, call them out and expose their corruption of the public interest.[13]

JOHN PILGER has been a war correspondent, author, and filmmaker. An Australian based in London, he is only one of two to win British journalism's highest award twice. He has been International Reporter of the Year and winner of the United Nations Association Peace Prize and Gold Medal. For his documentary films, he has won an Emmy and a British Academy Award. His first film, *The Quiet Mutiny*, made in 1970, revealed the rebellion within the US Army in Vietnam. His epic 1979 *Cambodia Year Zero* is ranked by the British Film Institute as one of the ten most important documentaries of the twentieth century. His *Death of a Nation*, filmed secretly in East Timor, had a worldwide impact in 1994. His books include *Heroes, Distant Voices, Hidden Agendas, The New Rulers of the World*, and *Freedom Next Time*. His website is www.johnpilger.com.

Notes

1. This is an expanded and updated version of an article originally published in the *New Statesman*, July 7, 2011, http://www.newstatesman.com/world-affairs/2011/07/pilger-foundation-obama-film, also at http://johnpilger.com/articles/the-strange-silencing-of-liberal-america.
2. John Pilger, *Heroes* (London: Vintage, 2001[1986]), 411–412.
3. Ibid., 516–520.

4. "CIA Activities in Chile," Central Intelligence Agency, September 18, 2000, https://www.cia. gov/library/reports/general-reports-1/chile/; Church Report, "Covert Action in Chile 1963– 1973," US Department of State, December 18, 1975, http://foia.state.gov/reports/churchreport. asp; Mark Zepezauer, *The CIA's Greatest Hits*, 2nd ed., (Berkeley, CA: Soft Skull Press, 2012), 40–41.
5. Paul Weideman, "Pilger: Claim of Too Few Tickets for Lannan Talk is Absurd," *Santa Fe New Mexican*, June 15, 2011, http://www.sfnewmexican.com/Local%20News/Pilger--Claim-of-too-few-tickets--absurd-#.UbZMKOvR2aw.
6. Ibid.
7. Ibid.
8. Ibid.
9. Ibid.
10. See especially "John Pilger: Global Support for WikiLeaks is 'Rebellion' Against U.S. Militarism, Secrecy," *Democracy Now!*, December 15, 2010, http://www.democracynow. org/2010/12/15/john_pilger_journalists_must_support_julian. See also "John Pilger Calls UK National Health Service a Treasure, Blasts US Lawmakers for Being 'in Bed with Powerful Interests' and Neglecting 'Their Own People's Basic Human Rights,'" *Democracy Now!*, July 2, 2009, http://www.democracynow.org/2009/7/2/john_pilger_blasts_us_lawmakers_on; "John Pilger on Honduras, Iran, Gaza, the Corporate Media, Obama's Wars, and Resisting the American Empire," *Democracy Now!*, July 6, 2009, http://www.democracynow.org/2009/7/6/ filmmaker_journalist_john_pilger_on_honduras; and "John Pilger: There Is a War on Journalism," *Democracy Now!*, June 29, 2010, http://www.democracynow.org/2010/6/29/john_pilger_there_is_a_war.
11. See Bob Feldman, "'Democracy Now!' Program Underwriter, Lannan Foundation, Censors Anti-War Journalist John Pilger," Educate-Yourself, July 9, 2011, http://educate-yourself.org/ag/ feldmanlannanfoundation09jul1.shtml; "'Democracy Now!' Show Funder Censors Anti-War Journalist John Pilger," *Where's the Change?*, July 9, 2011, http://wherechangeobama.blogspot. com/2011/07/democracy-now-show-funder-censors-anti.html; and Bob Feldman, "Lannan Foundation's Tactical Air Defense Services/Nation Magazine Link?" February 10, 2010, *Where's the Change?*, http://wherechangeobama.blogspot.com/2010/02/lannan-foundations-tactical-air-defense.html. Amy Goodman and Lannan connections are further elaborated here: http:// www.lannan.org/bios/amy-goodman.
12. Chris Hedges, *The Death of the Liberal Class* (New York: Nation Books, 2010), 215.
13. Robert M. Christie, "Purging Pilger Damages Public Interest," *Santa Fe New Mexican*, July 4, 2011, http://www.sfnewmexican.com/Opinion/Looking-In--Robert-M--Christie-Purging-Pilger-damages-public-in.

CHAPTER 8

Screening the Homeland
How Hollywood Fantasy Mediates State Fascism in the US of Empire

Rob Williams

Every day . . . our children learn to open their imaginations, to dream just a little bigger . . . I want to thank all of you tonight for being part of that vitally important work.

—First Lady of the United States Michelle Obama on *Argo*, via White House satellite feed to the Academy Awards television audience, 2013[1]

Interested in livening up a sleepy cocktail party in the Homeland? Here's one way—suggest to your fellow guests that Hollywood plays a deep and abiding role as popular propaganda provider for an ever-expanding United States of Empire bent on "full-spectrum dominance" of the planet and the demonization of all things Muslim. I know what you're thinking. Most American moviegoers cannot be bothered with so-called "conspiracy theories" about how US film projects advance a larger imperial agenda. Filmmakers and their audiences often argue that movies are just mindless eye candy for purely entertainment purposes. However, if ever a single year of popular film culture were to prove them wrong, it would have to be this past one, which featured some of the most sophisticated propaganda of our post-9/11 era, including two this essay will explore in more detail—*Argo* and *Zero Dark Thirty*. Unless you have killed your television dead (not a bad idea) and stopped watching movies, you've no doubt heard of these two films, which have received mountains of critical acclaim (and a bit of controversy) in the US popular press.

A few points of clarification: I use the word "screening" in this chapter title as a *double entendre*, to describe both the technique of the narrative process—propaganda disseminated 24/7/365 via ubiquitous screens, including movie theaters, TV, and all manner of mobile devices—*and* the political process by which the Hollywood industry "frames" audiences' understandings of vital issues of import, filtering and censoring our cultural understanding of what we might call "real life." When Hollywood filmmakers insist that certain of their films are "based on actual events" (a claim made by the production crews of both *Argo* and *Zero Dark Thirty*), discriminating audiences ought to reach for their collective cultural crap detectors.[2]

According to popular mythology and rabid pit bull pundits of the Faux News variety, Hollywood "liberals" and the Washington DC Beltway crowd are locked in a perpetual ideological war. The truth is exactly the opposite—Hollywood and DC not only need each other, they are sleeping together in serial multiplex fashion. As former president Lyndon B. Johnson's White House aide and Motion Picture Association of America (MPAA) CEO Jack Valenti once tellingly explained, "Washington and Hollywood spring from the same DNA."[3] It is here, at the intersection of realpolitik and art, where Hollywood pop culture plays a critically significant political role—producing and deploying powerful image-driven stories designed to legitimize US imperialism abroad. In other words, if we apply to US foreign policy the radical cultural critiques of scholar bell hooks—that Hollywood "fantasy" continually mediates US state "fascism"—what can we conclude?[4] That via the silver screen, Hollywood's job is to prepare American hearts and minds for embracing the collective actions of the state—both domestically and globally—on behalf of advancing US hegemony in the Middle East and around the world.[5]

A few words about the "fascism": let's start with some basics about the United States—"facts submitted to a candid world," as Thomas Jefferson famously stated in 1776. The twenty-first century US is no longer a self-governing republic, but an out-of-control empire that is essentially ungovernable, unreformable, and unsustainable. Easily accessible federal government documents, such as the vision articulated by the Project for a New American Century (PNAC),[6] make clear that the chief goal of the twenty-first century US is nothing less than world domination in the name of waging a sequential, global war for the planet's remaining fossil fuel energy resources. Looking back over the decade since the 9/11 tragedy,[7] the US has quickly morphed into a military–industrial–surveillance state that is obsessed with homeland security and marked by a rapid reorganization and centralization of federal agencies, the curtailing of constitutional rights and liberties under the USA PATRIOT Act and related legislation, and the expansion of corporate commercial power, wedded to an expanding state bureaucracy.[8] None of this is news to longtime Project Censored readers, who aren't afraid to call this "new normal" by its real name— "fascism," which Benito "Il Duce" Mussolini in the 1930s defined as the marrying of corporate and state power. And Fascism, Mussolini said, ought more rightly be called *corporatism*.

Looking globally, two-thirds of the planet's recoverable oil reserves are located in the greater Middle East, a region hotly contested by the US, Russia, and China, featuring repressively governed "client states" propped up with loans from the "international community" (read: International Monetary Fund, World Bank, and the US), which are currently experiencing a series of turbulent economic and political upheavals—Tunisia, Bahrain, Egypt, Yemen, Libya, and now Syria—simplistically dubbed the "Arab Spring." A complex and highly misunderstood region of the world, the Middle East is home to the modern Jewish state of Israel—which, since its creation in 1948, has been an intimate ally of the US—as well as the majority of the world's Arab peoples (most, but not all, of whom are Muslim), who trace Bedouin tribal lineage back thousands of years. To control this strategically vital region, the US has historically blended diplomacy's "hard power" with "soft power"—sticks and carrots—as well as relying on domestic popular propaganda like Hollywood films and television shows, as researcher Jack Shaheen explains in his book *Reel Bad Arabs*, to create enduring regional and cultural stereotypes for Western moviegoing audiences. The result? "Islamophobia," a deeply rooted media-induced fear of the Arab "Other."[9] Not surprisingly, then, do our highly visible Hollywood movies focus audience attention on the relationship between the US and the greater Middle East.

ARGO: "REEL BAD ARABS" REDUX

Consider the seven Academy Award nominations received by the hugely popular film *Argo*, Hollywood's 2013 Oscar winner for Best Picture, as well as Best Film Editing and Best Adapted Screenplay (#irony?), directed by Ben Affleck—who credits the film's popularity with reviving his Hollywood career. In case you missed *Argo* (spoiler alert), the story revolves around Central Intelligence Agency operative Tony Mendez (played by Affleck), who convinces the Agency to build a fake movie production agency from scratch, slip into post–Revolutionary Iran, and liberate six Americans stranded in hiding at the Canadian embassy under siege in Tehran.[10]

Regarding *Argo*, Affleck himself went public on many occasions with the "truthful" nature of his film. "It's okay to embellish, it's okay to compress, as long as you don't fundamentally change the nature of the story and of what happened," Affleck explained to *Fresh Air* radio host Terry Gross. And to the *London Evening Standard*: "This movie is about this story that took place, and it's true, and I go to pains to contextualize it and to try to be evenhanded in a way that just means we're taking a cold, hard look at the facts."[11] Given the long history of Central Intelligence Agency (CIA) and Hollywood connections, and the subject matter at hand, this seems to be a tall order.[12]

So, what's the story? *Argo* recounts a tiny footnote to the drama of the 1979 US/Iranian hostage crisis, and does lend itself to a Hollywood retelling based on sheer creative audacity alone. Adoring American moviegoing audiences and critics turned out in force, and were subjected to the film's remarkable flaws: the almost complete lack of historical context and/or misrepresenting of the decades-long US/Iranian political relationship, the odd downplaying of the Canadian embassy's central role in rescuing US hostages (real-life former Canadian ambassador Ken Taylor was outspoken in his criticism of *Argo*, noting that the film portrayed the Canadians as being just along for the ride), and major moments from *Argo* that Affleck's production team invented whole cloth, including *Argo*'s climax, featuring machine gun–toting Iranian soldiers pursuing the hostage's departing airplane down a Tehran runway in a high-speed Jeep chase that ends badly (for the Iranians) and triumphantly (for the Americans).

Note: According to everyone involved in the real-life escape, the sheer lack of drama and ease of exit proved to be their escape's most defining feature.[13] But, in the world of American cinematic triumphalism, such details are easily replaced by more Hollywood-esque endings, complete with obligatory national high-fiving, scorekeeping, and nose-thumbing toward Tehran; the film's final few intoxicatingly nationalistic minutes would make any pro-American public relations professional sit up and cheer.

American film critics' collective adoration of *Argo*, particularly by progressive and liberal observers occasionally critical of US imperial policy and propaganda, is perhaps best captured in Manohla Dargis's celebratory *New York Times* column. Calling *Argo* a "smart jittery thriller," Dargis concludes that "in the end, this is a story about outwitting rather than killing the enemy, making it a homage to actual intelligence and an example of the same." Indeed, perhaps what won over *Argo* audiences is this time-honored trope of proven Hollywood hokum—the "good guys" (Americans and Canadians) outmaneuver the "bad guys" (Iranians) with smarts and creativity instead of smart bombs and shock troops.[14] Most disturbing, however, is how this fictitious framing of 1979 events—"white hats" versus "black hats"—papers over *Argo*'s Islamophobic tendencies, at a time when real-life US/Iranian relations, including mutual saber-rattling and the US government's "all options are on the table" approach, are edgy, at best. Devoid of any mention of the US-backed Shah's autocratic government or the Iranian people's genuine grievances (remember, Persians, not Arabs, for anyone who is keeping track of such cultural differences), *Argo* paints a stereotype of Middle Eastern people that reeks of the worst cultural clichés. A few mainstream US critics picked up on this disturbing stereotype. "Instead of keeping its eye on the big picture of Revolutionary Iran, *Argo* settles into a retrograde 'white Americans in peril' storyline, recasting the oppressed Iranians as a raging, zombie-like horde," observed *Slate*'s Kevin B. Lee, who called *Argo* the year's "worst Best Picture Nominee."[15] But Lee's critical voice was drowned out by the film's Hollywood hype, culminating in the Best Picture award being given to *Argo* on Oscar night by none other than First Lady of the United States Michelle Obama via live video feed from the White House, surrounded by US military men and women in their uniformed finest. Citing "movies that lift our spirits, broaden our minds, and transport us to places we have never imagined," Ms. Obama went on to note that "these movies made us laugh, they made us weep, and they made us grip our armrest just a little tighter." (Full disclosure—I did all three while watching *Argo*, but not for the reasons Michelle Obama mentioned above). Here's Affleck's tortured rationalizing about accuracy in another interview about *Argo*:

> I tried to make a movie that is absolutely just factual. And that's another reason why I tried to be as true to the story as possible—because I didn't want it to be used by either side. I didn't want it to be politicized internationally or domestically in a partisan way. I just wanted to tell a story that was about the facts as I understood them."[16]

"I didn't want [*Argo*] to be politicized," insisted Affleck.[17] But, as Affleck himself must know, all movies are political, using powerful image-driven media to entertain, educate, and inspire (as *Argo* certainly does) with narratives that shape our hearts and minds. In the final analysis, we can thank *Argo* for perpetuating destructive Middle Eastern stereotypes, distorting history, and eroding cross-cultural understandings among peoples. The envelope, please . . .[18]

ZDT: REVEALING BLACK OPS, FEMINIZING IMPERIALISM, CONDONING TORTURE AND EXTRAJUDICIAL KILLING

If *Argo* was the big winner on 2013 Oscars night, Kathryn Bigelow's acclaimed film *Zero Dark Thirty* (ZDT) proved the big loser. Or was it? As a director, the talented Bigelow has crafted a deserved reputation for gritty realistic depictions of war—think Jeremy Renner as an emotionally detached bomb squad leader in *The Hurt Locker*. *Zero Dark Thirty*, which garnered multiple Oscar nominations, emerged as a gripping story—"witness the greatest manhunt in history"—based on Bigelow and screenwriter Mark Boal's recasting of facts garnered from "unusual access to senior officials at the Pentagon and CIA who were deeply involved in the hunt for Osama bin Laden."[19] (More on this in a moment.)

Critics initially praised the film on release for its "realistic" depiction of the search for Osama bin Laden (OBL), including the famous raid on the Abbottabad compound that resulted in his alleged death (a story that, like 9/11, leaves us with a number of unanswered questions). But the film subsequently came under fire for claiming to be historically accurate, particularly with regard to the film's opening scenes in which an actor/CIA agent tortures another actor/al-Qaeda detainee to unearth a crucial piece of information that leads CIA investigators to discover bin Laden's whereabouts.

The resulting firestorm of criticism of the film from congressional leaders, drawing on Senate Select Committee on Intelligence investigations from the previous year, attacked the ZDT team for misrepresenting (sort of) the facts in the OBL hunt—"the US may torture alleged terror suspects, but the US did *not* torture terror suspects to find Osama bin Laden"[20]—and sank the film's chances for an Oscar. "Since [Bigelow and Boal] presented their film as a form of history it has been judged on historical grounds and it has been found wanting," explains noted terrorism researcher Peter Bergen in a *Time* magazine cover story on Bigelow. "*Zero Dark Thirty* is a great piece of filmmaking; it's a far weaker work of history."[21]

True enough, Mr. Bergen, but the film's function as an imperial propaganda piece has proved far more useful to the US of Empire, legitimating a whole host of US post-9/11 policies and directives. Begin with *Zero Dark Thirty*'s opening sequence, featuring 9/11 audio footage of dying victims (used by Bigelow's production team without permission from 9/11 victims' families),[22] set against a black screen followed by an immediate "jump cut" to a CIA Middle Eastern black ops site. This explicit edit from the destruction of the World Trade Center building to Middle East torture sites reinforces the dominant popular US political narrative that "19 box cutter–wielding Muslim fanatics acting alone" carried out the 9/11 attacks, and reminds American filmgoers that, whatever nasty business the US may do in the Middle East, it is being done as a response to that "horrific" 9/11 attack on US soil.[23] *Zero Dark Thirty* also reveals to American audiences (because US newspapers of record seem unable to consistently report on CIA activities worldwide) that the US has crafted a network of "black sites" around the world, beyond public scrutiny, where the dirty business of the empire's maintenance is routinely handled. The presence of this so-called "secret government" may come as a surprise to many pop-corn-snorting Americans in their comfy theater seats, but, after all, in real life, the guys deemed "bad" by said secret government must be apprehended and brought to justice—or, better yet in our brave new post-9/11 world, broken, abused, and/or assassinated if they've already been deemed guilty as charged. ZDT's main character, a CIA agent named Maya (played by Jessica Chastain) functions as an audience surrogate in this role.

The flame-haired Chastain—playing a "lone-wolf female" in a man's world—winces on first witnessing the torture of an al-Qae-da detainee. In short order, though, Maya steels herself to the task, single-mindedly devoting herself to capturing bin Laden and facing down numerous more-powerful male higher-ups along the CIA chain of command. Some critics have followed female director Bigelow in interpreting Maya as a "feminist folk hero"—tenacious, scrappy, and determined to succeed in a man's world.[24] Others, including this writer, see Maya's constructed composite character as an unconvincing bone thrown to would-be feminists who are happy to see Maya kick some chauvinistic white male ass (while brown male asses get the life beaten out of them). "Do not now cleanse the wars of/on terror with the face of a white blonde female. Do not detract from the heinous aspects of the terror war by making it look gender neutral," declared Al Jazeera's Zillah Eisenstein.[25] Referring to "imperial feminism" in her column, Eisenstein well articulated my own feelings about Maya as a constructed composite Hollywood character who is more impe-rial cliché than real life:

> Maya is not believable to me. She is an awful stereotype: a driven, obsessive woman, alone with no friends. She has no depth. She is all surface. She says she prefers to drop a bomb rather than use the SEAL team. She says she knows 100 per cent that Osama is in the building. She says she is the "mother---er" who found the safe house in the first place. She assures the men of the SEAL team that Osama is there and that they must kill him for her.[26]

Or, as PolicyMic writer Hannah Kapp-Klote succinctly summarized, "In *Zero Dark Thirty*, Jessica Chastain's character's femininity and slight frame justify US policies that are unjustifiable."[27]

Beyond playing the diversionary "gender card" by using a female CIA agent as distraction, the propaganda machine of the Bigelow/ Boals team runs much deeper. In May 2013, independent journalists broke a news story that revealed the extent to which the CIA's Office of Public Affairs collaborated with Bigelow and Boals in drafting *Zero Dark Thirty*'s script through a series of "five conference calls" designed to "help promote an appropriate portrayal of the Agency and the bin Laden operation."[28] Script changes made by Boals at the CIA's request included removing the use of intimidating attack dogs in a key torture scene, censoring a scene involving a CIA officer and "drunken firearms abuse" at a party, and, perhaps most importantly, downplaying main character Maya's involvement in the film's opening torture scene from active participant to passive observer. Apparently, "reel" life does not mirror real life in the CIA's mind when it comes to representing the truth about the global war on terror on the silver screen. Perhaps *Gawker* said it best: jokingly referring to ZDT as "The CIA Director's Cut," Adrian Chen observed that "Kathryn Bigelow's Osama bin Laden revenge-porn flick *Zero Dark Thirty* was the biggest publicity coup for the CIA this century outside of the actual killing of Osama bin Laden."[29]

Zero Dark Thirty's most powerful use as a propaganda piece involves using the silver screen to convince American audiences to accept torture and extrajudicial killings in the name of the greater imperial good—a particularly troubling example of fantasy mediating fascism, to reinvoke bell hooks' insight. ZDT "teaches us that brown men can and should be killed with impunity, in violation of international law, and that we should trust the CIA to act with all due diligence," observed *Mondoweiss*'s Deepa Kumar. "At a time when the key strategy in the 'war on terror' has shifted from conventional warfare to extrajudicial killing, here comes a film that normalizes and justifies this strategy."[30] Kumar's provocative article linking Hollywood propaganda and US political policies is vital reading for anyone interested in the relationship between fantasy and fascism in the US of Empire. Kumar concluded her analysis of ZDT by observing:

Here then is the key message of the film: the law, due process, and the idea of presenting evidence before a jury should be dispensed with in favor of extrajudicial killings. Further, such killings can take place without public oversight. The film not only uses the moral unambiguity of assassinating bin Laden to sell us on the rightness and righteousness of extrajudicial killing, it also takes pains to show that this can be done in secret because of the checks and balances involved before a targeted assassination is carried out.[31]

Interestingly, scientific studies are now revealing that Hollywood movies can, in fact, play an active role in promoting the acceptance of specific kinds of formerly aberrant behavior within the mind of the collective audience. Consider researcher Luke Mitchell's insightful observations in his *Popular Science* article, "The Science of 'Zero Dark Thirty': When We Can Condone Torture." Mitchell described Kurt Gray and Daniel Wegner's work on "cognitive dissonance" and proximity to torture as it is being performed. Mitchell explained how Gray and Wegner conducted experiments with observers witnessing staged acts of torture. Those observers removed from the scene tended to feel the pain of torture less acutely, and, paradoxically, assumed the tortured was innocent, while observers closer to the event tended to assume guilt on the part of the tortured.[32] Why? Here's Mitchell's explanation:

> Gray's research suggests that torture's very repugnancy is what causes some of us to defend its use—we feel terrible about it, so we think there must be a reason for it. *In movies, the effect may be more pronounced: The giant screen brings us even "closer" to an interrogation. We condone the torture because the cinematic intimacy causes us, the audience, to feel complicit.* This proximity bias—a variation of confirmation bias we might call the Zero Effect—is relevant for scientists engaged in all kinds of observational research. It is also a crucial consideration for those of us watching interrogators at work, on-screen or in life.[33] (Emphasis added.)

In other words, fictionalized recreations of graphic torture, when set in the context of a film that is presented as "based on real life events"—like ZDT—push audiences to an acceptance of behavior they might normally deem reprehensible. Constructing a bad-ass lone-wolf fiery female agent to legitimize torture, promoting extrajudicial killing, revealing black sites, and steeling American audiences for the hard work of empire—*Zero Dark Thirty* does all of this in powerful and provocative fashion.

CONCLUSION: BEYOND THE IMPERIAL SILVER SCREEN

We all go to movies for different reasons, hoping to be entertained, educated, inspired—and sometimes all three. Because of film's unique power to move us emotionally, and now, in the Internet Age, to be available everywhere to everybody at any time, movies occupy a central place in our national storytelling culture like no other medium. And yet, too often, movie audiences fail to watch with a skeptical eye, and movie reviewers fail to report on films critically, while influential corporate commercial and political interests are quick to exploit Hollywood's uniquely powerful reach to propagandize, rather than to educate.

We all bear some responsibility for the perpetuation of fantasy film propaganda that plays a vital role in justifying twenty-first century US fascism. "Such a system requires an equally powerful system of propaganda to convince the citizenry that they need not be alarmed, they need not speak out, they need not think critically, in fact they need not even participate in the deliberative process except to pull a lever every couple of years in an elaborate charade of democracy," concluded Deepa Kumar. "We are being asked, quite literally, to amuse ourselves to death."[34]

If we are to take the Oscar night words of Michelle Obama at all seriously, if we really want "our children [to] learn to open their imaginations, to dream just a little bigger," then we'll need to work collectively to move our Hollywood moviemaking culture beyond simplistic stereotypes, rehashed storylines, and political propaganda, to a new reality that acknowledges cross-cultural complexity, multiple points of view, and a shared sense of community and global purpose.

It's no easy task—but let us begin by being honest about the films that Hollywood produces, and push for new mediated fantasy worlds that bring out the best in us as human beings rather than simply pandering to nationalistic goals and imperialistic designs.

───────────────

DR. ROB WILLIAMS is a media educator, musician, historian, journalist, and professor who teaches online and face-to-face courses at the University of Vermont and Champlain College, and serves as publisher of *Vermont Commons: Voices of Independence* newspaper.

Notes

1. Michelle Obama, Academy Awards 2013 *Argo* White House video feed presentation, https://www.youtube.com/watch?v=FtLKn5YlulcJ.
2. The phrase "crap detectors" comes from Neil Postman and Charles Weingartner, *Teaching As A Subversive Activity* (New York: Dell, 1969), 1–16.
3. Jack Shaheen, "Reel Bad Arabs: How Hollywood Vilifies A People," Media Education Foundation PDF, 206, http://www.mediaed.org/assets/products/402/transcript_402.pdf.
4. bell hooks, "Cultural Criticism and Transformation," Media Education Foundation PDF, 1997, http://www.mediaed.org/assets/products/402/transcript_402.pdf. And for more on the history of the connections between Hollywood and the political establishment of Washington DC, especially among conservatives and the GOP (which challenges the conventional wisdom of the Hollywood liberal stereotype), see Steven J. Ross, *Hollywood Left and Right: How Movie Stars Shaped American Politics* (New York: Oxford University Press, 2011); and hear an interview with Ross covering the contents of the book, both historically and in current context, by Pacifica Radio's Mitch Jeserich on the show, *Letters and Politics*, KPFA Radio, April 17, 2013, archived online at http://www.kpfa.org/archive/id/90755.
5. See, for example, Jim Garamone, "Joint Vision 2020 Emphasizes Full-Spectrum Dominance" American Forces Press Service, June 2, 2000, http://www.defense.gov/news/newsarticle.aspx?id=45289.
6. For more on the Project for the New American Century (PNAC), see http://www.newamericancentury.org. For a summary and link to full documents from PNAC published September 2000, "Rebuilding America's Defenses: Strategy, Forces and Resources for a New Century," see http://www.informationclearinghouse.info/article3249.htm.
7. John Farmer, *The Ground Truth: The Untold Story of America Under Attack on 9/11* (New York: Riverhead Books, 2009); David Ray Griffin, *The 9/11 Commission Report: Omissions And Distortions* (Northampton: Olive Branch Press, 2005); Architects and Engineers for 9/11 Truth, http://ae911truth.org.
8. See, for example, Elliot D. Cohen, "The Police State and Civil Liberties," *Censored 2013: Dispatches from the Media Revolution*, eds. Mickey Huff and Andy Lee Roth (New York: Seven Stories Press, 2012), 45–60.
9. Shaheen, "Reel Bad Arabs." See also Deepa Kumar, *Islamophobia and the Politics of Empire* (Chicago: Haymarket Press, 2012).
10. Kevin Russell, "Oscar Prints The Legend: Argo's Upcoming Academy Award and the Failure of Truth," Wide Asleep in America, http://www.wideasleepinamerica.com/2013/02/oscar-prints-the-legend-argo.html. Some may be noting while reading this paragraph, Iran is not part of the Arab Middle East, Iranians are not Arabs (Persians by cultural descent), and Iranians speak

Farsi, not Arabic. But in the minds of most heavily conditioned Westerners (an image helped along by mass media), Iran is just another uppity Middle Eastern country whose own self-interests inconveniently clash with US imperial designs for the region.

11. Quoted in "Ben Affleck, 'I Didn't Want Argo To Be Politicized,'" *London Evening Standard*, October 18, 2012, http://www.standard.co.uk/showbiz/celebrity-news/ben-affleck-i-didn't-want-argo-to-be-politicised-8215965.html. Given the topic of the film, that seems a difficult task, but Affleck's consulting with CIA analysts for this and other films, and his public praise for the Agency, make his claims of not wanting to politicize the film seem misleading.

12. The CIA actually has something called the Entertainment Industry Liaison that openly states they welcome working with Hollywood for consulting, online at https://www.cia.gov/offices-of-cia/public-affairs/entertainment-industry-liaison/index.html. The site states, "If you are part of the entertainment industry, and are working on a project that deals with the CIA, the Agency may be able to help you. We are in a position to give greater authenticity to scripts, stories, and other products in development." For more on CIA involvement in Hollywood, see Tom Hayden, "The CIA in Hollywood," *Los Angeles Review of Books*, February 24, 2013, http://lareviewofbooks.org/article.php?id=1438&fulltext=1; and Washington's Television: "The Winners of the Academy Award and Golden Globe Are . . . Government Propagandists," Global Research, January 16, 2013, http://www.globalsearch.ca/the-cia-and-other-government-agencies-dominate-movies-and-televison/53119262; See also note 26 below.

13. Noted in a number of critical reviews in the independent press. See, for example, Kevin Russell, "Oscar Prints the Legend: Argo's Upcoming Academy Award and the Failure of Truth," Wide Asleep in America, February 23, 2013, http://www.wideasleepinamerica.com/2013/02/oscar-prints-the-legend-argo.html.

14. Manohla Dargis, "Outwitting the Ayatollah With Hollywood's Help," *New York Times*, October 11, 2012, http://movies.nytimes.com/2012/10/12/movies/argo-directed-by-ben-affleck.html?r=1&.

15. Kevin B. Lee, "Argo, F--k Yourself," *Slate*, February 25, 2013, http://www.slate.com/articles/arts/culturebox/2013/01/down_with_argo_ben_affleck_s_iran_hostage_movie_is_the_worst.html.

16. Mike Ryan, "Ben Affleck, 'Argo' Director and Star, On Pinpointing the Resurrection of his Career," *Huffington Post*, October 8, 2012, http://www.huffingtonpost.com/2012/10/07/ben-affleck-ago_n_1946884.html.

17. Ibid.

18. David Walsh, "2013 Academy Award Nominations: 'And the Winner is . . . the CIA,' " Global Research, February 25 2013, http://www.globalresearch.ca/2013-academy-award-nominations-and-the-winner-is-the-cia/5318811.

19. Peter Bergen, "Is Washington Overreacting To Zero Dark Thirty?" *Time*, January 24, 2013, http://ideas.time.com/2013/01/24/is-washington-overreacting-to-zero-dark-thirty.

20. "CIA Disputes 'Zero Dark Thirty' Accuracy: Acting CIA Director Issues Public Statement," *Huffington Post*, December 22, 2012, http://huffingtonpost.com/2012/112/22/cia-disputes-accuracy_n_23522811.html.

21. Bergen, "Is Washington Overreacting?"

22. See "'Zero Dark Thirty' Used 9/11 Phone Call Without Permission," Project Censored's Media Freedom International, March 8, 2013, http://www.mediafreedominternational.org/2013/03/08/zero-dark-thirty-used-911-phone-call-without-pemission/; and "'Zero Dark Thirty' 9/11 Phone Calls Used Without Permission, Says Upset Mom Of Victim," *Huffington Post*, February 27, 2013, http://www.huffingtonpost.com/2013/02/27/zero-dark-thirty-911-phone-calls_n_2773255.html.

23. For further coverage of debate and controversy regarding the official 9/11 narrative see previous Project Censored annual books, all published by Seven Stories Press, including *Censored 2005, Censored 2007, Censored 2008, Censored 2009*, and *Censored 2011*.

24. Lauren Sandler, "Zero Dark Thirty and the Problem With Lone Wolf Heroines," *Cut*, December 18, 2012, http://nymag.com/thecut/2012/12/zero-dark-thirtys-lone-wolf-heroine-problem.html.

25. Zillah Eisenstein, "Dark, Zero-Feminism," Al Jazeera, January 21, 2013,http://www.aljazeera. com/indepth/opinion/2013/01/2013120121530123614.html.

26. Ibid.

27. Hannah Kapp-Klote, "Is 'Zero Dark Thirty' a Feminist Manifesto or a Picture of American Imperialism?," Policymic, February 2013, http://policymic.com/articles/24836/is-zero-dark-thirty-a-feminist-manifesto-or-a-picture-of-american-imperalism.

28. Adrian Chen, "Newly Declassified Memo Shows CIA Shaped Zero Dark Thirty's Narrative," Gawker, May 6, 2013, http://gawker.com/declassified-memo-shows-how-cia-shaped-zero-dark-thirty-493174407. For more on the history of CIA involvement in Hollywood, which is far more pervasive than some may understand, see Matthew Alford and Robbie Graham, "Lights, Camera . . . Convert Action: The Deep Politics of Hollywood," Global Research, January 21, 2009, http://www.globalresearch.ca/screen-propaganda-hollywood-and-the-cia/5324589. It should be noted that Ben Affleck worked on another movie with CIA ties in 2002 (where he consulted with CIA analysts), The Sum of All Fears.

29. Ibid. See also Julie Lévesque, "Screen Propaganda, Hollywood and the CIA," Global Research, February 28, 2013, http://globalresearch.ca/screen-propaganda-hollywood-and-the-cia/5324589; and John Cook, "If You Want to Know the CIA's bin Laden Secrets, Just Make a Movie About His Assassination," Gawker, May 23, 2012, http://gawker.com/5591284/if-you-want-to-make-a-movie-about-his-assissination. And for more on the controversy regarding the many reported deaths of Osama bin Laden, see David Ray Griffin, Osama bin Laden: Dead or Alive? (Northampton: Olive Branch Press, 2009), 1–17, and the endnote section particularly. The CIA is not only involved with Hollywood, they have long been active influencing and manipulating, when not outright scripting, news reporting in the US. See Carl Bernstein, "The CIA and the Media: How Americas Most Powerful News Media Worked Hand in Glove with the Central Intelligence Agency and Why the Church Committee Covered It Up," Rolling Stone, October 20, 1977, http://www.carlbernstein.com/magazine_cia_and_media.php.

30. Deepa Kumar, "Rebranding the War on Terror for the Age of Obama: 'Zero Dark Thirty' and the Promotion of Extra Judicial Killing," January 15, 2013, Mondoweiss, http://mondoweiss. net/2013/01/rebranding-promotion-judicial.html.

31. Ibid.

32. Luke Mitchell, "The Science of 'Zero Dark Thirty': When We Can Condone Torture," Popular Science, February 22, 2013, http://www.popsci.com/science/article/2013-02/fma-why-we-condone-torture.

33. Ibid.

34. Kumar, "Rebranding." And regarding the origination of the phrase "amusing ourselves to death," which Kumar expands upon, see Neil Postman, Amusing Ourselves to Death: Public Discourse in the Age of Show Business (New York: Penguin, 1985).

CASE STUDIES OF "UNHISTORY" IN THE MAKING—AND HOW TO BUILD A BETTER FUTURE

Historical understanding defines people's very sense of what is thinkable and achievable. As a result, many have lost the ability to imagine a world that is substantially different from and better than what exists today.

—Oliver Stone and Peter Kuznick[1]

In their book, *The Untold History of the United States,* Oliver Stone and Peter Kuznick observed that "Americans believe they are unbound by history," preferring myth to fact.[2] Their observations are salient to this section, especially if applied directly to contemporary establishment journalism in the United States.

Because most people do not witness news—history in the making—as it happens, we see, hear, or read about it in accounts provided by journalists. And those accounts reflect not only the world but also the social forces and professional conventions that shape journalism as a field. As sociologist Michael Schudson has famously observed, "The power of the media lies not only (and not even primarily) in its power to declare things to be true, but in its power to provide the forms in which the declarations appear."[3]

One consequence of establishment journalism's formal power—perhaps an unintended one, in some instances—is that certain types of stories consistently fall outside the scope of its attention. In such instances the result is that establishment journalism, instead of contributing to a "first rough draft of history," promotes one version of what Noam Chomsky has called "unhistory."[4]

The chapters in this section examine sources overlooked or ignored by the corporate media, to prevent some of the most important news stories of this era from joining the annals of unhistory. From the concentration of wealth in a global financial "superclass" (Peter Phillips and Brady Osborne, Chapter 9), to the voices of Chinese workers who protest against Apple and its subcontractors (Nicki Lisa Cole and Tara Krishna, Chapter 10), to Africa, where Brian Martin Murphy disambiguates US interests and the role of the indigenous Tuareg in Mali's crisis (Chapter 11), and the catastrophic impacts of climate change on the world's nonhuman species (Julie Andrzejewski and John C. Alessio, Chapter 12), these chapters challenge us to deal with the realities of global economics and our lives as consumers. These chapters also indicate how we might alter our behavior in order to create a different, better world.

It is not by chance, then, that Michael Nagler's chapter, "The New Story: Why We Need One and How to Create It," concludes both this section and the book as a whole. Drawing on the principled nonviolence of Gandhi and Martin Luther King Jr., among others, Nagler makes the case that "cooperation is a more potent driver of evolution than competition" and "compassion in us leads to more long-lasting change than hatred." Tacit in his argument is the point that all of us— not only journalists but everyday people and community members— have a central role to play in the development of this new, better story.

Notes

1. Oliver Stone and Peter Kuznick, *The Untold History of the United States* (New York: Gallery Books, 2012), ix.
2. Ibid., xiii.
3. Michael Schudson, "The Politics of Narrative Form," *The Power of News* (Cambridge, MA: Harvard University Press, 1995), 54.
4. Noam Chomsky, "Anniversaries from 'Unhistory," *In These Times*, February 6, 2012, http://inthesetimes.com/article/12679/anniversaries_from_unhistory. See also Mickey Huff and Andy Lee Roth with Project Censored, *Censored 2013: Dispatches from the Media Revolution* (New York: Seven Stories, 2012), 25, 217, 333–334.

CHAPTER 9

Exposing the Financial Core of the Transnational Capitalist Class

Peter Phillips and Brady Osborne

INTRODUCTION

The specific names of the power elites running the financial centers of the world are rarely identified in the context of a world-class system. Corporate media and mainstream academics choose to leave undisclosed the names of the most powerful people in the world at the financial core of the transnational capitalist class.

In this study, we decided to identify the people on the boards of directors of the top ten asset management firms and the top ten most centralized corporations. Because of overlaps, there is a total of thirteen firms, which collectively have 161 directors on their boards. We think that this group of 161 individuals represents the financial core of the world's transnational capitalist class. They collectively manage $23.91 trillion in funds and operate in nearly every country in the world. They are the center of the financial capital that powers the global economic system. Western governments and international policy bodies work in the interests of this financial core to protect the free flow of capital investment anywhere in the world.

A BRIEF HISTORY OF RESEARCH ON THE
AMERICAN POWER ELITE

A long tradition of sociological research documents the existence of a dominant ruling class in the United States, whose members set policy and determine national political priorities. The American ruling class is complex and competitive, and perpetuates itself through interacting families of high social standing with similar lifestyles, corporate affiliations, and memberships in elite social clubs and private schools.[1]

The American ruling class has long been determined to be mostly self-perpetuating,[2] maintaining its influence through policy-making institutions such as the National Association of Manufacturers, the US Chamber of Commerce, the Business Council, Business Roundtable, the Conference Board, American Enterprise Institute for Public Policy Research, Council on Foreign Relations, and other business-centered policy groups.[3] These associations have long dominated policy decisions within the US government.

In his 1956 book, *The Power Elite*, C. Wright Mills documented how World War II solidified a trinity of power in the US that comprised corporate, military, and government elites in a centralized power structure motivated by class interests and working in unison through "higher circles" of contact and agreement. Mills described how the power elite were those "who decide whatever is decided" of major consequence.[4] These higher-circle decision makers tended to be more concerned with interorganizational relationships and the functioning of the economy as a whole, rather than with advancing their particular corporate interests.[5]

The higher-circle policy elites (HCPE) are a segment of the American upper class and are the principal decision makers in society. Although these elites display some sense of "we-ness," they also tend to have continuing disagreements on specific policies and necessary actions in various sociopolitical circumstances.[6] These disagreements can block aggressive reactionary responses to social movements and civil unrest, as in the case of the labor movement in the 1930s and the civil rights movement in the 1960s. During these two periods, the more liberal elements of HCPE tended to dominate the decision-making process and supported passing the National Labor Relations and Social Security Acts in 1935, as well as the Civil Rights and Economic Opportunities Acts in 1964. These pieces of national legislation were seen as concessions to the ongoing social movements and civil unrest, and were implemented without instituting more repressive policies.

However, during periods of threats from external enemies, as in World Wars I and II, more conservative/reactionary elements of the HCPE successfully pushed their agendas. During and after World War I, the United States instituted repressive responses to social movements, for example through the Palmer Raids and passage of the Espionage Act of 1917 and the Sedition Act of 1918. After World War II, the HCPE allowed and encouraged the McCarthy-era attacks on liberals and radicals and, in 1947, passage of the National Security Act and the antilabor Taft-Hartley Act. In the past twenty-five years, and especially since the events of 9/11, the HCPE in the US has been united in support of an American empire of military power that maintains a repressive war against resisting groups—typically dubbed "terrorists"—around the world. This war on terror is much more about protecting transnational globalization, the free flow of financial capital, dollar hegemony, and access to oil, than it is repressing terrorism. Increasingly, the North Atlantic Treaty Organization (NATO) is a partner with US global dominance interests.[7]

THE TRANSNATIONAL CAPITALIST CLASS

Capitalist power elites exist around the world. The globalization of trade and capital brings the world's elites into increasingly interconnected relationships—to the point that sociologists have begun to theorize the development of a transnational capitalist class (TCC). In one of the pathbreaking works in this field, *The Transnational Capitalist Class* (2000), Leslie Sklair argued that globalization elevated transnational corporations (TNC) to more influential international roles, with the result that nation-states became less significant than international argreements developed through the World Trade Organization (WTO) and other international institutions.[8] Emerging from these multinational corporations was a transnational capitalist class,

whose loyalties and interests, while still rooted in their corporations, was increasingly international in scope. Sklair wrote:

> The transnational capitalist class can be analytically divided into four main fractions: (i) owners and controllers of TNCs and their local affiliates; (ii) globalizing bureaucrats and politicians; (iii) globalizing professionals; (iv) consumerist elites (merchants and media). . . . It is also important to note, of course, that the TCC and each of its fractions are not always entirely united on every issue. Nevertheless, together, leading personnel in these groups constitute a global power elite, dominant class or inner circle in the sense that these terms have been used to characterize the dominant class structures of specific countries.[9]

William Robinson followed in 2004 with his book, *A Theory of Global Capitalism: Production, Class, and State in a Transnational World.*[10] Robinson claimed that 500 years of capitalism had led to a global epochal shift in which all human activity is transformed into capital. In this view, the world had become a single market, which privatized social relationships. He saw the TCC as increasingly sharing similar lifestyles, patterns of higher education, and consumption. The global circulation of capital is at the core of an international bourgeoisie, who operate in oligopolist clusters around the world. These clusters of elites form strategic transnational alliances through mergers and acquisitions with the goal of increased concentration of wealth and capital. The process creates a polyarchy of hegemonic elites. The concentration of wealth and power at this level tends to over-accumulate, leading to speculative investments and wars. The TCC makes efforts to correct and protect its interests through global organizations like the World Bank, the International Monetary Fund, the G20, World Social Forum, Trilateral Commission, Bilderberg Group, Bank for International Settlements, and other transnational associations. Robinson claimed that, within this system, nation-states become little more than population containment zones, and the real power lies with the decision makers who control global capital.[11]

Deeper inside the transnational capitalist class is what David Rothkopf calls the "superclass." In his 2008 book, *Superclass: The Global Power Elite and the World They Are Making*, Rothkopf argued that the superclass constitutes 6,000 to 7,000 people, or 0.0001 percent of the world's population.[12] They are the Davos-attending, Gulfstream/ private jet–flying, money-incrusted, megacorporation-interlocked, policy-building elites of the world, people at the absolute peak of the global power pyramid. They are 94 percent male, predominantly white, and mostly from North America and Europe. Rothkopf reported that these are the people setting the agendas at the G8, G20, NATO, the World Bank, and the WTO. They are from the highest levels of finance capital, transnational corporations, the government, the military, the academy, nongovernmental organizations, spiritual leaders, and other shadow elites. (Shadow elites include, for instance, the deep politics of national security organizations in connection with international drug cartels, who extract 8,000 tons of opium from US war zones annually, then launder $500 billion through transnational banks, half of which are US-based.)[13]

Rothkopf's definition of the superclass emphasized their influence and power. Although there are over 1,500 billionaires in the world, not all are necessarily part of the superclass in terms of influencing global policies. Yet these 1,500 billionaires possess two times as much wealth as the 2.5 billion least wealthy people, and they are fully aware of these vast inequalities. The billionaires inside the TCC are similar to colonial plantation owners. They know they are a small minority with vast resources and power, yet they must continually worry about the unruly exploited masses rising in rebellion. As a result of these class insecurities, the TCC works to protect its structure of concentrated wealth. Protection of capital is the prime reason that NATO countries now account for 85 percent of the world's defense spending, with the US spending more on military than the rest of the world combined.[14] Fears of rebellions motivated by inequality and other forms of unrest motivate NATO's global agenda in the war on terror.[15]

NATO is quickly emerging as the police force for the transnational capitalist class. As the TCC more fully emerged in the 1980s, coinciding with the collapse of the Soviet Union, NATO began broader operations. NATO first ventured into the Balkans, where it remains, and then into Afghanistan. NATO started a training mission in Iraq in 2005, has recently conducted operations in Libya, and, as of July 2013, is considering military action in Syria. Superclass use of NATO for its global security is part of an expanding strategy for US military domination around the world, whereby the US/NATO military–industrial–media empire operates in service to the TCC for the protection of international capital anywhere in the world.[16]

The most recent work on the TCC is William K. Carroll's *The Making of a Transnational Capitalist Class* (2010).[17] Carroll's work focused on the consolidation of the transnational corporate-policy networks between 1996 and 2006. He used a database of the boards of directors of the global 500 largest corporations, showing the concentrated interconnectedness of key corporations and a decreasing number of people involved. According to this analysis, the average size of corporate boards has dropped from 20.2 to 14.0 in the ten years of his study. Furthermore, financial organizations are increasingly the center of these networks. Carroll argued that the TCC at the centers of these networks benefit from extensive ties to each other, thus providing both the structural capacity and class consciousness necessary for effective political solidarity.

A 2011 University of Zurich study completed by Stefania Vitali, James B. Glattfelder, and Stefano Battiston at the Swiss Federal Institute of Technology, reported that a small group of companies—mainly banks—wields huge power over the global economy.[18] Applying mathematical models—usually used to model natural systems—to the transnational corporations in the world economy, the study found that 147 companies controlled some 40 percent of the world's wealth.[19]

PROJECT CENSORED RESEARCH ON THE 2013 TRANSNATIONAL CAPITALIST CLASS

Although sociological theorists conduct studies of the world's power elite, these researchers rarely identify specific members of the transnational capitalist class, preferring instead to build theory for other academics to read and discuss, while avoiding the particulars of who is actually involved.

The world's corporate media pay absolutely no attention to academic concepts like "transnational capitalist class." Thus, a LexisNexis search of news coverage, completed on June 3, 2013, using the term "transnational capitalist class," returned only three news stories in the past decade—two from foreign media, and the third a letter to the editor by Leslie Sklair. The concept of a transnational capitalist class is absent from corporate news coverage, which also does not address who constitutes this most elite, powerful group.

We think that the world needs to know who comprises the TCC and thus who makes the financial decisions regarding global capital.

This is actually a fairly straightforward—if labor-intensive—research effort: most of the information is not only public but also online. We started with the top ten most centralized companies from the previously cited 2011 Swiss study.[20] This identified the world's most centralized and interconnected financial organizations. We also wanted to consider those groups managing the largest volumes of financial capital, so we added the top asset management firms from 2012 to our data set.[21] The following chart shows the rankings in trillions of dollars of assets managed for the top thirty-five asset management firms in the world.

TABLE 1: THE WORLD'S TOP 35 ASSET MANAGEMENT FIRMS, IN TRILLIONS OF DOLLARS (2012)

1	BlackRock	US	$3,560
2	UBS	Switzerland	$2,280
3	Allianz	Germany	$2,213
4	Vanguard Group	US	$2,080
5	State Street Global Advisors (SSgA)	US	$1,908
6	PIMCO (Pacific Investment Management Company)	US	$1,820
7	Fidelity Investments	US	$1,576
8	AXA Group	France	$1,393
9	JPMorgan Asset Management	US	$1,347
10	Credit Suisse	Switzerland	$1,279
11	BNY Mellon Asset Management	US	$1,299
12	HSBC	UK	$1,230
13	Deutsche Bank	Germany	$1,227
14	BNP Paribas	France	$1,106
15	Capital Research and Management Company	US	$1,071
16	Prudential Financial	US	$961.0
17	Amundi	France	$880.0
18	Goldman Sachs Group	US	$836.0
19	Wellington Management Company	US	$719.8
20	Natixis Global Asset Management	France	$710.9
21	Franklin Resources (Franklin Templeton Investments)	US	$707.1
22	Northern Trust	US	$704.3
23	Bank of America	US	$682.2

24	Invesco	US	$646.6
25	Legg Mason	US	$631.8
26	Nippon Life Insurance Company	Japan	$600.0
27	Legal & General Investment Management	UK	$598.5
28	Generali Group	Italy	$581.5
29	Prudential	UK	$570.2
30	Ameriprise Financial	US	$543.6
31	T. Rowe Price	US	$541.7
32	Wells Fargo	US	$534.9
33	Manulife Financial	Canada	$513.8
34	Sun Life Financial	Canada	$496.3
35	TIAA-CREF	US	$481.0

Seven of the top ten asset management firms were in the top ten of the most centralized firms from the Swiss study. We decided to identify the people on the boards of directors of the top ten asset management firms and the top ten most centralized corporations. With overlaps there is a total of thirteen firms in our study: Barclays PLC, BlackRock Inc., Capital Group Companies Inc., FMR Corporation: Fidelity Worldwide Investment, AXA Group, State Street Corporation, JPMorgan Chase & Co., Legal & General Group PLC (LGIMA), Vanguard Group Inc., UBS AG, Bank of America/Merrill Lynch, Credit Suisse Group AG, and Allianz SE (Owners of PIMCO) PIMCO-Pacific Investment Management Co. The boards of directors of these firms, totaling 161 individuals, represent the financial core of the world's transnational capitalist class (for more details see Appendix). Collectively, they manage $23.91 trillion in funds and operate in nearly every country in the world. The $23.91 trillion does not include the equity balances—which number in the billions of dollars—that each of these firms holds in company assets. Nor does it include the $18.8 trillion controlled by the next twenty-five most valuable asset management firms.

The bank Barclays, the most wealth-centralized corporation in the world, sold its global asset management division to BlackRock in 2009. The result is that Blackrock is now the single largest asset management firm, though Barclays remains one of the most wealth-centralized firms with company assets of $2.42 trillion.[22]

UNDERSTANDING THE FINANCIAL CORE OF THE TRANSNATIONAL CAPITALIST CLASS

The 161 directors of the thirteen mostly centralized/largest asset management firms represent the central core of international capital. As such, these 161 people share a common goal of maximum return on investments for their clients and will seek to achieve returns sometimes by any means necessary—legal or not.

Authorities have deemed the largest banks "too big to fail," and have responded to the banks' criminal activities with weak reforms and no prosecutions.[23] The American government has refused to prosecute any officials from the multitude of banks who have laundered billions of dollars for illegal drug cartels. Powerful banking corporations, such as JPMorgan Chase, have continually refused to comply with American anti-money laundering (AML) laws.[24]

This refusal to prosecute is often hailed as an honorable move that serves to protect all individuals from devastation. Thus, Assistant Attorney General Lanny A. Breuer explained the refusal to prosecute the bank HSBC:

> Had the US authorities decided to press criminal charges, HSBC would almost certainly lost its banking license in the US, the future of the institution would have been under threat and the entire banking system would have been destabilized.[25]

Not only are these powerful corporations considered "too big to fail," they appear to have become too big to tell apart. Traditionally, banks have been understood as separate entities, competing against one another in order to entice consumers to deposit funds and invest. Such competition theoretically forces banks to compete to offer the best rates. However, in reality, these banks found that competing against one another was less profitable than working together. Realizing that their interests lie side by side, the financial core of the TCC have been highly motivated to join forces—legally or not—to manipulate laws, policies, and governments to their advantage. The ramifications of the lack of competition in the banking industry are devastating. Consider, for example, price-fixing scandals such as Libor or ISDAfix. JPMorgan Chase, UBS, and Barclays (among thirteen others) were implicated in the Libor scandal, falsifying the data that was used to create benchmark rates.[26] Based on faked data, those rates affected the prices of everything from auto, home, and student loans to credit cards to mortgage and commercial loans, and even the price of currencies themselves. The Financial Services Authority in the United Kingdom fined Barclays $450 million, and several other banks are still under investigation.[27]

The ISDAfix scandal looks a lot like the Libor case. The same superpower banks are currently under investigation to determine whether or not they manipulated ISDAfix, a benchmark number used to calculate the prices of global interest rate swaps.[28] Because cities and sovereign governments use interest rate swaps to help manage their debts, manipulation of those rates has far-reaching impacts, particularly for the poor and working classes, as economic safety nets are subject to "austerity" measures—i.e., budget cuts—that favor protection of financial capital.

Not only were rates illegally fixed and data falsified, but the offending banks also used individual consumers' investments to engage in criminal activity. The Vanguard Group was accused of investing its clients' money into illegal offshore gambling sites, prompting a class-action lawsuit under the Racketeer Influenced and Corrupt Organizations (RICO) Act. Vanguard did not deny such wrongdoing, but a judge determined that when the plaintiffs (Vanguard's clients) were harmed, they lost their money due to the government's crackdown on such illegal gambling, rather than due to Vanguard's investing in such sites.[29] However, it is clear that if Vanguard had not invested client money in illegal ventures, there would have been no negative repercussions from such a government crackdown. As journalist Matt Taibbi declared, "Everything is rigged."[30] Indeed it seems that the superpower corporate elite will never be made to pay for their crimes against consumers—we have yet to see such a prosecution.

Vanguard Group and BlackRock are major investors in Sturm, Ruger & Co., a leading firearms manufacturer.[31] Though there is nothing illegal about such investments, we can wonder about the consequences of such a pairing. With the expansion of private police and military companies, the power elite are investing in the violent means with which to maintain and further their power.

With money comes power, influence, and propaganda. BlackRock and numerous other banks and Wall Street institutions are financially backing groups like Parent Revolution and StudentsFirst, whose agendas are to privatize and subsequently corporatize the public school system.[32] The transnational capitalist class is laying the foundation for the privatization of the world. If public, democratic institutions—including schools, post offices, universities, the military, and even churches—become privately owned entities, then corporate interests will truly dominate. Then, we become neo-feudal societies where the reign of kings is replaced by private corporate ownership and the people serve as peasants.

We do not claim that any single person identified in this study, as one of the 161 individuals at the financial core of the TCC, has done anything illegal. We only point out that the institutional, structural arrangements within the money management systems of global capital relentlessly seek ways to achieve maximum return on investment, and that the conditions for manipulations—legal or not—always hold. As these institutions become "too big to fail," their scope and interconnections pressure government regulators to shy away from criminal investigations, much less prosecutions. The result is a semi-protected class of people with increasingly vast amounts of money, seeking unlimited growth and returns, with little concern for consequences of their economic pursuits on other people, societies, cultures, and environments.

Estimates are that the total world's wealth is close to $200 trillion, with the US and Europe holding approximately 63 percent of that total; meanwhile, the poorest half of the global population together possesses less than 2 percent of global wealth.[33] The World Bank reports that in 2008, 1.29 billion people were living in extreme poverty, on less than $1.25 a day, and 1.2 billion more were living on less than $2.00 a day.[34] Thirty-five thousand people, mostly young children, die every day from starvation.[35] So while millions suffer, the TCC financial elites seek returns that speculate on the rising cost of food, and they do this in cooperation with each other in a global system of TCC power and control.

Who are the financial core of the transnational corporate class? As indicated above, the financial core of the TCC are directors of banks and asset management firms. The 161 directors who manage the top thirteen firms have very similar backgrounds and training. (See Appendix for names and affiliations. The full, detailed list is online at: http://projectcensored.org/financial-core-of-the-transnational-corporate-class/).

FINANCIAL CORE OF THE TRANSNATIONAL CORPORATE CLASS

One hundred thirty-six of the 161 core members (84 percent) are male. Eighty-eight percent are whites of European descent (just nineteen are people of color). Fifty-two percent hold graduate degrees—including thirty-seven MBAs, fourteen JDs, twenty-one PhDs, and twelve MA/MS degrees.

Almost all have attended private colleges, with close to half attending the same ten universities: Harvard University (25), Oxford University (11), Stanford University (8), Cambridge University (8), University of Chicago (8), University of Cologne (6), Columbia University (5), Cornell University (4), the Wharton School of the University of Pennsylvania (3), and University of California–Berkeley (3), which is a public institution. Forty-nine are or were CEOs, eight are or were CFOs; six had prior experience at Morgan Stanley, six at Goldman Sachs, four at Lehman Brothers, four at Swiss Re, seven at Barclays, four at Salomon Brothers, and four at Merrill Lynch.

People from twenty-two nations make up the central financial core of the TCC. Seventy-three (45 percent) are from the US; twenty-seven (16 percent) Britain; fourteen France; twelve Germany; eleven Switzerland; four Singapore; three each from Austria, Belgium, and India; two each from Australia and South Africa; and one each from Brazil, Vietnam, Hong Kong/China, Qatar, the Netherlands, Zambia, Taiwan, Kuwait, Mexico, and Colombia. They live in or near a number of the world's great cities: New York, Chicago, London, Paris, and Munich.[36]

Members of the financial core take active parts in global policy groups and government. Five of the thirteen corporations have directors as advisors or former employees of the IMF. Six of the thirteen firms have directors who have worked at or served as advisors to the World Bank. Five of the thirteen firms hold corporate membership in the Council on Foreign Relations in the US. Seven of the firms sent nineteen directors to attend the World Economic Forum in February 2013. Seven of the directors have served or currently serve on a Federal Reserve board, both regionally and nationally in the US. Six of the financial core serve on the Business Roundtable in the US. Several directors have had direct experience with the financial ministries of European Union countries, the G8, and the G20. Almost all of the 161 individuals serve in some advisory capacity for various regulatory organizations, finance ministries, universities, and national or international policy-planning bodies.

These 161 directors are part of Rothkopf's superclass. Given their control over $23.91 trillion, Western governments and international policy bodies serve the interests of this financial core of the TCC. Wars are initiated to protect their interests, and to promote the free flow of global capital for investment anywhere that returns are possible. Identifying the people with such power and influence is an important part of any democratic movement seeking to protect our commons so that all humans might share and prosper.[37]

APPENDIX

FINANCIAL CORE OF THE TRANSNATIONAL CAPITALIST CLASS (2013)

BOARD OF DIRECTORS

Barclays PLC (assets $2.4 trillion)

Antony Peter Jenkins, Sir David Alan Walker, Frits van Paasschen, Michael Ashley, Hugh E. "Skip" McGee III JD, Tim Breedon, Fulvio Conti, Ashok Vaswani Brysam, Diane de Saint Victor, Shaygan Kheradpir, David George Booth, Simon John Fraser, Reuben Jeffery III, JD, Dambisa Moyo, Sir Michael Rake, Sir John Sunderland, Maria Ramos

BlackRock Inc. (corp. assets $22.3 billion; assets in management: $3.7 trillion)

Laurence Fink, Robert S. Kapito, James Rohr, Hsueh-Ming Wang, Murry S. Gerber, Thomas H. O'Brien, Jr, Sir Deryck Charles Maughan, David Komansky, James Grosfeld, William S. Demchak, Susan Lynn Wagner, Dennis D. Dammerman, Mathis Cabiallavetta, Abdlatif Al-Hamad, John Silvester Varley, Ivan Seidenberg, Thomas Montag, Marco

Antonio Slim Domit, Fabrizio Freda, Jessica P. Einhorn,

Capital Group Companies Inc. Assets Management: $1.07 Trillion
David Isador Fisher, Martin E. Diaz Plata, Ashley Dunster, Koenraad Foulon, Shaw B. Wagener, Leonard L. Kim, Guilherme Lins, Lam Nguyen-Phuong,

FMR Corporation: Fidelity Worldwide Investment (Family Controlled) Assets Management: $1.7 Trillion
Edward Crosby Johnson III, Abigail Pierrepont Johnson, Ned C. Lautenbach,

AXA (Assets Management: $1.4 Trillion)
Claude Bébéar, Henri de Castries, Norbert Dentressangle, Jean-Pierre Clamadieu, Denis Duverne, Jean-Martin Folz, Anthony Hamilton, Isabelle Kocher, Suet Fern Lee, Stefan Lippe, François Martineau, Deanna Oppenheimer, Ramon de Oliveira, Michel Pébereau, Dominique Reiniche, Marcus Schenck

State Street Corporation (Assets management: $1.9 trillion)
Joseph (Jay) L. Hooley, Kennett F. Burnes, Peter Coym, Patrick de Saint-Aignan, Dame Amelia C. Fawcett, David P. Gruber, Linda A. Hill, Robert S. Kaplan, Richard P. Sergel. Ronald L. Skates, Gregory L. Summe, Robert E. Weissman,

J. P. Morgan Chase & Co. (Assets management: $1.34 Trillion)
James A. Bell, Crandall C. Bowles, Stephen B. Burke, David M. Cote, James S. Crown, James Dimon, Timothy P. Flynn, Ellen V. Futter, Laban P. Jackson, Jr., Lee R. Raymond William C. Weldon,

Legal & General Group PLC (LGIMA) (Assets management: $598 Billion)
John Morrison Stewart, Nigel Wilson, Mark Zinkula, Mark Gregory, John Pollock, Henry Staunton, Mike Fairey, Rudy Markham, Stuart Popham, Nick Prettejohn, Julia S. Wilson, Lindsay Tomlinson

Vanguard Group Inc. (Assets management: $2.1 Trillion)
F. William McNabb III, Emerson U. Fullwood, Rajiv L. Gupta, Amy Gutmann, JoAnn Heffernan-Heisen, F. Joseph Loughrey, Mark Loughridge, Scott C. Malpass, André F. Perold, Alfred M. Rankin, Jr., Peter F. Volanakis,

UBS AG (Assets management: $2.3 Trillion)
Axel A. Weber, Michel Demaré, David Sidwell, Rainer-Marc Frey, Ann F. Godbehere, Axel P. Lehmann, Wolfgang Mayrhuber, Helmut, William G. Parrett, Isabelle Romy Beatrice Weder de Mauro, Joseph Yam Chi-kwong, Luzius Cameron, Sergio P. Ermotti,

Bank of America/Merrill Lynch (Assets management: $2.3 trillion)
Charles O. Holliday, Jr., Susan S. Bies, Frank P. Bramble, Sr, Arnold W. Donald, Charles K. Gifford, Monica C. Lozano, Thomas J. May, Brian T. Moynihan, Lionel L. Nowell, Sharon Allen, Jack Bovender, Linda Parker Hudson, David Yost,

Credit Suisse Group AG (Assets management: $1.8 Trillion)
Urs Rohner, Peter Brabeck-Letmathe, Jassim Bin Hamad, J.J. Al Thani, Iris Bohnet, Noreen Doyle, Jean-Daniel Gerber, Walter B. Kielholz, Andreas N. Koopmann, Jean Lanier,

Kai S. Nargolwala, Anton van Rossum, Richard E. Thornburgh, John Tiner,

**Allianz SE (Owners of PIMCO) (Assets Management; $ 2.3 Trillion) and
PIMCO-Pacific Investment Management Co. (Assets Management; $1.8 Trillion)**
Michael Diekmann, Oliver Bäte, Manuel Bauer, Gary C. Bhojwani, Clement B. Booth, Dr. Helga Jung, Christof Mascher, Jay Ralph, Dieter Wemmer, Werner Zedelius, Maximilian Zimmerer

---

PETER PHILLIPS is professor of sociology at Sonoma State University and president of Media Freedom Foundation/Project Censored.

BRADY OSBORNE is a senior level research associate at Sonoma State University.

Sonoma State University's KIMBERLY SOEIRO, KATELYN CLATTY, and GARRETT LYONS provided research assistance with this study. Portions of the literature review in this chapter were previously published in earlier Censored yearbooks.

Notes

1. See G. William Domhoff, *Who Rules America?*, 5th ed. (New York: McGraw Hill, 2006), and Peter Phillips, "A Relative Advantage: Sociology of the San Francisco Bohemian Club," 1994, http://library.sonoma.edu/regional/faculty/phillips/bohemianindex.php.
2. Early studies by Charles Beard, published as *An Economic Interpretation of the Constitution of the United States* (1913), established that economic elites formulated the US Constitution to serve their own special interests. Henry Klein, in a 1921 book entitled *Dynastic America and Those Who Own It*, argued that wealth in America had power never before known in the world and was centered in the top 2 percent of the population, which owned some 60 percent of the country. In 1937, Ferdinand Lundberg published *America's Sixty Families*, which documented intermarrying, self-perpetuating families, for whom wealth was the "indispensable handmaiden of government." In 1945, C. Wright Mills determined that nine out of ten business elites from 1750 to 1879 came from well-to-do families ("American Business Elites," *Journal of Economic History*, December 1945).
3. See Robert A. Brady, *Business as a System of Power* (New York: Columbia University Press, 1943); and Val Burris, "Elite Policy Planning Networks in the United States," *Research in Politics and Society*, 4th ed. Gwen Moore and J. Allen Whitt (Greenwich, Connecticut: JAI Press, 1992), 111–134, http://pages.uoregon.edu/vburris/policy.pdf.
4. C. Wright Mills, *The Power Elite* (New York: Oxford University Press, 1956).
5. See Michael Soref, "Social Class and Division of Labor within the Corporate Elite," *Sociological Quarterly* 17 (1976); and two works by Michael Useem: "The Social Organization of the American Business Elite and Participation of Corporation Directors in the Governance of American Institutions," *American Sociological Review* 44 (1979), and *The Inner Circle* (New York: Oxford University Press, 1984).
6. Thomas Koenig and Robert Gogel, "Interlocking Corporate Directorships as a Social Network," *American Journal of Economics and Sociology* 40, no. 1 (1981); and Peter Phillips, "The 1934–35 Red Threat and the Passage of the National Labor Relations Act," *Critical Sociology* 20, no. 2 (1994).

7. For a discussion of principals inside the HCPE who pursue US military domination of the world as their key agenda, see Peter Phillips, Bridget Thornton, and Celeste Vogler, "The Global Dominance Group: 9/11 Pre-Warnings & Election Irregularities in Context," http://www.projectcensored.org/top-stories/articles/the-global-dominance-group.

8. Leslie Sklair, *The Transnational Capitalist Class* (Oxford, UK: Blackwell, 2001).

9. Leslie Sklair, "The Transnational Capitalist Class and the Discourse of Globalization," *Cambridge Review of International Affairs* 14, no. 1, (2000), 67–85, http://www.lse.ac.uk/collections/globalDimensions/globalisation/theTransnationalCapitalistClassAndTheDiscourseOfGlobalization.

10. William I. Robinson, *A Theory of Global Capitalism: Production, Class, and State in a Transnational World* (Baltimore: John Hopkins University Press, 2004).

11. Ibid., 155–156.

12. David Rothkopf, *SuperClass: The Global Power Elite and the World They are Making* (New York: Farrar, Straus, and Giroux, 2008).

13. Peter Dale Scott, *American War Machine, Deep Politics, the CIA Global Drug Connection, and the Road to Afghanistan* (Lanham, MD: Rowman & Littlefield Publishers, 2010). See also *Censored* story #22, "Wachovia Bank Laundered Money for Latin American Drug Cartels," *Censored 2013: Dispatches from the Media Revolution*, Mickey Huff and Andy Lee Roth with Project Censored (New York: Seven Stories Press, 2012), 66–68.

14. David Rothkopf, Superclass, Public Address: *Carnegie Endowment for International Peace*, April 9, 2008.

15. "Defense Against Terrorism Programme of Work (DATPOW)," North Atlantic Treaty Organization, September 24, 2012, http://www.nato.int/cps/en/SID-EBFFE857-66071109D/natilive/topics_50313.htm?selectedLocale-en.

16. Nazemroaya, Mahdi Darius, *The Globalization of NATO* (Atlanta: Clarity Press, 2012).

17. William K. Carroll, *The Making of a Transnational Capitalist Class: Corporate Power in the 21st Century* (London and New York: Zed Books, 2010).

18. Stefania Vitali, James B. Glattfelder, and Stefano Battiston, "The Network of Global Corporate Control," *PLoS ONE*, October 26, 2011, http://www.plosone.org/article/info%3Adoi%2F10.11 3711%2Fjournal.phone.0025995. See also *Censored* story #6, "Small Network of Corporations Run the Global Economy," *Censored 2012*, 69–70.

19. More details on this University of Zurich study, and the list of the top twenty-five of the 147 super-connected companies, is printed in full in Mickey Huff and Andy Roth with Project Censored, *Censored 2013*, 247–248.

20. Vitali, et al., "Network of Global Corporate Control."

21. "The Top Asset Management Firms 2012, Banks around the World," June 30, 2012, http://www.relbanks.com/rankings/largest-asset-managers.

22. "Barclays Total Assets: 2.426T for Dec. 31, 2012," http://ycharts.com/companies/BCS/assets.

23. See the Censored News Cluster, "Iceland, the Power of Peaceful Revolution, and the Commons," in this volume, for coverage of Iceland as a notable exception to the international trend of banks not being held accountable for systemic misconduct.

24. Dylan Murphy, "Money Laundering and The Drug Trade: The Role of the Banks," Global Research, May 7, 2013, http://www.globalresearch.ca/money-laundering-and-the-drug-trade-the-role-of-the-banks/5334205. See also Scott, *American War Machine*.

25. Ibid.

26. Kylie MacLellan and Matthew Tostevin, "Factbox: Banks drawn into Libor rate-fixing scandal," Reuters, July 11, 2012, http://www.reuters.com/article/2012/07/111/us-banking-libor-panel-idUSBRE86A0P020120711.

27. "Barclays Fined for Attempts to Manipulate Libor Rates," BBC News, June 27, 2012, http://www.bbc.co.uk/news/buisness-18612779.

28. Matthew Leising, Lindsay Fortado and Jim Brunsden, "Meet ISDAfix, the Libor Scandal's Sequel," April 18, 2013, *Bloomberg Businessweek*, http://businessweek.com/articles/2013-04-118/meet-isdafix-the-libor-scandes-sequel.

29. Dan Margolies and Ross Kerber, "Vanguard Sued again for 'Illegal Gambling' Investments," Reuters, April 8, 2010, http://www.reuters.com/article/2010/04/08/vanguard-lawsuit-idUSN0818833420100048.

30. Matt Taibbi, "Everything is Rigged: The Biggest Price-Fixing Scandal Ever," Rolling Stone, April 25, 2013, http://www.rollingstone.com/politics/news/everything-is-rigged-the-biggest-financial-scandal-yet-20130425.

31. John Rudolf and Chris Kirkham, "Gunmaker Investments Under Review By California Teachers' Fund After Newton Massacre," Huffington Post Business, December 18, 2012, http://huffingtonpost.com/2012/12/118/gunmaker-investments-newton_n_2325323.html.

32. Yasha Levine, "Exposed: The Billionaire-Backed Group Strong-Arming Parents into Destroying Their Kids' Public Schools," AlterNet, April 26, 2013, http://www.alternet.org/education/exposed-billionare-backed-group-strong-arming-parents-destorying-their-kids-public. On efforts to privative public education, see also, Adam Bessie, "GERM Warfare: How to Reclaim the Education Debate from Corporate Occupation," Censored 2013, 271–296.

33. Tyler Durgen, "A Detailed Look at Global Wealth Distribution," Zero Hedge, October 11, 2010, http://www.zerohedge.com/article/detailed-look-global-wealth-distribution.

34. "World Bank Sees Progress Against Extreme Poverty, but Flags Vulnerabilities," The World Bank, February 29, 2012, http://www.worldbank.org/en/news/press-release/2012/02/29/world-bank-sees-progress-against-extreme-poverty-but-flags-vulnerabilities.

35. Mark Ellis, "The Three Top Sins of the Universe," http://www.starvation.net.

36. Please see http://projectcensored.org/financial-core-of-the-transnational-corporate-class/for a searchable chart of the members of the superclass.

37. On the heritage of the commons, see http://www.fairsharecommonheritage.org.

CHAPTER 10

Apple Exposed
The Untold Story of Globalization

Nicki Lisa Cole and Tara Krishna

Critical readers might have the impression that they are fully informed about labor and environmental abuses within Apple's supply chain in China. In fact, the *New York Times* would have us believe that Apple has made significant progress in addressing issues that have been brought to light over the last year and a half.[1] However, based on a comparative analysis of news coverage in the United States and China, we find that US reporting has been clouded by a Western lens, and that it has overwhelmingly ignored the voices of workers themselves: rural Chinese citizens affected by environmental pollution, and those displaced by ongoing construction of new factories. US coverage has focused nearly entirely on just one supplier, Foxconn, without specifying which factory location, and has disproportionately focused on the brand image of Apple. Our comparison to Chinese coverage of these issues reveals the US coverage to be unbalanced and narrow in focus, and thus it has missed the bigger picture of the systemic and extensive labor and environmental abuses coursing throughout Apple's Chinese supply chain.

Drawing on Chinese news media reports, a series of reports on Apple and its suppliers from a coalition of Chinese nongovernmental organizations (NGOs), and scholarly research from Chinese sociologists who study labor conditions and resistance, including numerous accounts of Chinese citizens, we offer a more robust and chilling account of the untold story of globalization in China. In this essay, we present worker perspectives on the rash of suicides at Foxconn factories, to counter the corporate media account of Chinese workers as grateful and passive, and to reposition them as people who regularly resist, protest, and fight tirelessly for their rights. We highlight Chinese and English language news stories on the coerced enslavement of college students as "interns" at Foxconn factories, the forced relocation and reconfiguration of rural Chinese communities, and the destruction of agriculture as land is razed for ongoing factory construction. And we reveal that most Chinese factory workers are young migrants from rural peasant communities who face long-term and psychologically damaging isolation from their families and friends when they enter factory jobs. This trend not only affects the workers themselves, but also has negative consequences for Chinese elders who are left without a younger generation to assist in their care, and for "left-behind children" who grow up in rural communities without their parents. The combined pull of young adults into urban factories and the displacement of rural communities is resulting in a major geo-spatial and social reorganization of Chinese society, the implications of which have not been addressed at all in US news coverage.

And, while some recent coverage, including that by Project Censored authors, has pointed to the environmental problems that stem from technological production in China,[2] we draw on a series of Chinese NGO reports to reveal the long-term, systemic nature of this problem, and identify Apple as the most offensive and least-responsive tech contractor operating in the region. We illuminate the vast and intensely dangerous problem of air, water, and soil pollution that has ravaged mainland China and the health of its residents over the last decade. While the *New York Times* offered praise for minor changes in labor policy at one Foxconn factory, and while Chinese NGOs report that Apple has overseen some targeted and limited—though successful—environmental corrections at a couple of suppliers, we hesitate to applaud these moves because of the vast and mostly unaddressed scope of the implications of China's role as the world's factory.

MIKE DAISEY: THE SPARK THAT IGNITED A FIRESTORM OF COVERAGE

As readers of last year's *Censored 2013* are aware, on January 6, 2012, the popular public radio program *This American Life* aired an adapted version of performer Mike Daisey's monologue, *The Agony and the Ec-*

stasy of Steve Jobs.[3] In the radio episode, Daisey explained that he became curious about the manufacturing process behind Apple products after an iPhone customer found photos of Chinese workers on his device. The customer shared these photos with the Cult of Mac website frequented by Apple devotees, which is how Daisey came upon them.

Inspired by these photos, Daisey took a trip to Shenzhen, China, to visit one of several Foxconn factories in the region where Apple's mobile devices—iPods, iPhones, and iPads—are assembled. After meeting with workers and visiting their dormitories, he was saddened to learn of the dangerous, sickening, and oppressive work conditions that young Chinese laborers endure in the factories. Consumer outcry and criticism of Apple followed these revelations.[4]

On March 16, 2012, *This American Life* host Ira Glass retracted the story and characterized Daisey's claims as lies.[5] While many were dismayed that Daisey had not witnessed firsthand all that he described in his monologue, he nonetheless deserved credit for sparking interest in Apple's highly secretive supply chain.

Since January 2012, corporate media have paid significant attention to Apple and to Foxconn, the Taiwanese company incorporated as Hon Hai that holds contracts for assembly of Apple products.[6] Building on Daisey's monologue, Western media outlets relayed reports of suicides at Foxconn factories, provided details about the health risks that assembly workers face because of long, break-free hours and chemical exposure, and described the crowded dorm rooms where workers live.[7] News sources, most notably the *New York Times* in its "iEconomy" series, prominently feature testimonies from Apple executives who explain the slow management of these problems by citing complex corporate procedures, and insist that Apple is doing its best to address the plight of workers. The series in the *Times* has been widely read, and was awarded a Pulitzer Prize for "Explanatory Reporting" on April 15, 2013.

THE US MEDIA INVESTIGATES FOXCONN: UNDERLINES APPLE, ECLIPSES WORKERS

After reviewing print media coverage of labor issues in Apple's supply chain, from sources including the *New York Times*, the *Atlantic*, *PC Mag*, the *San Francisco Chronicle*, Mashable.com, *International Business Times*, the *Los Angeles Times*, Yahoo!, and the Cult of Mac, among others, we find significant disparity in Chinese versus US coverage. US corporate media coverage has been overly focused on one of many suppliers, Foxconn, and on the brand image of Apple, while Chinese coverage includes the voices of workers and speaks to issues throughout the entire Chinese supplier base. This narrow focus of corporate media coverage in the US does a disservice to Chinese workers and citizens, as it suggests that Apple's image is more important than their suffering. We recognize that significant decreases in funding for investigative reporting, even among major print news outlets like the *New York Times*, contributes to this problem, and that journalists themselves are not to blame.[8] Nonetheless, it is important that we recognize the full scope of the problem, and come to understand what has limited our ability to see the full scope.

Troublingly, US coverage of locations of labor abuses is uniformly vague. Although Foxconn, a Taiwanese-owned company that contracts production and assembly for Apple, has been the focus of reports on labor abuses, specific factory sites go unmentioned. This gives us pause, as we have found that Foxconn has over twenty different production facilities throughout China, and five alone in Shenzhen.[9] We also note that this focus is curious, as there are dozens of other suppliers operating on Apple's behalf in China, and of those, only Wintek, where the workers have been subject to poisoning with n-hexane gas, has been included in US coverage.[10]

We are more disturbed by the finding that across the coverage, with the exception of a couple of articles from the *New York Times*' "iEconomy" series, writers consistently contribute to the dehumanization of Foxconn's already-exploited factory workers by not including firsthand accounts of the conditions from workers themselves, and typically, do not even name those whose workplace suicides are reported. Instead, coverage of labor abuses tends to focus on the brand and reputation of Apple, Inc., and on the Western activist group SumOfUs.

To this end, coverage of the SumOfUs "Ethical iPhone" campaign eclipses all the efforts that workers themselves have expended to fight for their rights, which we will elaborate later. Workers have been fighting labor battles at Apple suppliers in China for years, but it was only when SumOfUs refocused attention on consumer rights that corporate media picked up the story.[11] While it is the workers' voices that should matter most here, theirs are missing from US corporate media coverage.

Finally, the *New York Times* seems to have closed the door on conversation about these issues with its final installment in the iEconomy series published on December 26, 2012. Reporters Charles Duhigg and Keith Bradsher reviewed some changes at one Foxconn location in Shenzhen, which have happened since scrutiny has focused on the supplier. The piece champions Apple for joining the Fair Labor Association, and lauds minor changes to workplace safety and comfort made at Foxconn under the leadership of embarrassed founder and CEO Terry Gou.[12] The article seems to suggest that the media attention has done its job, yet Apple, Foxconn, and many other Apple suppliers have affected the lives of workers in more intimate and extensive ways than audits can uncover, in addition to wreaking environmental devastation and health and safety issues throughout Chinese communities on a mass scale.

WORKERS TELL A DIFFERENT STORY

Factory workers' accounts complicate the reports provided by Western media sources. Research completed by Hong Kong Polytechnic University Associate Professor of Applied Social Sciences Pun Ngai and her colleagues at production sites throughout China reveals that workers experience many more problems than US corporate media accounts suggest.[13] Foxconn's leaders and factory supervisors demand that the workers execute their tasks efficiently and mechanistically, and workers recognize the company's "human subordination," putting into more serious terms the problems glossed over by US corporate media sources. In Pun's report, one male worker offered an explanation for the widespread suicides by attributing worker deaths to the fear caused by assembly line superiors and the immense amount of scrutiny faced by any frontline worker who has made a mistake—a perspective lacking, for example, in the *Los Angeles Times* coverage from June 2012.[14] Another worker, Tian Yu, survived her jump from the fourth floor of the Shenzhen Longhua dormitory but continued to feel the exhaustion of long work hours and the loneliness that had prompted her suicide attempt. Numerous reports, spanning several years' time, from Fiona Tam, reporter for the *South China Morning Post*, offer additional evidence of the poor working conditions and psychological distress that factory workers suffer.[15] Contributing to the oppression and stress of workers is that most are not given legally required employment contracts, and consequently lack job stability, rights, and resources.[16]

A January 2011 report from a group of Chinese NGOs including Friends of Nature, the Institute of Public and Environmental Affairs, and Green Beagle, titled *The Other Side of Apple*—which has been referenced in previous Project Censored coverage—offered further documentation of this problem.[17] The report stated that an examination by Xinhua News Agency of a worker paycheck found that 60 percent of the workers' monthly income was based on overtime.[18] One worker logged over 136 hours of overtime—100 hours more than what is legal in China. The report further stated that a random check by the Shenzhen Human Resources and Social Security Bureau found that nearly three-quarters of all workers had significantly exceeded the overtime limit.

Workers do, nevertheless, find ways to mitigate these stressors and put pressure on managers, factory owners, and the Chinese government to obey labor laws and improve working conditions. Pun and her research team found that some combat feelings of powerlessness by "[making] fun of their line leaders in their daily life."[19] Others participate in more revolutionary behavior. Fieldwork completed from 2003 to 2007 at a Taiwanese-owned factory in Shenzhen details the worker networks created in their dormitories. The small amount of space available to workers in these dormitories facilitates kinship and encourages collective action.

Pun's report explained that workers organized a strike in 2004 without much help from trade unions or labor organizations.[20] The 2011 NGO report also documented an April 2009 strike of 7,000 workers at Dongguan Wanshida in protest over high-volume production demands and thirteen-hour workdays. Interviews with and studies focused on the factory workers thus elucidate their frustration and strategic rebellion, whereas in US corporate media accounts, workers are portrayed either as victims or happy to have a job, if they are touched upon at all. Further, the absence of coverage of the work of Chinese labor groups, unions, and NGOs, in addition to the workers themselves, contributes to the erroneous Western perspective that China is a lawless land of capitalism run amok.

US corporate media coverage also suggests that the Chinese themselves are to blame for the labor and environmental abuses, rather than the American corporations, like Apple, that create these conditions by allotting suppliers the slimmest possible profit margin, which encourages suppliers to sidestep regulations and labor laws in the economic interest of their companies.[21]

The NGO report also provides evidence of worker mistreatment and unsafe workplace conditions as far back as 2007, when Apple launched the iPhone to consumers. The report reveals through interviews of workers at Apple touchscreen supplier Lian Jian Technology, a Taiwanese-owned facility located in the Suzhou Industrial Park, that workers had been poisoned and left with long-term illnesses. They were sickened while cleaning touchscreen glass for the iPhone after n-hexane was substituted for an alcohol-based cleaner, and the report notes that exposure to this poison "leads to peripheral neuropathy, numbness of the limbs, and impedes movement and sense of touch."[22] Workers reported losing strength in their bodies, fainting and collapsing at work, and doctors found nerve damage to be a result of the poisoning. Of the forty-nine young workers that were admitted to hospital for treatment, many are now classified with an occupational disability, and were given only a modest stipend by the company, which will not cover their lifelong medical bills. Workers reported that Apple representatives had visited the facility before workers became ill, and that Apple never communicated with any of the sickened workers.

At Yun Heng Hardware and Electrical, a factory of about thirty employees, poisoning of workers was also a problem. In 2010, five workers were still in hospital after being poisoned by n-hexane. Workers stated that they were never informed of the hazards, and reported the same ailments as those at Lian Jian. At the Yun Heng factory, Yuhan Photoelectric Technology (Suzhou) Co., Ltd., contracted workers to clean Apple logos and affix them to film. Workers reported the poisonings to the Wujiang Health Bureau in January 2010, and the Worker Safety Bureau subsequently found that the toxic work was done between April 2009 and January 2010. The investigation revealed that workers had labored in unventilated spaces without safety equipment, which led to eight cases of n-hexane poisoning. For some, the cost of treatment decimated family funds, which caused them to stop medical treatment before they were well. The report indicated that workers were also sickened in 2009 at Dongguan Wanshida, a sister company of Lian Jian. The Dongguan Health Bureau found that 234 workers had a history of exposure to occupational hazards, and that some had suffered hearing loss and anemia.

In *The Other Side of Apple II*, the second report of the three-part series, published in August 2011, the coalition of NGOs pointed out that despite Apple's claims that it rigorously audits its supply chain, the Foxconn Chengdu facility, which was contracted by Apple to manufacture the iPad2, was the site of an explosion that resulted in the death of three workers and the injury of fifteen others.[23] The production facility was constructed in just seventy-six days, and through a media investigation it was found that workers had only been trained for a maximum of three days before entering the production line.[24]

The report noted that the granting of this contract to Foxconn raises serious questions about Apple's auditing process.

In addition to serious health and safety hazards, the first report recounted that workers suffered humiliation at the hands of management. At Dafu Scientific Building Material Co., Ltd., in Changsu, the *Southern Daily* news outlet found and published in December 2009 that women workers were forced to remove belts and submit to a body inspection when leaving the workplace. An anonymous worker posted on a website about this and stated that she left her job because of it. The worker recounted, "Watching a younger girl stand on the inspection platform with her pants suddenly falling down and run away as everyone laughed at her, my eyes filled with tears and I did not laugh. That day, I don't know how I ended up leaving. To this day I still do not dare recall those humiliating memories."[25]

This first report noted that Apple speaks broadly about how it manages its supply chain and never mentions specific sites in the supplier responsibility reports it publishes on its website, which prevents external monitoring of its claims of compliance with its supplier code. The report also spotlights Apple's pattern of nonresponse, denial, and stated nondisclosure when complaints are registered from Chinese NGOs or state and regional Chinese authorities. Apple denied using Lian Jian Technology as a supplier of touchscreens, despite worker-provided evidence of Apple-related production. More damning, the report stated that poisoned workers from this site wrote a letter to Steve Jobs in 2011, but they never received a response from Apple.

COMMUNITY IMPACTS OBSCURED BY CORPORATE MEDIA ACCOUNTS

US corporate media reports additionally contribute to the simplification of the factory workers' situation by ignoring their backgrounds and their motivations to work for Apple suppliers. Chinese news stories note that many Foxconn workers are student interns who do not fall under the protections provided by labor laws.[26] The US news outlets do not explain, however, as Pun and Chan found in their research, that students in vocational schools report that pro-growth priorities in China encourage the government officers in charge of their schools to connect students to Foxconn internships.[27] A Chinese story written by Xiaotian Ma, titled "Interns Behind the iPhone 5" and published online for *Nanfang People Weekly* on September 21, 2012, explained that school officials who arrange "involuntary internships" threaten to withhold degrees from college students who leave their Foxconn jobs and ask the interns to sign forms that suggested that they willingly took part in the internships.[28] Records of these interns' workdays fail to capture the overtime hours assembly line leaders demanded from them. Western media sources leave out the emotional consequences of the interns' forced labor, especially the reactions from the parents of the interns who feel that the school fees they pay are going toward the exploitation of their own children.[29]

Additionally, the US corporate media ignores the fact that most workers are migrants who have left their homes in rural areas for stable jobs in cities. A Chinese article published in Henan Social Sciences in 2011 by scholar Fang Qixiong sheds light on this issue.[30] Qixiong analyzed thirty-nine reports from the *Nanfang Weekend* on the topic of China's migrant workers and found that, for rural Chinese, Foxconn has provided a source of consistent, if not significant, income. A letter from Shenzhen migrant worker Feng Ji to Steve Jobs, written in September 2011, highlighted the difference between the state of the Chinese factory worker and the American Apple executive, illustrating the way Apple's leaders—and Americans in general—can distance themselves from the feelings of assembly line workers. Feng Ji reminded Steve Jobs that his employees in Cupertino return to their homes at the end of a workday and spend time with their spouses and children. Migrant workers, on the other hand, are physically separated from their own families for months or even years at a time.

The distance between the migrant workers and their families, in combination with the stress of factory work, makes the workers especially prone to psychological distress and is damaging to familial relationships. As Qixiong details, *Nanfang Weekend* reports that migrant workers who wish to see their families during major holidays like the Chinese New Year are thwarted by limited numbers of train tickets.

Many workers remain stranded in the city, the site of their difficult work lives, during periods of national celebration. Workers face disappointment and helplessness in this unfamiliar city and are cut off from the kind of intimate emotional care they would receive at home. In fact, many—10 percent, according to Fiona Tam in 2008—Shenzhen-based migrant workers who are able to return to their rural-area homes for the Lunar New Year resolve to stay there.[31] They may forgo the stable factory wages for farming work that will resume only in the spring, but they restore the healing familial bonds the factory environment fails to offer.[32]

Additionally, Tam reported in 2008 that relocated migrant workers are not granted residency in their place of work and thus do not have voting rights in their districts.[33] In June 2010, this policy was changed, though workers felt the change was mostly symbolic because most of them do not meet the educational and community activities requirements for residency.[34] This means that in addition to suffering the stress of being separated from their families, being regularly overworked, and sometimes injured on the job, they are politically disenfranchised too.

The children of workers, their parents, and extended families also suffer the burden of the flight of young Chinese from rural areas to factory jobs. A July 2010 Chinese report published in *China Business News* details the phenomenon of "left-behind kids" who remain in rural villages with grandparents or other kin when one or both parents leave to work in a factory for an extended period of time. In a very sad case, four "left-behind" children about thirteen years of age attempted suicide together by consuming an agricultural chemical mixed with beer.[35] Fortunately all of the children survived, but their suicide attempt is indicative of the struggles children face when growing up without their parents, which is a widespread problem for Chinese families.

China's role as the world's factory not only sucks its young adults out of their communities, but sometimes factories encroach upon and displace rural communities too. A December 2010 report in *Nanfang Weekend* exposed the social effects of village displacement with the story of a ten-year-old child who is now the only pupil in her school because all other residents accepted the terms of forced relocation offered by Foxconn while her parents have not.[36] The story showcases a sad, lonely child who bursts into tears at a school staffed by a few dedicated teachers who insist on providing her education.

All but one of the school's 161 pupils left within a month of relocation notice, signaling the scattering of rural families and the disruption of community and social networks.

In fact, fourteen villages across fifteen square kilometers were displaced by Foxconn's building plans in Deyuan Town to clear the way for factory dormitories.[37] *South China Morning Post* reporter Fiona Tam emphasized in 2009 that rural citizens have been most affected by the mainland's shift to a manufacturing economy, as they have had to send their resources, including people, into the city for production.[38] Reports like these illustrate that Apple's presence in China has changed the geographic location, migratory patterns, familial structures, and even democratic participation of Chinese citizens in significant and harmful ways. These facts have been completely and irresponsibly ignored by both corporate and independent US media outlets.

AN ENVIRONMENT DESTROYED

Although corporate media have recently reported on air quality in China, and some independent media have covered China's "cancer villages," US establishment media have ignored the pollution of China's rivers, lakes, reservoirs, and ground water as a result of wastewater disposal at tech production facilities. This is particularly egregious in the case of Apple and its suppliers; a study of twenty-nine information technology (IT) brands operating in China found that most had similar problems in their supply chains, however Apple was hands down the most evasive and resistant to hearing complaints and taking appropriate action in response to them.[39]

As of the August 2011 publication of the NGO report *The Other Side of Apple II*, Apple had continued to fail to act on the complaints detailed in the first report,[40] though other brands had publicly responded and taken responsibility. Some of the chronic and systemic problems that have been documented at Apple suppliers in China include hazardous and excessive wastewater runoff and toxic airborne emissions. The NGO report found that more than twenty-seven suspected Apple suppliers had significant environmental problems, and noted that Apple had not reported any of them in its *2011 Supplier*

Responsibility Report.[41] Because Apple has only recently begun to respond, the company was ranked last of all twenty-nine IT brands in terms of environmental responsibility.

Meiko Electronics, a Japanese company, is one of Apple's admitted suppliers of printed circuit boards (PCBs) for the iPad 2. The report states that the Guangzho site is a known serious polluter in the region. The state has regularly monitored the site since 2009, and it has been found in breach of state standards for wastewater and gas emissions and listed as one of seven violators in need of enforcement. One resident of Nansha District reported a noxious smell that irritates the throat—evidence that points to the serious health implications of these emissions. Investigation by the Nansha District Environmental Supervision Unit found that the site was discharging gases from three outlets without use of required carbon scrubbers, and the facility was fined at the time for emitting exhaust from a generator that violated standards. Investigations also found that the company routinely attempted to conceal its violations.

The NGO report also cited another Meiko site in the Wuhan Economic and Technological Development Zone, located in Hubei province, also in violation of Chinese environmental laws.

Research found that residents have long been concerned about the growth of the production facility, as its wastewater discharge contains the heavy metals nickel and copper. Local investigation of the wastewater discharge found contamination in both a channel that leads to Nantaizi Lake and in the lake itself. A sample of the water tested by the Hongshan district's Wuhan Environmental Protection Bureau monitoring station was found to contain copper and nickel, and that the concentration of nickel was 11.15 times over the legal standard for water destined for human consumption. The report describes the lake as "an ash grey color with white bubbles accompanying groups of black floating objects." The report notes that the contamination in the lake has spread to the Yangtze River, where the copper level is 56 to 193 times the normal amount. The amount of copper found indicates that the likelihood of harmful toxicity is very high.

Another known Apple supplier, Kaedar Electronics located in Kunshan, Jiangsu province, holds the 2006 pollution record in the organization's Pollution Map Database for its excessive levels of untreated wastewater discharge.[42] Another facility in the region, Unimicron Electronics, owned by the Taiwanese Unimicron Group, is a suspected PCB supplier to Apple, and also holds a pollution record for 2005. Kaedar is noted to produce exteriors and interiors of notebook computers, which result in emissions from sprays used in the production process, while Unimicron emits acid gas and dust.

An audit found that, given the proximity to residential areas, even if Kaedar abided by official standards, their operations would still be disruptive to residents.[43] Some residents reported that they have been living in fear of poisonous gases for six years. They do not open their windows because of this, and if they leave them open while sleeping, "they will wake in the middle of the night choking." The report noted that Tong Haiyi, a student at a kindergarten that abuts the factory, said to his mother, "Sometimes when I come back home and I'm studying, I have chest pains, and when you come to fetch me, I feel really dizzy. Sometimes there is a really strange smell at school." The mother noted that the child suffers from regular headaches, dizziness, and nose bleeds.

The report also noted that residents of nearby Tongxin Village explained that, prior to Kaedar Electronics coming to their area, their village was thriving. However, the facility consumed much of the arable land and blackened their previously clean stream. Residents noted a sharp increase in cancer rates since the facility was established, and said that when the state inspects the factory, the smell disappears—but it always returns. One villager, Zhu Guifen, had to have her stomach removed due to gastric cancer. The researchers reported that she and others fell to their knees and begged for help during the conversation. Following up on the cancer reports, the researchers found that more than nine people in a village of just sixty had contracted or died from cancer in recent years, while in the 1970s only one person from the village died of cancer. Some residents have sent their children to live in other locations over fears for their health.

BEWARE OF CORPORATE WASHING

In early 2013, the coalition of Chinese NGOs released its third report, titled *Apple Opens Up: IT Industry Supply Chain Investigative Re-*

port.[44] In it, they stated that in response to the pressure brought by the previous two reports, Apple has begun working with them and with third-party auditors to remedy some environmental problems in its Chinese supplier base. In a few cases, suppliers have made significant and satisfactory improvements, while in others more still needs to be done. The report noted that significant improvements to the wastewater management system were made at the Meiko Electronics facility described previously after the company agreed to an audit in April 2012. Action was also taken at Tripod (Wuxi) Electronic Co., Ltd., which had been identified in the previous report as a generator of massive amounts of hazardous waste, and a water-recycling program was instituted at Ibiden Electronics (Beijing) Co., Ltd., to significantly reduce water consumption at the PCB production plant. We emphasize, however, as does the report, that much of the supply chain remains unexamined.

On the labor side, the final installment of the *New York Times'* iEconomy series reported that targeted improvements in labor conditions had been made at one Foxconn site in Shenzhen.[45] Yet, critics have pointed out that Apple's partnership with the Fair Labor Association (FLA) to provide auditing of labor conditions at Chinese suppliers raises serious questions, as the FLA was founded in part by leading corporations in the global garment industry to monitor themselves.[46] Apple was also applauded by Gene Sperling, director of the US president's National Economic Council, when it announced in late 2012 that it would make some Macbooks here in the US in a move to bring production back home.[47]

While we praise Apple and these few suppliers for taking action in these cases, we point out that this level of response leaves much to be desired given the systemic nature of the problems in the supply chain. Given the scope of the issue, these moves strike us as a mostly symbolic response designed to protect Apple's brand, rather than a commitment to the well-being of Chinese citizens. For instance, although it is nice that Apple will create some US jobs for Macbook production, when over 70 percent of company revenue comes from iPods, iPads, and iPhones made in China, it is clear that this is not a substantive change in their production model.[48] Further, while the "amenities" available to Foxconn workers have been touted in both corporate and independent media, in 2010 workers reported such long hours that they are not able to swim in the Olympic-sized swimming pool onsite at one of the Shenzhen factories, and that they spend their lunch break in a crowd of over 400,000 trying to access the provided meals.[49]

Until Apple makes systemic changes in its economic and managerial relations with its suppliers, these targeted efforts will be nothing more than symbolic management of the company's public relations problem. The third NGO report stated that it would like Apple to do systemic and in-depth environmental audits throughout its supply chain, not just at the sites identified in the previous reports.[50] They also call for Apple to take responsibility for checking China's Pollution Map Database for its suppliers who are in violation, to urge suppliers to publish discharge data regularly, and manage materials suppliers. In other words, they want Apple to be proactive instead of reactive in managing its supply chain. We add to this a call for systemic audits of labor conditions and Chinese labor law violations, and register our dismay that changes in this regard seem to have only been made at one Foxconn site, while abuses have been reported throughout the Chinese supply base. We applaud Apple for taking some baby steps in the last year to improve its deeply problematic supply chain, but we urge the company to give these long-term and systemic problems the committed and critical attention they deserve, and to recognize the company's role as the *driver* of these problems.

CONCLUSIONS

Through a comparison of US corporate media coverage and Chinese news, scholarly research, and NGO reporting, we found that the story of labor and environmental abuses happening at Apple suppliers in China has not been fully or truly told. The Western-centric and narrow focus of US coverage has done a disservice to Chinese workers and citizens, and to American consumers who still do not know the extent of the problems generated by our demand for Apple products. The collective sweeping-under-the-rug by corporate media of Mike Daisey's account, and the *New York Times'* celebration of recent changes at one Foxconn site suggest that Apple consumers have nothing to be concerned about. Ira Glass even went so far as to suggest in the *This American Life* retraction that difficult labor conditions are to be expected in "industrializing" economies, and that ultimately all of this is benefitting the Chinese.[51] However, when the Chinese perspective is considered, it is clear that the benefits, if any at all, are few—and when the profits from iPhones and iPads are examined, we see that only the slimmest margin of economic benefit goes to the Chinese.[52]

Labor abuses in Apple's supply chain, and the social and psychological distress that follow, are not isolated to just one Foxconn facility, but are systemic, significant, and ongoing, and include enslavement of Chinese college students. China's migrant workers and their families are far from content with this situation, in which there is sometimes not even enough work to go around for all those who flock to the factory zones.[53] They regularly express their dismay through resistance in the workplace, strikes, and broad-based labor rights campaigns, and in some cases, even express their dissent through suicide.[54] And beyond the impacts on workers themselves, Chinese accounts illuminate the community-wide social impacts of the forced relocation of villages, the economic impacts of the razing of agricultural land, and the widespread and systematic destruction of the environment, which produce serious health problems and compromise the well-being of many.

As sociologists, we recognize that these problems in Apple's supply chain are typical of globalized production, and so too are Apple's targeted and mostly symbolic responses to critics.[55] Symbolic response has historically proven to be a successful tactic when those in power seek to retain their power. For this reason, we urge readers to sustain the criticism of Apple and its suppliers, and to continue to press the company to make meaningful change in its supply chain. The fight for rights cannot be left to workers, because as has proven to be true in the garment industry,[56] among others, Chinese workers can only push so hard for their rights in a globalized system in which factories can leave their country for cheaper labor pools elsewhere.[57]

In addition to the focused effects of Apple's globalized production system in China, we encourage readers to consider the chasm of global wealth inequality that these relations of production and trade yield. As we write this conclusion, news of Apple's massive tax avoidance scheme has just come to light.[58] Not only does Apple vastly undervalue the labor of those who make its products, thus ripping off the Chinese, the company also rips off American citizens to the tune of *$74 billion dollars* in avoided tax liability between 2009 and 2012.[59] Most recently, as Isaiah J. Poole wrote for *Truthout*, Apple's cleverly financed $55 billion payout to shareholders was executed in order to avoid paying $9.2 billion in taxes for this year. Poole noted that had Apple paid that bill, all of the recent cuts to the federal budget known as "the sequester" would have been unnecessary.[60] The way Apple does business is not just bad for the Chinese, it is bad for us and our nation.

We encourage readers who wish to stay up to date on these issues to follow the work of Fiona Tam at the *South China Morning Post*, who offers consistent, critical, English-language coverage based on firsthand accounts of workers and citizens.

NICKI LISA COLE, PHD, is a visiting assistant professor of sociology at Pomona College in Claremont, California. She earned a PhD in sociology at the University of California–Santa Barbara in 2011, and since then has been committed to the practice of a critical, public sociology. With a general focus on consumer culture and global production and trade, she is currently researching the brand power, supply chain, and financial structure of Apple, Inc. She is the founder and head writer of the blog *21 Century Nomad*, where she has written extensively on fair trade and ethical consumption.

TARA KRISHNA is currently completing her final year at Pomona College, where she is studying sociology and public policy analysis with a focus on biology. Tara is interested in the impact of globalization on environmental justice, collective action, media responsibility, and public health.

The authors wish to acknowledge Li Zhao for providing invaluable Chinese news media research and translation services, as well as localized insights into Foxconn's presence in China. Ms. Zhao is a native of Shenzhen and a student at Pomona College. We also thank Yi Luo and Dingyun Zhang for providing insider perspectives on Apple's presence in Shenzhen, Richard P. Appelbaum for tipping us off to Fiona Tam's excellent coverage in the *South China Morning Post*, and Christine Shearer for editorial assistance on an earlier version of this essay. Finally, we thank Andy Lee Roth for dedicated guidance, support, and editorial expertise throughout the writing process.

Notes

1. Keith Bradsher and Charles Duhigg, "Signs of Changes Taking Hold in Electronics Factories in China," *New York Times*, December 26, 2012, http://nytimes.com/2012/12/27/buisness/signs-of-changes-taking-hold-in-electronics-in-electronics-factories-in-china.html.

2. See *Censored* story #16,"Sweatshops in China Are Making Your iPods While Workers Suffer," *Censored 2012: Sourcebook for the Media Revolution*, Mickey Huff and Project Censored (New York: Seven Stories Press, 2011), 91–93; and follow-up coverage in *Censored 2013: Dispatches from the Media Revolution*, Mickey Huff and Andy Lee Roth with Project Censored (New York: Seven Stories Press, 2012), 145–147 and 168–169.

3. Project Censored's previous coverage, ibid., mistakenly identified *This American Life* as a National Public Radio program. Chicago Public Radio produces the program and Chicago Public Radio distributes it. Some NPR-affiliated stations broadcast it.

4. For coverage of consumer protests at Apple stores following Daisey's appearance on *This American Life*, see Amy Goodman, "Apple Accustomed to Profits and Praise, Faces Outcry for Labor Practices at Chinese Factories," *Democracy Now!*, February 10, 2012, http://democracynow.org/2012/10/apple_accustomed_to_profits_and_praise.

5. For more on this episode and what it entailed, see Ira Glass, "Retraction," *This American Life*, Chicago Public Radio, March 16, 2012, http://podcast.thisamericanlife.org/special/TAL_460_Retraction_Transcript.pdf; and also "Who's the Rotten Apple? *This American Life* Goes Daisey Crazy," *Censored 2013*, 168–169.

6. "Group Profile," Foxconn Electronics Inc., accessed May 23, 2013, http://www.foxconn.com/GroupProfile_En/GroupProfile.html.

7. For one such example, see David Sarno, "Worker from Foxconn, Apple's Chinese Factory, Jumps to Death," *Los Angeles Times*, June 14, 2012, http://articles.latimes.com/2012/jun/14/business/la-fi-tn-foxconn-worker-20120614.

8. See, for example, Mary Walton, "Investigative Shortfall," *American Journalism Review* (September 2010), http://www.ajr.org/Article.asp?id=4904; and James T. Hamilton, "Subsidizing the Watchdog: What Would It Cost to Support Investigative Journalism at a Large Metropolitan Daily Newspaper?," Duke Conference on Nonprofit Media, May 4–5, 2009, http://sanford.duke.edu//nonprofitmedia/documents/dwchamiltonfinal.pdf.

9. "Supplier List 2013," Apple, Inc., http://images.apple.com/supplierresponsibility/pdf/Apple_Supplier_List_2013.pdf.

10. For example, see David Barboza, "Workers Poisoned by Chemical at Apple Supplier in China," *New York Times*, February 22, 2011, http://www.nytimes.com/2011/02/23/technology/23apple.html?pagewanted=all&_r=0.

11. See, for example, Chenda Ngak, "SumOfUs Launches Apple, Foxconn Watchdog Site," *CBS News*, May 21, 2012, http://www.cbsnews.com/8301-501465_162-57438213-501465/sumofus-launches-apple-foxconn-watchdog-site.

12. Bradsher and Duhigg, "Signs of Changes."

13. Pun Ngai and Jenny Chan, "Global Capital, the State, and Chinese Workers: The Foxconn Experience," *Modern China* 38 (2012): 383–410.

14. Ibid., 397. On *Los Angeles Times* coverage, see Sarno, "Worker from Foxconn, Apple's Chinese Factory, Jumps to Death," cited in note 7, above.

15. See, for example, Fiona Tam and Danny Mok, "New Foxconn Suicide after Boss Visits Shenzhen Plant," *South China Morning Post*, May 27, 2010, http://www.scmp.com/print/article/715408/new-foxconn-suicide-after-boss-visits-shenzhen-plant; and Fiona Tam, "Foxconn Rallies Urge 800,000 to 'Treasure Life,'" *South China Morning Post*, August 18, 2010, http://www.scmp.com/print/article/722411/foxconn-rallies-urge-800000-treasure-life.

16. Tam, "Only a Third of Migrant Workers Given Contracts," *South China Morning Post*, January 22, 2010, http://www.scmp.com/print/article/704346/only-third-migrant-workers-given-contracts.

17. Mike Kolbe, "Sweatshops in China Are Making Your iPods While Workers Suffer," *Censored 2013*, 145–147.
18. Friends of Nature, IPE, Green Beagle, *The Other Side of Apple*, January 20, 2011, http://www.business-humanrights.org/media/documents/it_report_phase_iv-the_other_side_of_apple-final.pdf.
19. Pun and Chan, "Global Capital, the State, and Chinese Workers," 397.
20. Chris King-Chi Chan and Pun Ngai, "The Making of a New Working Class? A Study of Collective Actions of Migrant Workers in South China," *China Quarterly* 198 (2009): 287–303.
21. For a detailed breakdown of how profits from iPhones and iPads are distributed primarily to Apple and not to its suppliers, see Kenneth L. Kraemer, Greg Linden, and Jason Dedrick, "Capturing Value in Global Networks: Apple's iPad and iPhone," paper, Personal Computing Industry Center, July 2011, http://pcic.merage.uci.edu/papers/2011/Value_iPad_iPhone.pdf.
22. *The Other Side of Apple.*
23. Friends of Nature, IPE, Green Beagle, Envirofriends, Green Stone Environmental Action Network, *The Other Side of Apple II: Pollution Spreads Through Apple's Supply Chain*, August 31, 2011, http://www.greenbiz.com/sites/default/files/63637255-Apple-II-Final-20-14.pdf
24. Ibid., 4.
25. *The Other Side of Apple*, 17.
26. Xiaotian Ma, "'Interns' Behind the iPhone 5," *Nanfang People Weekly*, September 21, 2012, http://www.nfpeople.com/News-detail-item-3661.html.
27. Pun and Chan, "Global Capital, the State, and Chinese Workers," 393.
28. Xiaotian, "'Interns' Behind the iPhone 5."
29. Ibid.
30. Fang Qixiong, "Traits of Nanfang Weekend's Coverage on the Topic of Migrant Workers," *Henan Social Sciences*, no. 4 (2011) (Huazhong University of Science and Technology, School of News and Communications).
31. Fiona Tam, "Delta Short of Workers Even as Migrants Return," *South China Morning Post*, February 23, 2008, http://www.scmp.com/print/article/627273/delta-short-workers-even-in-migrants-return.
32. Fiona Tam, "Migrants Left No Choice after Falling Victim to the Global Economic Downturn," *South China Morning Post*, January 5, 2009, http://www.scmp.com/article/665862/migrants-left-no-choice-after-falling-victim-global-economic-downturn.
33. Fiona Tam, "Moves to Help Migrants Fail to Convince Critics," *South China Morning Post*, April 8, 2008, http://www.scmp.com/print/article/632918/moves-help-migrants-fail-convince-critics.
34. Fiona Tam, "Migrant Workers Get Chance for Urban Residency," *South China Morning Post*, June 9, 2010, http://www.scmp.com/print/article/716615/migrant-workers-get-chance-urban-residency.
35. "Five Primary School Students Made Pact to Suicide by Drinking Agricultural Chemical; Most Left-Behind Kids," *China Business News*, July 5, 2010.
36. Jin Ran, "Foxconn and the Ten-Year-Old 'Nail,'" *Nanfang Weekend*, December 13, 2010, http://www.infzm.com/content/53351.
37. Ibid.
38. Fiona Tam, "Chongqing to Raise Migrant, Rural Incomes," *South China Morning Post*, January 3, 2009, http://www.scmp.com/print/article/665654/chongqing-raise-migrant-rural-incomes.
39. *The Other Side of Apple*, 25.
40. *The Other Side of Apple II.*
41. "Apple Supplier Responsibility 2011 Progress Report," Apple Inc., http://images.apple.com/supplierresponsiblity/pdf/Apple SR 20111 Progress Report.pdf.
42. Ibid.
43. *The Other Side of Apple II.*
44. Friends of Nature, The Institute of Public & Environmental Affairs, Envirofriends, Nature University, Nanjing Greenstone, *Apple Opens Up: IT Industry Supply Chain Investigative Re-*

port—*Phase VI*, January 29, 2013, http://switchboard.nrdc.org/blogs/lgreer/Report-IT-Phase-VI-Draft-EN.pdf.

45. Bradsher and Duhigg, "Signs of Changes."

46. Steven Greenhouse, "Critics Question Record of Fair Labor Association, Apple's Monitor," *New York Times*, February 13, 2012, http://www.nytimes.com/2012/02/114/technology/ critics-question-record-of-fair-labor-association-apples-monitor.html.

47. Catherine Rampell and Nick Wingfield, "In Shift of Jobs, Apple Will Make Some Macs in U.S.," *New York Times*, December 6, 2012, http://www.nytimes.com/2012/12/07/technology/apple-to-resume-us-manufacturing.html?pagewanted=all&_r=0.

48. For Apple revenue breakdown, see "Revenue by Product (as Percentage of Revenues)," Bare Figures, http://barefigur.es.

49. Fiona Tam, "All Work and No Play Makes It a Dull Plant," *South China Morning Post*, May 27, 2010, www.scmp.com/print/article/715430/all-work-and-no-play-makes-it-dull-plant.

50. *Apple Opens Up: IT Industry Supply Chain Investigative Report—Phase VI*, 33.

51. Ira Glass, "Retraction."

52. Kraemer et al., "Capturing Value in Global Networks: Apple's iPad and iPhone."

53. Fiona Tam, "Number of Migrant Workers in Delta Outstrips Job Vacancies," *South China Morning Post*, March 4, 2009, http://www.scmp.com/print/article/671980/number-migrant-workers-delta-outstrips-job-vacancies.

54. Pun and Chan, "Global Capital, the State, and Chinese Workers: The Foxconn Experience."

55. See, for example, William I. Robinson, *Latin America and Global Capitalism: A Critical Perspective* (Baltimore: John Hopkins University Press, 2008); Mike Davis, *Planet of Slums* (London: Versa, 2007); and Pun Ngai, *Made in China: Women Factory Workers in a Global Workplace* (North Carolina: Duke University Press, 2005).

56. Edna Bonacich and Richard P. Appelbaum, *Behind the Label: Inequality in the Los Angeles Apparel Industry* (Berkeley: University of California Press, 2000).

57. Fiona Tam, "Million to Be Trained to Fight Labour Shortage," *South China Morning Post*, February 26, 2008, http://www.scmp.com/print/article/627636/million-be-trained-fight-labour-shortage; and Fiona Tam, "300,000 Foxconn Staff in Move to Henan," *South China Morning Post*, June 30, 2010, http://www.scmp.com/print/article/718493/300000-foxconn-staff-move-henan.

58. Nelson D. Schwartz and Charles Duhigg, "Apple's Web of Tax Shelters Saved It Billions, Panel Finds," *New York Times*, May 20, 2013, http://www.nytimes.com/2013/05/21/business/apple-avoided-billions-in-taxes-congressional-panel-says.html?hp&_r=1&.

59. Ibid.

60. Isaiah J. Poole, "Apple Dodges Enough Taxes to Cover Much of the Sequester," *Truthout*, May 5, 2013, http://truth-out.org/opinion/item/116177-apple-dodges-enough-taxtes-to-cover-much-of-the-sequester.

CHAPTER 11

The "New" American Imperialism in Africa
Secret Sahara Wars and AFRICOM

Brian Martin Murphy

In January 2013, a new African conflict burst into world headlines. The French Air Force and Army invaded the Saharan nation of Mali, launching attacks on an advancing force of rebels who had occupied the north of the country and imposed Islamic sharia law.

The official story, circulating in most international media, was that a network of jihadists had emerged from the wilds of the Sahara to sow radical Islam, led by the self-declared "Al-Qaeda in the Islamic Maghreb." French troops, supported by soldiers from the nations of West Africa grouped under the flag of the Economic Community of West African States (ECOWAS), pushed north, and the rebels slowly dispersed back into the desert, to the joy of the occupied Malians.

In reality, what the world witnessed was a tragic new chapter in a conspiracy to create a terrorist threat in the Sahara. The main player has been Algeria, with the involvement of various arms of the United States government. Dating back to the months after the attacks on September 11, 2001, the program started as part of the US global war on terror and has since run parallel with the creation of the US military's Africa Command (AFRICOM), in 2007–2008.[1] Together they signal a "new" American imperialism in Africa,[2] with the primary aim of securing access to oil for US corporations.[3]

Aside from Antarctica, the Sahara is the largest desert mass in the world. It covers over 3.5 million square miles, or roughly 10 percent, of the continent. Parts of several African nations occupy the space, including Algeria, Chad, Egypt, Libya, Mali, Mauritania, Morocco, Niger, Sudan, and Tunisia. Famous for its large sand dunes, most of the terrain in fact features rough, rocky, windswept plains dotted by low mountains of up to 2000 feet. Although the population is estimated at twelve million, most live in towns and villages around the desert's edges. In southern Algeria, northern Mali, northern Niger, and northern Chad—where corporate media have largely ignored a decade of war—the primarily pastoralist population does not number more than five million.

The roots of the secret wars trace back to the 1990s, a period of bloody civil strife in Algeria that pitted Islamist rebels against a de facto military government. The decade featured mass imprisonments, massacres and counter-massacres, and free-floating networks and affiliations among various opposition Islamist guerrilla armies. There were continuous allegations that the Algerian military's secret intelligence service, the *Département du Renseignement et de la Sécurité* (DRS), had infiltrated many of the rebel groups. The numbers of the dead and the injured have never been officially counted, but estimates run beyond 100,000.[4]

By 1999–2000, the war had wound down as amnesties were offered, an army-backed president was elected, and most of the Islamist groups were disbanded. One group vowed to fight on: Salafist Group for Preaching and Combat (GSPC). A leading figure was a shadowy Algerian DRS operative with a string of aliases and the nickname "El Para." In the mid-1990s, he had trained with the Green Berets (US Army Special Forces) at Fort Bragg.[5]

At war's end, the Algerian government sought to modernize and rearm. In early 2001, Algeria's newly elected president Abdelaziz Bouteflika met with President George W. Bush in Washington DC. He requested military assistance to counter "terrorism." There was no interest. After September 11, 2001, all this changed, when the US formulated the global war on terror.

One US focus was on the "arc of unstable Muslim countries" from Afghanistan through the Middle East to North Africa. The Pentagon believed it could work with two nations in North Africa: Morocco and Algeria. Military assistance flowed to them right away.[6] A year later, in 2002, a Congressional Research Service report on potential transnational terrorism on the continent did not mention the Sahara or even GSPC as a threat.[7] But by then both Algeria and the US needed the world to see that roving international terrorists populated the Sahara. In February 2003, the GSPC, led by El Para, abducted thirty-two Europeans touring the southern Sahara in Algeria. European media reported the story every day. For a month, the GSPC kidnappers and their captives moved in convoy through southern Algeria en route to northern Mali. They were apparently undetected, despite combined US/Algerian electronic monitoring capabilities. For example, some hostages said later that, from time to time, they saw US Air Force Boeing E-3 Sentry planes, carrying the distinctive Airborne Warning and Control System (AWAC) dishes, flying low over the convoy.[8]

Later, troops from Chad and Niger, backed by US Special Forces, tracked down and cornered El Para. But instead of capturing the GSPC leader, they mysteriously left him to fall into the hands of yet another rebel group, the Movement for Democracy and Justice (MDJT), which sought liberation of Chad. The MDJT handed El Para over to the Algerians and he was sent north to the capital city, Algiers, for trial. A few months later, Algeria quietly released him. One Algerian official said he was no longer needed.[9]

The US propaganda machine went into action, kicked off by an article in *Air Force Magazine* describing the Sahara as "a swamp of terror," and ripe for military action.[10] By 2013, documentation of these endless activities could handily make the case for Congress that the rise of a network of jihadists was responsible for every protest and bombing across North and West Africa.[11]

The abductions dovetailed with the first official US military pushes into the region. In late 2002, the State Department had launched the Pan Sahel Initiative. US Special Forces deployed to Chad, Mali, Mauritania, and Niger to train and support border patrolling. Then in July 2003, Algeria, Chad, Niger, and Nigeria signed a counterterrorism cooperation agreement with the US, which promised them increasing levels of military training and assistance. By 2005 the programs had been folded into a broader Trans-Sahara Counter-Terrorism Partnership (TSCTP) with Morocco, Senegal, and Tunisia added to the mix. Management was moved from the State Department to the Department of Defense, who would coordinate small projects launched

by the State Department, the Agency for International Development (USAID), and the Department of the Treasury. In effect, four years before the official formation of AFRICOM, US program profiles in Africa—and, specifically, in the Sahara—had been reorganized within a military framework. Funding increased steadily, from an initial sixteen million to thirty million dollars in 2006, the year AFRICOM was announced, to an estimated hundred million dollars in 2011.[12] The first "official" arrival of US "boots on the ground" was 500 troops to Mauritania in 2004. A steady increase of US military trainers, Special Forces, and a new and regular program of US naval maneuvers up and down the African west coast followed.

TUAREG, PEOPLE OF THE DESERT: FROM RESISTANCE SOCIETY TO "TERRORISTS"

Of course, the southern Sahara is not "empty." Approximately 2.5 million indigenous Tuareg inhabit much of the central Sahara and southern Sahara. Their largest number, estimated at 800,000, live in

Mali, followed by Niger, with smaller populations in Algeria, Burkina Faso, and Libya. This nomadic people, most of who live by herding goats and camels, controlled trans-Sahara trade routes for almost a thousand years, with the peak in the sixteenth century. In more modern times they have developed cultures of rebellion and resistance as wave after wave of outsiders have sought to take their territory, disrupt their traditional social structure, and end their pastoralism.

Tuareg resisted French invasion in the late nineteenth century. After that, there were rebellions in one part or another of Tuareg territory about every fifteen years, leading up to the withdrawal of the French in the 1960s. Boundaries of new nations were drawn without Tuareg consultation; instead, the new governments continued attempts to crush their pastoral culture.[13]

Rebellion continued. In Mali, a simmering conflict with the state marked the 1960s. Then there was relative peace for about twenty-five years, but by 1990, more widespread revolt rocked northern Niger and Mali. The Tuareg occupied most of northern Mali and declared an independent state, Azawad. Thousands were killed on all sides. France and Algeria brokered a brooding peace in Niger (1992) and in Mali (1995). Both agreements called for decentralization of national power and guaranteed integration of Tuareg resistance fighters into the countries' respective national armies.

By most accounts, the agreements' promises were only marginally implemented or ignored altogether, leaving the Tuareg as ethnic outsiders. Sporadic fighting continued with spikes in 2004 and 2007 in Niger, and 2006 in Mali. Meanwhile, many Tuareg men were attracted to serve and train in Colonel Muammar Gaddafi's Libyan armies, where they were not only welcomed but also benefited from a period of relatively steady income. Gaddafi made well-publicized speeches encouraging the formation of a Tuareg state.

Arguably, the rolling Tuareg rebellions after 2004 were responsive to new offensives against them. Newly armed and trained by US Special Forces, the governments of Chad, Mali, and Niger launched sustained attacks in Tuareg communities, killing civilians as well as militants. In 2005, a mob said to be of Tuareg origin attacked and burned the center of the southern Algerian city of Tamanrasset. Subsequent legal proceedings revealed that Algerian security police acting as *agents provocateurs* had led the riot. Similarly, the 2006 rebellion in Mali was found to have been orchestrated by Algerian intelligence operatives assisted by US Special Forces. Someone was trying to frame the rebellious Tuareg as Saharan terrorists.[14]

A "NEW" AMERICAN EMPIRE IN AFRICA?

Empire-making is a two-way street. A dominant power needs a threat to justify its action: "We can thus recognize the initial and implicit source of imperial right in terms of police action and the capacity of the police to create and maintain order."[15]

Before 9/11, the last time the US had had an official military presence in Africa was 1941–1943, during the Allies' North Africa campaign in the Second World War. Although there had been sporadic intelligence operations, quiet material and logistical support for proxies, as well as the singular disaster in Somalia in the early 1990s, since World War II, the US had expressed no strategic interest in the continent, much less the intent to establish a permanent military presence there. As recently as the 2000 presidential campaign, George Bush had referred to Africa as a continent "of little strategic interest to the US."[16]

Africa may not have been on Bush's (public) agenda during his 2000 presidential campaign, but it was on the Pentagon's new map by 1995. And yet the policy forces that would identify Africa—and specifically the Sahara—as targets for military expansion, culminating in AFRICOM, trace back to early 1991. Rudderless in the wake of Soviet demise, the Pentagon initiated its global search for continued strategic relevance. By the mid-1990s, military academics provided the Pentagon with a new map of the world, detailing how to perceive strategic allies and threats.[17]

The simplistic map was based on how well nations were integrated into the "global capitalist system." The first, "core" states, were closely aligned with the US, primarily through the Organisation for Economic Co-Operation and Development (OECD). Second were "seam states," partially integrated nations that might be occasional strategic allies. Third were "gap states": disorganized, failed, unintegrated, and clear threats to current and future core states' interests. In this view,

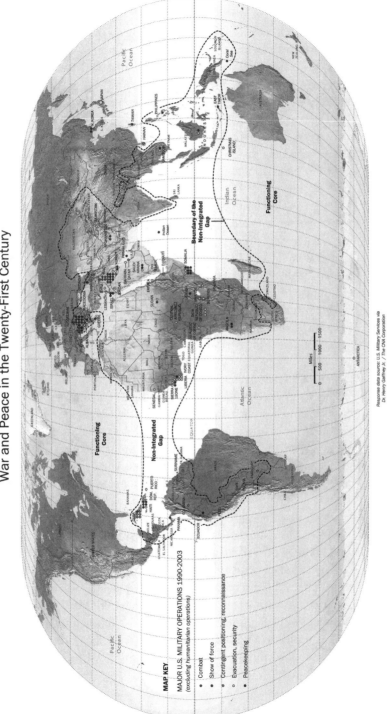

The Pentagon's New Map:
War and Peace in the Twenty-First Century

MAP KEY

MAJOR U.S. MILITARY OPERATIONS 1990–2003
(excluding humanitarian operations)

- Combat
- Show of force
- Contingent positioning, reconnaissance
- Evacuation, security
- Peacekeeping

Boundary of the Non-Integrated Gap

Functioning Core

Non-Integrated Gap

Response data source: U.S. Military Services via
Dr. Henry Gaffney Jr. / The CNA Corporation

© 2003 by William McNulty.
Reprinted by permission of G.P. Putnam's Sons and Thomas P.M. Barnett.

more than half of the world's gap states were African. South Africa was deemed a core state. But two African nations—Morocco and Algeria—were deemed "seam states" with which the US might work for strategic management of surrounding "gap states."

There was no major US corporate presence in Africa after World War II, although there was a heavy focus on resource extraction. Yet, year after year, economic data showed that, despite extreme levels of poverty across the continent, some of the highest profit margins gained by international corporations came from African investments. In 1992, 180 major US corporations formed the Corporate Council on Africa (CCA) to lobby the US government to facilitate more access to African markets.[18] One major strand in their discussions with government departments was the need for more security in potential markets—to declare West Africa (and its oil) of US strategic interest and to establish a military presence in the region, if necessary.[19] CCA was joined in this effort by the Washington-based Institute for Advanced Strategic and Political Studies (IASPS), an Israeli lobby group linked to the Likud party. The IASPS wanted creation of a US military "sub-command" for African oil states, in hopes that increased security would reduce the US's need for oil from Middle Eastern states, particularly Saudi Arabia.[20]

The policy mechanisms for the creation of a continent-wide, military-led imperial initiative were in place by the late 1990s. When a new focus on Africa was integrated into the global war on terror in 2002, plans had already been made and military treaties had already been signed with a range of African states. The Pentagon designated three theaters: West Africa, particularly oil-producing countries; the Sahara, as a major world "gap" zone; and the Horn of Africa (northeast Africa bordering the Red Sea), as an enduring command center (based in the nation of Djibouti) for surveillance and intervention throughout the Persian Gulf region, North Africa, and Somalia.[21]

When the Pentagon and President Bush announced AFRICOM in 2006–2007, the discourse of official statements focused on its humanitarian–security–development mandate. But the data show that, in the period leading up to 2008, the US administration shifted its African profile to a military focus.

Despite the outflow of military aid, AFRICOM has not been well received. Every African government except Liberia's has refused to host the military command, and the Pentagon decided, in 2011, to have its infrastructure remain with the US European Command in Germany. In addition, the US government has refused to align and share the resources of AFRICOM with the emerging regional military and peacekeeping units of the African Union, causing diplomatic rifts.[22]

Finally, every known instance of AFRICOM material assistance has proved disastrous, further corrupting already shady governments, destabilizing and increasing local rivalries, and causing many civilians deaths:

> ▸ Somalia, 2006: AFRICOM Special Forces murdered thousands of civilians fleeing the civil war.[23]
> ▸ Niger, 2008: Government troops armed and supported by AFRICOM attacked Tuareg nomadic camps, which were also bombed by light planes. Termed an "ethnocide," it has been reported by the United Nations High Commissioner for Refugees and denounced as genocide by Amnesty International and Human Rights Watch.[24]
> ▸ Uganda/Congo, 2011: a Ugandan army/US Special Forces attack on the camp of the well-known Lord's Resistance Army fails, and the guerrillas flee, leaving a path of thousands of civilians dead in the Congo.[25]

In context, then, the events of 2012–2013 in northern Mali are best understood as the latest in a growing list of tragic destabilizations intended to provide excuses for a US imperial initiative on the continent. After El Para's departure, the hapless GSPC fell to bickering and slowly disintegrated. In 2006, a rump of the group renamed itself, "Al-Qaeda in the Islamic Maghreb" (AQIM).[26] The GSPC breakup spawned a cluster of new jihadist groups. Rumors persisted that at least AQIM was firmly under the control of the Algerian DRS, which aimed to use it to destabilize northern Mali.[27]

By 2011, the Tuareg had been drawn into this conspiracy. In 2012, angry Tuareg soldiers, fleeing developments in Libya, initiated another in the 200-year history of rebellions for self-determination.

They organized under the name *Mouvement National de Libération de l'Azawad* (MNLA). They were immediately countered by AQIM and two new "jihadist" groups—led by local Tuareg leaders—*Ansar al-Din* and *Jamat Tawhid wal Jihad fi Garbi Afriqqiya* (Movement for Oneness and Jihad in West Africa, or MOJWA). The four groups formed a loose alliance and occupied the three northern provinces of Mali, once again declaring it the independent state of Azawad.[28]

But it was soon clear that the three Islamic groups were determined to impose strict sharia laws. MNLA broke from the coalition. Fighting broke out. The three Islamist groups, heavily armed and provisioned by the Algerian DRS, won the day, moving on from that victory to march south. That is what alerted Western corporations and ultimately led to the French invasion. More than 100,000 people were made refugees. Thousands were killed.

Corporate media have portrayed events in Mali, and the factions involved, as irrational, but as informed insiders and independent journalists have reported, six basic facts are clear:

1. When the US administration and the Pentagon declared the Sahara a dangerous "empty zone" populated by international terrorists, the situation did not exist.

2. Agents of the Algerian military intelligence service (DRS) co-opted a hapless local jihadist group, GSPC, to execute acts that gave US and international media an opportunity for speculation that the Sahara based "international terrorists."

3. This fabrication gave the US government and Pentagon the cover and excuse to initiate military programs (many in planning since the mid-1990s) signaling the start of a "new" American imperialism on the continent.

4. Algerian security agents and intelligence operatives highjacked the indigenous Saharan Tuaregs' 200-year struggle for self-determination, further destroying Tuareg social structure and reframing their society as a force in international terrorism.

5. Algeria, one of only two "seam states" on the Pentagon's new map, has used the global war on terror and AFRICOM destabilization to establish itself as the dominant regional-imperial political economy in North Africa and the Sahara.

6. AFRICOM, sold as a humanitarian/development initiative, is at

the front edge of a new military-based American imperialist project in Africa.[29]

The ongoing crisis in Mali may lead to that nation's permanent destabilization, resulting in the kind of "failed state" that the US needs to enforce its "new" imperialism in Africa.

BRIAN MARTIN MURPHY, PHD, passed away on June 14, 2013. He was an African affairs analyst and associate professor of communication studies at Niagara University. His reportage appeared in publications like *New African* and *African Business*. For six years he was editor in chief of the Inter Press Service's African bureau, Africa Information Afrique. He continued to serve as editorial advisor and contributor with the New York–based globalinfo.org, which distributes weekly African news reports to US subscribers. He was chair and associate professor of communication studies at Niagara University, where he taught investigative reporting, media history and theory, and international communication. In March 2012, the *Niagara Index* recognized him as one of the university's twenty "most intriguing professors," identified by students in response to a campus survey asking which professors had the "greatest impact" on their lives.

Notes

1. For Project Censored's previous coverage of AFRICOM, see, for example, *Censored* story #3, "AFRICOM: US Military Control of Africa's Resources," *Censored 2008: The Top 25 Censored Stories of 2006–2007*, Peter Phillips and Andrew Roth with Project Censored (New York: Seven Stories Press, 2007), 44–48.

2. Abayomi Azikiwe, "US Imperialism in Africa: From Cairo to Cape Town the African Masses Struggle for Justice and Self-Determination," Global Research, December 29, 2012, http://www.globalresearch.ca/us-imperialism-in-africa/5317219.

3. Mike Crawley, "With Mideast Uncertainty, the US Turns to Africa for Oil," *Christian Science Monitor*, May 23, 2002; Jean-Christophe Servant, "The New Gulf Oil States," *Le Monde Diplomatique*, January 2003; Daniel Volman, "The Bush Administration and African Oil: The Security Implications of US Energy Politics," *Review of African Political Economy* 30 (December 2003), 573–584; Brian Martin Murphy, "Africa: Communication Intelligence and 'Clientelism,'" in *Enduring Freedom or Enduring War?: Prospects and Costs of the New American 21st Century*, ed. Carl Mirra (Washington DC: Maisonneuve Press, 2005), 117–118; and Jeremy Keenan, *The Dark Sahara: America's War on Terror in Africa* (London: Pluto Press, 2009), ch. 7.

4. Luis Martinez, *The Algerian Civil War 1990–1998* (New York: Columbia University Press, 2000); and Hugh Roberts, ed., *The Battlefield Algeria: Studies in a Broken Polity* (London: Verso, 2003).

5. Keenan, *Dark Sahara*, 101.

6. Thomas P. M. Barnett, *The Pentagon's New Map: War and Peace in the Twenty-First Century* (New York: Penguin, 2004), 182–188.

7. Ted Dagne, "Africa and the War on Terrorism," Congressional Research Service (CRS), Report for Congress, January 17, 2002, http://fpc.state.gov/documents/organization/7959.pdf.

8. Keenan, *Dark Sahara*, 107.

9. Robert G. Berschinski, "AFRICOM's Dilemma: The 'Global War on Terrorism,' 'Capacity Building,' Humanitarianism, and the Future of U.S. Security Policy in Africa," Strategic Studies Institute, US Army War College (November 2007), 24–25.

10. Stewart M. Powell, "Swamp of Terror in the Sahara," *Air Force Magazine*, November 2004, http://www.airforcemag.com/MagazineArchive/Pages/2004/November 2004/1104sahara.aspx.

11. Rudolph Atallah, "Conflict and Instability in the Sahara and Sahel: Local Dilemas, Global Implications," prepared statement before United States House of Representatives, Committee on Foreign Affairs, Sub-committee on Africa, Global Health, Global Human Rights, and International Organizations; Sub-committee on the Middle East and North Africa; Sub-committee Terrorism, Non-proliferation and Trade, Tuesday, May 21, 2013, http://docs.house.gov/meetings/FA/FA16/20130521/100886/HHRG-113-FA16-Wstate-AtallahR-20130521.pdf.

12. J. Peter Pham, "AFRICOM: Terrorism and Security Challenges in Africa," in *US Strategy in Africa: AFRICOM, Terrorism and Security Challenges*, ed. David J. Francis (Oxford: Routledge, 2010), 64–77.

13. Jeremy Keenan, *The Tuareg: People of Ahaggar* (London: Allen Lane, 1977; reprinted London: Sickle Moon Books, 2002).

14. Jeremy Keenan, "AFRICOM: Its Reality, Rhetoric and Future," in *US Strategy in Africa*, 125.

15. Michael Hardt and Antonio Negri, *Empire*, (Cambridge: Harvard University Press, 2001), 17.

16. Salih Booker, "Africa off the Agenda?," *Foreign Policy in Focus* (Institute for Policy Studies), January 25, 2001, http://www.fpif.org/commentary/2001/0101africa.html.

17. Barnett, *The Pentagon's New Map*.

18. Murphy, "Africa: Communication Intelligence and 'Clientelism,'" 117.

19. Ibid., 119.

20. Ibid., 121.

21. Jeremy Keenan, "AFRICOM: Its Reality, Rhetoric and Future," 125.

22. Ibid.

23. Ibid., 124.

24. Ibid., 125.

25. Ibid., 122.

26. Ibid., 123.

27. Jeremy Keenan, "How Washington Helped Foster the Islamic Uprising in Mali," Global Research, February 2, 2013, http://www.globalresearch.ca/how-washington-helped-foster-the-islamist-uprising-in-mali/5321468.

28. Ibid.

29. Jeremy Keenan, *The Dying Sahara: US Imperialism and Terror in Africa* (London: Pluto Press, 2013).

CHAPTER 12

The Sixth Mass Extinction

Julie Andrzejewski and John C. Alessio

Quietly, globally, billions of bees are dying.

—Avaaz, 2013[1]

Biodiversity has declined globally by around 30 percent between 1970 and 2008; by 60 percent in the tropics.

—*Living Planet Report* 2012[2]

Although individual news items about particular endangered species or a general mention of extinction may find their way into the US corporate media here and there, a comprehensive picture of the sixth mass extinction of species is fragmented, denied, trivialized, distanced, "resolved," or missing altogether. As a result, people in the United States are either completely unaware that such a crisis exists, or are lulled into thinking the problem is not that bad, faraway in time or space, or that science will solve it. In a word, the real extinction story has been *censored* so that the industries profiting from the drivers of extinction can continue to extract the Earth's resources while decimating other forms of life and/or their means of survival.

This brief overview presents key aspects of the sixth mass extinction, the confluence of harms leading to this extreme event, the current state of environmental and species censorship, the obstacles to accessing and taking the information seriously, and key organizations—including some independent news outlets—providing leadership for actions.

THE MASS EXTINCTION CRISIS

Scientists estimate that approximately 99 percent of all species that have ever lived on Earth have become extinct, most of them during five previous mass extinctions on Earth. Since the 1970s, scientists have documented a contemporary massive decline in species. Evidence clearly indicates that with ever increasing technological sophistication, human activities are causing what is now known as the sixth mass extinction of life on Earth. These extinctions are happening so rapidly that they are disrupting the intricate web of life whereby species rely upon each other in complex ways. As explained by the Center for Biological Diversity:

> Although extinction is a natural phenomenon, it occurs at a natural "background" rate of about one to five species per year. Scientists estimate we're now losing species at 1,000 to 10,000 times the background rate, with literally dozens going extinct every day.[3]

Scientists are already reporting that one of the drivers of extinctions, global warming, is causing ecosystems to "cascade and collapse."[4] If this process is not arrested and reversed, even more species will become extinct. Besides the ongoing suffering and deaths endured by animals themselves, such escalating extinctions will cause extreme hardships for human beings, threatening the survival of our own species. Clearly, the extent and import of the scientific research, conclusions, and predictions pertaining to the sixth mass extinction have not been communicated to the US public.

In 2002, the world's governments agreed to stop the rate of biodiversity loss by 2010. That goal was not met; the rate of extinctions continues unabated.[5] US corporate media have generally ignored scientific reports released through credible noncorporate sources in attempts to bring public attention to the extinction crisis.[6] A few key nonprofit organizations are leading the challenge to stop species extinctions. One of these, the Species Alliance, summarizes the scientific research as follows.

Today, scientists believe that we are entering the 6th Mass Extinction. But unlike the previous five, this one will not take centuries to unfold—in fact, it will take place in our lifetimes. As scientists begin to realize the severity of the crisis and new worldwide assessments are made, the news is difficult to believe. At least half of all plant and animal species are likely to disappear in the wild within the next 30–40 years, including many of the most familiar and beloved large mammals: elephants, polar bears, chimpanzees, gorillas and all the great apes, all the big cats, and many, many others. Bird species are similarly imperiled, songbird populations have declined by 50% in the last 40 years. One out of every eight species of plant life worldwide and almost one third of the plant species within the United States already face extinction. Populations of large ocean fish have declined by 90% since the 1950s. All around the world, birds, reptiles, mammals, amphibians, fish, and invertebrates, as well as trees, flowering plants, and other flora, are all in steep decline.[7]

Many striking descriptions explaining the magnitude of the problem are available in the United Nations (UN) Global Biodiversity Outlook.[8] If the corporate media were doing their job, it would be clear to all that humans have created an oscillating condition that is spiraling out of control. As Barnosky et al. report, the Earth is rapidly moving into a dramatically different state of existence, from which there may be no return.[9]

This process of oscillation toward a "state shift" is explained by using the concepts of "cascade and collapse," frequently used to describe power grid and computer network collapses. The cascade and collapse concepts are now being applied to biological systems, as demonstrated in the award-winning film, *Call of Life: Facing the Mass Extinction*.[10] While our tendency is to think in linear relations of cause and effect, ecological systems are so complicated and interconnected that the removal of just one critical component within such a system can result in a downward spiral of an entire ecosystem or a significant portion of it. What does the extinction or dramatic reduction of a particular fish species mean to a crab, and what is the significance of the crab to an entire ecosystem? Altieri et al. answer these questions by examining the cascading phenomenon in marsh ecology.[11] Reductions in large fish dramatically increase crab numbers, which in turn dramatically reduce the plant life and, hence, the infrastructure of an entire marsh. Of course, their reported research only captures one small area of one marsh.

The number of these interconnections in a large geographical area representing a complex ecology is so great that, despite what some humans—including many researchers—might think, they are too complicated and vast to "manage." Our only recourse is to protect these species and interconnections by means of minimized disturbance and a healthy surrounding environment. Once a confluence of significant interconnections is violated, a cascade effect is imminent, and collapse will be sudden and permanent. The cascade and collapse concepts inform us that the existence of any one species, regardless of its current state, can be suddenly and irretrievably brought into jeopardy. Ultimately, this includes the human species as well, a species no less a part of the web of life than the other species on Earth.

CORPORATE MEDIA'S CENSORSHIP OF THE SIXTH MASS EXTINCTION

Our ProQuest Newsstand and LexisNexis searches of the terms "sixth mass extinction" or "biodiversity loss" from 2011 through May 2013 yielded relatively few hits for a subject of this import. In the searches we conducted, we received from 32 to 169 results depending on the terms used. About one-quarter of the articles had no relationship at all to the mass extinction of plants and animals, and most of the rest were from foreign publications. Only forty-six articles from the US corporate press mentioned the sixth extinction, and none of these articles provided clear, comprehensive material on the subject. Eighteen of these articles mentioned the sixth mass extinction only as part of a book review, or as a tangential component of another topic, and the remaining articles undermined its significance and urgency in various ways. Only two fairly good, albeit short, articles were located during this time period. One was an *opinion* piece, not a news article, in the *New York Times*.[12] The other was an article on the UN State of the Ocean Report, picked up by a few papers on the East Coast, which identified key causes of the mass extinctions but focused mostly on only one component, oceans.[13] Despite its value, this single, short article cannot be considered adequate coverage.

It is important to describe and characterize some of the types of articles available to the US public in order to get a sense of how the corporate press avoids discussing the true extent and seriousness of the sixth mass extinction. This analysis will also reveal how selectively this topic is packaged for public consumption. Through omissions, manipulations, and diversions, readers are misinformed and placated in ways that constitute censorship of the real causes and consequences of the current mass extinctions.

Denial

In one ProQuest Newsstand search for "biodiversity loss," the first "relevant" US press article (*South Florida Sun*) was titled, "We Need to Manage Climate Change, Not Avert Catastrophe."[14] This article argued that too much money is being spent to prevent climate change and should, instead, be spent on helping people adapt to it now. Further, it claimed that serious environmental damage and animal losses are being caused by . . . environmental projects. This article is not really about biodiversity loss at all; rather, it is a climate change denial article that blames environmental funding and projects for causing harm to the world.

For a different example, the *Miami Herald* published a review of a new book, *Fate of the Species: Why the Human Race May Cause Its Own Extinction and How We Can Stop It*, by Fred Guterl. This review outlined some aspects of the sixth mass extinction but ended with denial by the reviewer: "And while it is easy to see how millions, and even billions, of humans could die as a result of these adventures, it is hard to see how even these prodigious die-offs could cause the human species [to] disappear."[15]

Another form of denial is to focus on one study that challenges the crisis. In this case, the *Los Angeles Times* fostered doubt about extinction predictions in an article titled, "Less Dire View of Extinction: Scientists Using a New Method to Calculate the Rate at Which Species Are Dying Out Say the Crisis Is Bad but Overestimated," suggesting the predictions are exaggerated. And the first sentence undermines the seriousness of the issue further by a snide introduction, "Hit the snooze on the ecological doomsday clock for a minute: The world's species may not be going extinct quite as fast as we thought they were. Scientists may be overestimating the crisis by as much as 160%, according to a new study."[16]

Following this pattern, the *Philadelphia Inquirer* published an article titled, "Mass Extinction: Humans Have Edge." The article is punctuated with trivializing statements like, "Mass extinctions are interesting," and they "periodically reboot the system." The final sentences, however, demonstrate a level of denial of the consequences that is hard to comprehend:

> If it's any reassurance, humans have the profile of survivors. We live in a wide variety of habitats across a huge geographic range. If we're in a self-inflicted mass extinction, we may lose billions of people, but as a species, our odds are good, Jablonski said. "Humans will be the hardest thing to kill off."[17]

Another article in the *Patriot-News* (Harrisburg PA) speculated illogically, "During the current mass extinction, humans will be able to adapt, but our crops and animals might not." In the *Christian Science Monitor* article "Mass Extinction? Man May Still Have Time to Catalog Earth's Species," the human destruction of other species is ignored by focusing on whether there is time left to discover and catalog them.[18] All these forms of denial serve to pacify the public and downplay the reality and gravity of extinctions.

Trivialization and Exploitation

In some articles focused on profiling individuals, or the authors of books, extinction is mentioned only peripherally. In an article about Richard Leakey, for instance, the *New York Times* focused on his adventurous life with one short quote about five mass extinctions and a mention of "the sixth."[19]

Another *New York Times* article, introducing basic information about the *possibility* of a sixth mass extinction, quickly devolved into a debate among scientists about the use of statistical models, the precision of predictions, whether the extinction of a particular species could be linked to climate change, and so on. When this major report predicted a great loss of species, one scientist cautioned, "We don't want to give a false impression of what our confidence is."[20] Instead of reporting on the rapidity and extent of extinctions to create a sense of urgency and concern, the article trivialized the evidence and encouraged readers to doubt it.

In yet a third *New York Times* article, endangered species are actually touted as an enticement for tourism in Cambodia, complete with a list of resorts. "Thanks to this new accessibility, travelers are now discovering the area's awe-inspiring biodiversity, which includes one of Southeast Asia's largest tracts of virgin rain forest; some 60 threatened species, including the endangered Asian elephants, tigers, Siamese crocodiles and pileated gibbons."[21]

Impractical or Imprudent Solutions

Finally, a few articles take the extinction crisis seriously and report some alarming data, but present one type of "solution" or another that may serve to pacify readers or lull us into a false sense that scientists are addressing the problem. None of the solutions proposed addressed the actual drivers (root causes) of extinction as discussed below. For instance, a BBC article reported that conservationists think "we should accept ecosystems that incorporate non-native species, value them and try to conserve them,"[22] rather than more accurately portraying conservationists as preservers of native species. It also referred readers to another article about how science is working on cloning extinct animals.[23] One article addressed the issue of rapid urbanization, a key driver of habitat loss, and recommended creating and maintaining green spaces in urban areas.[24] Activism for more green areas is an urgent cause that can slow down the process of extinction, but actions to address global extinctions must certainly go beyond green spaces in cities.

Newsweek, however, takes the prize for human arrogance and reckless "solutions." In the longest and most detailed article located, the causes of mass extinctions were cavalierly dismissed with "assigning blame is less important than figuring out how to prepare for the inevitable and survive it." The answer: "What we need to do is actually quite unnatural. . . . we need to adapt the planet to suit humanity." Calling humans "extremely cunning," author Annalee Newitz proceeded to lay out various geo-engineering schemes including sun blockage efforts referred to as "solar management." Ships could spray "aerosols high into the air" or "inject reflective particles into the stratosphere." Admitting that unintended consequences could be disastrous, Newitz declared,

> Nonetheless, if the planet starts heating up rapidly, and droughts are causing mass deaths, it's very possible that we'll become desperate enough to try solar management. . . . However we do it, we need to begin to maintain the climate at a temperature that's ideal for human survival. Instead of allowing the planet's carbon cycle to control us, we would control it.[25]

If these sci-fi proposals aren't preposterous enough, Newitz seriously suggested that humans must "find ways of escaping [the planet] to build cities on the moon and on other planets." To investigate the plans for this idea further, she attended a conference where scientists were planning a sixty-two–mile high space elevator.

So, the corporate media reserves little to no space for scientific evidence informing the public about the activities and policies actually causing mass extinctions, policies that might actually be changed by an aroused public. At the same time, there appears to be ample room to tout grandiose technological projects that are imprudent at best and patently dangerous at worst, given that human technologies have wrought the extinction crisis in the first place.

Fragmentation

Many scientific studies focus on the decline or loss of a particular species. These reports, and the accompanying media articles, are important, but they often neglect to explain how the decline of a particular species is part of the sixth mass extinction. So, one can find items in the US corporate media on the "loss" of bees, a study on the world's oldest giant trees dying, or a report on the plight of the polar bear—as if these events have nothing to do with each other. This fragmentation, as Herbert Schiller pointed out many years ago, is one of the key strategies of manipulation used by the corporate media.[26]

Distance through Time and Space

Like the quotation about bees at the start of this chapter, extinctions are quiet, difficult-to-observe events. In fact, a species is confirmed as extinct only when it has not been seen for fifty years. This lengthy waiting period, and the tendency of the corporate media to focus on species that live in other countries, distances readers from the actual imminence and proximity of extinctions. For instance, the article "In Haiti, a Trek to Save Rare Animals: As Its Forests Disappear, Other Life Does, Too," reads more like an adventure story of the hardships endured by an intrepid biologist trying to capture endangered frogs and lizards than a wake-up call about the impact of extinctions on the whole planet.[27]

Since we do not see animals dying in mass numbers in our daily lives or in our immediate spaces, and thus are not attuned to observing key changes in our natural environments, we do not feel a sense of urgency about this issue.

Distance through Language

Language strongly affects how information is received, and whether emotions are aroused enough to move people to action. The terms "biodiversity" and its "loss" distance a reader from the trauma and realities of extinctions. They do not evoke images of frightened, hungry, exhausted, homeless animals; the violence of clear-cutting of forests; or the deaths of oil-soaked birds. The term "loss" can imply that there are no persons or actions causing these annihilations. Such "cool" language does not really communicate the intensity with which human policies and technologies are killing animals and species; the killings are happening even though the "deciders" may not be there to witness the deaths.

Further, many articles and reports only highlight how the deaths and extinctions will affect human beings. The loss of other beings is completely contextualized as a loss of services and products for humans. They do not educate the public about how all life is intricately intertwined and why all ecosystems and forms of life should be valued in and of themselves.

Missing Information

Of course, censorship is fundamentally characterized by what is omitted. While some articles about the sixth extinction can be located in the corporate media, the most important pieces of information are either ignored or purposefully suppressed, as they may conflict with the business interests of corporate owners. Missing from these corporate press articles, a few of which were picked up by several corporate news outlets, are the human-based root causes of extinctions, and what actions and policies must be immediately undertaken to stop and reverse these root causes if we hope to ameliorate the extinction crisis. There is no discussion of how the pattern of extinctions threatens life everywhere on Earth and disrupts the complex interactions among species that is necessary for the survival and well-being of all species and ecosystems.

SPECIESISM AND HUMAN IGNORANCE

Even though human beings are a recent species on this planet and did not exist during the millions of years that most other forms of life evolved, many human societies have adopted unwarranted beliefs that humans are superior to all other living beings, and that the Earth and other forms of life are here specifically for our use. Some religions have encouraged this disposition, but industrialized societies that extract resources through massive projects, and capitalist societies that emphasize the accumulation of wealth, especially promote this thinking. This lack of regard for the lives and well-being of other animals and plants has provoked the most egregious human abuses of the land, air, water, and other species. The name of this belief and the actions that follow from it is called *speciesism*.[28]

Many people do not understand the extreme seriousness of animal extinctions. People have been taught to think of animals as "other," peripheral to the lives of humans. Unless they are companions, they can be sold, used for work, or killed so that their body parts can be eaten or turned into other consumer products. At the same time, we often are not educated to understand the significance of each plant or animal to the intricate web of life.

Further, because industrialized humans are "busy" with the projects promoted by our societies and media, we often do not pay attention to nature and thus do not notice the extinctions happening around us. In our ignorance, indifference, or arrogance toward other species, we do not seek to understand how the precipitous extinction of many amphibians, deaths of bees and pollinators, the killing of top predators, drastic loss of bat populations, massive deforestation, extreme declines in bird populations, contamination of ecosystems, and so on, affect other forms of life or even our own human lives. Indeed, as we know at some level, we are animals ourselves—although we are taught to think of ourselves as separate from, and superior to, all other life.

The Human Activities Driving Species Extinctions

There is widespread scientific agreement on the key drivers of extinctions and their human origin: "Habitat loss, invasive species, pollution, climate change, over-exploitation of resources, and above all—the factor that magnifies all the others—human overpopulation."[29] Human overpopulation, as an ecological burden, is exacerbated by the complex web of institutions and social psychological processes that humans have created and rigorously defend. Sociologists have been analyzing the social consequences of these phenomena for many decades, but not in an integrative manner that includes the relevance of speciesism within the fabric of all life and thus within all social and ecological systems.[30]

Greed, wealth accumulation, and economic systems that foster the concentration of wealth in the hands of a few have exacerbated the cruel and destructive projects that humans have initiated to make money. Many of these projects are identified below as part of a list of human activities that are harmful to life, and thus species survival. UN Under-Secretary General Achim Steiner of the UN Environment Programme (UNEP) identified economics as a key reason that the UN Convention on Biodiversity goal was not met:

> One key area is economics: many economies remain blind to the huge value of the diversity of animals, plants and other life-forms and their role in healthy and functioning ecosystems from forests and freshwaters to soils, oceans and even the atmosphere. . . . The real benefits of biodiversity, and the costs of its loss, need to be reflected within economic systems and markets. . . . Perverse subsidies and the lack of economic value attached to the huge benefits provided by ecosystems have contributed to the loss of biodiversity. We can no longer see the continued loss of and changes to biodiversity as an issue separate from the core concerns of society: to tackle poverty, to improve the health, prosperity and security of our populations, and to deal with climate change. Each of those objectives is undermined by current trends in the state of our ecosystems, and each will be greatly strengthened if we correctly value the role of biodiversity in supporting the shared priorities of the international community.[31]

Human beings have drastically altered every ecosystem on the planet. Societies and economic systems that emphasize material wealth, overconsumption, and maximization of profits incentivize "taking more than you need and not leaving the rest." Products are extracted from the Earth, or from plants, animals, and even humans with little to no concern for the consequences of the extraction or production processes. The "precautionary principle," whereby an activity should not proceed until proven safe for the public and the environment, is rarely followed.[32] Instead, corporations are permitted to engage in harmful activities until some weak government "regulatory" agency can demonstrate that the activity is causing harm—typically direct harm to humans only, and occasionally to the environment in general. Federal and state regulatory agencies, led by politically appointed and approved directors, run the gamut from good intentions with insufficient enforcement capabilities to intentional neglect of duty on behalf of corporations—often the very corporations the regulatory directors once led. Under these circumstances, even piecemeal environmental impact statements, to whatever extent they exist, provide minimal, if any, protection for the environment.

What constitutes "harm" is always a negotiated item within a legal process that favors those with the most legal resources, and most often that is the corporation conducting the harmful activity. Thus, legal definitions of harm to some aspect of the environment, or life in general, are never set at an actual zero point: the complete absence of harm, allowing corporations to seamlessly externalize large portions of their costs—environmental and natural resource protection—to the general public.[33] Only in the most egregious cases, after significant harm has been done, is the public able to address the problem in some small way—though legal remedies, when available, seldom repair the damage that has been done to the ecosystem or deter future violations. Negotiated definitions of harm create an artificial zero point that is well above the actual absence of harm. The assumption implied within this process is that the environment and/or life within an ecosystem can tolerate a certain amount of poison, destruction, exploitation, and/or overutilization. But following that assumption is still not enough to satisfy corporate interests within an economic system based on greed. Once an industry-friendly definition of harm is legally established, corporations expend huge portions of their resources to go considerably beyond those legal limits.[34]

The corporate media do not take responsibility for educating the public about the importance of the precautionary principle. No activity that involves changing the natural state of an ecosystem should be allowed to take place unless the change has been demonstrated to have absolutely no negative consequences for that ecosystem. Indeed, with the sixth mass extinction occurring as a result of past neglect, corporations should now have to go beyond an actual zero-harm requirement, to prove that their actions will have a positive effect on the environment. Some Native American cultures inform us that we can create artificial laws defining what constitutes "harm," but if human laws are not consistent with natural law they are meaningless.[35]

The harm of a mass extinction is not captured by the sum of the individual losses: its greatest damage can only be understood in terms of the consequent interaction effects, which scientists are only beginning to understand. The dynamics of "cascade and collapse" mean that mass extinctions are likely to produce many more negative consequences than scientists have yet considered.[36]

Humans have invaded and dramatically altered almost all the lands and waters on Earth. Throughout the world, humans control or affect nonhuman life in two major ways: corporate projects and overconsumption, and direct killing.

Corporate projects harm all life—including humans—through the processes of extraction, production, dissemination, overconsumption, and disposal.[37] Consider the combined effects of the following projects and products causing harm, disease, and/or death in humans, animals, and plants:

▶ Nuclear, chemical, biological, and conventional weapons and their waste products;[38]
▶ Fossil fuels causing global climate changes, ocean acidification, and air and water pollution;[39]
▶ Nuclear power plants, their waste products, and the release of radioactivity into the air and water;[40]
▶ Genetically modified organisms in food, at factory farms, and released into the environment;[41]
▶ Toxic chemicals and poisons in building materials, clothing, furniture, foods, personal care products, and pharmaceuticals;[42]
▶ Toxic chemicals used for mining or extraction processes such as hydraulic fracturing (a.k.a. fracking);[43]
▶ Oil spills and "cleanups" using toxic chemicals to disburse the oil;[44]
▶ Electromagnetic waves and microwaves (e.g. wireless technologies and cell phones);[45]
▶ Nanotechnology;[46]
▶ Five ocean gyres of plastics and garbage, their tiny particles altering ocean ecosystems;[47]
▶ Destruction of entire ecosystems (e.g. mountaintop removal, tar sands oil, and navy testing of explosives in oceans);[48]
▶ Urbanization, urban sprawl, and impermeable surfaces.

Secondly, animals and plants are used and/or killed outright, without regard for the quality and significance of their lives or their role in their ecosystems, in the following ways:

▸ Deforestation and agricultural monocultures (plant and animal);
▸ Dams and the alteration of natural waterways;
▸ Factory farms, aquaculture, and concentrated animal feeding operations (CAFOs);
▸ Massive extraction of sea life through factory fishing;[49]
▸ Killing animals for sport and/or profit (e.g. the gun industry, the hunting industry, bushmeat, the global trade in animals and animal parts, and the killing of predators by US Fish and Wildlife);
▸ Killing animals, insects, and "pests" for human convenience;
▸ Animal entertainment industry (e.g. zoos, marine parks, films, and puppy mills);
▸ Scientific experimentation on animals.

The above list provides only a partial accounting of the most egregious human impacts on other species, as well as on humans. Each by itself is worthy of intensive daily news coverage—and yet, because of conflicting interests, corporate media do little to cover these stories. The real story, however, is in the confluence of factors. If all segments of the media do not begin informing the public of the serious imminent dangers the world now faces, the sixth mass extinction will be over before we know it, with untold suffering along the way.

WHAT HUMANS CAN DO

As gloomy as the above picture might be, key organizations, individually and in collaboration, are leading activism to address the sixth mass extinction. If they are able to gain substantial public support, they have a chance to ameliorate the extinction process, which includes human extinction. If we can reduce or reverse the activities and processes causing the harms listed above, we can possibly slow or arrest the extinction processes, diminish the threat of cascade and collapse, and thus moderate the dangers associated with the current

mass extinction. This means contending with all the forces driving extinctions simultaneously, so individual beings, species, and ecosystems might have a chance to heal. Some important steps humans can take are below.

1. Join and support organizations directly working on extinctions, working to prevent further damage to life systems, or working to bring the plight of animals to public attention: the Center for Biological Diversity, Earthjustice, Endangered Species Coalition, World Wildlife Fund, Species Alliance, Izilwane, Defenders of Wildlife, Sierra Club, Natural Resources Defense Council, Navdanya, 350.org, Earth First!, Idle No More, and many others.

2. Support international agreements related to environmental protections: for example, the UN Convention on Biological Diversity has been endorsed by every country in the world except the United States. Work in conjunction with organizations to pressure political representatives to support all legislation and international agreements that will help protect the environment.

3. Read and support independent news media that make it a point to include articles on plants, animals, ecosystems, and extinctions: Common Dreams regularly highlights and publishes articles on animals and plants. It provides an excellent platform for linking progressive organizations working tirelessly to save species, the environment, and the planet. Other outstanding sources of information are the Environmental News Network, *Yes! Magazine*, *E: The Environmental Magazine*, *Endangered Earth*, and *OnEarth Magazine*.

Secondly, participate in pressuring corporate media to attend to their responsibility to keep the public informed about this very serious issue. Write letters to the editor on extinctions. Join and support organizations that monitor and hold corporate media accountable, like Project Censored, Center for Media and Democracy, Center for Public Integrity, Institute for Public Accuracy, and Free Press.

4. Initiate local activism to change local policies and stop harmful projects. Ultimately, everything happens in a local environment. When towns and counties refuse to let a large factory, mining operation, or retail chain disrupt their communities, they are practicing sound local ecological decision-making. If local communities effectively resist having their environments harmed, global problems could be mitigated considerably. One example is the Declaration on Local Authorities and Biodiversity, signed by many mayors and local politicians in a number of countries as a commitment to protect their local environments from harm.

5. Change our own lives to stop killing or harming animals, including bees, bats, spiders, and more. Stop killing animals in and around our houses. Stop using poisons of any kind. Stop or drastically reduce eating animals and/or animal products.[50] Stop supporting the harming or killing of animals in the wild, in science, in entertainment, and elsewhere.

6. Participate in mass movements and demonstrations, to pressure governments to respond to the needs of the public and ecosystems rather than corporations, and to hold corporations accountable for their actions.

Overall, it is important to remember that all social and environmental justice issues are interconnected—not just in an ecological sense, but in a politico-economic sense as well. For example, working for peace in the world is one of the most important things you can do to slow down the sixth mass extinction. One of the best kept secrets is that the United States military is the greatest contributor to environmental harm in the world, and it makes this onerous "contribution" in a multitude of ways at home and abroad.[51] Why isn't the corporate media continually reporting this extremely important piece of information? We arrive at the same answer as to the question of why they are not reporting the sixth mass extinction: the corporations that benefit from polluting are also primary benefactors of war. Ultimately, the public must hold the media accountable to its responsibility if we are to avoid the ultimate cascade and collapse that the sixth mass extinction holds before us.

JULIE ANDRZEJEWSKI, EDD, is professor of human relations at St. Cloud State University, where she cofounded the Social Responsibility Program. Her recent publications include coediting *Social Justice, Peace, and Environmental Education* (Routledge, 2009) and authoring "War: Animals in the Aftermath" in *Animals and War: Confronting the Military Animal Industrial Complex* (Arissa, 2013). She serves as one of Project Censored's international judges, and her students regularly contribute stories to Project Censored's Top 25 list.

JOHN C. ALESSIO, PHD, is professor emeritus in sociology at St. Cloud State University, where he cofounded the Social Responsibility Program. He has taught at a number of universities and served as an academic dean at Marywood University, and Minnesota State University, Mankato. A widely published author, Dr. Alessio has published, most recently, *Social Problems and Inequality: Social Responsibility Through Progressive Sociology* (Ashgate Publishers, 2011).

Notes

1. "EU: Ban Bee Poison," Avaaz.org, January 29, 2013, http://www.avaz.org/en/hours to save the bees. Introduction to the AVAAZ petition signed by 2.6 million people to the European Union to ban neonicotinoid pesticides made by Bayer and other giant pesticide producers that are implicated in killing bees.
2. World Wildlife Fund in collaboration with the Global Footprint Network and the Zoological Society of London, *Living Planet Report* (2012), accessed May 2, 2013, http://awassets.panda.org/downloads/lpr 2012 summary booklet final.pdf.
3. "The Extinction Crisis," Center for Biological Diversity, http://www.biologicaldiversity.org/programs/biodiversity/elements_of_biodiversity/extinction_crisis; and Eric Chivian and Aaron Bernstein, eds., *Sustaining Life: How Human Health Depends on Biodiversity* (New York: Oxford University Press, 2008).
4. Andrea Germanos, "Report: Ecosystems in Upheaval, Biodiversity in Collapse," Common Dreams, December 12, 2012, https://www.commondreams.org/headline/2012/12/12. Germanos's article is based on Michelle D. Staudinger et al., "Impacts of Climate Change on Bio-

diversity, Ecosystems, and Ecosystem Services: Technical Input to the 2013 National Climate Assessment," Cooperative Report to the 2013 National Climate Assessment, July 2012, http://assessment.globalchange.gov.

5. United Nations Environment Programme (UNEP), "Global Biodiversity Outlook 3: Biodiversity in 2010,"http://www.cbd.int/gbo3.

6. Key reports available include US Geological Service with National Wildlife Federation and Arizona State University, *Emerging Consensus Shows Climate Change Already Having Major Effects on Ecosystems and Species*, December 18, 2012, http://www.ugs.gov/newsroom/article.asp?ID=3483; World Wildlife Fund in collaboration with Global Footprint Network and the Zoological Society of London, *Living Planet Report* (2012), http://wwf.panda.org/about our earth/all publications/ living planet report/2012 lpr/; the International Union for Conservation of Nature and the *Red List of Endangered Species*, 2013, http://www.iucnredlist.org; UNEP, especially the Convention on Biological Diversity, http://www.cbd.int and publications like *Nature* and *Science*.

7. Species Alliance, *Call of Life: Facing the Mass Extinction*, 2010, http://calloflife.org/p-story.htm

8. UNEP, "Global Biodiversity Outlook 3."

9. Anthony D. Barnosky et al., "Approaching a State Shift in Earth's Biosphere," *Nature* 486 (June 7, 2012): 52–58. http://www.stanford.edu/group/hadlylab/_pdfs/Barnoskyetal2012.pdf. See also UNEP, "Global Biodiversity Outlook 3."

10. Species Alliance, *Call of Life*.

11. Andrew H. Altieri et al., "A Trophic Cascade Triggers Collapse of a Salt-Marsh Ecosystem with Intensive Recreational Fishing," *Ecology* 93 (2012): 1402–1410, http://dx.doi.org/10.1890/11-1314.1.

12. Richard Pearson, "Are We in the Midst of a Sixth Mass Extinction?" *New York Times*, June 3, 2012, 5.

13. Seth Borenstein, "Panel: Problems with Oceans Multiplying, Worsening," *Brattleboro Reformer* (Brattleboro VT), June 21, 2011.

14. Tom Harris, "We Need to Manage Climate Change, Not Avert Catastrophe," *South Florida Sun-Sentinel* (Fort Lauderdale), August 15, 2012.

15. Gaylord Dold, "Are Humans Headed for Mass Extinction?" *Miami Herald*, July 29, 2012, http://www.miamiherald.com/2012/07/29/2915428/are-humans-headed-for-mass- extinction.html.

16. Amina Khan, "Less Dire View of Extinction: Scientists Using a New Method to Calculate the Rate at Which Species Are Dying Out Say the Crisis Is Bad but Overestimated," *Los Angeles Times*, May 21, 2011.

17. Faye Flam, "Mass Extinction: Humans Have Edge," *Philadelphia Inquirer*, July 9, 2012, C1.

18. Pete Spotts, "Mass Extinction? Man May Still Have Time to Catalog Earth's Species," *Christian Science Monitor*, January 25, 2013.

19. Jim Dwyer, "Warning of A World That's Hotter Wetter," *New York Times*, May 23, 2012, 16, http://www.nytimes.com/2012/05/23/nyregion/african-fossils-may-show-the-future-of-climate-change.html?_r=0.

20 Carl Zimmer, "Multitude of Species Face Threat of Warming," *New York Times*, April 5, 2011, D1.

21. Naomi Lindt, "The Call of the Wilds in Cambodia," *New York Times*, March 6, 2011, TR8.

22. Gaia Vince, "A Looming Mass Extinction Caused by Humans," British Broadcasting Company, November 1, 2012, http://www.bbc.com/future/story/20121101-a-looming-mass-extinction/1.

23. Ewen Callaway, "Cloning: Can it Resurrect Extinct Species?" BBC Future, February 29, 2012, http://www.bbc.com/future/story/20120229-can-we-resurrect-extinct-species.

24. Michelle Lalonde, "Biodiversity's Concrete Solution; Urban Accommodation of Wildlife and Green Spaces Needs to Be Championed More Actively by Politicians," *Montreal Gazette*, November 1, 2010, http://blogs.montrealgazette.com/2010/11/01/green-life-column-biodiversitys-concrete-solution.

25. Annalee Newitz, "Can Humans Survive?: Five Mass Extinctions Have Nearly Wiped Out Life on Earth. The Sixth Is Coming," *Newsweek*, May 6, 2013, http://www.thedailybeast.com/newsweek/2013/05/06/the-sixth-mass-extinction-is-upon-us-can-humans-survive.html.

26. Herbert I. Schiller, *The Mind Managers* (Boston: Beacon Press, 1973).
27. Faye Flam, "In Haiti, a Trek to Save Rare Animals: As Its Forests Disappear, Other Life Does, Too." *Philadelphia Inquirer*, September 13, 2011, A1.
28. For definitions and examples, see Peter Singer, *Animal Liberation* (New York: Avon Books, 1975); David Nibert, *Animal Rights/Human Rights: Entanglements of Oppression and Liberation* (Lanham, MD: Rowman & Littlefield Publishers, 2002); and Joan Dunayer, *Speciesism* (Derwood: Ryce Publishing, 2004).
29. Species Alliance, *Call of Life*; UNEP, "Global Biodiversity Outlook 3"; Center for Biological Diversity, "Owning Up to Overpopulation," *Endangered Earth* (Fall 2009): 1,7; and Paul and Anne Ehrlich, *One with Nineveh: Politics, Consumption, and the Human Future* (Washington DC: Island Press, 2004). One classic statement on this problem is William R. Catton, *Overshoot: The Ecological Basis of Revolutionary Change* (Champaign: University of Illinois, 1980).
30. For notable exceptions in the sociological literature, see John C. Alessio, *Social Problems and Inequality: Social Responsibility Through Progressive Sociology* (London: Ashgate Publishers, 2011); and Riley E. Dunlap et al., eds., *Sociological Theory and the Environment: Classical Foundations, Contemporary Insights* (Lanham MD: Rowman & Littlefield, 2002).
31. UNEP, "Global Biodiversity Outlook 3" 12–13. For one accessible account of efforts to model the economic value of undisturbed ecosystems, see Gretchen C. Daily and Katherine Ellison, *The New Economy of Nature: The Quest to Make Conservation Profitable* (Washington DC: Island Press, 2002).
32. United Nations Educational, Scientific, and Cultural Organization (UNESCO), *The Precautionary Principle: World Commission on the Ethics of Scientific Knowledge and Technology*, March 2005, http://unesdoc.unesco.org/images/0013/001395/139578e.pdf. While there are numerous definitions of the precautionary principle, a strong definition, when applied, requires all social actors who engage in economic/technological/social activities that could somehow affect the delicate balance within an ecosystem or otherwise bring harm to life—to first demonstrate that, indeed, no such harm will occur. Until then, no action should be taken. While weak versions of this principle are applied in some parts of Europe and non-European countries like New Zealand, there is little notable application of this principle in the United States, where the focus tends to be more on risk management related to cost-benefit analyses than on protecting life and the ecosystem.
33. Annie Leonard, *The Story of Stuff: How Our Obsession with Stuff Is Trashing the Planet, Our Communities, and Our Health* (New York: Free Press, 2010).
34. General Electric is one of many giant corporations that uses its nearly endless economic resources to defend its illegal activities—all the while doing cost-benefit assessments of being caught and prosecuted. For examples, see "GE Misdeeds," http://www.cleanupge.org/gemisdeeds.html; and Charlie Cray, "General Electric," CorpWatch, http://www.corpwatch.org/section.php?id=16. Corporations are also effective at using their resources to influence the political system and government "regulatory" agencies. Consider, for example, the relationship between Monsanto and the US Department of Agriculture (USDA), as covered in Censored story #24, "Widespread GMO Contamination: Did Monsanto Plant GMOs before USDA Approval?," in this volume.
35. See, for example, Winona LaDuke, "A Society Based on Conquest Cannot Be Sustained," in *Oppression and Social Justice: Critical Frameworks*, ed. Julie Andrzejewski (Needham Heights: Simon & Schuster Custom Publishers, 1996), 199–206.
36. Alterieri et al., "Trophic Cascade" and Species Alliance, *Call of Life*.
37. Leonard, *Story of Stuff.*
38. See, for example, *Censored* story #7, "The Merchants of Death and Nuclear Weapons," and story #12, "The US Has Left Iraq with an Epidemic of Cancers and Birth Defects," in this volume.
39. See, for instance, *Censored* story #15, "Food Riots, the New Normal?" in this volume.
40. See *Censored* story #3, "Fukushima Nuclear Disaster Worse Than Expected," in *Censored 2013: Dispatches from the Media Revolution*, Mickey Huff and Andy Lee Roth with Project Censored (New York: Seven Stories Press, 2012), 91–93; and story #8, "The Fairy Tale of Clean and Safe

Nuclear Power," in *Censored 2012: Sourcebook for the Media Revolution*, Mickey Huff and Project Censored (New York: Seven Stories Press, 2011), 101–107.

41. In this volume, for example, see *Censored* story #21, "Monsanto and India's 'Suicide Economy'" and story #24, "Widespread GMO Contamination: Did Monsanto Plant GMO's before USDA Approval?"

42. For example, see "Baby's Tub Still Toxic?" *Censored 2013*, 96–97.

43. See *Censored* story #18, "Fracking Our Food Supply."

44. For example, *Censored* story #18, "The True Cost of Chevron," in *Censored 2011: The Top Censored Stories of 2009–10*, eds. Mickey Huff, Peter Phillips, and Project Censored (New York: Seven Stories Press, 2010), 94–99.

45. See *Censored* story #14, "Wireless Technology a Looming Health Crisis," in this volume, and also story #15, "Dangers of Everyday Technology," in *Censored 2013*, 93–96.

46. For instance, *Censored* story #17, "Nanotech Particles Pose Serious DNA Risks to Humans and the Environment," in *Censored 2011*, 88–93; and story #22, "Nanotechnology Offers Exciting Possibilities But Health Effects Need Research," in *Censored 2006: The Top 25 Censored Stories*, eds. Peter Phillips and Project Censored (New York: Seven Stories Press, 2005), 110–111.

47. See, for example, *Censored* story #12, "Pacific Garbage Dump: Did You Really Think Your Plastic Bag Was Being Recycled?" in *Censored 2012*, 107–108.

48. For instance, *Censored* story #10, "Mountaintop Removal Threatens Ecosystem and Economy," *Censored 2006*, 75–78. On Navy testing, see "U.S. Military's War on Earth," *Censored 2004: The Top 25 Censored Stories*, eds. Peter Phillips and Project Censored (New York: Seven Stories Press, 2003), 79–82.

49. See *Censored* story #2, "Oceans in Peril," *Censored 2013*, 87–89.

50. International Panel for Sustainable Resource Management, "Assessing the Environmental Impacts of Consumption and Production," UNEP, June 2, 2010, http://www.eurekalert.org/pub releases/2010-06/udot-ffu0530110.php.

51. Project Censored reported this as the *Censored* story #2, "US Department of Defense is the Worst Polluter on the Planet," *Censored 2011*, 15–24.

CHAPTER 13

The New Story
Why We Need One and How to Create It

Michael Nagler

*The deepest crises experienced by any society are those
moments of change when the story becomes inadequate
for meeting the survival demands of a present situation.*

—Thomas Berry[1]

1. A CRISIS OF MEANING

Every social movement needs two resources to succeed: *unity*, or a
sense of *shared purpose*; and a long-term *strategy*. That is acutely true
of the movements swirling around the globe today in response to crisis after crisis unleashed by the failing institutions of the prevailing
order. Environmentalist and author Paul Hawken has convincingly
shown that, while there are literally a million or more worthy projects
being carried out in "the largest social movement in history," they
are working in isolation, thus forfeiting their potential effectiveness.[2]
And nonviolence scholars (yes, there are some) have realized for
some time that spontaneous popular uprisings, hopeful and dramatic
as they may be, soon lose momentum for want of long-term strategy, thus unintentionally giving rise to elements as destructive as the
regimes they dislodged, when those elements rush into the vacuum
created by those popular uprisings.

Inspired by Mahatma Gandhi's iconic campaign for India's freedom, which was conspicuously endowed with both unity and strategy,

we at the Metta Center for Nonviolence have created a platform called Roadmap that provides a framework for both shared purpose and long-term strategy.

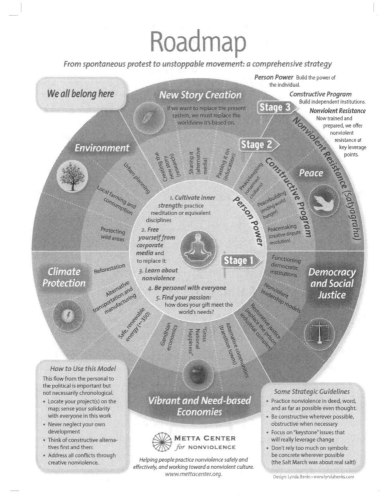

Roadmap

From spontaneous protest to unstoppable movement: a comprehensive strategy

Person Power Build the power of the individual.

We all belong here

New Story Creation
If we want to replace the present system, we must replace the worldview it's based on.

Stage 3

Constructive Program Build independent institutions.
Nonviolent Resistance Now trained and prepared, we offer nonviolent resistance at key leverage points.

Nonviolent Resistance (Satyagraha)

Environment

Creating the new story (research)
Sharing it (alternative media)
Passing it on (education)

Stage 2

Urban planning

Local farming and consumption

Peacekeeping (unarmed civilians)

Constructive Program

Peace

1. **Cultivate inner strength:** practice meditation or equivalent disciplines

Peacebuilding (ending world hunger)

Protecting wild areas

2. **Free yourself from corporate media** and to replace it:

Person Power

Peacemaking (creative dispute resolution)

Stage 1

Climate Protection

Reforestation

3. **Learn about nonviolence**

Functioning democratic institutions

Democracy and Social Justice

Alternative transportation and manufacturing

4. **Be personal with everyone**

5. **Find your passion:** how does your gift meet the world's needs?

Nonviolent leadership models

Safe, renewable energy (+ 350)

Gandhian economics

"Gross National Happiness"

Alternative communities (transition towns)

Restorative justice (replace the prison industrial complex)

How to Use this Model
This flow from the personal to the political is important but not necessarily chronological.
- Locate your project(s) on the map; sense your solidarity with everyone in this work
- Never neglect your own development
- Think of constructive alternatives first and then:
- Address all conflicts through creative nonviolence.

Vibrant and Need-based Economies

METTA CENTER *for* NONVIOLENCE

Helping people practice nonviolence safely and effectively, and working toward a nonviolent culture.
www.mettacenter.org.

Some Strategic Guidelines
- Practice nonviolence in deed, word, and as far as possible even thought.
- Be constructive wherever possible, obstructive when necessary
- Focus on "keystone" issues that will really leverage change
- Don't rely too much on symbols: be concrete wherever possible (the Salt March was about real salt!)

Design: Lynda Banks • www.lyndabanks.com

Nonviolence is the Roadmap's operative principle. By emphasizing nonviolence, we provide an alternative to the established culture, which sees coercive force as the fundamental basis of both change and order.

But nonviolence is more than a method; it is itself a new story of reality and human significance. The Roadmap reflects this understanding by placing the power of the individual at its center, in direct contradiction to the passivity and powerlessness that characterize the old story. The individual is not just the beneficiary of this new model but its source. The energy of change arises from personal empowerment as it did in Gandhi's scenario, and moves outward through "constructive program" to confrontational nonviolent resistance, if necessary.[3]

Among the areas that serve as guidelines for essential change and regeneration in the Nonviolent Resistance ring around the Roadmap, we give primary consideration to the creation of a new story. Observing that ballads and stories "socialize us into our roles as men and women and affect our identities," the pioneer of cultivation theory, George Gerbner, often quoted Scottish patriot Andrew Fletcher (1655-1716), "If I were permitted to write all the ballads, I need not care who makes the laws of the nation."[4] The powerful resonance of a person-centered movement—armed, as it were, with a new story that makes clear *why* the person is the center of global meaning and power—has an incredible potential for change. Why care about other peoples' health care, especially if there might be more to go around if they weren't there? Why look for an alternative to brute force, even if its destructive side effects outweigh any possible gains, if we live in a regime of competing interests and there's no other way? What, after all, do human trafficking, high rates of murder and suicide, weak gun safety laws, election fraud, banksterism, and war have in common? These all rest upon a flawed vision of the human being. In fact, "flawed" is an understatement. The prevailing image of a human being today—an image consistent across the mainstream of our art forms, education, policy-making, the news media, and a majority of scientists (though their number is shrinking somewhat)—is that of a material body separate from other creatures and the environment, doomed to compete for ever scarcer resources in a universe that has come about by chance. "What liberals and progressives don't seem to understand," wrote Lynn Stuart Parramore recently, "is that you don't counter a myth with a pile of facts and statistics. You have to counter it with a more powerful story."[5] That more powerful story is beginning to take shape.

THE NEW STORY

What we have lost in the modern desacralization of nature and the degradation of the human image—and what we stand to gain by reversing it—can be thrown into relief by this passage from a four-teenth-century text of Christian mysticism, *The Cloud of Unknowing*: "Beneath you and external to you lies the entire created universe. Yes, even the sun, the moon, and the stars. They are fixed above you, splendid in the firmament, yet they cannot compare to your exalted dignity as a human being."[6]

Seven centuries later, University of California–Berkeley's quantum physicist Henry P. Stapp wrote:

> Rational arguments lead to the conclusion that all aspects of nature, including our own mental aspects, must be interacting parts of one mental whole. This conclusion opposes, and therapeutically so, the materialist message that each of us is a separate and isolated collection of mechanical parts that, in some incomprehensible (and useless) way, can think, know, and feel. Perceiving oneself to be an integral part of the mental whole can elicit a feeling of connectivity, community, and compassion with fellow sentient beings, whereas the materialist message of isolation and survival of the fittest tends to lead to selfish actions.[7]

Present-day visionaries frame this new narrative in terms of three inter-related stories: the *Universe Story* (which is also the title of Brian Swimme and Thomas Berry's excellent book);[8] the *Earth Story*, sometimes called Sacred Earth or the Gaia Hypothesis; and finally the *Person Story*. Although these stories overlap, it is the third story, about the new image of the human being, that is critical for significant social change. Unfortunately, it has been the least studied. But, to appreciate all fully, we must start with the biggest picture.

The Universe Story

For our purposes, the postclassical or quantum-era story of the universe can be summed up in two propositions:

1. All reality is an interconnected whole. It is "nonlocal," in the language of physics; but in the plain words of Swami Vivekananda, "The whole universe is one."[9] Nothing that we do, say, or even think is without effects, whether measurable or not, that extend everywhere. This interconnected perspective resonates with the observation of Martin Luther King Jr. that "injustice anywhere is a threat to justice everywhere. We are caught in an inescapable network of mutuality, tied in a single garment of destiny. Whatever affects one directly, affects all indirectly."[10]

2. All of evolution has been a steady unfolding of consciousness.

The two points are clearly related because unity, or "nonlocality," is utterly impossible in the material realm but begins to be imaginable as a feature of consciousness.

But two things must be added to the second point. First, "unfolding" means just that.[11] Consciousness itself, the underlying reality in both quantum physicists and the Vedantic and other traditions, did not evolve: it always was and still is, unchanging and indivisible. "I regard consciousness as fundamental," physicist Max Planck wrote in 1931. "I regard matter as derivative from consciousness. . . . Everything that we talk about, everything that we regard as existing, postulates consciousness."[12] Consciousness has been there, Rabbi Michael Lerner has argued, "[n]ot from the emergence of brains but from the very, very beginning of everything. . . . There never was a time when the universe wasn't equally conscious as it was physical."[13] Indeed, pursuing Lerner's line of inquiry, we may consider whether the universe is *more* conscious than physical.

What has evolved is not consciousness itself, then, but life-forms with greater abilities to use this consciousness—climaxing, as far as life on this planet is concerned, with the uniquely human (though not often fully utilized) capacity for self-awareness. This long process has been beautifully brought out by the popular meditation teacher, Sri Eknath Easwaran: "If we take the Gita's view, that God has become the world and mind and matter belong to the same field, we get a much loftier view of evolution: the eons-long rise of consciousness from pure energy until the simplest of life-forms emerges and the struggle for increasing self-awareness begins."[14]

Second, and even more significant: evolution *will continue to be* an unfolding of consciousness. As physiologists and sages alike say of our cognitive capacities, they have not begun to reach any known limitation. We nonetheless experience at least one serious limitation in our consciousness, which Albert Einstein, in a famous passage, identified and pointed out how to transcend:

> A human being is part of the whole called by us "universe," a part limited in time and space. He experiences himself, his thoughts and feeling as something separated from the rest, a kind of optical delusion of his consciousness. This delusion is a kind of prison for us, restricting us to our personal desires and to affection for a few persons nearest to us. Our task must be to free ourselves from the prison by widening our circle of compassion to embrace all living creatures and the whole of nature in its beauty.[15]

Here is the twentieth century's greatest scientific genius describing nothing less than the purpose of life, to "shatter the chains of egotism" that create the feeling of separateness between ourselves and others, as Gandhi put it.[16] This would seem to be the great leap that humankind has taken beyond other animals.

Scientists have calculated that the likelihood that this universe and its most spectacular achievement—life—came about by chance is about that of a strong wind blowing through a junkyard and assembling a Boeing 707. Clearly, as Nobel Prize–winning biologist George Wald said at a recent conference, this universe has been "headed for life from the Big Bang."[17] Heading for life and raising consciousness are two ways of looking at the same phenomenon. There is also a third. Since higher consciousness means an enhanced awareness of unity—because as evolutionary biology has discovered, cooperation has played a more potent role in evolution than competition and, as neuroscience has discovered, we higher animals are "wired for empathy"—then the universe exhibits what Buddhists call *mahakaruna* or "vast compassion." It exhibits what we might call—to paraphrase an expression from the sterile debate between creationism and science— "compassionate design"; and we participate in that design when we carry out projects of social change through nonviolence. This would explain why solving problems with nonviolence leads to more lasting solutions than doing so in the "traditional" way—with violence, which, from this perspective, is counter-evolutionary.

While animals exhibit many behaviors of appeasement and conflict transformation—far more than were recognized before the birth of "positive science"[18]—it would seem to be a human prerogative to consciously choose suffering as a way of opening the heart of the opponent for his or her own welfare. In Gandhian or "principled" nonviolence, we are never against the true well-being of the other even when we're compelled to resist their attitude, behavior, or institutions: in Christian terms, "We hate the sin, but not the sinner." Gandhi stated very simply: "Nonviolence is the law of our species," a spirit that "lies dormant in the brute."[19] Without a framing narrative to rationalize this law, nonviolent activists have nonetheless discovered it in their own experiences.

Christian Peacemaker Teams (CPT) is one of some twenty nongovernmental organizations that is now actively applying nonviolence across borders in situations of impending or open conflict—a development of Gandhi's *Shanti Sena* or "peace army" idea that has been expanding throughout the world beneath the radar of the mass media. Recently, a CPT field team member was conversing with an activist in Iraqi Kurdistan who announced his intention to use nonviolence in their struggle. The CPT member, perhaps to test his friend's resolve, pointed out that nonviolence can be dangerous (which is true, though not nearly as dangerous as violence), that sometimes nonviolence doesn't yield the hoped-for results right away (which may also be true but again is even more true of violence).[20] The activist replied, "Sometimes you are happy in nonviolence because you are not losing your soul. You might lose hope, or get tired, but you are not losing your soul." He does well to repeat the phrase; "I lost my soul in Iraq/Afghanistan" is frequently on the lips of veterans who, numbering in hundreds of thousands (actually, 1.7 *million* from Vietnam alone), are suffering post-traumatic stress disorder, which drives increasing numbers of veterans to the point of suicide.[21] A retired US Army psychiatrist recently said that the response to this tragedy of the Army and the Department of Veterans Affairs is to not talk about it, because to acknowledge the existence of this widespread phenomenon would be "to pathologize an absolutely necessary experience"[22]—namely, war. But there is another reason the military doesn't talk about it: it lies beyond the vision of the prevailing paradigm, with its assumption of alienation and separateness.

More positively, Aram Jamal Sabir, the executive director of the Kurdish Institute for Elections, reported: "I can't tell you exactly when I started to believe in nonviolence—sometime during all the wars and violence here. . . . I saw that violence didn't change the situation. In any person there is some humanity. Nonviolence tries to develop that part of a person."[23]

In other words, nonviolence, being perfectly in sync with human destiny, not only conveys a deep sense of fulfillment on the activist but also helps to awaken the opponent and the broader public.

The explosive quantitative and qualitative growth of nonviolence in the few decades since Gandhi and King[24] thus takes its place beside the birth of new science and the recovery of ancient wisdom as a potent factor in the change that David Korten, Joanna Macy, and others have referred to as the Great Turning.[25] Now that political science has begun looking at this phenomenon, we already have some impressive studies of its efficacy to dislodge oppressive regimes. But the growth of nonviolence, and knowledge about it, has not only political but also cultural and even evolutionary significance.

The Earth Story

Of the three intersecting stories that comprise this new narrative, the ecological has been the most recognized and thus requires less review here—not that solving the problem of global climate disruption is not urgent! In fact, it's the most urgent task in the category Joanna Macy identified as "stopping the worst of the damage." But its primary urgency is to preserve the nourishing capacity of the Earth so as to cradle the continuation of the great experiment called life. Indeed, as Vandana Shiva has stated, "If you stop the pollution in people's minds, they will stop their pollution of the environment."[26] While we must stop mountaintop removal, the Keystone XL pipeline, etc.—and quickly!—the "worst of the damage" has been industrial civilization's damage to the human image.[27]

The desacralization of Earth that Carolyn Merchant called the "death of nature," which began at the dawn of the industrial revolution, meant that the ancient myth of a living earth was deliberately, if not always consciously, deconstructed. This process must be reversed, for even if the modern mind cannot reimagine earth as actually living, we can at least regain a *respect* for life, and by extension, for our planet's exquisite life-support system. Along with that reimagining must come a change in the collective psyche that creates our vulnerability to greed by propagating a misleading image of ourselves as empty physical beings in need of fulfillment from outside objects. When he was only twenty-two years old, the great modern Indian sage Ramana Maharshi replied to a questioner: "Happiness is the very nature of the Self. There is no happiness in any object of the world."[28] Fuller awareness of this fundamental fact of our nature, which is at present rigorously obscured by advertising and other aspects of our culture, would point us to the end to our extractive economy and the way we're despoiling the Earth to service it.[29]

The Person Story

We now begin to see through the critical lens: our human image. As Huston Smith said years ago, "For our culture as a whole, nothing major is going to happen until we figure out who we are. The truth of the matter is . . . we haven't a clue who we are today."[30] Or rather, we have imposed on ourselves a theory that violates our deepest intuitions and is ultimately a travesty of what science, wisdom traditions, and our own best judgment are saying. Ancient Indian tradition offers a set of potent formulas called *mahāvākyas* ("core statements"), which encapsulate the vision of reality that the Vedanta had created—for example, *prajñānām brahma*, "All reality is consciousness."[31] We might try to set out a few core statements for our present age even though we may not be able to match the *mahāvākyas'* brevity; that takes time, and genius. Supported as they are by science and wisdom, and offered here with confidence, we nonetheless treat them as hypotheses to be lived and tested in the living.

▸ We are not merely material beings. To use a popular formula: we are body, mind, and spirit, but spirit (consciousness) is our first and fundamental identity.

▸ We are not separate, despite appearances. All of us—for that matter, all of life—is one, and this oneness can be discovered in the depths of our consciousness.

▸ We are not violent by nature. We have a *capacity* for violence inherited from our evolutionary past, but just as cooperation is a more potent driver of evolution than competition, compassion in us leads to more long-lasting change than hatred. Injustice and cruelty are not absent from our world, but they are not fundamental to it. Life doesn't punish; it teaches.[32]

▸ We are not determined by our DNA, our hormones, or our neurotransmitters any more than we are by the position of the stars or anything outside of us: we make our own destiny primarily with our *will*.

▸ We are not a finished product. The miraculous human body that has taken five billion years to evolve (since the emergence of life-forms on this planet) may have reached a plateau—for instance, it may not be possible to run a three-minute mile—but we are far from realizing the full potential of our *consciousness*. (Except that some of us have: Jesus, the Buddha, and, as thought by many people in our own age, Mahatma Gandhi, and a handful of other women and men of realization, who represent what each of us can become.)

WHAT'S KEEPING THE OLD STORY ALIVE?

It's interesting to observe how the new story is struggling to be told in the shell of the old. For example, Barbara Fredrickson, developing an important aspect of positive psychology, has written an important book called *Love 2.0: How Our Supreme Emotion Affects Everything We Feel, Think, Do, and Become,* but the headline of a review on *AlterNet* tells exactly the opposite (and depressingly familiar) story: "Your Brain on Love: The Fascinating *Biochemical Reactions That Make Sparks Fly*" (emphasis added).[33] Even on this otherwise quite progressive blog, the categories used to frame this scientific finding are taken from the old, materialistic narrative. While it is virtually ubiquitous in public discourse, the most effective medium imposing this inhibiting and demoralizing narrative is modern advertising. Examples abound: an old advertisement touts a brand of cigarettes as "alive with pleasure," or a more recent picture of some diamond rings carries the label, "This is what extraordinary love looks like." Bear in mind that, according to recent studies, we are exposed to between 3,000 to 5,000 of these commercial messages a day; their cumulative impact—including their underlying "story," or message of a self that is empty, needing fulfillment from the outside world, separate from others and the environment—cannot be ignored.

The six-part BBC documentary *Century of the Self* demonstrates the power of advertising—including, for example, how the Nazis enthusiastically adopted advertising techniques in their propaganda with devastating clarity that we needn't elaborate on here. Those who have become alarmed by Citizens United, the Supreme Court–approved doctrine that corporations have the same rights as natural persons, have mainly been roused by its baleful consequences for democracy, as well they should; but even if corporations never take advantage of this court's ruling to sway political decisions, the decision still does serious harm by propagating a shallow, inert image of personhood, which has come to dominate our collective sense of self.

An earlier version of *Century of the Self* was called *Happiness Machines*, borrowing from a quote by President Herbert Hoover, who fell all over himself to offer this fulsome praise to a group of advertisers: "You have taken over the job of creating desire, and have *transformed people into* constantly moving happiness *machines*—machines which have become the key to economic progress" (emphasis added).[34]

Since Hoover's time, as audiences have become more and more desensitized and indoctrinated to this message of their own dehumanization, advertisers have become increasingly forthright about transferring humanity to inanimate objects. "Meet Gwen," invites a billboard. Gwen likes music and good restaurants. But there's a problem: "Gwen" is a smartphone. This is not a joke. Recall that the atomic bombs dropped on Hiroshima and Nagasaki were given the cute, euphemistic, and equally pseudo-personal names "Little Boy and "Fat Man," while the cities they destroyed were referred to not as cities but "targets."

Reviewing Nick Turse's Vietnam War book, *Kill Anything That Moves*, Chris Hedges describes how "the god-like power that comes with the ability to destroy . . . along with the intoxicating firepower of industrial weapons, rapidly turns those who wield these weapons into beasts. *Human beings are reduced to objects*" (emphasis added).[35] The degradation inflicted by these messages is double-edged, injuring first oneself, and then the intended victim.[36] Conflict scientists have long recognized that dehumanization is a fundamental precondition of violence; indeed to deny the humanity of another and/or oneself is a kind of spiritual violence in itself. From dehumanization to inhumanity is a short step.

Dehumanization begins long before an army recruit shouts in unison for his drill sergeant that the purpose of a bayonet is to "kill, kill, kill without mercy." As is well known, before becoming California's governor, Arnold Schwarzenegger starred in a particular type of action film. According to a *New Yorker* profile of Stan Winston, whose special effects studio designed monsters and robots for these movies, Winston found it exciting to "scare the crap out of people."[37] This sounds uncomfortably similar, does it not, to the way governments try to keep us cowed and in line? For instance, in 1947 when the American people *were* turning from militarism in disgust, Senator Arthur H. Vandenberg told President Harry S. Truman that if he wanted to rearm he would have to "scare the hell out of the American people."[38] But the Winston studio team was convinced that their projects were humanitarian. *The New Yorker* account also quoted Donald Norman, a professor of computer science and psychology and "an influential writer on technological design." According to Norman, "Robots need to display their emotions so that humans will be able to tell at a glance what's going on inside them."[39] *Emotions? Inside* them? And, according to Cynthia Breazeal, an MIT computer scientist who collaborated with Wintston, in countries like the US and Japan where demand for elder care is projected to surpass the supply of caretakers, "The solution could be a sociable robot, something that lives with you and that you can have a *meaningful emotional* relationship with."[40]

To seriously believe that you can have a meaningful relationship with a machine epitomizes our civilization's pathology. It is perhaps the worst possible delusion, for it becomes all too easy to dehumanize persons in a culture that dehumanizes *personhood*.

FROM THE CULTURAL TO THE POLITICAL

Nonviolent Peaceforce (NP) is a remarkable organization that places trained, unarmed field team members in select regions of conflict. It's now a seven million dollar worldwide organization with teams in five countries. When NP was just getting underway, I had lunch with a colleague, a distinguished political scientist with a special interest in peace, which was not commonplace in that discipline. I explained to Ernie what NP and other nonviolent intervention groups were doing (the field is now known as Unarmed Civilian Peacekeeping): such groups had rescued child soldiers; offered "protective accompaniment" to hundreds of threatened human rights workers in Latin America and elsewhere; stood ready to interpose themselves, if necessary, in outbreaks of fighting—all without losing a single member. "Fascinating, Mike," he said, with genuine interest.

So I said, "Let's put together a seminar and I can share this with some of your colleagues."

"No," he said.

No? Wouldn't his colleagues want to know about an earthshaking development in their own field? After a few days I got over my shock and pressed Ernie to tell me why he thought they would not, and after thinking for a moment he put very simply: "That's not their culture." Two decades on, it still isn't. Nor is it the culture of policy-makers, funders, or the millions of ordinary men and women who go into military "service" for a variety of personal reasons and one cultural one: in their worldview, there is no alternative to coercive force.

The debate between Democrats and Republicans is not taking place on a level playing field: politically conservative perspectives are premised on the old story, which is still the default notion of reality for a large majority in the industrialized world. For example, in this view, torturing our enemies may be acceptable if their suffering benefits us and hurts only them. However, recent findings in neuroscience suggest that inflicting pain is harmful to both victim and perpetrator alike.[41] The prevailing story came into existence, after all, for political reasons: as my colleague Carolyn Merchant has shown in her critical study, *The Death of Nature: Women, Ecology, and the Scientific Revolution*, the rationalism of the "Enlightenment" was seized upon to supplant the image of "sacred Earth"[42] and to replace it with the notion of Earth as an inert block of matter—thus making the industrial revolution possible, unleashing much despoliation of the earth, then by mines, and now by poisoning, climate disruption, mountaintop removal, and so on. David Korten, Joanna Macy, and other brilliant visionaries are now in effect trying to reverse that narrative shift, to restore the image of a living or sacred Earth. They are quite correct in pointing out that repressive forces are strongly invested in keeping the prevailing story of a lifeless Earth inhabited by human beings with no agency, who are radically dissociated from one another and the planet and thus fit victims of elite control and exploitation. This is why, when we come down to an "inexplicable" catastrophe like Iraq, Tom Hayden reported one member of Congress declaring, "Republicans can declare victory and leave, but the Democrats can only declare failure and be blamed."[43]

THE OPPORTUNITY OF NOW

Despite appearances, we have reached a time of great possibility. On the one hand, the prevailing story is causing untold suffering and, consciously or not, millions of people yearn to discard it: no one takes joy in thinking of themselves as a mechanical thing in a random universe. On the other hand, two parallel and remarkable developments in the twentieth century have made it possible to reunite two great streams of human understanding and belief that have long been at odds in the West: religion and science. "New science"—including the positively oriented social sciences that walked through the door thrown open by the astounding breakthroughs of quantum theory— and the wisdom traditions of human spirituality that have become somewhat more available to the general public, have begun to reveal quite complementary models of reality. While the findings of science and spiritual awareness do not always overlap, the former's systematic exploration of the outer world, and the latter's equally systematic exploration of the world within, are telling the same story where they do. When you distinguish, as Rupert Sheldrake has done, between the *dogma* of science—i.e. the belief, sometimes called scientism, that only things that can be measured and weighed are real—and the scientific *method*, which relies on hypothesis and testing, these two great inquiring systems are again complementary, because spiritual investigation also relies on hypotheses and testing, though by other means. Gandhi seems to be at home in both realms. When challenged to substantiate his claim that the directive for his spectacularly successful fast against untouchability in 1932 came from "the voice of God," he said, "I have stated *a simple scientific truth*, thus to be tested by all who have the will and the patience to acquire the necessary qualifications."[44]

The basic tenets of the wisdom tradition, with their powerful teachings of human interconnectedness and the norms that follow, are nowhere in conflict with the discoveries of new science, though each has developed its distinctive idiom. Where physicists have spoken of "nonlocality," sages have called it the unity of life (or the whole of existence). Where the latter have spoken of the primacy of consciousness (or, in popular terms, "mind over matter"), physicist Amit Goswami has coined the term "downward causality."[45] And when both have spoken of the critical concept of unity in diversity—without which no resolution of social, economic, or other tensions is possible—Gandhi came up with a fundamental guiding principle he called "Heart Unity,"[46] the norm that there is no underlying, unresolvable competition in the universe, that differences convert from threats to challenges when we gain a feeling for the other's welfare. Martin Luther King Jr. was very clear that when that happens we actually *need* diversity on the surface: "I can never be what I ought to be until you are what you ought to be; and you cannot be what you ought to be until I am what I ought to be."[47] Add to the fact that science and traditional wisdom converge around a "new" image of humanity the lesser-known fact that nonviolence, which arises from that image, is proving such a successful tool of social change and we have compelling support for the new story, or what we have taken to call in Metta documents the Story of Belonging.

HOW TO TELL THE NEW STORY

Tellers of the new story can build upon it by articulating the details— and they are rich indeed when one studies the subject in any depth— of nonviolence.[48] Few people today can be reached by scientific abstractions, much less the tenets of traditional wisdom, but the story is hard to ignore when dictators are deposed and oppressing regimes are brought down by an unfamiliar form of resistance.

Whether they realize it or not, countless people are depressed by the old story, yearning to believe that they really are conscious agents whose choices are endowed with meaning, that they are not condemned to competition and violence. There is powerful motivation to accept the message on which science, spirituality, and nonviolence now converge. And in embracing the new story they would find themselves relinquishing many kinds of injustice to which they might have continued to succumb. When done in the wrong spirit, pointing out others' misbehaviors often serves only to alienate further, thus perpetuating the depressing plotline of the old story.

The time is right, then, to avoid corporate media and to replace their toxic culture with the affirming study of nonviolence (which, as Gandhi said, is "not the inanity it has been taken for," but a rich science) as a personal practice, as we suggest in the inner circle of Roadmap, and to familiarize ourselves with the other scientific and wisdom teachings available to us.[49]

Then, tell our new story: let's not be shy about explaining where we're coming from on the innumerable projects encircled by the Roadmap, at a deeper level than usually figures into political discourse. *Waging Nonviolence* editor Nathan Schneider gave a great example from the Occupy movement journal *Tidal:*

> The psychology of debt impels us to think at every level about who and what Palestinians owe. But *since we refuse to value fellow human beings by their relationship to capital*, we should be asking the opposite question. We owe to Palestinians at least what we demand for ourselves: freedom from occupation, freedom from new forms of colonization, freedom to return to, inhabit, and live in a territory which we or our par-

402   CENSORED 2014

ents and grandparents called home, without annexation, . . . without the destruction of the common resources that nurture and sustain life.[50] [Emphasis added.]

Statements like this will increase our effectiveness. They will build to a tipping point the long-awaited and now essential shift of culture toward belonging instead of alienation, toward agency and responsibility instead of an imagined passivity. We'll be building a future—when we can tell political scientists, policy-makers, journalists, and the general public about a newly discovered nonviolent practice, and they will hear it with joy—because it's become their culture.

MICHAEL NAGLER, PHD, is professor emeritus of classics and comparative literature at the University of California, Berkeley, where he founded the Peace and Conflict Studies Program; founder and president of the Metta Center for Nonviolence (MettaCenter.org); and author of *Our Spiritual Crisis*, and *The Search for a Nonviolent Future*, which received a 2002 American Book Award and has been translated into Arabic, Italian, Korean, Croatian, and several other languages. Other writings of his have appeared in the *Wall Street Journal* among other venues. Among other awards, he received the Jamnalal Bajaj International Award for Promoting Gandhian Values Outside India in 2007. Michael is a student of Sri Eknath Easwaran, founder of the Blue Mountain Center of Meditation (Easwaran.org) and has lived at the Center's ashram in Marin County since 1970.

Notes

1. Wendell Berry, *Dream of the Earth* (San Francisco: Sierra Club Books, 1988), xi. Quoted in David Korten, "Religion, Science and Spirit: A Sacred Story for Our Time," *YES! Magazine*, January 17, 2013, http://cms.yesmagazine.org/happiness/religion-science-and-spirit-a-sacred-story-for-our-time.

2. Paul Hawken, *Blessed Unrest: How the Largest Social Movement in History Is Restoring Grace, Justice, and Beauty to the World* (New York: Penguin, 2008).

3. More on each of these steps in the Roadmap section of our website, http://www.mettacenter.org.

4. See, for example, *Truths Among Us: Conversations on Building a New Culture*, ed. Derrick Jensen (Oakland: PM Press, 2011), 14. Also see, George Gerbner, "The Stories We Tell," World Association for Christian Communication, http://www.waccglobal.org/en/19964-communication-and-conflict/954-The-Stories-We-Tell.html.

5. Lynn Stuart Paramore, "What if Liberals and Progressives Could Learn to Talk to White Southern Men?" *AlterNet*, November 2, 2012, http://www.alternet.org/election-2012/what-if-liberals-and-progressives-could-learn-talk-white-southern-men.

6. William Johnston, ed., *The Cloud of Unknowing* (New York, Doubleday, 1973), 129.

7. *On The Nature of Things: Thoughts, Actions, And The Fundamentally Mental Character of Nature*, 26.

8. Brian Swimme and Thomas Berry, *The Universe Story: From the Primordial Flaring Forth to the Ecozoic Era—A Celebration of the Unfolding of the Cosmos* (New York: Harper Collins, 1992).
9. Swami Vivekananda, *The Complete Works of Swami Vivekananda*, vol. 2 (Calcutta: Advaita Ashrama, 1978–1987), 461.
10. Martin Luther King Jr., Letter from Birmingham Jail, April 16, 1963.
11. See David Bohm, *Wholeness and the Implicate order* (London: Ark, 1988).
12. C. E. M. Joad, *The Philosophical Aspects of Modern Science* (London: George, Allen and Unwin, 1932), 12.
13. "Life and Mind in the Universe," paper delivered at National Council of Educational Research and Training seminar, New Delhi, February, 1987, quoted in Swami Jitatmananda, *Holistic Science and Vedanta* (Bombay: Bharatiya Vidya Bhavan, 1991), 74.
14. Sri Eknath Easwaran, *Essence of the Bhagavad Gita: A Contemporary Guide to Yoga, Meditation, and Indian Philosophy Gita* (Tomales, CA: Nilgiri Press, 2011), 51.
15. Letter reprinted in the *New York Times*, March 29, 1972.
16. Mahatma Gandhi, *Selected Writings* (Mineola, NY: Dover, 2005), 52.
17. This was at the Bhaktivedanta Institute's First Conference on Consciousness within Science, San Francisco, 1998. Since then the science of astrobiology has added a great deal of evidence.
18. See, for example, the works of Frans deWaal, e.g. *The Age of Empathy: Nature's Lessons for a Kinder Society* (New York: Random House, 2009).
19. See Eknath Easwaran, *Gandhi the Man: the Story of his Transformation* (Blue Mountain Center of Meditation, 1997), 150.
20. See, for example, Erica Chenoweth and Maria Stephan, *Why Civil Resistance Works: The Strategic Logic of Nonviolent Conflict* (New York: Columbia University, 2011).
21. "More US Soldiers Committed Suicide than Died in Combat," *Censored 2012: The Top Stories and Media Analysis of 2010–11*, ed. Mickey Huff and Project Censored (New York: Seven Stories Press, 2011), 43–54. Cf. also the illuminating concept of Perpetration Induced Traumatic Stress (PITS) coined by psychologist Rachael MacNair.
22. Dan Baum, "Coming Home in the 21st Century," *New Yorker*, September 12, 2004.
23. Christian Peacemaker Teams, annual report, October 2010.
24. Richard Deats, "The Global Spread of Active Nonviolence," in Walter Wink, ed., *Peace is the Way* (Maryknoll, MD: Orbis, 2000), 163–295. Note how much—including, for example, the Arab Spring—has happened since this publication.
25. See, *inter alia*, David C. Korten, *The Great Turning: From Empire to Earth Community* (Bloomfield CT, and San Francisco: Kumarian Press and Barrett-Koehler, 2006), and Joanna Macy, "Three Dimensions of the Great Turning," http://www.joannamacy.net/three-dimensions-of-the-great-turning.html.
26. Vandana Shiva, quoted in Azim M. Khamisa, "From Grief to Gratitude," *Peace Movements Worldwide: History and Vitality of Peace Movements*, vol. 2, ed. Marc Pilisuk and Michael N. Nagler (Santa Barbara, CA: ABC-CLIO, 2011), 199.
27. I am grateful to Stephanie Van Hook, executive director of the Metta Center, for this insight.
28. Bhagavan Sri Ramana Maharshi, *Who Am I? The Teachings of Bhagavan Sri Ramana Maharshi* (Tiruvannamalai: Sri Ramanashramam, 2007), 14.
29. In addition to Bhutan's Gross National Happiness index, there is rich new literature on human happiness; for one review, see Stacey Kennely, "Happiness Comes From Respect, Not Riches," *YES! Magazine*, August 3, 2012, http://www.yesmagazine.org/happiness-comes-from-respect-not-riches. On Bhutan, see Andrew C. Revkin, "A New Measure of Well-Being from a Happy Little Kingdom," *New York Times*, October 4, 2005, http://www.nytimes.com/2005/10/04/science/04happ.html?pagewanted=all&_r=0.
30. Quoted in Steven Glazer, *The Heart of Learning* (New York: Jeremy P. Tarcher/Putnam, 1999), 218.
31. Aitareya Upanishad 3.3. The other three are *ayam ātmā brahma*—"This Self (Atman) is Brahman" (Mandukya Upanishad 1.2), most famously *tat tvam asi*—"Thou art That" (Chandogya Upanishad 6.8.7) and finally *aham brahmāsmi*—"I am Brahman" (Brhadaranyaka Upanishad 1.4.10).
32. A forthcoming book by physicist Henry Stapp is called *Benevolent Universe?* Gandhi and King drop the question mark. See Henry P. Stapp, *Benevolent Universe?* Accessible online, http://www-physics.lbl.gov/~stapp/BUFin2.pdf.

33. Barbara Fredrickson, "Your Brain on Love: The Fascinating Biochemical Reactions That Make Sparks Fly," *AlterNet*, March 5, 2013, http://www.alternet.org/books/your-brain-love-fascinating-biochemical-reactions-make-sparks-fly.
34. See, e.g., Marc Pilisuk and Michael N. Nagler, "A Final Word," in *Peace Movements Worldwide: History and Vitality of Peace Movements*, vol. 2, ed. Marc Pilisuk and Michael N. Nagler (Santa Barbara, CA: ABC-CLIO, 2011), 370.
35. Chris Hedges, "Don't Look Away: We Must Confront the Horrific Industrial Violence the American Military Is Capable of," *AlterNet*, March 17, 2013, http://www.alternet.org/world/dont-look-away-we-must-confront-horrific-industrial-violence-american-military-capable.
36. Joe R. Feagin and Hernán Vera, *Liberation Sociology* (Boulder CO: Westview Press, 2001), 17. "Our humanity is affirmed in struggles to achieve freedom and social justice. Dehumanization marks and defines the oppressor as much as it torments the oppressed. For Freire, the struggle to recover humanity is a struggle of the oppressed 'to liberate themselves and their oppressors as well.'"
37. John Saybrook, "It Came From Hollywood," *New Yorker*, December 1, 2003, 54.
38. On Senator Vandenburg advising President Truman to "scare the hell out of the American people," see, e.g., Gore Vidal, *Imperial America: Reflections on the United States of America* (New York: Avalon, 2004), 97.
39. Saybrook, "It Came From Hollywood," 62.
40. Ibid., emphasis added.
41. Marco Iacoboni, *Mirroring People: The New Science of How We Connect With Others* (New York: Farrar, Strauss, and Giroux, 2008), 124. "Although we commonly think of pain as a fundamentally private experience, our brain actually treats it as an experience shared with others."
42. Carolyn Merchant, *The Death of Nature: Women, Ecology, and the Scientific Revolution* (New York: HarperCollins, 1990[1980]).
43. Tom Hayden, "Calls for Withdrawal from Iraq Echoing in Washington," *AlterNet*, September 19, 2005, http://www.alternet.org/story/25686/calls_for_withdrawal_from_iraq_echoing_in_washington.
44. *Bombay Chronicle*, November 18, 1932. See http://www.mkgandhi.org/momgandhi/chap05.htm.
45. See, e.g., Amit Goswami, *God Is Not Dead: What Quantum Physics Tells Us about Our Origins and How We Should Live* (Charlottesville, VA: Hampton Roads Publishing Co., 2012[2008]).
46. See the glossary on our website, MettaCenter.org.
47. Rev. Dr. Martin Luther King, Jr., "Remaining Awake Through a Great Revolution," Oberlin College Commencement Address, June 1965, http://www.oberlin.edu/external/EOG/BlackHistoryMonth/MLK/CommAddress.html.
48. By stark contrast, the US military also attempts to use the image and words of Martin Luther King Jr. to legitimize its military mission. In January 2013, the US Air Force's Global Strike Command published a promotional piece titled "Dr. King's Dream for the Global Strike Team." Independent media have been quick to point out the travesty, but this shows that King and his legacy *have* a moral cachet that the military feels a need to appropriate. See, e.g., Glenn Greenwald, "US Military Says Martin Luther King Would Be Proud of Its Weapons," *Guardian*, January 22, 2013, http://www.guardian.co.uk/commentisfree/2013/jan/22/martin-luther-king-military-weapons; and David Sirota, "Martin Luther King Jr., Champion of Military Defense?," *Salon*, February 1, 2013, http://www.salon.com/2013/02/01/martin_luther_king_jr_champion_of_military_defense.
49. For a good example of how independent media can provide more "New Story" insights, see Sarah van Gelder's foreword to this volume.
50. Folks in Strike Debt and Occupy Wall St., "Colonizer as Lender: Free Palestine, Occupy Wall Street, Strike Debt," *Tidal*, February 2013, http://tidalmag.org/issue4/colonizer-as-lender, as quoted in Nathan Schneider, "A New Kind of Palestine Solidarity—The Strike Debt Analysis," *Waging Nonviolence*, March 4, 2013, http://wagingnonviolence.org/2013/03/a-new-kind-of-palestine-solidarity-the-strike-debt-analysis.

Acknowledgments

Mickey Huff and Andy Lee Roth

We would like to thank everyone that has contributed to Project Censored over the past thirty-seven years. For those who contributed directly to this year's volume, we offer thanks and pay our respects:

To the courageous independent journalists who continue to file real news, without which the Project would be impossible. Your work inspires us.

To the faculty evaluators and student researchers at our college and university affiliates around the world, as the eyes and ears of Project Censored, you help us keep up with the cutting edge of independent journalism.

To the authors in *Censored 2014*, your research and writing connects the dots among the Top 25 stories, and your contributions exemplify fearless speech in fateful times.

To our national and international judges, your dedication and expertise assures that our Top 25 list includes only the best, most significant independent news stories each year.

To our stalwart publishers at Seven Stories Press in New York, including the intrepid Dan Simon at the helm; Veronica Liu, our sharp-eyed, tireless editor; Jon Gilbert for his impeccable design layout; Crystal Yakacki for publicity; and Stewart Cauley for cover design. You, and the entire Seven Stories crew—including Liz DeLong, Ruth Weiner, Anne Rumberger, Silvia Stramenga, Amber Qureshi, Sadie Trombetta, and Jesse Lichtenstein, as well as interns Arielle Holstein, Tiffany Xu, Erin Carden, and Ellen Waddell—have our deepest respect and appreciation for making the commitment to publish the Project's research, and for doing so in record time each year.

To Marcia Annenberg, artist, who graciously gave us permission to use detail from her piece, "No News Is Good News," as the striking image on the cover of *Censored 2014*.

To Dr. Carl Jensen, founder of Project Censored in 1976, whose original vision and defiance of the status quo continue to inspire this Project.

To Dr. Peter Phillips, who has dedicated so much of his life to extending Project Censored's influence through his teaching, writing, and speaking. Peter is an exemplar of the educator as public intellectual, engaging people in discussions about media, democracy, and human liberation wherever he goes.

To Christopher Oscar and Doug Hecker, with Hole in the Media Productions, for *Project Censored: The Movie—Ending the Reign of Junk Food News*, a six-year labor of love that brings the Project to the attention of an even broader audience.

To the board of directors at the Media Freedom Foundation, the nonprofit parent of Project Censored, who provide organizational structure, and invaluable counsel. You keep us on course in pursuing Project Censored's mission.

To our friends and supporters at Pacifica and KPFA 94.1 FM, Free Speech Radio in Berkeley CA, which broadcasts The Project Censored Show on The Morning Mix each Friday morning. Summer Reese, Tracy Rosenberg, Andrew Phillips, Veronica Faisant, Anthony Fest, Dennis Bernstein, Miguel Molina, Kirsten Thomas, and Rod Akil all contribute to making The Project Censored Show a strong presence on the air.

To Adam Armstrong, who helps Project Censored reach its global Internet audience.

To the inimitable Khalil Bendib, whose cartoons again add luster and edge to our annual volume.

To Abby Martin, host of *Breaking the Set* on RT, founder of Media-Roots, colleague and ally in media freedom.

To Dr. Michel Chossudovsky and the Centre for Research on Globalization, which maintains the website GlobalResearch.ca.

To Allan Rees of No Lies Radio and Ken Jenkins, who record and broadcast our events online.

To the team at the Progressive Radio Network, for rebroadcasting *The Project Censored Show* each week.

To colleagues and staff at Diablo Valley College for their support and informed conversation, including Hedy Wong, Greg Tilles, Dr. Matthew Powell, Melissa Jacobson, Dr. Manual Gonzales, Nolan Higdon, Dr. Jacob Van Vleet, Adam Bessie, David Vela, Obed Vazquez, Dr. Lyn Krause, Dr. Steve Johnson, Dr. Jeremy Cloward, Dr. Amer Araim, and Dr. Mark Akiyama.

To T. M. Skruggs, Richard and Janet Oscar, Brian Martin Murphy, Steve Outtrim at Majitek, and the late Elizabeth Shariff for their generous financial support.

To Dorothy Andersen, and the late Alfred F. Andersen, of the Fair Share of the Common Heritage, for helping us to reestablish the Commons as a crucial element of public life.

On a personal note, to Meg, Liz, and our families and close friends, who have supported and encouraged us.

And to you, our readers, supporters, and global citizen-agitators, you share our goal of creating a truly free press, one that champions the voice of the People, in service of democratic self-government.

MEDIA FREEDOM FOUNDATION/PROJECT CENSORED BOARD OF DIRECTORS

Carl Jensen (founder), Peter Phillips (president), Mickey Huff, Andy Lee Roth, Bill Simon, Elaine Wellin, Derrick West, Kenn Burrows, Nora Barrows-Friedman, Abby Martin, Brian Martin Murphy, and T. M. Skruggs; with thanks to outgoing board member, Mary Lia.

Project Censored 2012–13 National And International Judges

JULIE ANDRZEJEWSKI, professor of human relations, cofounder of the Social Responsibility Program, St. Cloud State University. Publications include *Social Justice, Peace, and Environmental Education.*

ROBIN ANDERSEN, associate professor and chair, Department of Communication and Media Studies, and director of Peace and Justice Studies, Fordham University. Publications: *Critical Studies in Media Commercialism.*

OLIVER BOYD-BARRETT, professor in the Department of Journalism and Public Relations, Bowling Green State University. Publications: *The International New Agencies* (1980), *The Globalization of News* (1998), *Media in Global Context* (2009), and *Hollywood and the CIA: Cineman, Defense and Subversion* (2011).

KENN BURROWS, faculty member for the Institute for Holistic Health Studies, San Francisco State University. Director of the Holistic Health Learning Center and producer of the biennial conference, Future of Health Care.

ERNESTO CARMONA, journalist and writer. Director of the Chilean Council of Journalists. Executive secretary of the Investigation Commission on Attacks Against Journalists, Latin American Federation of Journalists (CIAP-FELAP).

ELLIOT D. COHEN, freelance journalist. Director, Institute of Critical Thinking: National Center for Logic-Based Therapy. Executive director, National Philosophical Counseling Association (NPCA). Editor and founder, *International Journal of Applied Philosophy*. Recent books: *Mass Surveillance and State Control* (2010), *Critical Thinking Unleashed* (2009), and *The Dutiful Worrier: How to Stop Compulsive Worry without Feeling Guilty* (2011).

JOSÉ MANUEL DE-PABLOS, professor at University of La Laguna (Tenerife, Canary Islands, Spain). Founder of scientific journal *Revista Latina de Comunicación Social* (RLCS), Laboratory of Information Technologies and New Analysis of Communication.

GEOFF DAVIDIAN, investigative journalist and editor, *The Putnam Pit* (Milwaukee). Publications include Reuters, the *Chicago Sun-Times*, the *Globe and Mail* (Toronto), the *New York Daily News*, *Albuquerque Journal*, *Seattle Post-Intelligencer*, and the *Vancouver Sun*.

LENORE FOERSTEL, Women for Mutual Security. Facilitator of the Progressive International Media Exchange (PRIME).

ROBERT HACKETT, professor at the School of Communication, Simon Fraser University. Co-director of News Watch Canada since 1993. Cofounder of Media Democracy Day (2001) and openmedia. ca (2007). Publications include *Expanding Peace Journalism* (coedited with I. S. Shaw and J. Lynch, 2011) and *Remaking Media: The Struggle to Democratize Public Communication* (with William K. Carroll, 2006).

KEVIN HOWLEY, professor of media studies, DePauw University. Author of *Community Media: People, Places, and Communication Technologies* (2005). Editor of *Understanding Community Media* (2010) and *Media Interventions* (2013).

CARL JENSEN, professor emeritus of communication studies, Sonoma State University. Founder and former director of Project Censored. Author of *Censored: The News That Didn't Make the News and Why* (1990–96), *20 Years of Censored News* (1997), and *Stories that Changed America: Muckrakers of the 20th Century* (2002).

NICHOLAS JOHNSON,* professor at College of Law, University of Iowa. Former FCC Commissioner (1966–73). Author of *How to Talk Back to Your Television Set*.

CHARLES L. KLOTZER, founder, editor, and publisher emeritus of *St. Louis Journalism Review*.

NANCY KRANICH, lecturer, School of Communication and Information, and special projects librarian, Rutgers University. Past president of the American Library Association (ALA).

DEEPA KUMAR, associate professor of media studies and Middle East studies at Rutgers University. Author of *Outside the Box: Corporate Media, Globalization and the UPS Strike* (2007) and *Islamophobia and the Politics of Empire* (2012).

MARTIN LEE, investigative journalist and author. Cofounder of Fairness and Accuracy in Reporting, and former editor of FAIR's magazine, *Extra!* Director of Project CBD, a medical science information service. Author of *Smoke Signals: A Social History of Marijuana*, *The Beast Reawakens* and *Acid Dreams: The Complete Social History of LSD: The CIA, the Sixties and Beyond*.

DENNIS LOO, associate professor of sociology at California State University Polytechnic University–Pomona. Coeditor of *Impeach the President: The Case Against Bush and Cheney*.

PETER LUDES, professor of mass communication, Jacobs University Bremen. Founder in 1997 of German initiative on news enlightenment, publishing the most neglected German news (Project Censored Germany). Editor, *Algorithms of Power: Key Invisibles* (2011).

WILLIAM LUTZ, professor emeritus of English, Rutgers University. Former editor of *The Quarterly Review of Doublespeak*. Author of *Doublespeak Defined* (1999); *The New Doublespeak: Why No One Knows*

What Anyone's Saying Anymore (1996); *Doublespeak: From Revenue Enhancement to Terminal Living* (1989); and *The Cambridge Thesaurus of American English* (1994).

SILVIA LAGO MARTINEZ, professor of sociology, Universidad de Buenos Aires. Codirector, Gino Germani Research Institute Program for Research on Information Society.

CONCHA MATEOS, faculty in the Universidad Rey Juan Carlos (Madrid). Journalist for radio, television, and political organizations in Spain and Latin America. Coordinator for Project Censored in Europe and Latin America.

BRIAN MARTIN MURPHY, associate professor and chair of communications studies, Niagara University.

JACK L. NELSON,* Distinguished Professor Emeritus, Graduate School of Education, Rutgers University. Former member, AAUP Academic Freedom Committee. Author of seventeen books, including *Critical Issues in Education*, 8th ed. (2013), and approximately 200 articles.

PETER PHILLIPS, professor of sociology, Sonoma State University. Director, Project Censored, 1996–2009. President, Media Freedom Foundation. Editor/coeditor of fourteen editions of *Censored*, and coeditor, with Dennis Loo, of *Impeach the President: The Case Against Bush and Cheney* (2006).

NANCY SNOW, professor of communications, California State University–Fullerton, and adjunct professor of communications and public diplomacy, Annenberg School for Communication and Journalism, University of Southern California. Author/editor of seven books, including *Information War* and *Propaganda, Inc.*

SHEILA RABB WEIDENFELD,* president, DC Productions, Ltd. Emmy Award–winning television producer. Former press secretary to Betty Ford.

ROB WILLIAMS, media educator, musician, historian, journalist, and professor, University of Vermont and Champlain College. Publisher of the newspaper *Vermont Commons: Voices of Independence*.

*Indicates having been a Project Censored judge since our founding in 1976.

Report from the Media Freedom Foundation President

Media Freedom Foundation (MFF) is a nonprofit 501(c)(3) corporation that sponsors Project Censored and all its various programs. MFF has a ten-person board of directors that is responsible for monitoring the budget and setting policy for our operations. Mickey Huff is director of Project Censored and has overall responsibility for its day-to-day management and for production of the annual *Censored* yearbook. Associate Director Andy Lee Roth serves in a similar administrative capacity and has been heavily involved in writing and researching *Censored 2014* and earlier yearbooks. This report details some of Project Censored's daily work and annual endeavors on behalf of media democracy in action.

We each are regularly invited speakers at community events, college campuses, academic conferences, and independent bookstores, addressing the issues of media censorship, propaganda, and the importance of accurate independent media in society. To arrange for a member of our speaking team to come to your community or campus, see ProjectCensored.org/speakers.

We are approaching our third year of producing and hosting the weekly one-hour *Project Censored Show* on *The Morning Mix* for KPFA/ Pacifica Radio. *The Project Censored Show* presents original content every Friday at 8:00 a.m., Pacific Standard Time, at 94.1 FM in the San Francisco Bay region and online at KPFA.org. Our affiliate stations include the Progressive Radio Network, No Lies Radio, and several Pacifica Radio stations around the country. Please ask your local public/ nonprofit radio station to air our weekly shows. See ProjectCensored. org/radio-archive for a listing of past broadcasts and guests. These archived public affairs broadcasts—available at no charge—make excellent classroom listening for high school and college classes.

We currently have students and faculty from nearly twenty colleges and universities researching and posting Validated Independent

News stories (VINs), which are news stories reported in the independent media that have been ignored by corporate media. Students and professors affiliated with Project Censored vet and research these stories, which Project Censored then posts on its website. These VINs become the candidates for our annual list of the Top 25 censored news stories. Reading independent news and comparing it to corporate media coverage is an important part of many high school and college critical thinking classes. Teaching college classes, helping students to learn about alternative news outlets, and mentoring them in writing VINs are hands-on components of our effort to create a more media literate society. We welcome inquiries from faculty and students at college and university campuses interested in becoming Project Censored affiliates.

MFF/Project Censored continues to maintain a website, CensoredNews.org, with daily RSS newsfeeds from approximately twenty sources that we trust for quality news. Helping the public identify and evaluate trustworthy sources of daily news is an important part of freedom of information, which is vital to all democratic societies. Adam Armstrong continues to serve as the webmaster for all the MFF/Project Censored websites, including our Spanish-language site, ProyectoCensurado.org. We have around 400,000 unique views each month, with millions of monthly hits. Adam also founded and maintains the blog DailyCensored.com, which has over fifty regular writers posting news stories and opinion. As we redesign and upgrade all our websites to state-of-the-art status, we will have movie- and book-downloading capabilities and increasingly stronger daily news and information. Adam is a vital part of the Project Censored team.

We are pleased to announce that MFF board member Abby Martin of Media Roots is continuing her program *Breaking the Set* on *Russia Today* in Washington DC. In addition to her duties at RT, she remains on the MFF board, and continues to update video content for Project Censored and Media Roots (MediaRoots.org).

Another MFF board member, Nora Barrows-Friedman, staff editor and reporter with *Electronic Intifada*, is currently working on a book focusing on how college students in the United States are organizing for justice in Palestine and are using direct action to protest their universities' complicity in Israel's occupation. The book will be published by Just World Books, due out in fall 2014.

We were saddened to learn this winter of the passing of our good friend and supporter Elisabeth Sherif.

In Memoriam
Elisabeth Anne Sherif
Social Justice Activist, Friend of Project Censored,
Artist, and Poet
June 28, 1933–February 11, 2013

Over the past three years, MFF/Project Censored has engaged in developing the idea of a fair share of the common heritage. With special funding from Dorothy Andersen of Santa Rosa, California, in honor of her late husband Alfred Andersen's beliefs, MFF has held public events, organized essay contests, produced radio shows, and maintained a website, all highlighting the importance of acknowledging that the world's material resources and cultural wealth belong to all living beings. For full information of the philosophy of the fair share of the common heritage, see FairShareCommonHeritage.org.

In addition to our longstanding relationship with our book publisher Seven Stories Press, Project Censored has extended its influence over the past five years through weekly radio broadcasts, development of the campus affiliates program, and improved websites. This year, we add an incredible new Project Censored documentary to our set of outreach tools. *Project Censored: The Movie—Ending the Reign of Junk Food News* hit the film festival circuit this summer and is slated for full release in fall 2013. Produced and directed by former Project Censored student and Sonoma State University alum Doug Hecker, and longtime Project Censored supporter Christopher Oscar, the film features original interviews about the Project and media censorship with Noam Chomsky, Howard Zinn, Michael Parenti, Greg Palast, Oliver Stone, Daniel Ellsberg, Peter Kuznick, Cynthia McKinney, Nora Barrows-Friedman, John Perkins, Jonah Raskin, Khalil Bendib, Pacifica and KPFA Free Speech Radio personalities, Abby

Martin of *Breaking the Set*, and many more Project-affiliated faculty and students. It also highlights Project founder Dr. Carl Jensen, former director and president of the Media Freedom Foundation Dr. Peter Phillips, current director Professor Mickey Huff, and associate director Dr. Andy Lee Roth. Watch for *Project Censored: The Movie* screenings in your area (ProjectCensoredTheMovie.com).

MFF/Project Censored is primarily affiliated with colleges, universities, independent media, and social justice organizations. In this capacity, we are constantly writing, researching, and promoting important human rights issues and news. As we enter our thirty-seventh year, the team at Project Censored has not only been looking back at how much we have done, but also ambitiously planning ahead. In efforts to broaden our impact, we are partnering with other outstanding organizations in our endeavors to fight media censorship. These include the National Coalition Against Censorship and the Union for Democratic Communications as well as film projects on solutions-based journalism like What the World Could Be.

We all know that the establishment news media in the US is in woeful condition; to address this, we at Project Censored continue to do all we can to support independent journalism, promote media literacy, and teach critical thinking skills—not only on college and university campuses across the country but also in the communities beyond those campuses.

These efforts and others too numerous to list engage us everyday. We currently do all of this on less than $80,000 a year. In order to stabilize our expanded affiliates program and to extend our influence in the future, we really need your help. Those who already subscribe to our electronic e-mail list know that we do not do a great deal of mass appeal fundraising. But, we have to be more honest with our readers and our supporters: we cannot continue to do all that we do unless we increase our budget.

Project Censored currently receives no funding of any kind from foundations or universities. For thirty-seven years, we have relied on support from personal donors, monthly subscribers, and book sales. (In past years when we have had some small foundation grants, that funding only augmented the individual donations that have always been the Project's economic lifeblood.) We hope that you will consider us among the most important nonprofits that you support, and we ask you to consider helping in any way or amount that you can. Increased revenues will help us meet our goals of doubling the size of our campus affiliates program in the next two years, hiring a part-time staff person to help with daily administrative tasks, and expanding our Internet content.

A new option this year has been for donors to pledge five dollars or more a month. In return, monthly subscribers receive our great appreciation and a copy of the annual *Censored* yearbook. Over 200 of you have so far joined as monthly subscribers. If you have not yet done so, please consider making a monthly pledge online at Project-Censored.org. If you are affiliated with a nonprofit foundation, or can make a larger gift in support of one or all of our activities, we would sincerely appreciate hearing from you and we would welcome the opportunity to tell you in more detail how you can be a crucial supporter in helping the Project to realize our future plans.

We humbly thank you for considering our appeal, and we are grateful for your support as we continue to fight censorship, deconstruct propaganda, and support fearless speech in fateful times.

Peter Phillips, PhD

President—Media Freedom Foundation/Project Censored

June 2013

PO Box 571

Cotati CA 94931

(707) 874-2695

peter@projectcensored.org

How to Support Project Censored

NOMINATE A STORY

To nominate a *Censored* story, send us a copy of the article and include the name of the source publication, the date that the article appeared, and page number. For news stories published on the Internet, forward the URL to mickey@projectcensored.org; andy@projectcensored.org; and/or peter@projectcensored.org. The deadline for nominating *Censored* stories is March 15 of each year.

Criteria for Project Censored news story nominations:

A *Censored* news story reports information that the public has a right and need to know, but to which the public has had limited access or exposure.

The news story is recent, having been first reported no more than one year earlier. For *Censored 2014*, the Top 25 list includes stories reported between April 2012 and March 2013. Thus, stories submitted for consideration in *Censored 2015* should be no older than April 2013.

The story has clearly defined concepts and solid, verifiable documentation. The story's claims should be supported by evidence—the more controversial the claims, the stronger the evidence necessary.

The news story has been published, either electronically or in print, in a publicly circulated newspaper, journal, magazine, newsletter, or similar publication from either a domestic or foreign source.

MAKE A TAX-DEDUCTIBLE DONATION

Project Censored is supported by the Media Freedom Foundation, a 501(c)(3) nonprofit organization. We depend on tax-deductible donations to continue our work. To support our efforts on behalf of independent journalism and freedom of information, send checks to the address below or call (707) 874-2695.

Donations can also be made online at ProjectCensored.org.

Please consider helping us fight news censorship and promote media literacy.

Media Freedom Foundation
PO Box 571
Cotati CA 94931
Phone: (707) 874-2695
Mickey Huff: mickey@projectcensored.org
Andy Lee Roth: andy@projectcensored.org
Peter Phillips: peter@projectcensored.org

No News Is Good News

Marcia Annenberg, cover artist for *Censored 2014*
www.mannenberg.com

It is not an overstatement to say that American journalism is endangered. In the 1990s, it was simply a question of the insertion of entertainment news into the news hour. By 2012, the news hour had shrunk—on some stations—to eighty seconds around the world. Does market research really find that the average American citizen can maintain interest in world news for only eighty seconds?

With media consolidation came the closing of news bureaus overseas, to increase profit margins. What if Osama bin Laden's articles, published in London, were publicized in 1998, instead of Monica Lewinsky's blue dress stains? Would our national security apparatus have been more focused? Probably. Where is the news that informs, instead of titillates? More recently, it is the underreporting of domestic news that should concern us. My artwork, *No News Is Good News*, grew out of an inadvertent discovery of a critically important news story that was omitted from national news—namely, the signing of the NDAA, on New Year's Eve, by the president in 2012. I was startled to discover on the Internet, a week after the signing, that it had in fact taken place the prior week.

Why does this matter? A bill, which even FBI Director Robert Mueller objected to, gave the army the same power as the police—to arrest terrorism suspects. Since when did the army become an adjunct police force? This news caused barely a ripple in the national press. I couldn't believe that I had missed this news, so I started to send away for national newspapers, for example, the *New York Times*, the *Wall Street Journal*, the *Washington Post*, the *Philadelphia Enquirer*, the *Los Angeles Times*, the *Dallas Free Press*, the *Detroit Free Press*, and the *Tampa Bay Times*. What I found was that it simply wasn't reported—except for page 22 in the *New York Times* and the front page of the *Dallas Free Press*. How did it come to this?

As our Fourth Amendment protections slip away, against unreasonable search and seizure, under the cover of the war on terror, with warrantless access to our e-mail and phone calls—allowing the gathering of data without encryption—we have to wonder why the press has acquiesced, without protest. As investigative journalism moves into the web of the Internet, the American people are left in a state of unknowing. Not only do we not know what the government is doing on our behalf in the fight against terrorism, due to the absence of reporting, we don't know that we don't know what it is that we are missing.

In this bubble of mostly entertainment and crime news the public is fed on a daily basis, how can we make critical judgments on policy without any background in world affairs? Political contests become sound bites. Photogenic leaders are given scripts that play to designated interest groups. Perhaps the greatest deceit of our time is the obfuscation of the science behind global warming. As the level of greenhouse gas rises above 400 parts per million, will any politician take to the floor of Congress to demand action? How many newspapers and how many newscasts reported the implications of that number? When the greatest threat to our future has been suppressed for years—can we still say that America has a free press?

ABOUT THE EDITORS

MICKEY HUFF is director of Project Censored. He is a professor of social science and history at Diablo Valley College in the San Francisco Bay Area, where he is cochair of the history department. Huff is cohost with former Project Censored director Dr. Peter Phillips of *The Project Censored Show*. The program airs weekly as part of *The Morning Mix* on Pacifica's KPFA Free Speech Radio in Berkeley, California, and rebroadcasts on several stations including No Lies Radio and the Progressive Radio Network out of New York City. He is also on the executive committee of Banned Books Week working with the National Coalition Against Censorship, of which Project Censored is a member.

ANDY LEE ROTH is associate director of Project Censored. He earned a PhD in sociology at the University of California–Los Angeles and a BA in sociology and anthropology at Haverford College. He teaches sociology at Sonoma State University and the College of Marin.

For more information about the editors, or to invite them to speak at your college, in your community, or to schedule interviews, please visit ProjectCensored.org.

Index

1 Percent, 5, 26, 42, 85, 89, 90, 94, 96, 99, 194, 246
1948 Universal Declaration of Human Rights, 56
2013 Farm Bill, 53
700 Club, 266
9/11, 184, 213, 266, 267, 272, 278, 279, 282, 284, 287, 298, 300, 304, 305, 309, 310, 316, 330, 360
99 Percent, 15, 95, 97, 367
Abbottabad, 304
ABC News, 191, 205
Abercrombie and Fitch, 194
Abu Dhabi, 199
Abu Ghraib, 263
Academy Award, 170, 296, 298, 301, 309, 310
Accountability Review Board, 189
ACLU, see American Civil Liberties Union
ACTA, see Anti-Counterfeiting Trade Agreement
Affleck, Ben, 301, 310
Afghanistan, 41, 69, 70, 71, 115, 120, 161, 180, 188, 212, 259, 319, 330, 355, 394
Afghanistan War, 212, 259
Africa, 11, 28, 32, 55, 64, 66, 124, 133, 134, 313, 326, 354, 355, 357, 360, 361, 363, 364, 365
Africa Command (AFRICOM), 354
Age of Turbulence, The, 122, 126
Agency for International Development (USAID), 357
Agricultural Appropriations Bill, 195
Ahmadinejad, Mahmoud, 52
Ahmed, Nafeez Mosaddeq, 16, 55, 127, 133, 140
Air Force Magazine, 357, 365
Airborne Warning and Control System (AWAC), 355
Al Jazeera, 41, 65, 82, 84, 102, 111, 126, 127, 136, 141, 167, 169, 203, 305, 432
al-Din, Ansar, 363
al-Qaeda, 30, 74, 156, 157, 161, 162, 166, 167, 168, 169, 172, 185, 188, 189 265, 304, 305, 354, 362
al-Shariam, Ansar, 189
Alfred P. Murrah Federal Building, 280, 286
Algeria, 354, 355, 356, 357, 358, 361, 362, 363, 364
Allen, General John, 188
Allende, Salvadore, 289
Allianz, 48, 321, 322, 329
Alternative Radio, 290
America's Newsroom, 191
American anti-money laundering laws, 323
American Civil Liberties Union (ACLU), 160, 172, 174, 212, 219
American Enterprise Institute for Public Policy Research, 315
American Jewish Joint Distribution Committee (JDC), 107, 111
Amnesty International, 362
Amos 'n' Andy, 266

Amusing Ourselves to Death, 177, 179, 185, 200, 202, 311
Anderson, Rocky, 196
Anti-Counterfeiting Trade Agreement (ACTA), 151
Apple, 32, 313, 332, 334–52
Arab, 66, 79, 80, 84, 114, 166, 270, 300, 309, 405
Argo, 31, 115, 251, 298, 299, 301, 302, 303, 309, 310
Arias, Jodi, 274
Arizona, 141, 227, 228, 229, 230, 233, 234, 248, 274, 384
Armstrong, Neil, 190
Assange, Julian, 71, 149, 150, 159, 212
Associated Press, 27, 68, 70, 81, 110, 158, 175, 190, 199, 204, 205, 213
Associated Whistle-Blowing Press (AWP), 149
Atlantic, 114
Aurora, CO, 273
Austria, 75, 150, 326
Autism, 129
AWP see Associated Whistle-Blowing Press
Azawad, 357, 362
Bahrain, 66, 74, 80, 84, 299
Balkan, 80
Bank for International Settlements, 42, 317
Bank Interests, 48, 86, 94
Bank of America, 48, 182, 320, 321, 327
Barclays, 48, 164, 166, 182, 203, 321, 322, 323, 325, 326, 329
Barnett, Andre, 196
Barsamian, David, 126, 289, 292, 294
Basra, 52, 121
Battiston, Stefano, 320, 330
BBC News, 101, 111, 129, 140, 141, 153, 166, 169, 198, 206, 329
Beck, Glenn, 280, 285
Belgium, 325
Benghazi, 188, 189, 204, 205
Bergen, Peter, 204, 303, 309
Berman, Morris, 200, 202
Bernays, Edward, 272, 285
Bernstein, Dennis, 270, 293, 409
Big Oil, 114, 123, 126
Bigelow, Kathryn, 306
Bilderberg Group, 318
bin Laden, Osama, 162, 171, 191, 282, 287, 303, 304, 306, 311, 422
Birth control, 63, 102, 107, 108, 111, 256
birth defects, 52, 113, 120, 121, 126, 385
Bitter Seeds, 60, 137, 141
Black Friday, 192, 193, 205
BlackRock, 48, 321, 322, 323, 325, 327
BNP Paribas, 48, 321
Boal, Mark, 303
Boeing E-3 Sentry, 356
Borgnine, Ernest, 190
Borromeo, Leah, 60,137

Boston Marathon, 274, 283, 287
Bouteflika, Abdelaziz, 355
Bradsher, Keith, 336,350
Bratich, Jack, 278
Brazil, 56, 326
Breuer, Lanny A., 323
Broadwell, Paula, 188
Bt cotton, 60, 136, 137
Bureau of Investigative Journalism, 258, 268
Burnett, Erin, 261, 269
Bush administration, 80, 123, 124, 171, 252, 253, 259, 262, 264, 363
Bush Agenda, The, 123
Bush, George W., 75, 118, 171, 252, 289, 354
Business Council, 314
Business Roundtable, 314, 326
caesium, 187
Cal/West Seeds, 63
Carbon sequestration, 128, 132, 133, 140
Carlin, George, 200
Carroll, William K., 329, 410
CBS, 70, 162, 163, 180, 186, 200, 206, 265, 349
CC, see Creative Commons
Center for Constitutional Rights, 173
Central Intelligence Agency (CIA), 27, 44, 73, 117, 188, 278, 288, 300, 310
Chad, 354–357
Changsu, 339
Chastain, Jessica, 304, 305
Chavez, Hugo, 199, 206
Chen, Adrian, 33, 305
Chile, 43, 92, 296
Chilean Telephone Company, 288
China Business News, 341, 350
Chinese New Year, 341
Chomsky, Noam, 34, 180, 203, 288, 290, 313, 416, 432
Christie, Robert M., 295, 297
CIA, see Central Intelligence Agency
Citizen's Global Trade Watch, 43
Civil Rights Act, 102
Clean Water Act, 187, 204
Clear Skies Act of 2003, 256
Clemente, Tim, 261
Clifford, W. K., 254, 264, 269
Clinton, Bill, 50, 105, 221
Clinton, Hillary, 130
CNN, 66, 79, 80, 81, 84, 123, 124, 126, 178, 182, 183, 184, 195, 202, 203, 204, 205, 241, 257, 269, 281, 286
CNN International (CNNi), 80
COINTELPRO, see Counter-Intelligence Program
Colombia, 125, 242, 325
Comcast, 260
Commission on Presidential Debates, 196
Committee to Protect Journalists (CPJ), 56, 76
Conference Board, 314
Congo, 361
Congressional Research Service, 354, 363
Conrad, Jessica, 49, 143, 146, 152
conspiracy theories, 28, 31, 104, 278, 281, 285, 297
Constitution Party, 196

Convention on the Prevention and Punishment of the Crime of Genocide, 108
Corexit, 187, 204
Cornell University, 325
Corporate Council on Africa, 360
Council on Foreign Relations, 314, 326
Counter-Intelligence Program (COINTELPRO), 163
Covert, Brian, 26, 29, 37, 65, 81, 176
CPJ, see Committee to Protect Journalists
Creative Commons, 27, 57, 143, 144, 145, 150, 151, 154, 159
Cult of Mac, 334, 335
Cultural Freedom Public Events, 289
"Culture of Cruelty," 50, 101, 105, 110
Curtis, Liz, 288
Dafu Scientific Building Material Co., Ltd., 339
Daily Kos, 83, 192, 205
Daily Show, The, 184
Daisy, Mike, 333, 346
Darfur, 259
Dargis, Manohla, 309
Dark Alliance, 279
Deep Water Horizon, 187
Defense of Marriage Act, 194
Département du Rensiegnementet la Sécurité (DRS), 354
Department of Defense (DOD), 169, 356, 385
Department of Justice, 68, 149, 172, 174, 187
Department of the Treasury, 357
Depo-Provera, 64, 107, 108
Deyuan Town, 342
Diller, Phyllis, 190
Diplomatic Security, 189
direct reimbursement, 49
Dirty White Gold, 60, 127, 137, 141
Disney, 31, 191, 251, 252, 260, 268
Djibouti, 360
DOD, see Department of Defense
domestic terrorism, 45, 103
Downing Street, 254, 259, 268
Drake, Thomas, 44, 73, 82
Drone strikes, 37, 38, 116, 117, 156, 172, 173, 174, 268
Dubai, 199
Duhigg, Charles, 349, 351
Duncan, Clarke, 190
EBay, 192
Economic Community of West African States (ECOWAS), 353
Economic Opportunities Act, 315
EFTA, see European Free Trade Association
Egypt, 195, 300, 355
Ehrlich, Anne, 55, 385
Ehrlich Paul, 55, 127, 385
Eisenste, Zillah in, 305
El Mercurio, 288
El Para, 355, 356
Electronic Intifada, 62, 102, 107, 111, 414
electromagnetic radio frequency radiation, 54, 131
Ellsberg, Daniel, 159, 207, 208, 213, 293, 416, 432
Elmo, 186, 187, 204

Enlightenment, 274, 276, 401, 412
Environmental Protection Agency (EPA), 130
Equal Protection Clause, 194
Espionage Act of, 1917, 44, 316
Ethics of Belief, 253, 268, 269
Ethiopian immigrants, 63, 102, 107, 108, 111
European Free Trade Association (EFTA), 145
Everhart, Sue, 264, 269
Fair Labor Association, 335, 351
Fairness and Accuracy in Reporting (FAIR), 70, 199
Fallujah, 52, 113, 121, 126
Farmer Assurance Provision, 195
Burkina Faso, 357
Father Knows Best, 265
Federal Bureau of Investigation (FBI), 73, 149, 188, 261
FDA, *see* Food and Drug Administration
Federal Bureau of Investigation (FBI), 73, 149, 188, 261
Federal Reserve Board, 327
Final Environmental Impact Statement, 63
Financial Services Authority, 324
First Amendment, 41, 218, 219, 220, 221, 222, 223, 224, 225, 258, 262
Flashpoints, 292
Focke-Wulf, 288
FOIA, *see* Freedom of Information Act
Food and Agricultural Organization of the United Nations, 98
Food and Drug Administration (FDA), 130
food crisis, 55, 129, 133, 134, 135
food riots, 22, 55, 127, 133, 140, 384
food stamps, 184, 193
Forbes Magazine, 191, 193, 205
Fort Bragg, 354
Foucault, Michel, 25–27, 33, 250
Foundation for National Progress, 289
Fourteenth Amendment, 194
Fourth Amendment, 257, 263,422
Fox News, 73, 158, 164, 169,173, 176, 180, 182, 183, 186, 191, 193, 198, 200, 202, 203, 204, 206, 255, 265, 286
Foxconn, 332–36, 339–42, 346–48, 350–52
fracking, *see also* hydraulic fracturing, 18, 22, 26, 57, 58, 61, 66, 78, 79, 84, 127, 128, 132, 133, 140, 378, 385
Free Speech TV, 287
Freedom of Information Act (FOIA), 171-2
Freedom of the Press Foundation, 149, 154, 158
French Air Force and Army, 352
Friedman, Milton, 198
Friends of Nature, 336, 350
Fromm, Erich, 31, 263, 270, 275, 276, 286
Fuel on Fire, 123
Fukushima Daiichi Nuclear Power Plant, 187
Fukushima Ocean Impacts Symposium, 187
G20, 90, 318, 327
G8, 90, 318, 327
Gaddafi, Muammar, 189
gag laws, 26, 37, 42, 44, 57, 62, 65, 79, 84, 176
Garrison, Jim, 279

Gawker, 33, 305
Gaza blockade, 59, 101, 102, 106, 111, 139
General Electric, 258, 384
genetically modified, 63, 129, 135, 137, 138, 141, 195, 272, 378
Geneva Conventions, 262
Georgia, 264
Germany, 20, 22, 48, 49, 50, 119, 219, 289, 321, 326, 362, 412
Gisha, 59, 106, 111
Glass, Ira, 333, 347, 349, 351
Glattfelder, James B, 320, 330
Global economy, 156, 164, 165, 166, 320, 330
global food crisis, 55, 129, 133, 135
Global Research, 37, 38, 63, 85, 86, 93, 99, 127, 128, 129, 140, 141, 168, 189, 204, 205, 285, 287, 310, 330, 364, 365
Global Terrorism Index (GTI), 180
GMO contamination, 63, 128, 141, 385, 386
GMO labeling, 129
GMO-free crops, 63
GMO, *see also* genetically modified, 60, 63, 128, 129, 136, 137, 138, 139, 141, 142, 385, 386, 135, 195
Goldman Sachs, 98, 321, 326
Goldman, Emma, 272
Good Morning America, 191
Goode, Virgil, 196
Goodman, Amy, 174, 206, 243, 293, 294, 296, 349
Gosztola, Kevin, 26, 65, 71, 82, 160, 176
Gou, Terry, 336
Government Accountability Project, 72
Gray, Kurt, 306
Great Britain, 198
Green Beagle, 336, 350
Green Berets, 355
Green Party, 196, 197, 206
Greenspan, Alan, 123, 126
Greenwald, Glenn, 26, 65, 66, 80, 82, 84, 158, 160, 173, 175, 203, 204, 269, 405
Grey, Barry, 189, 205
Griffith, Andy, 190
gross domestic product (GDP), 87
GTI, *see* Global Terrorism Index
Guangzho, 343
Guantánamo, 160, 173, 175, 240, 269
Guggenheim, 199
Guifen, Zhu, 345
Gulf of Mexico, 183, 187
Gulf of Tonkin, 282
Haiyi, Tong, 345
Hamas, 59, 107, 166
Harvard University, 125, 312, 325, 364
Hauben, Ronda, 189
HB 683, 79
Hedges vs. Obama, 157
Hedges, Chris, 34, 157, 158, 160, 172, 202, 206, 293, 294, 296, 398, 405
Helmsley, Sherman, 190
Henan Social Sciences, 341, 350
Henry, James S, 42, 85

Herman, Carl, 26, 85, 91, 99
Higher Circle Policy Elites, 314
Hitselberger, James, 74
Hollingsworth vs. Perry, 194
Hollywood, 31, 115, 203, 269, 297–301, 304–10, 405, 409
Holmes, James, 274
Hong Kong Polytechnic University, 337
Hongshan, 344
Honkala, Cheri, 197, 206
Horn of Africa, 361
Hostess, 191, 192, 205
Houston, Whitney, 198
HR 933, 195
HSBC, 48, 182, 321, 323
Hubei Province, 343
Huffington Post, The, 180, 186, 191, 192, 196, 218
Human Rights Watch, 362
Hurt Locker, The, 303
Hussein, Saddam, 80, 114, 255, 265
hydraulic fracturing, see also fracking, 18, 57, 61, 78, 128, 129, 132, 379
IAEA, *see* International Atomic Energy Agency
Ibiden Electronics Beijing Co., Ltd., 346
ICAN, *see* International Campaign to Abolish Nuclear Weapons
Iceland, 23, 27, 37, 49, 57, 58, 59, 99, 130, 140, 143–54, 176, 329
Icelandic Modern Media Initiative (IMMI), 148–50
IEP, *see* Institute for Economics and Peace
IMMI, *see* Icelandic Modern Media Initiative
India, 21, 60, 118, 128, 135, 136, 137, 138, 141, 325, 403
Institute for Advanced Strategic and Political Studies, 360
Institute for Economics and Peace (IEP), 180
Institute of Public and Environmental Affairs, 336
International Atomic Energy Agency (IAEA), 52
International Business Times, 78, 84, 333
International Campaign to Abolish Nuclear Weapons (ICAN), 47
International Monetary Fund, 42, 299, 317
International Press Institute, 75, 83
International Telephone and Telegraph Corporation, 288
Invisible War, The, 115, 170, 171
Iran, 5, 50, 52, 73, 82, 113, 115, 117, 118, 119, 120, 125, 126, 168, 296, 300, 301, 308, 309
Iran nuclear deal, 50, 113, 117
Iranian Nuclear Crisis, The, 51, 118
Iraq War, 41, 114, 122, 123, 125, 126, 252, 261, 265
iReveltion: Online Warrior of the Arab Spring, 79
Iron Lady, 198, 206
ISDAfix, 165, 323, 329
Islam, 138, 269, 353
Islamophobia, 125, 270, 300, 309, 412
Israel, 59, 60, 63, 64, 101, 102, 106–11, 118, 125, 139, 168, 299
Israeli Education Television, 64, 107
Israeli Health Ministry, 107
Israeli Ministry of Defense, 59

Jackson, Michael, 198
Jamat Tawhid wal Jihad fi Garbi Afriqqiya, 363
J.C. Penney, 194
JDC, *see* American Jewish Joint Distribution Committee
Jefferson, Thomas, 298
Ji, Feng, 341
Jiangsu Province, 344
Jobs, Steve, 333, 339, 340
Johnson, Gary, 196
Johnson, LaVena, 169
Johnson, Lyndon B., 298
Joint Base San Antonio-Lackland, 190
JPMorgan Chase, 48, 98, 182, 321–23
Juhasz, Antonia, 123, 126
Justice Party, 196
Kaedar Electronics, 343, 344
Kant, Immanuel, 275
Kelley, Jill, 188, 204
Kennedy, John F., 211, 277, 278
Kennedy, Margrit, 49, 94, 99
"Kill the Gays" law, 183
Kim, Stephen, 73, 82
Kimmitt, General Mark, 281
King Jr., Martin Luther, 312, 391, 401, 404, 405
Kiriakou, John, 44, 74, 83, 159
Klein, Mark, 260
KPFA/Pacifica, 292, 413
Kumar, Deepa, 269, 305, 307, 308, 310, 411
Kunshan, 343
Kuznick, Peter, 285, 311, 312, 415, 431
Kuwait, 114, 325
laissez faire, 46
Lannan Foundation, 288–96
Lannan, Patrick, 288–95
Lee, Kevin B., 302, 310
Lehman Brothers, 326
Leibniz, Gottfried Wilhelm, 274
Leibowitz, Shamai, 73
Lensic, 292, 293
Lexis Nexis, 40, 282, 320, 369
Lian Jian Technology, 338, 340
Liberia, 362
Libertarian Party, 196
Libor *see* London Interbank Offered Rate
Libya, 120, 126, 135, 188, 189, 190, 204, 300, 319, 355, 358, 362
Likud Party, 196
Lindorf, Dave, 56, 66
London Evening Standard, 301, 310
London Interbank Offered Rate (Libor), 164, 165, 166, 181, 182, 203, 324, 330
Lord's Resistance Army, 362
Los Angeles Times, 55, 78, 84, 133, 140, 150, 154, 194, 204, 205, 335, 337, 350, 370, 384, 422
Loughner, Jared Lee, 274
Louvre, 199, 200
Luftwaffe, 289
Ma, Xiaotian, 341, 351
Madison, James, 257
Mali, 32, 354, 355, 356, 357, 358, 360, 362, 363, 364, 365

Manning, Bradley, 5, 26, 41, 44, 65, 68, 71, 72, 73, 82, 158, 159, 160, 176, 195, 212, 274
Marcellus Shale, 57
Marrs, Jim, 280
Martha Gellhorn Prize, 289
Mashable.com, 335
Mauritania, 355, 357
Mazuera Davis, Christie, 292
McCarthy-Era, 316
McClelland, J. S., 274, 286
McVeigh, Timothy, 281
MEFTA, see Middle East Free Trade Area
Meiko Electronics, 343, 345
Merrill Lynch, 322, 326, 328
Mexico, 26, 43, 50, 58, 92, 101, 105, 106, 110, 132, 183, 187, 234, 235, 288, 325
Middle East, 55, 77, 79, 80, 101, 102, 110, 111, 118, 124, 133, 169, 259, 298, 299, 303, 308, 354, 364, 411
Middle East Free Trade Area (MEFTA), 124
Migratory Bird Act, 187
Miller, Judith, 80
Mills, C. Wright, 31, 88, 92, 98, 274, 276, 285, 314, 328
Mitchell, Luke, 310
Mondoweiss, 310
Monsanto, 6, 60, 63, 127, 128, 129, 130, 136, 137, 138, 139, 140, 141, 142, 194, 195, 206, 385, 386
Monsanto Protection Act, 195, 206
Morgan Stanley, 326
Morocco, 355, 357, 361
Morsi, Mohamed, 195
Mother Jones, 61, 65, 66, 84, 163, 172, 174, 204, 287, 289
Motion Picture Association of America, 299
Mousavian, Seyed Hossein, 50
Mouvement National de Libération de l'Azawad (MNLA), 363
Movement for Democracy and Justice (MDJT), 356
Muammar, Colonel, 358
Mussolini, Benito, 300
Muttitt, Greg, 114, 123
My Plate, 191
Nafis, Quazi Mohammad, 162
NAFTA, see North American Free Trade Agreement
Nanfang People Weekly, 341, 351
Nanfang Weekend, 341, 342, 351
Nansha District, 344
Nansha District Environmental Supevision Unit, 344
Nantaizi Lake, 344
Nation Institute, 212, 288
National Association of Manufacturers, 315
National Coalition for Syrian Revolutionary and Opposition Forces, 167, 168
National Defense Authorization Act (NDAA), 44, 156, 197
National Economic Council, 346
National Labor Relations Act, 193, 329
National Labor Relations Board, 193
National Oceanic and Atmospheric Administration (NOAA), 135

National Resources Defense Council, 54
National Security Act, 316
National Security Agency (NSA), 73, 261
NATO, 90, 126, 317, 318, 319, 330
Naureckas, Jim, 199
NBC News, 169, 171, 172, 174, 198, 206
NBC Universal, 259
NDAA, see National Defense Authorization Act
Near Eastern Affairs, 189
Netherlands, 326
News Corp., 191
Ngai, Pun, 337, 350, 351, 352
Niger, 355, 356, 357, 358, 362
No More Deaths, 50, 101, 105, 110
NOAA, see National Oceanic and Atmospheric Administration
North Africa, 55, 124, 133, 355, 360, 361, 363, 365
North American Free Trade Agreement (NAFTA), 50, 93, 105, 106
North Atlantic Treaty Organization, 317, 330
Northern Ireland, 289
NSA, see National Security Agency
nuclear weapons, 47, 50, 113, 116, 117, 118, 119, 212, 385
Obama, Barack, 18, 67, 72, 81, 83, 104, 156, 196, 198, 215, 240, 290
Obama, Michelle, 298, 302, 303, 308, 309
Occupy, 21, 90, 162, 163, 164, 166, 232, 233, 234, 236, 237, 248, 263, 270, 403, 406
Oceana, 135, 141
OECD, see Organisation for Economics Co-operation and Development
Oklahoma City, 110, 281, 282, 287
On the Commons, 49, 146
Organisation for Economics Co-operation and Development (OECD), 47, 360
Organization United for Respect at Walmart, 193
Other Side of Immigration, The, 105
Oxford University, 98, 286, 309, 326, 329, 383
Pakistan, 56, 118, 125, 135, 156, 171, 180, 259, 269, 282
Palestine, 106, 110, 125, 406, 415
Palmer Raids, 222, 316
Pan Sahel Initiative, 357
Parenti, Michael, 269, 416, 432
parrhesia, 25, 30, 33
Pasatiempo, 292
PBS, 70, 179, 186, 288, 289
PC Mag, 335
Peled, Micha X., 60, 141
Persian Gulf, 361
Petraeus, General David, 188
Physicians for Social Responsibility, 47
Pinochet, Augusto, 199, 289
Plato, 250, 265, 270
PolicyMic, 306
Poole, Isaiah J., 349, 352
Popular Science, 218, 307, 311
Porter, Gareth, 51, 113, 117, 119, 126
Postman, Neil, 177, 179, 185, 200, 202, 309, 311
Pot, Pol, 288
poverty line, 87

"power elite" 31, 88, 89, 91, 92, 99, 279, 315, 317, 318, 320, 325, 329, 330
Printed Circuit Boards (PCBs), 344
PRISM, 158, 270
privatization, 46, 58, 93, 198, 224, 296, 325
Project for Excellence in Journalism, 202
Project for the New American Century, 260, 309
propaganda, 30, 66, 80, 84, 104, 118, 130, 159, 185, 198, 251, 254, 265, 272, 273, 281, 283, 285, 287, 298, 299, 300, 302, 304, 306, 308, 325, 357, 398, 413, 414, 418, 432
Proposition 8, 137, 138, 146, 194, 195
"propietary secrets," 61, 66, 77
Prouty, Colonel L. Fletcher, 280
Psy, 182, 183, 203
Qatar, 167, 326
Qixiong, Fang, 341, 351
Racketeer Influenced and Corrupt Organizations Act, 324
Red Sea, 361
Reform Party, 196
Reitman, Janet, 26, 65, 82
Reporters Without Borders, 75, 83
Revolutionary War, 259
Riesman, David, 275, 286
Risk List, 56
Robertson, Pat, 270, 266
Robinson, William, 317
Romero, Anthony, 174
Romney, Mitt, 186, 196, 256
Rothkopf, David, 89, 99, 330, 318
Royal Society, 55, 127
Russell, Katherine, 261
Ryan, Paddy, 192, 205
Ryan, Paul, 256
Sahara, 232, 354, 356, 357, 358, 360, 361, 363, 364, 365
Said, Edward, 295
Salafist Group for Preaching and Combat (GSPC), 355
Salinas, Carlos, 50, 105
Salomon Brothers, 326
San Francisco Chronicle, 335
San Jose Mercury News, 280
Sandy Hook Elementary School, 283
Santa Fe New Mexican, 291, 292, 295, 297
Schudson, Michael, 312, 313
Second Amendment, 257
Sedition Act, 316, 230
Senate Select Committee, 304
Senegal, 357
September 11, 2001, *see also* 9/11, 354, 355
Sesame Street, 187, 185, 186
Sexual Assault Prevention and Response Program, 170
Sexual violence, 171, 238, 239, 156, 169
Shaheen, Jack, 300, 309
Sharia Law, 354
Shenzen Human Resources and Social Security Bureau, 337
Shenzen, China, 334
Shiva, Vandana, 60, 126, 136, 141, 243, 395, 405
Sigurardóttir, Jóhanna, 49

Simpson, O. J., 274
Simpson, Pamela, 199
Singapore, 43, 92, 326
Sklair, Leslie, 317, 320, 330
Slate, 310
Smart grids, 131
smart meters, 54, 131
SNAP, *see* Supplemental Nutrition Assistance Program
Snowden, Edward, 148, 153, 157, 158, 175, 270
Social Security Act, 316
SOF, *see* Special Operations Forces
Somalia, 156, 171, 360, 361, 362
South China Morning Post, 337, 343, 349, 350, 351, 352
Southern Daily, 340
Southern Poverty Law Center (SPLC), 44, 103
"sovereign citizens," 45
Soviet Union, 319
Special Operations Forces (SOF), 167
Sperling, Gene, 346
SPLC, *see* Southern Poverty Law Center
Stanford University, 74, 326
State Department, 70, 73, 167, 189, 204, 357
Stein, Jill, 196, 197, 206
Sterlin, Jeffrey, 73
Stevens, Christopher, 188
Stewart, Jon, 184, 203
Stone, Oliver, 312, 313, 416, 432
Sturm, Ruger & Co, 325
Sudan, 260, 355
"suicide economy," 60, 127,136, 386
SumOfUs, 336, 350
"superclass," 28, 32, 89, 90, 99, 313
Supplemental Nutrition Assistance Program (SNAP), 53
Supreme Court, 14, 88, 138, 149, 154, 158, 194, 195, 202, 205, 218, 220, 221, 223, 228, 230, 263, 398
Suzhou Industrial Park, 338
Swartz, Aaron, 150, 159
Switzerland, 48, 321, 326
Swiss Federal Institute of Technology, 320
Swiss Re, 326
Syria, 30, 156, 166, 167, 168, 169, 188, 204, 300, 319
Taft-Hartley Act, 316
Taibbi, Matt, 159, 160, 165, 166, 176, 324, 331
Tail-hook Scandal, 190
Taiwan, 326
Tam, Fiona, 349, 350, 351, 352, 337, 342, 343
Tamanrasset, 358
tax enforcement, 46
tax havens, 26, 42, 85, 90, 91
tax rates, 46, 87
Taylor, Ken. 301
Tehran, 117, 301, 302
Thatcher, Margaret, 198, 199, 200, 206
This American Life, 334, 348, 350
ThisCantBeHappening!, 56, 66
Thomas, Jesse, 191, 205
Three Trillion Dollar War, The, 115, 125
Time Magazine, 160, 176, 304

Tongxin Village, 345
TPP, *see* Trans-Pacific Partnership
Trans-Pacific Partnership (TPP), 43, 92, 151
Trans-Sahara Counter-Terrorism Partnership
    (TSCTP), 357
Transaction Tax, 62, 86, 97
Transnational Capitalist Class, 32, 98, 165, 314,
    317, 318, 319, 320, 322, 323, 325, 327, 330
Transnational Corporation, 164, 317, 318, 320
Trilateral Commission, 318
Tripod Wuxi Electric Co., Ltd, 346
Truthout, 82, 85, 86, 96, 99, 152, 349, 352
Tsarnaev, Dzhokhar, 274
Tsarnaev, Tamerlan, 261
Tunisia, 300, 355, 357
Turkey, 56, 167, 195
Turner Diaries, The, 281
Twinkie, 30, 177, 185, 190, 191, 205
Tyranny of Oil, The, 123
UBS, 48, 182, 321, 322, 324, 328
Uganda, 362
Umicron Electronics, 345
Universal Declaration of Human Rights, 33, 56,
    77, 84
UNESCO, *see* United Nations Educational, Scien-
    tific and Cultural Organization
"unhistory," 31, 32, 312, 313
United Food and Commercial Workers Interna-
    tional Union, 193
United Kingdom, 50, 119, 128, 132, 167, 324
United Nations, 52, 67, 75, 76, 77, 81, 83, 84, 86,
    98, 109, 120, 133, 134, 135, 154, 166, 168, 260,
    296, 362, 368, 384, 385
United Nations Educational, Scientific and Cul-
    tural Organization (UNESCO), 75, 81, 385
United Nations High Commissioner for Refu-
    gees, 362
United Nations Human Rights Council, 76
United Nations Security Council (UNSC), 52
United States Department of Agriculture (USDA),
    63, 130, 140, 191
United States vs. Windsor, 194
Unmanned Aerial Vehicles, 259
UNSC, *see* United Nations Security Council
US Army, 69, 73, 120, 169, 281, 296, 355, 365, 394
US Border Patrol, 105, 50
US Chamber of Commerce, 315
USA PATRIOT Act, 197, 221, 256, 300
USA Today, 164, 174, 175, 200, 203, 206
USDA, *see* United States Department of Agriculture
Vacuum, 64, 107
Valenti, Jack, 299
Validated Independent News Stories (VINs), 35, 39
Vanguard Group, 321, 322, 324, 325, 328
Venezuela, 198, 199
Ventrello, Barbara, 290, 291, 292
Vidal, Gore, 190, 406
Vietnam; Vietnam War, 43, 56, 92, 213, 282, 289,
    296, 326, 394, 399
Vitali, Stefania, 330, 320
Wall Street Journal, 15, 21, 150, 153, 154, 164, 166,
    198, 206, 404, 422

Wallach, Lori, 43, 85
Walmart, 192, 193, 194, 205
Wanshida, Dongguan, 338, 339
War You Don't See, The, 31, 290, 293, 294
Warren Commission Report, 280, 286
weapons of mass destruction (WMDs), 122, 260
Webb, Gary, 280, 287, 288
Wegner, Daniel, 307
West Africa, 354, 357, 361, 363
whistleblower, 44, 65, 68, 69, 70, 72, 74, 82, 148,
    153, 157, 158, 159, 175, 210, 261, 270
Whistleblower Protection Enhancement Act, 44
WikiLeaks, 41, 44, 69, 70, 71, 82, 107, 144, 149,
    150, 153, 154, 158, 167, 274, 297
Windhoek Declaration of 1991, 77
Wintek, 336
WIPO, *see* World Intellectual Property Organization
WMDs, *see* weapons of mass destruction
Worker Safety Bureau, 339
World Bank, 16, 20, 22, 42, 90, 300, 318, 325,
    327, 331
World Economic Forum, 327
World Intellectual Property Organization (WIPO),
    151, 154
World Press Freedom Day, 77, 81, 66, 67
"World Press Freedom Index," 75, 83
World Social Forum, 318
World Socialist Web Site, 168, 189
World Trade Center, 304
World Trade Organization (WTO), 317
World War I, 69, 316
World War II, 56, 361, 360, 316, 315, 122, 87
Wuhan Economic and Technological Develop-
    ment Zone, 344
Wuhan Environmental Protection Bureau, 343
Wujiang Health Bureau, 339
Xinhua News Agency, 337
Yahoo!, 214, 335
Year Zero, The Silent Death of Cambodia, 288
Yemen, 171, 156, 300
Yu, Tian, 337
Yuhan Photoelectric Technology Co., Ltd., 339
YunHeng Hardware and Electrical, 339
Zambia, 326
Zepezauer, Mark, 289, 297
Zero Dark Thirty, 27, 31, 34, 115, 251, 298, 299,
    303, 304, 306, 307, 308, 310, 311

PROJECT CENSORED THE MOVIE
ENDING THE REIGN OF JUNK FOOD NEWS

Written, Directed and Produced by Doug Hecker and Christopher Oscar
Edited by Mike Fischer

AVAILABLE ONLINE AND ON DVD FALL OF 2013!

This new documentary, six years in the making, takes an in-depth look at what is wrong with the news media in the United States and what we can do about it. The film highlights the work of thirty-seven-year veteran media democracy organization Project Censored and their commitment to providing solutions through media literacy and critical thinking education, while celebrating the best in underreported, independent journalism. Therein lies the antidote to top-down, managed news propaganda and censorship so pervasive in the US today.

Project Censored—The Movie: Ending the Reign of Junk Food News features original interviews with Noam Chomsky, Howard Zinn, Daniel Ellsberg, Michael Parenti, Greg Palast, Oliver Stone, Peter Kuznick, Cynthia McKinney, Nora Barrows-Friedman, Laurel Krause, Susan Rahman, Kevin Danaher, Dan Rather, Phil Donahue, John Perkins, Jonah Raskin, Khalil Bendib, Pacifica and KPFA Free Speech Radio personalities, Abby Martin of Breaking the Set, Al Jazeera English, several Project Censored–affiliated faculty and students, Project founder Dr. Carl Jensen, former Project director and Media Freedom Foundation president Dr. Peter Phillips, current Project director Professor Mickey Huff, current Project associate director Dr. Andy Lee Roth, plus much, much more!

Winner, Best Directing of a Documentary Feature, Madrid International Film Festival
Winner, Most Viewed Film, Sonoma International Film Festival

See ProjectCensoredTheMovie.com for details about how to screen this film in your community or your local college campus.